City University
Library Information Services
Law Innovation Centre
WITHDRAWN

AF765974

BEN

Inn on
T
or v,

Library Services
City, University of London
Innovation Centre
Whiskin Street, London, EC1R 0JD
T: 020 7040 8191
W: www.city.ac.uk/library

LONG LOAN

Return or renew this item by the
date on your library account to
avoid overdue charges

Constitutional Policy in Multilevel Government

Transformations in Governance

Transformations in Governance is a major new academic book series from Oxford University Press. It is designed to accommodate the impressive growth of research in comparative politics, international relations, public policy, federalism, and environmental and urban studies concerned with the dispersion of authority from central states up to supranational institutions, down to subnational governments, and sideways to public–private networks. It brings together work that significantly advances our understanding of the organization, causes, and consequences of multilevel and complex governance. The series is selective, containing annually a small number of books of exceptionally high quality by leading and emerging scholars.

The series targets mainly single-authored or co-authored work, but it is pluralistic in terms of disciplinary specialization, research design, method, and geographical scope. Case studies as well as comparative studies, historical as well as contemporary studies, and studies with a national, regional, or international focus are all central to its aims. Authors use qualitative, quantitative, formal modeling, or mixed methods. A trade mark of the books is that they combine scholarly rigor with readable prose and an attractive production style.

The series is edited by Liesbet Hooghe and Gary Marks of the University of North Carolina, Chapel Hill, and the VU Amsterdam, and Walter Mattli of the University of Oxford.

With, Without, or Against the State? How European Regions Play the Brussels Game
Michaël Tatham

A Postfunctionalist Theory of Governance (5 Volumes)
Liesbet Hooghe and Gary Marks et al.

Democrats and Autocrats: Pathways of Subnational Undemocratic Regime Continuity within Democratic Countries
Agustina Giraudy

Organizational Progeny: Why Governments are Losing Control over the Proliferating Structures of Global Governance
Tana Johnson

Constitutional Policy in Multilevel Government

The Art of Keeping the Balance

Arthur Benz

In cooperation with Dominic Heinz, Eike-Christian Hornig, Andrea Fischer-Hotzel, Jörg Kemmerzell, and Bettina Petersohn

OXFORD
UNIVERSITY PRESS

OXFORD
UNIVERSITY PRESS

Great Clarendon Street, Oxford, OX2 6DP,
United Kingdom

Oxford University Press is a department of the University of Oxford.
It furthers the University's objective of excellence in research, scholarship,
and education by publishing worldwide. Oxford is a registered trade mark of
Oxford University Press in the UK and in certain other countries

© Arthur Benz 2016
© Chapter 3 with Andrea Fischer-Hotzel and Bettina Petersohn
© Chapter 4 with Dominic Heinz, Eike-Christian Hornig, Andrea Fischer-Hotzel,
and Bettina Petersohn
© Chapter 5 with Jörg Kemmerzell and Bettina Petersohn

The moral rights of the author have been asserted

First Edition published in 2016

Impression: 1

All rights reserved. No part of this publication may be reproduced, stored in
a retrieval system, or transmitted, in any form or by any means, without the
prior permission in writing of Oxford University Press, or as expressly permitted
by law, by licence or under terms agreed with the appropriate reprographics
rights organization. Enquiries concerning reproduction outside the scope of the
above should be sent to the Rights Department, Oxford University Press, at the
address above

You must not circulate this work in any other form
and you must impose this same condition on any acquirer

Published in the United States of America by Oxford University Press
198 Madison Avenue, New York, NY 10016, United States of America

British Library Cataloguing in Publication Data
Data available

Library of Congress Control Number: 2016936267

ISBN 978–0–19–878607–8

Printed in Great Britain by
Clays Ltd, St Ives plc

Links to third party websites are provided by Oxford in good faith and
for information only. Oxford disclaims any responsibility for the materials
contained in any third party website referenced in this work.

Acknowledgments

This book summarizes the results of a comparative research project on reforming federal constitutions, but has been inspired by a broader research agenda on dynamics of multilevel political systems. While I have been interested in this subject matter for a long time, the idea to study processes of constitutional reform and change originated when I participated as an expert in a commission on the "modernization of federalism," established by the German federal parliament and the *Bundesrat* (2003–4). At about the same time, I gained some insight into the "Convention on the Future of the EU" (also known as the Constitutional Convention) when I participated in a group of scholars and higher civil servants of the Land government in North Rhine-Westphalia discussing on matters of the Convention. The experiences of these different processes and arrangements to negotiate constitutional amendments in multilevel polities led me to start a systematic research on this issue, not the least when I realized that processes of constitutional change in general and those affecting the allocation of powers in federal or regionalized states in particular have not been studied extensively. Apart from case studies, research has tended to focus on formal amendment rules but has neglected the processes of drafting amendments. Thus, there appeared to be a lack of studies, especially comparative ones, on the interplay between formal amendment procedures, actual constitutional reform negotiations, the course of ratification, and the success or failure of constitutional reform. As my experiences suggested, the various arrangements of these processes are highly relevant for explaining outcomes of constitutional change. As they can be designed for each reform project, understanding processes of constitutional change has not only academic but also practical relevance.

The research project was generously funded by the German Research Foundation between 2008 and 2011 (grant number DFG 1667/9-1). This allowed me to pursue my plan with a group of young scholars. During the three-year period of funding, Nathalie Behnke, Andrea Fischer-Hotzel, Dominic Heinz, Eike-Christian Hornig, Jörg Kemmerzell and Bettina Petersohn contributed to the project. Nathalie supported me as a post-doc in preparing and coordinating the project, until she left the team in 2009 to become a professor at the University of Bochum and then at Konstanz. Our cooperation in the first year of the project led to our editing a special issue of *Publius: The Journal of Federalism* (2009). The other members of the team contributed to the empirical research summarized in this book. Although I wrote several individual chapters and finished the final manuscript, they each contributed a substantial share in the respective chapters, as indicated at the appropriate places.

The empirical work summarized in this book is based on nine country case studies. For the research outside Germany, we were fortunate to receive expert opinions submitted by a number of partners in the other eight countries. I owe gratitude to Barbara Blümel, Christoph Konrath, Peter Bußjäger, Helmut Hörtenhuber and Johannes Fischer (Austria); Nicolas Lagasse, Jean-Benoit Pile and Dave Sinardet (Belgium); Marc-Antoine Adam, Martin Fournier, Anna-May Choles, Greg Clarke and Nadia Verrelli (Canada); Patrick Le Lidec and Romain Pasquier (France); Carlo Fusaro, Francesco Palermo and Matteo Nicolini (Italy); Dieter Freiburghaus and Gérard Wettstein (Switzerland); César Colino and José A. Olmeda (Spain); Jonathan Bradbury and James Mitchell (UK). Most of these experts met in a conference we organized with the support of the Forum of Federations, the Dimitris-Tsatsos-Institut für Europäische Verfassungswissenschaften (DTIEV) at the University of Hagen, and the Bundesrat in Berlin. I would like to thank these institutions for their generous assistance, in particular Felix Knüpling from the Forum and Gerd Schmidt and his team in Berlin for the excellent cooperation in making the conference a successful event and a fruitful experience for all participants. I also owe gratitude to the DTIEV and its director, Peter Brandt, for providing an interdisciplinary research environment for the project, and for his continued support even after I moved to the Technische Universität Darmstadt.

During my work on this project, I had the opportunity to discuss with many scholars. It is impossible to mention all of them. Two of them, Richard Simeon and Ronald Watts, recently passed away, and I will remember our meetings, long talks and exchange of opinions on federalism. The influence of Fritz W. Scharpf becomes obvious throughout the book. Moreover, I benefited from many inspiring discussions with Thomas O. Hueglin. With Jörg Broschek, I worked on theories of institutional change and federal dynamics, and our cooperation culminated in the volume *Federal Dynamics*, published in 2013 by Oxford University Press. My theoretical approach and empirical knowledge on comparative federalism has been very much influenced by these colleagues.

After Jörg had left Darmstadt to become research professor at Wilfrid Laurier University in Canada, Jared Sonnicksen joined my team at Darmstadt and contributed to the quality of this book with many substantial comments. Moreover, Jörg Kemmerzell, who is meanwhile involved in other research projects, not only commented the final manuscript but also participated in the editorial work, together with my student assistants Florian Ostertag and Nicolas Schrader. I am grateful for their excellent and valuable work.

Arthur Benz
Darmstadt
October 2015

Contents

List of Tables

List of Abbreviations

AC, ACs	Autonomous Community; Autonomous Communities
CDU	*Christlich Demokratische Union* (Christian Democratic Union)
CiU	Convergència i Unió (Convergence and Union, alliance of two moderate nationalist parties in Catalonia)
COSTA/COREE	*Conferentie voor de Staatshervorming / Conférénce pour la réforme de l'Etat* (Intergovernmental and Interparliamentary Conference for Institutional Renewal in Belgium)
CSU	*Christlich Soziale Union* (Christian Social Union, Bavarian party)
ERC	*Esquerra Republicana de Catalunya* (Leftist Republican Party of Catalonia)
FDF	*Fédéralist démocrates francophone* (liberal party of Wallonia)
FDP	*Freie Demokratische Partei* (Liberal Democratic Party of Germany)
FPÖ	*Freiheitliche Partei Österreichs* (Austrian Liberal Party)
LibDems	Liberal Democrats
MR	*Movement réformateur* (liberal party of Wallonia)
NFA	*Neugestaltung des Finanzausgleichs und der Aufgabenverteilung zwischen Bund und Kantonen* (Renewal of fiscal equalization and allocation of powers between the federation and Cantons)
ÖVP	*Österreichische Volkspartei* (Austrian People's Party)
PP	*Partido Popular* (Spanish People's Party)
PSC	*Partit dels Socialistes de Catalunya* (Catalan Socialist Party)
PSOE	*Partido Socialista Obrero Español* (Socialist Worker's Party of Spain)
PSOE-A	*Partido Socialista Obrero Español de Andalucía* (Socialist Workers' Party of Andalucia)
QCA	Qualitative Comparative Analysis
SCC	Scottish Constitutional Convention
SNP	Scottish Nationalist Party
UMP	*Union pour un mouvement populaire* (Union for a Popular Movement)
VU	*Volksunie* (Peoples Union, Flemish nationalist party)
WLP	Welsh Labour Party

1

Introduction

Multilevel structures of governments are on the rise. While in the first half of the twentieth century, scholars observed the evolution of centralized, unitary nation states and declared federalism obsolete (Laski 2005 [1939]), division of powers in multilevel political systems, either in a federal or regionalized state or in a political union of states (like the EU) has attracted attention during the second half of the twentieth century. Integration of states, federalism, decentralization and regionalization have become key concepts and research topics in political science (Loughlin 2013). In political discourses, ideas expressed with these concepts are taken as guidelines for creating institutions of good governance. In reality, processes of transnational integration and regionalization of nation states reshaped the structures at least of Western democracies (Hooghe, Marks and Schakel 2010).

These processes have generated a variety of territorial organizations of governments. Old typologies of state theory could no longer cover the emerging forms; new attempts to adjust concepts contributed more to confusion than to clarification. The simple dichotomy between unitary and federal states has been replaced by more differentiated terminologies (Watts 2013), more general concepts like hybrid states (Loughlin 2009), multilevel governance (Piattoni 2010) or territorial governance (Loughlin 2007b). While governance addressed structural dynamics or patterns of policy-making, the term hybrid states, although meant to emphasize recent trends in state development, avoids any conceptual distinction and responds to variety with a catch-all category. The term multilevel government applied in this book may not solve these conceptual problems. However, it allows us to cover federal and regionalized unitary states facing similar problems of how to organize their territorial structures and stabilize the balance of power between tiers of government. The concept refers to political systems (i.e. institutionalized structures of a polity), which divide powers of government (including legislative, executive and fiscal powers) into at least two levels.

All these political systems are confronted with the problem of keeping the balance despite the continuous pressure of change and in the face of ongoing shifts of power. Stabilizing this balance is fundamental for the legitimacy and operation of multilevel governments, and for preserving the constitutional order. This problem has been discussed in studies on federalism, following William Riker's assumption that federal systems are necessarily instable (Riker 1964). As it is not federalism as such that causes instability, but the division of power between territorial units of government, instability can challenge regionalized unitary governments no less than federal governments. Under the pressure of regionalist movements or confronted by regional parties claiming to represent a distinct national community of citizens, unitary governments can even face more instability than federal states. And in these cases, federalization, i.e. a constitutional change of the territorial structure of the state leading to an extension of regional authority and autonomy as such is no solution if it does not end in a stable balance. For this reason, regionalized governments or those that introduced elements of federalism (federalizing states) should be included in research on this issue. Therefore, we regard them as instances of multilevel government.

This fundamental problem of multilevel government in fact concerns two basic issues discussed in the literature on federalism. One is the problem of stabilizing a balance of power between levels against unintended "authority migration" leading either to a concentration of power at the central level or a fragmentation of power among lower level governments. Some scholars have confirmed William Riker's suggestion that an integrated party system rather than a constitution provides for stability (Filippov et al. 2004). Others emphasize the relevance of institutions and constitutional rules (Lemco 1991), whereas Jenna Bednar has suggested that a combination of interacting mechanisms of control ("safeguards") can protect federal systems against authority migration (Bednar 2009). Yet mechanisms stabilizing a distribution of power can have two negative consequences. Either they can make a political system rigid and unable to adjust to changing conditions, or they induce countervailing dynamics against destabilizing trends, but with the risk of setting off unintended processes.

Therefore, the problem of balancing powers in multilevel governments needs to be reframed as an issue of constitutional politics and policy-making. Consequently, research on safeguards has to be complemented by research on constitutional change. In order to stabilize existing divisions of power between governmental levels, constitutional rules have to be changed, either in order to improve the quality of governance and to respond to changes in society, or to redress trends in authority migration that evolve in a problematic direction and threaten to destabilize a constitutional order. Multilevel governments are not only instable, they are always dynamic, and designs aiming at stability can turn dynamics into rigidity. Therefore, in addition to the research on how to deal with instability, the issue is how multilevel constitutions can maintain their flexibility to adjust and how they can be changed in order to restore the balance of power. It is this second aspect of the constitutional problem of federal or multilevel government that is addressed in this book. In contrast to scholars who have contributed to these research fields, we claim that the key to maintaining a flexible balance of power lies in constitutional policy, in processes of reviewing and correcting destructive dynamics of power structures in multilevel government.

At first glance, this poses a seemingly paradoxical argument. Indeed, according to most theories of federalism and multilevel governance, changing a constitution is extraordinarily difficult. This stems, for instance, from numerous competing interests among units of governments and the existence of many veto-players. In particular, the concept of the joint-decision trap now widely applied in the literature on multilevel governance implies that constitutional change is especially unlikely if it aims at a reallocation of powers among levels of government (Scharpf 1988, 2011). Theories of institutional change support the assumption that complex political systems can at best be changed gradually, and scholars working on federalism have supported this view (e.g. Bednar 2013). Accordingly, significant modification of the allocation of power or resources seems to be unlikely, except under specific historical circumstances ("critical junctures") or if strong leaders or powerful change agents reduce the impact of veto players, two not very promising alternatives. In line with this perspective, research on change in multilevel government has focused on mainstream parties, i.e. parties predominating politics at the central level, and tried to explain their willingness to decentralize power.

These are important contributions to research on dynamics of federalism or multilevel government (Benz and Broschek 2013a). Yet constitutional policy and constitutional change result from multifaceted processes, and it is the interplay of different dimensions, i.e. the institutions and arenas at the different levels, the overlapping sequences of agenda setting, negotiation and decision-making, and of formal amendment and informal change, which drives the dynamics of constitutional policy. Therefore, we argue that complex processes rather than simple power structure (majority parties, veto positions, bargaining among veto-players, strong leadership) promise to achieve the necessary institutional stability and allow for constitutional change. We look at the more or less multidimensional process and its potential for change. As we will explain, specific process designs can increase the probability that constitutional policy generates stabilizing dynamics, whereas others may cause rigidity or destabilizing effects. We also show, in clear contrast to institutionalist and actor-centered theories prevailing in political science, that complex designs of constitutional policy are necessary to stabilize multilevel governments.

This conclusion will be supported in the following chapters by theoretical reasoning and comparative case studies. From a normative point of view, this reasoning is in line with requirements of democracy. In constitutional matters, decisions need to be made by rules, which guarantee that all citizens and political actors can accept them. In a similar vein, the constitutional principle of federalism, which also should apply to regionalized states (and de facto or de jure does so), requires that a constitution should not be changed without representatives of lower level jurisdictions being able to participate. Therefore, our findings have practical implications by showing how changing multilevel structures is feasible in processes conforming to standards of democracy.

Based on this theoretical perspective, this study focuses on constitutional change in multilevel governments. It intends to show under which conditions change is possible and contributes to maintaining or restoring the balance of power, despite the fact that many actors participate in constitutional policy with diverse interests and the ability to obstruct intended amendments. This particular approach adds to theories of institutional change, federal dynamics and multilevel politics and policy-making. Our approach is unique in linking these theories with a theory of constitutional policy-making and suggests a new understanding of how complex multilevel systems work.

In our research project, we applied the theoretical perspective to compare constitutional policy in federal and regionalized governments systematically. During this project, we studied processes of constitutional reform and change in nine federal or regionalized democratic governments, where we found reforms or reform attempts or intensive political discussions relating to the territorial structure of the state and/or the vertical or horizontal (re-)distribution of powers between levels or units of government. The cases selected represent states differing in their constitutional framework (established federations, new federal states still undergoing federalization, regionalized states) and confronted by different constitutional problems (deficits in governance performance or problems with integrating different regions). Moreover, they differ in the outcome of reform processes we studied in detail. Most importantly in view of our theoretical approach, they all reveal different patterns of constitutional policy. Thus our comparative study considered not a limited set of variables derived from a theory, but rather was designed to take account of different conditions and to discover mechanisms of change or stagnation by tracing processes in case studies.

In order to present our research results, we organized the book as follows. Chapter 1 explains our focus and research questions by more extensively introducing the constitutional problem of multilevel governments. Here we outline the basic dilemma of instability and rigidity confronting constitutional policy in these political systems. Moreover, we briefly review the solutions, which scholars so far have proposed and discussed.

Starting from an account of the state of research, Chapter 2 develops the theoretical framework that has guided our research work. In contrast to other theories on institutional or constitutional change, our own approach emphasizes agenda setting and—in particular—negotiations on amendment proposals as most important conditions to be considered. It suggests looking at the whole process of policy-making, instead of either agenda setting, or negotiations, or decision-making and veto power. Moreover, while external conditions like economic crises, pressure from interest organizations or party politics are not neglected, the way constitutional negotiations are framed and organized is accentuated as a most significant condition affecting the outcome of constitutional policy. Finally, formal (explicit) and informal (implicit) constitutional change (Voigt 1999) are taken as closely linked processes contributing to the dynamics of change. At the end of Chapter 2, we present our research design, explain the selection of cases and outline how outcomes of constitutional policy can be characterized and how they are operationalized for the empirical research.

Chapter 3 categorizes the cases according to varieties of the basic constitutional problem of multilevel political systems. It sheds light on the particular conditions that give rise to various expressions of the instability–rigidity dilemma and different kinds of imbalances either due to over-centralization or asymmetries, fragmentation or over-decentralization. Problems of integration in divided societies are distinguished from problems of ineffective governance. Accordingly, we can identify different reform agendas in federal and regionalized states. Presumably, constitutional amendment is more likely to fail if integration problems predominate. For these reasons, scholars have recommended avoiding ambitious projects of constitutional reforms (Lerner 2011). However, the case studies presented in the book do not confirm the assumptions justifying this proposal.

Chapter 4 presents the results of the empirical research. The nine case studies, which include federal and regionalized (federalizing) states confronted by either performance or integration problems, are presented in short reports. These reports cover the particular historical situation of the reform process under consideration, agenda setting and evolution of the agenda, constitutional negotiations, the ratification process and the outcome of constitutional policy. The chapter ends with a comparative summary of the results. Thus, success stories are identified and distinguished from stories of failure occurring in states where a balance of power could not be achieved or where the constitution became more rigid. The study reveals that formal constitutional amendments do not always restore the balance of a multilevel system and that a rejection of a constitutional amendment bill in ratification need not necessarily be characterized as failure of constitutional policy.

The following chapters place the case studies in a comparative perspective. Chapter 5 deals with a particular issue, which has been discussed, in the literature over the last decade. It examines the relevance of amendment rules, i.e. those rules relevant for ratification of an amendment bill. Yet, while researchers following veto-players theory could not find any effect of amendment rules on the outcomes of constitutional reforms, be they defined as frequency of amendments or scope of change, the research presented in the book draws attention to the impact of amendment rules on negotiations. Negotiators try to anticipate potential vetoes. However, this is not always possible, and it is the particular linkage of negotiations and ratification that makes a difference.

Chapter 6 addresses another particular aspect. In theories on federal constitutions (Livingston 1956) and in constitutional economics (Voigt 1999), evolution of informal constitutional norms (or implicit constitutional change) has been emphasized as a most significant mode of change. This study on the other hand shows that implicit and explicit change are often linked. Moreover, implicit change can be legitimized by negotiated agreements, provided that they are found in inclusive constitutional negotiations, even if ratification fails due to specific circumstances. On the other hand, negotiations can end with an ineffective but nonetheless ratified compromise. In this case, implicit change of an ineffective constitutional amendment can solve some of the ensuing problems, but lacking the legitimacy of an agreement usually invites further dispute. Case studies on Canada and Germany illustrate both patterns of change.

By including the aspects dealt with in the previous chapters, Chapter 7 extends the analysis and systematically compares the cases following the theory presented in Chapter 2. Moreover, alternative explanations are taken into consideration. While those theories should not be discarded based on our empirical evidence, the research results support the theory presented in Chapter 2. Accordingly, successful constitutional change in multilevel systems leading to a stable and flexible balance of power is not only possible even under difficult institutional or political conditions. The results also show that the design of constitutional policy can improve the conditions for effective change. Chapter 8 summarizes the results of the research and draws conclusions for theory of federalism and multilevel governance and for further research in this field. Moreover, it discusses the practical relevance of the results presented in the previous chapter and the theoretical reasoning.

Political science draws conclusions from theoretical reasoning and empirical studies. Both never fully grasp the real complexity of political practice. For these reasons, it can discover mechanisms which cause problems under particular circumstances, and derive principles or ideas from observing cases of problem solving. But science always remains abstract, and its conclusion should not be confused with recommendation for policy-makers. Our study ends with some general ideas, which we think are relevant for politics and governments confronted with the challenge to make multilevel governance work and stabilize its structures. Nevertheless, political scientists neither can determine how powers should be distributed and organized, nor can they say in which particular processes relevant constitutional change can be achieved. For political actors, finding a stable and flexible balance of power remains an art.

2

Theoretical Framework and Research Design

Studies on multilevel governance and comparative federalism have dealt extensively with issues of effectiveness and legitimacy. They also have described the reconfiguration of structures and ongoing processes of integration and disintegration. Based on this research, this chapter explains our research question and presents the theoretical framework of the empirical study. We start by clarifying the basic constitutional problem each democratic government with division of powers between levels is confronted with, and explicate how this general problem finds expression in different federal and regionalized states. The core of our framework consists of an analytical model of a multidimensional process of constitutional policy. We applied this concept to compare processes identified in the case studies. It is based on the assumption that the complexity of the constitutional problem and of multilevel governments has to be reflected in patterns of constitutional policy-making, and success or failure depends to a considerable extent on particular arrangements and linkages of different arenas of policy-making. Finally, we spell out how we distinguish success or failure of constitutional policy and describe the design of our empirical research.

2.1 The Constitutional Problem of Multilevel Government

2.1.1 *Balancing Power—Enabling Change*

Whereas the division of power between the executive, parliament and courts can be defined by abstract functions, the division of powers between levels of government refers to particular tasks. For this reason, federalism necessarily implies constitutionalism, and this also applies to regionalized states. In the exceptional case among Western states, the UK, where for historical reasons no written constitution exists, devolution, like European integration, was established by a set of laws that are to be considered as elements of a constitutional order. Hence, rule of law is a decisive precondition of multilevel governance, just as the existence of a constitution has always been conceived as a basic feature of federalism and a precondition of its stability and operation (Hueglin and Fenna 2006: 43). From another angle, division of powers among levels of governments can be considered a second source of constitutionalism beyond the idea of dividing powers between state and private citizens in a free society. Consequently, constitutionalism meanwhile has "traveled" to international politics, which is particularly exemplified by the European Union.

As essential as they are, constitutional rules of multilevel governments generate genuine problems for governance and democracy. These rules should define the powers of central and regional or local governments including their relations and the necessary fiscal resources in a way which is considered appropriate to conform to expectations of citizens. Powers are in balance if they fulfil this requirement and as long as they are not deemed inappropriate or contested by legitimate means. What balance of power means depends on public opinions, political judgments and collective decisions on the respective constitutional rules and norms. Since opinions and judgments about the appropriate distribution of power are in flux, balance in this context does not imply a static equilibrium, but a moving target.

From this follows a second problem. Being a precondition for the operation of a government, constitutions in general need to be protected against rulers seeking to change the law to their advantage. According to the normative theory of federalism, constitutions have to fix the "federal bargain" (Riker 1964), i.e. the basic compromises on the distribution of power and on rules of operation. On the other hand, there are reasons to postulate that those constitutional rules determining the division of power between levels of government need to be highly flexible in order to allow the system to adapt to changing circumstances. Thus, rigidity and flexibility turn out as conflicting requirements.

One reason for the inherent conflict between constitutional rigidity and flexibility stems from the ambiguity of constitutional norms and rules in multilevel systems. Here rules are often formulated in a manner that they hold disputes in abeyance. Regarding the allocation of powers between levels of government, normative theories provide criteria, those emphasizing effectiveness of "scaling" as well as those referring to the interests of communities in preserving their identity (Hooghe and Marks 2009). But given the political implications of decisions on centralization and decentralization or different ways to separate or share powers, their effects on the way policies are made, the particular structure can always be contested (Treisman 2007). The justification of particular rules either emphasizes non-discrimination between territories or refers to distinctness of particular territories. Moreover, the relative weight of the criteria suggested in normative theories depends on social and economic developments or changes in policy concepts, if new political coalitions gain influence. Therefore, decisions on decentralization or centralization and the respective constitutional law usually remain ambivalent. The same applies for constitutional decisions determining the degree of autonomy of regional governments between shared rule and self-rule. Autonomy enables groups to pursue their particular goals, while limiting possibilities to deal with common problems of the whole community of citizens and increasing the challenges for coordination between jurisdictions and levels. Shared rule, on the other hand, increases transaction costs in policy-making, depending on the particular pattern of multilevel governance. It also constrains governments' ability to pursue the will of their citizens, while autonomy may have a "*demos*-enabling" effect (Stepan 1999). Beyond that, democratic federations and regionalized governments imply a normative conflict expressed in a "continual tension between persons and places" (Kincaid 2002: 134). The principle of equality of citizens vested with individual rights tends to require uniform decisions and supports centralization of power. But democracy also requires considering particular concerns of territorially organized groups.

Another reason favoring constitutional flexibility concerns the inevitable tensions between the requirements of constitutional government and of effective and democratic governance in a multilevel system. Although these tensions vary depending on the particular features of a government, they cannot be ruled out by institutional design. In theory, the territorial organization of a state, constitutionalism, democracy and good governance can be justified as ideal principles of government; in reality, they combine to a multidimensional polity institutionalizing conflicting requirements. Division of powers between levels of government and constitutional rules constrain the sovereignty of the people or parliaments; effective policy coordination between levels can strengthen the executive against parliaments, but is complicated due to accountability of the executive. Democratic processes at the different levels can cause conflicts, which may weaken the constitutional rules on a division of powers. Moreover, the need to settle these conflicts can cause tensions between constitutional courts and democratic politics. Therefore, multilevel governments reveal a high "contradictory potential of institutions" (Onoma 2010: 65).

The consequences of these normative ambiguities and inevitable tensions have been spelled out in theories underlining the notorious instability of federalism (Lemco 1991). They have pointed out different mechanisms and sources bringing forth unintended changes that threaten the balance of power. Accordingly, instability is usually caused by "authority migration" due to attempts by political actors at the central and lower levels to increase their power and exploit ambiguities and conflicts. It results from changing socio-economic conditions, which affect power structures and the legitimacy of claims to maintain or extend powers. It may also be prompted by changes in the definition of public policies influencing the weighting of reasons for a particular multilevel structure.

- The mechanism of authority migration has been emphasized in rational choice models of federalism (Riker 1964). Accordingly, the structure of a federal system results from bargaining among governmental actors who convene on binding rules in order to solve collective choice dilemmas and to enable effective governance, but who are also interested in extending their power. Due to these mixed motives of actors, federal systems are subject to an ongoing power game between levels of government and thus are inherently instable. For similar reasons, actor-centered theories of multilevel governance highlight the dynamics of structures (Hooghe and Marks 2001; Marks 1996).
- Society-centered theories of federalism (Friedrich 1968; Livingston 1967) either focus on the influence of social groups and economic development on the distribution of powers or they regard institutions as an expression of societal norms. In both variants, it is social change that explains dynamics of federal systems. While economic developments affecting interests and resources of territorial units cause continuous, but in the longer term significant changes, social values and norms support the persistence of structures and patterns of policy-making. From this perspective, instability emerges if societies are divided by extreme economic disparities or cultural cleavages, in particular if minorities feel oppressed by central or uniform policies (Heinemann-Grüder 2002). But the vertical dimension of the distribution of power can also become unstable, for instance if intense mobility of actors across the territorial boundaries causes external effects of decentralized governance, if citizens express increasing or decreasing loyalties to regional communities, or if the political structuring of collective interests in a society changes, which in particular finds expression in the territorial dimension of the party system (Benz 2013).
- From a policy-science perspective, multilevel government is highly dynamic due to functional tensions between unity and diversity. Territorial scopes of tasks assigned to the different levels often change in processes of "rescaling" of tasks (Brenner 2004) or when new policies are set on the agenda of central or regional governments. The fiscal balance, too, is in constant flux. Regional communities demanding autonomy or fair redistribution of resources tend to mobilize countervailing power against the central government responsible for fiscal equalization. Central governments often try to shift the burden of public investments and services to lower levels.

Depending on the territorial organization of governments, these dynamics of the balance of power lead either towards over-centralization or towards disintegration, and both developments can end in the dissolution of a political system. This constitutional problem has extensively been discussed in literature on federalism, and scholars have suggested different solutions. Rational choice theorists, who assume that actors are inclined to extend their power, have expressed their skepticism that constitutional rules can guarantee stability of a federal order. Instead, they rely on a party system integrated across levels (Filippov et al. 2004; Riker 1964) or on coalitions formed by regions in order to defend their claims against a central government (De Figueiredo and Weingast 2005). This way, an institutional equilibrium of countervailing forces should emerge "whereby formal rules and individual motives generally and over time remain in agreement" (Filippov et al. 2004: 13). But shaping a federal system according to these suggestions requires constitutional change. At the end of their compelling analysis, Filippov, Ordeshook and Shvetsova (2004: 226–94) argue for an appropriate institutional design, particularly for rules guaranteeing regional and local autonomy and an electoral system supporting an integrated party system to evolve. Apparently, successful constitutional policy is necessary in order to stabilize federalism. However, the design principles leading to a vertical integration of a party system make constitutional design difficult. These structures of policies are, as illustrated by cases of German or Austrian federalism, one of the causes of constitutional rigidity. In a federal system with an integrated party system, constitutional change requires an agreement of governments from different levels which are likely to adhere to competing parties. While such a constellation indeed guarantees stability, it might become too rigid in view of the need to adjust the federal balance to changes in society.

Other scholars have emphasized the capacity of federal systems to adjust and find a dynamic equilibrium (Landau 1973). This flexibility should be achieved by countervailing safeguards and the opportunities for experimental policies (Bednar 2009; Nicolaïdis 2001). Furthermore, a reinterpretation of constitutional rules legitimized by constitutional courts has been said to allow for incremental change (Galligan 2008). Accordingly, scholars have regarded constitutions as incomplete contracts (Héritier 2007: 46) and concluded that any allocation of powers and rules of intergovernmental relations need to be continuously renegotiated. However, a balance of power does not necessarily emerge as a result. The technical terminology of system theory introduced by Landau conceals mechanisms of "error-control and error correction" (Landau 1973: 181) as political processes. What is defined as an error and how it must be corrected is an issue of political decision-making and raises the problem of legitimacy. Therefore, while flexibility by continuous renegotiations or reinterpretations may allow for adjustment, we have to take into account the possibility that it can be exploited by actors who want to extend their power. Moreover, incremental adjustments of constitutional norms by governments or courts can lead to an increasing discrepancy between effective and written constitution and, accordingly, lead to an erosion of legitimacy.

Apparently, theories formulated so far only confirm the basic dilemma of multilevel government. On the one hand, if a constitutional order is fixed by an equilibrium of power among actors of the federal and regional level or by effective safeguards of the constitution, adjustment of a federal constitution to changing impacts of state–society relations can turn out as impossible or at least rather difficult. On the other hand, flexible mechanisms for adjustment cannot guarantee that a balance of power emerges or that the legitimacy of a federal constitution can be preserved. In this case, instability can result either due to illegitimate authority migration, or it can be due to self-enforcing intergovernmental conflicts threatening the cohesion of the polity if the first mechanisms apply. If the existing rules cannot prevent centrifugal or centripetal shifts in power or if they ignite conflicts on basic norms of federalism, stability can be restored only by legitimate processes of constitutional change (Héritier 2007; Ostrom 1990).

Therefore, in order to prevent multilevel government from becoming instable, not only do constitutional rules have to be flexible, but they also need to be revised from time to time, be it to maintain the balance of power or to respond to functional needs of societies. In consequence, constitutional policy offers a core mechanism to maintaining a federal balance. If federalism has to be designed by a constitution and if an allocation of power determined and legitimized by a constitution is always in flux and cannot be fixed finally, continuous renegotiations of the constitutional agreement and amendments of a constitution are of fundamental relevance for making federalism work and persist. This is the reason why a theory of federalism and multilevel governance must include an understanding of how and why constitutional policy succeeds under the particular institutional conditions of multilevel governance. The relevance of this research topic cannot be emphasized enough, for two reasons: First, constitutional change is quite difficult to achieve due to the complexity of "multidimensional regimes" (Benz and Broschek 2013b: 3) with a comparatively large number of veto points and interacting rule systems. Second, constitutional policy as such does not guarantee a stable balance of power, and even bears the risk of contributing to increasing instability or rigidity.

In multilevel governments, the high number of institutional and partisan veto-players pursuing divergent interests apparently causes particular difficulties of changing constitutional rules dividing powers between levels of governments. Requirements of democracy make the problem more complicated. In multilevel polities, constitutions combine features of a treaty among governments and a basic consent among citizens. Different varieties of multilevel government emphasize either treaty-based legitimacy or legitimacy by agreement of the *demos* or *demoi* (Hueglin 2013). Regardless of these variations, constitutional amendments are negotiated among representatives of governments and passed by parliaments. In real policy-making, intergovernmental negotiations among executives are linked to parliamentary processes determined by competition among political parties or conflicts between two chambers of the legislative, and in many cases of federal or regionalized states a combination of both. If negotiating executives require the support of majorities in legislative institutions or consider the presumed will of the people which they claim to represent (Saward 2010), they are bound to varying, and often contradicting, positions. Parties may have different opinions about the division of power, and the public interest of the whole community of citizens in a polity (the "*demos*") can clearly diverge from the interest of regional "*demoi.*" Beyond that, executives have an interest in the distribution of power between levels on their own, which rarely are in accordance with the corresponding interest of members of parliament. As a consequence, constitutional policy-making not only needs to cope with conflicts over a redistribution of power, but these conflicts vary according to the actors involved and imply different, but not necessarily overlapping cleavages, and the positions of participating actors are often fixed due to their accountability to parties or citizens.

In general, the constitutional problem of federal or multilevel systems can be explained as follows: The rule of law requires the persistence of an existing constitutional order that should be protected by particular amendment procedures against manipulation by those holding power in government. Thus changing a constitution must be difficult, and certainly entail higher thresholds than ordinary legislation. However, the inherent ambiguity of basic constitutional decisions on structuring multilevel government and the instability of structures caused by authority migration and institutionalized tensions always requires constitutional change. What has been debated as a challenge for constitutionalism in general (Elkins et al. 2009) is a serious quandary of constitutions in multilevel governments: Constitutional change is necessary, and it appears on the political agenda more often than in unitary polities. But institutional conditions of federalism or multilevel governance make it rather difficult to achieve necessary constitutional change. It affects many actors who exert veto power according to amendment rules and who more often than not pursue diverging interests on a redistribution of powers or resources. Therefore, federal systems are threatened at the same time by instability and rigidity (Bednar 2005).

Problems identified in theory are challenges for responsible political actors and policy-making. They engage in constitutional policy to confront the dilemma. In fact, empirical studies on federalism have revealed astonishing dynamics of constitutional change, including reforms (Banting and Simeon 1985a; Behnke and Benz 2009; Benz and Knüpling 2012a; Lorenz 2011). Apparently, the constitutional dilemma of multilevel government, which has been identified in theory, can be resolved in practical policy-making.

Certainly, the outcomes of constitutional policy vary. Emphasizing its relevance to maintain the balance of power in a multilevel government does not mean that constitutional change brings about stability per se. Like every social mechanism, constitutional policy can fail, depending on the particular conditions. As mentioned, the basic obstacle is caused by amendment rules protecting the federal constitutions against change. Usually, qualified majorities are required, mostly in both houses of a legislature. In multinational federations, modifications of constitutional rules affecting regional governments often are subject to veto rights of individual governments. In times of instability, meeting these procedural requirements seems all the more difficult, with the effect of constitutional policy being at the particular risk of ending in a deadlock and thus federalism being doomed to *stagnation*.

Yet if multilevel governments are inherently dynamic, this must be taken into account when reasoning about constitutional policy. While this policy aims at changing basic rules of governance, it is embedded in ongoing shifts in power and patterns of interactions in politics. These dynamics can constitute both a source of instability to be addressed and a condition influencing the outcome of constitutional change. In view of the rigidity of constitutions, endogenous dynamics even provide a source for stabilizing a multilevel balance, as Martin Landau rightly pointed out (1973). In this perspective, constitutional change is not restricted to amending the written text ("explicit constitutional change" or constitutional reform) but can also result from "implicit constitutional change," practices which modify the effective constitution by application and interpretation and which, in contrast to authority migration, achieve this result in a legitimate way (Voigt 1999).[1] Hence, to remain balanced, a federal constitution must be open to dynamics.

Independent of its sources and the driving mechanism, constitutional change can reinforce *destabilizing dynamics*. We cannot rule out that constitutional amendments resulting from flawed policy-making can trigger self-enforcing processes of concentration of powers in a center or fragmentation of regionalized powers. But we also cannot rule out that implicit change is exploited by powerful actors, that it is insufficient for responding to societal or economic developments or that it continues along a problematic path. Although it regularly proceeds incrementally, thus generating more "continuity of change" than discontinuity ("change of continuity"), implicit constitutional change can

[1] Implicit constitutional change is achieved by non-constitutional means, but it needs to be distinguished from "non-constitutional amendments" (Albert 2009).

Table 2.1. Different directions of multilevel dynamics

		Allocation of power	
		more balanced	more imbalanced
Constitution	more rigid	(unlikely)	*stagnating, instable*
	more flexible	*robust*	*destabilizing*

destabilize a federal system. For this reason, federal dynamics must be controlled according to a common understanding about what constitutes a stable balance of power guaranteeing good governance. As Jenna Bednar, who further elaborated the systems theory of Landau, emphasized, a federal system appears robust if its structures evolve in accordance with public interests (Bednar 2013), i.e. if they facilitate, under changing conditions, effective policy-making conforming to the needs of citizens in the federation and in its constituent units. What qualifies as stable must be defined in a democratic process; and changes in structures of a federal system restoring stability require decisions on constitutional rules. Such a multilevel government in which legitimacy supports commitment to rules and flexibility allows for adjusting rules or norms could be regarded as *robust* (Bednar 2009: 3). A robust federation or multilevel government must be able to adjust and to renovate ("reform") its structures.

Multilevel dynamics can lead in different directions and constitutional policy can support or correct these developments (see Table 2.1). Constitutional policy can express the rigidity of a constitution if it fails to generate amendments, but it can also make it more rigid by extending regulation of multilevel governance. However, it can benefit from the flexibility of a constitution or make it even more flexible by an appropriate amendment of rules. As to the allocation of power, constitutional policy can contribute to increasing balance or imbalance. A rigid constitution hardly makes a government balanced as it cannot correct instability or adjust the distribution of power if necessary. Flexibility in combination with imbalance fosters destabilizing changes. Stagnation despite instability occurs if an imbalance of power cannot be corrected due to a rigid constitution. The aim of constitutional policy should be a balanced but flexible structure of a "robust" multilevel government.

These reasons explain why research on federalism and multilevel governance needs to address the issue of constitutional policy. It is a process determined to maintain the balance of power which is always contested by actors and which needs to be adjusted to changing societal and international conditions of governance. However, in view of the institutional conditions of multilevel government, the various sources of conflict and confrontation among involved policy-makers, the demanding requirements of democratic legitimacy, and the inevitable interplay of formal constitutional reform and informal, implicit change, constitutional policy is burdened by many obstacles, and a balanced multilevel government becomes unlikely. Much depends on the conditions and the particular way of policy-making. As the cases summarized in Chapter 4 demonstrate, we find many attempts to stabilize the constitutional order in federal and regionalized states, but only a few of them succeed. Therefore, we need a better understanding of what explains the different outcomes and which factors contribute to solving the constitutional problem.

So far, researchers cannot convincingly explain why some reforms succeed and why others do not. Moreover, research has utterly neglected to study what happens when reforms have failed. How federal systems solve the rigidity–flexibility dilemma and how they are able to maintain a stable balance of powers remains an open question. In research on constitutional policy, available empirical studies have focused on a limited set of dependent and independent variables and have neglected different patterns of constitutional policy.[2] Therefore, we lack a theory of constitutional dynamics in federal systems covering different modes of change, ranging from continuous incremental adjustment to discontinuous change by reform and explaining why and under which conditions a particular mode succeeds or fails. "The comparative study of 'constitutions' is some 2,300 years old; yet the field remains under-theorized, and we know little about what makes constitutions work and endure over time" (Kincaid 2012: 34).

2.1.2 *Varieties of the Constitutional Problem in Federal and Regionalized Governments*

While we focus our study on constitutional policy as an approach to resolve the dilemma of rigidity and flexibility of federal constitutions, we cannot

[2] Scholars studying comparative politics or federalism show a growing interest in constitutional policy, with the volume by Banting and Simeon (1985a) still providing the most important source of our knowledge. More updated information could be gained from studies dealing with constitution-making and constitutional change in particular countries, including countries with federal or federalizing political systems (Dawn and Fusaro 2011; Ginsburg et al. 2009). Meanwhile, comparative empirical studies of constitutional reform have been published, but they rarely considered agenda setting and negotiation processes. Instead, they dealt with the effects of ratification procedures in different unitary and federal countries (Lorenz 2005; Lutz 1994, 2006). Efforts to come to terms with federal constitutional change have resulted in a number of case-studies and case-specific explanations. Scholars have analyzed the factors that influence agendas or reform initiatives, reform discourses and ideas, or the importance of procedural or structural factors in relation to actors' strategies, resources, tactics or shared norms and perceptions. In cases of failed reforms, they have tried to explain the conditions of that failure observing, among other factors, the role of negotiation procedures, the power of elites and the intervention of the citizens in the design and the ratification of agreed reforms. Path-dependency or cultural and actors' interests have been used to explain outcomes. This research has not yet produced a theoretical framework that can support comparative research. Only recently have scholars begun to look for a more generalizable explanation that accounts for the variation among multilevel governments and across types of reforms (see Behnke and Benz 2009; Broschek and Schultze 2007; Lorenz 2008; Simeon 2009).

ignore that this fundamental problem as well as processes leading to its solution evolve in the context of particular multilevel political systems. In line with the reasoning outlined above, the analysis of constitutional policy that follows is based on a conception of dynamic regime, i.e. a complex, multidimensional setting of institutions structuring patterns of interaction between territorially demarcated jurisdictions and levels of government (Benz and Broschek 2013b). Dynamics is defined as the interplay of continuity and change, with both being perceived as processes evolving through time. Continuity means that a status quo persists over a certain time span, with the status quo signifying either an existing division of powers or an ongoing development of existing structures. Change is defined as a modification of the status quo by deliberate institutional amendment or by unintended effects of collective action. It can occur in a continuous evolution or in a discontinuous way. Depending on the particular conditions, both continuity and change can lead to instability due to rigidity, erosion and destruction or to stability due to sustainability, evolution or reform. This understanding of dynamics in multilevel government implies that driving forces can be traced back to policy-making, to state–society relations or to historical evolution of institutions including ideas legitimizing a power structure, rules and patterns of interaction (Benz and Broschek 2013c: 371). These processes result in varieties of state configurations and particular manifestations of the basic constitutional problem.

The challenge of stabilizing the balance of power by a flexible constitution confronts all political systems which divide powers between different levels. Yet the basic dilemma of multilevel governments finds different expressions depending on the particular type. Varieties result from historical sequences of state building, i.e. the drawing of boundaries and the establishment of governance capacities; nation building, i.e. the integration of diverse groups into a nation held together by imagined identities or solidarity among fellow citizens; and democratization, i.e. the creation of structures and institutions enabling citizen participation and accountable government (Bartolini 2005). Moreover, changes in state–society relations occurring under specific conditions shape multilevel government structures in different countries (Benz 2013). Scholars have made efforts to comprehend varieties and have distinguished different types (for a summary see Colino 2013: 51–4). For the purpose of this study, it is sufficient to focus on the dimensions of multilevel government affected by authority migration and addressed in processes of constitutional change.

In principle, these processes relate to three dimensions of multilevel government: First, the vertical distribution of power and modes of coordination between central and regional governments; second, the power and resources of regional units and their horizontal relations; and third, the relations between the executives and the legislative institutions (the intragovernmental dimension). In the reform processes which have occurred since the late 1970s, only the first two dimensions have been relevant, while the executive–legislative dimension has remained more or less unchanged or only indirectly affected by decentralization of powers or modifications of intergovernmental relations.[3] Therefore, the constitutional problems can be described by referring to the vertical and horizontal structures of multilevel systems, which in reality overlap.

According to the vertical intergovernmental dimension, we can distinguish between unitary states undergoing a process of regionalization and established federal states. Particular constitutional problems of multilevel government arise in both. In federal states, the distribution of powers between central and lower levels and rules of intergovernmental coordination have to be revised in order to maintain a legitimized balance or to find a new one. In regionalized states, constitutional policy aims at devolution or decentralization of powers from central government to regions and can include a revision of intergovernmental relations and the fiscal regime. In both processes, those governments losing powers have a decisive say in constitutional reform; hence they can be considered veto-players. De facto, if not pursuant to law, central and regional governments need to come to an agreement on constitutional amendments.

Concerning the horizontal dimension, federal or regionalized governments are challenged either by conflicts among governments or by conflicts among social groups. In integrated multilevel systems characterized by a homogeneous society, government-centered issues prevail, like the distribution of fiscal resources or institutional conditions for horizontal coordination of regional policies. In disintegrated federations, society-centered conflicts have to be managed. Accordingly, finding or maintaining a balance of power implies different challenges for constitutional policy depending on how problems of governance and integration are framed in constitutional policy.

Based on this reasoning, we can distinguish performance problems and problems of territorial integration which have to be dealt with in constitutional policy. *Performance problems* concern the effectiveness of governance of a multilevel system. They occur due to a divergence of space and scale (Brenner 2004), with space meaning the territorial scope of policy problems and scale meaning the scope of jurisdiction where policies are made. This divergence may result from a high degree of centralization, from uncoordinated external

[3] This stands in remarkable contrast to the European Union. Here the institutions participating in exerting executive and legislative powers of the Union and their relations evolved or were reformed in close connection with the delegation of powers from the national to the European level. Moreover, member states have adjusted their parliamentary systems to the conditions of European governance. In federal and regionalized governments, tensions between democracy and intergovernmental relations have been discussed, without major consequences for the constitutional design. In general, decentralization of power and regional autonomy have been considered to improve democracy.

effects in decentralized policies, or from the interlocking of politics or policy-making at the different levels either in legislation or administration. In general, these institutional conditions lead to suboptimal policy output at the central or regional level and to coordination deficits. Horizontal imbalances can also cause performance deficits, if redistributive conflicts between constituent units overburden a central government or cannot be solved in intergovernmental agreements. They can also surface as a consequence of ineffective governance in multilevel political systems. *Integration problems* are, simply put, caused by a divergence between community and scale (Hooghe and Marks 2009), with community meaning a group of citizens sharing a particular loyalty related to the production of public goods. Divergence is expressed in conflicts usually provoked by regionally concentrated groups expressing the need to accommodate diversity in heterogeneous societies. They are particularly intensive if communities share distinct cultural or linguistic backgrounds and are interested in a specific way of living together or in maintaining economic resources of their region for which they claim ownership. Communities of citizens with a strong intragroup loyalty but with lower attachment to the whole nation not only demand recognition, but also particular rights to defend their identities or interests, powers to govern themselves autonomously and fiscal support to maintain their distinct policies.

Both performance and integration problems require a redistribution of powers and resources for normative reasons, i.e. for guaranteeing legitimacy of governance and the constitutional order. But they also have implications for the operation and stability of the territorial structure, as they relate to different forces of dynamics and highlight different expressions of the rigidity–flexibility dilemma in a multilevel government. According to studies of constitutional change, problems of performance trigger reforms "aimed primarily at tidying up political and administrative processes in order to facilitate policy-making and co-ordination", and group or integration-related conflicts call for reforms "aimed at reshaping the fundamental relations among contending groups" (Banting and Simeon 1985b: 6).

Certainly, both types of problems do not appear as objectively given. Rather, powerful actors who are able to frame certain conditions as a constitutional issue define them. Hence, the specific matters of constitutional policy result from processes of agenda setting. Depending on the particular societal and institutional context, governments or political parties from the central or regional level define the problems to be addressed in reform debates and in constitutional reform. Together with interest groups or the media, they also frame how problems are perceived. Therefore, the following categorization of types of constitutional problems in federal or federalizing systems should not lead to a functionalist explanation of constitutional change. Rather it allows us to distinguish how powerful agenda-setters frame problems, which issues are addressed in or excluded from constitutional negotiations, and which types of conflicts predominate in constitutional politics.

Performance problems may, as indicated, be caused by over-centralization, fragmentation, or a tight interlocking of different levels of government or administration. Over-centralization breeds policy rigidity due to a lack of information, or information overload; it increases conflicts due to insufficient consideration of particular problems or interests arising in regions; and it is conducive to deficient implementation of central legislation. In reality, these problems are difficult to discern because costs of centralization always have to be set off against the costs of decentralization in particular policies. Although liberal societies tend to favor decentralization, this does not necessarily indicate problems of over-centralization (Treisman 2007). In political practice, different lines of reasoning support decentralization reforms, which can be summarized under the label of a "new regionalism." In contrast with the "old" conservative, premodern regionalism of the nineteenth century directed against the emerging nation state, proponents of the new version respond to the increasing regional differentiation of economic and social structures (Keating 1998). In this context, Social Democrats have emphasized the power of regions to provide public utilities and services and they have proposed regional cooperation between government, private firms and civic society organizations. Moreover, they argued that a centralized state offers its citizens too few opportunities for participation. They also point out that central bureaucrats may not feel the need for transparency, and accountability may be limited (Crook and Manor 2000: 4, 11). Due to this delegitimization of political action, loyalty and support for the state may be threatened. Neoliberal scholars and politicians attacked centralization as an inefficient organization of territorial government (Osborne and Gaebler 1993; Toffler 1970: 251). In this line of thinking, efficiency is expected to result from governance organized like markets (Loughlin 2007b: 389), with citizens being considered consumers of public services. Accordingly, policies should be tailored to the needs of the citizens and provided as closely to them as possible. Political performance, according to this view, is also improved by pressure of competition, if individual or corporate actors "vote with their feet" in order to express their preferences (even if this usually applies only to a rather small number of mobile people; De Vries 2000: 193–4; Ranson and Stewart 1994: 102). Neoliberalists also argue that over-centralized government causes suboptimal policy outcomes due to capacity overload of the center. They regard the centralized Western welfare state as being charged with too many tasks leading to excessive spending and rising public deficits. Instead, neoliberals propose that governments should concentrate on core functions and that in particular the central state be "dismantled" (Loughlin 2007b: 390–1).

Performance problems triggering constitutional reform may also result from a tight interlocking of levels. They find expression in ineffective joint decision-making and potentially the joint-decision trap (Scharpf 1988), in insufficient coordination between levels, or in distributive conflicts due to fiscal imbalances. Joint decision-making describes a particular constellation of power sharing between levels of government, where "central-level policy choices depend on the (nearly) unanimous agreement of lower-level government" (Scharpf 2011: 218). Under these institutional conditions, policy-making may end in deadlock with governments at the different levels being unable to act unilaterally ("compulsory negotiation system"; Scharpf 2011: 222), and policy outputs and outcomes turn out as suboptimal since governments tend to find compromises on the lowest common denominator. Even when situations require major policy changes, only incremental modification of the status quo can be achieved. In multilevel governments where powers are separated, the complexity of policies and the interconnectedness of central and regional decisions require coordination between different levels of government. Disentangling policies entirely between levels will therefore fail to achieve a sufficient quality of policy performance. Performance losses may also occur, if coordination between levels of government does not find support in the constituent units, or if accountability to parliaments or commitments to interests groups reduce the discretion of policy-makers to find compromises (Benz 2000b).

Finally, performance problems can find expression in fiscal imbalances, which may cause insufficient supply of public goods and services in certain territories or waste of fiscal resources by overspending. Again, the framing of constitutional problems depends not only on the given institutional setting but also on political ideologies. Liberals and Conservatives tend to emphasize the lack of transparency and efficiency of interlocking of levels, while Social Democrats tend to include the issue of fiscal balance, in particular if they perceive problems of distributive justice in a federal system.

Integration problems find expression in conflicts in a society and may be caused by insufficient recognition and accommodation of minorities, limited access to public goods or services in peripheral regions, the decline of interregional solidarity, and under-representation of certain groups. These conflicts trigger demands for constitutional reforms reallocating power among existing levels of government or guaranteeing representation or veto rights for minorities in federal institutions. They may also aim at creating institutions with administrative or legislative powers in regions, in which the minority finds a meaningful representation of their interests, thus allowing these groups to autonomously decide on significant policies and reduce their dependence on other groups.

The need to accommodate distinct cultural or linguistic communities or minority nations can be justified by normative as well as functional reasons.

After policies of assimilation or integration had prevailed in previous decades, the general understanding has turned towards different approaches of preserving cultural diversity or guaranteeing survival of linguistic communities (Kymlicka 2007). Constitutions in democratic countries regularly guarantee equality and individual rights to express identities and provide for a legal basis to prosecute discriminatory actions based on cultural, linguistic or ethnic grounds. However, proponents of communitarian theories have claimed that individual rights or equality rights are not sufficient to support cultural survival of minority groups or individual self-development (Taylor 1992). In order to achieve this goal, protection from majority decisions in certain policy domains, e.g. education, culture, but sometimes also social policy or health care are regarded as similarly important, not the least because regionalist movements arise primarily in regions interested in preserving and developing their economic resources. Otherwise, support of and loyalty to the state may decrease within these groups and may turn into civil disobedience, if not insurgency, and demands for secession. Constitutional reforms are therefore considered necessary in order to recognize distinct groups appropriately and to provide for constitutionally protected spaces of cultural autonomy and self-government for these constituencies (Kymlicka 1995; Tully 1995). They can be a way to restore a balance between loyalty to the state and demands for autonomy. Federalization has been suggested as a solution as it combines "forms of unity with forms of diversity" (Burgess 2006: 156f.) and supports the cohesion of the state while at the same time providing for some autonomy for substate entities (Simeon and Conway 2001). However, scholars have also cautioned against the potential spiral towards disintegration triggered by processes of federalization (Erk and Anderson 2009; Horowitz 1985; McGarry and O'Leary 2009; Roeder 2009).

In particular contexts defined by institutional settings of governments, these problems result in different driving forces for agenda setting in constitutional policy. Performance problems may be intensely debated in public, but as matters of the constitution and as problems requiring a reallocation of powers or resources, they primarily concern actors in governments, i.e. members of the executive, of parliaments or political parties. Integration problems often are raised by regionalist movements or regional parties. Thus processes of agenda setting are mainly pushed by societal forces and dynamics which cannot be controlled by governments. If integration is at stake, the need for constitutional change is much more pressing than if performance of multilevel governance is under debate, in particular as the exclusion of minorities and the threat of secession are regarded as fundamental problems in democracies. On the other hand, when performance deficits are diagnosed as problems of institutions, actors in governments often call for modest adjustments of constitutional rules rather than for fundamental reforms.

Institutions differing between regionalized or federal governments can also affect the way constitutional problems are defined. If integration and performance problems are traced back to over-centralization in regionalized states, the central government is expected to unilaterally devolve powers and fiscal resources to regions. In this case, the strongest player in the redistributive game of a constitutional reform must concede parts of its powers. It seems likely that the executive can profit from restructuring multilevel government. In line with theories of European integration and transnational politics, it can be expected that executives maintain power despite regionalization or decentralization by participating in intergovernmental relations, whereas parliaments mostly lose out (Moravcsik 1997; Wolf 2000). However, shared powers nevertheless imply limits compared to centralized powers, and regionalization in these states usually results from regionalist movements or parties framing the problems in terms of integration. Thus even if a central government may not be compelled to find support by regional governments as is typically required in federal states, constitutional change aiming at decentralization, regionalization or devolution is rather difficult to achieve due to the different framings of constitutional issues by the decisive actors. If governments search for a new balance of powers in federal states, redistributive effects may be concealed by emphasizing performance problems. If they are considered to result from the interlocking of levels the existing constitutional order appears as a constraint for all governments, with the consequence that constitutional reform turns out as a positive-sum game despite a redistribution of powers. Certainly, an effective solution of these problems nevertheless requires negotiating agreements proceeding as a mixed-motive game. Moreover, a vertical reallocation of powers often affects lower level governments in different ways and raises horizontal distributive conflicts. However, the degree of asymmetry of expected outcomes must not be obvious from the outset and conflicts evolve during the process of constitutional change rather than during agenda setting. Settling conflicts by package deals and compromises, however, may turn out impossible if constitutional rules under debate relate to fundamental values, as is the case in disintegrated societies. Here, the pressure for change goes along with intense conflicts making constitutional reform a particularly demanding task.

2.2 Constitutional Policy as Mechanism of Change

2.2.1 *State of Research: Theories of Constitutional Change and Empirical Evidence*

In comparative federalism, scholars tend to regard constitutions as rules determining the allocation of powers, the representation of regional communities or regional governments in central legislation and the role of courts as arbiters of federal–regional disputes. In many countries, they include rules concerning fiscal equalization schemes or intergovernmental relations. This "technical" understanding focuses on the static character of a fundamental law, but fails to capture the dynamics of federal constitutions. In a broader sense elaborated in political theory, constitutions are conceived not only as a formal legal framework of a government, but also as norms guiding social and political practice in a political system, and as fundamental principles shared in a political community or society (Fossum and Menendez 2010: 20–7). Accordingly, constitutional change appears either as amendment of formal rules, as modification of norms, i.e. accepted patterns of politics and policy-making or as reinterpretation of shared ideas justifying an allocation of rights, powers and resources. In reality, all three dimensions are affected by dynamics, in one way or another, and reveal more or less continuity or change.

Change in all three dimensions has been the subject of theories of institutional change and theories of multilevel policy-making, although the different approaches have emphasized selected aspects of a constitution. Overall, these theories mainly call attention to the constraining effects of principles, norms and rules or the limits of change in view of conflicts about the redistribution of power. They explain why institutions are "sticky" (Mahoney and Thelen 2010: 6) and, accordingly, emphasize rigidity not only of constitutions of multilevel polities but of institutions in general (Peters et al. 2005). Scholars applying institutionalism in a historical perspective point out the impact of historical legacies on constitutional reforms, be they entrenched in institutions or expressed in predominating ideas (Broschek 2011). Thus they account for continuity rather than change. Only a few contributions have explicitly addressed processes of constitutional change, but none of them has emphasized constitutional policy as a mechanism of change. Theories considering collective decisions on institutions or constitutions suggest that continuation of the status quo is more likely than substantial change.

Scholars theorizing in the framework of a rational choice approach refer to the character of institutions as rule systems enabling and constraining collective action. In a historical perspective, they point out the incentives for actors to follow a path of development set by earlier decisions on institutions. When confronted with constraints, actors are assumed to compare existing institutions to prospective benefits of change. From an economic perspective, institutions result from investments, which yield increasing returns for collective action when maintained, whereas they cause high costs when being changed (North 1990; Pierson 2000). In view of the complexity of institutions and the costs for transformation, historical institutionalism describes change as gradual, with the exception of unusual circumstances causing critical junctures (Thelen 1999). In these particular situations, a change of an institutionalized path may be possible. Yet the causal logic and effects of critical junctures still are not understood appropriately (Soifer 2012). Moreover, some studies have found out that external shocks or turbulences may lead actors to preserve the stability of institutions, which are more likely to be modified under rather stable conditions (Thelen and Karcher 2013).

Based on a similar conceptualization of institutions as rules, actor-centered institutionalism suggests that deliberate redistribution of powers is difficult to achieve, since amendment rules constitute many veto points. Even if converted into a positive-sum game, institutional change likely ends with a preservation of the existing balance of powers and resources. While the creation of new institutions adding to old ones seems to be possible, an outcome which recently has been categorized as "layering" (Mahoney and Thelen 2010: 16–17; Streeck and Thelen 2005: 31), any transformation of existing institutions seems nearly unachievable. This reasoning has guided Fritz W. Scharpf's analysis of the joint-decision trap (Scharpf 1988). By applying what was later elaborated as the veto-player theory (Tsebelis 2002) to policy-making and institutional reform, he explained why institutional or constitutional change is doomed to fail, even if actors consider such change necessary. In line with this approach, scholars studying constitutions have tried to trace back the probability of change to different decision rules that apply in the ratification of constitutional amendments. However, findings have not led to any general conclusions (Closa 2012a; Rasch and Congleton 2006; Lorenz 2005), and thus have at least raised some doubts as to the validity of the veto-player theory.

In an interesting extension of the actor-centered approach, Mahoney and Thelen have drawn attention to actors who try to extend their powers and thus trigger dynamics. Although they distinguish a different pattern of intended and unintended institutional development, they also describe change as more or less gradual due to antagonistic powers of change agents and actors profiting from the status quo (Mahoney and Thelen 2010). In constitutional policy referring to territorial organization of government, the conflicting positions are often reflected in party politics when regionalist parties confront mainstream parties. For these reasons, scholars have suggested considering the party system or party politics as the factor explaining success or failure of constitutional change in federal or regional states (Bolleyer, Swenden and McEwen 2014; Swenden and Maddens 2009; Toubeau and Massetti 2013; Toubeau and Wagner 2015). While this is relevant for many cases, not the least since parties influence agenda setting and participate in constitutional policy-making, this approach does not go beyond identifying party positions and political cleavages and tends to neglect institutional constraints and the particular impact of party politics on constitutional negotiations (see Petersohn, Behnke and Rhode 2015).

Sociological institutionalism frames institutions as norms shaped not only by political decisions on institutional designs, but also by permanent practices of actors guided by norms, values, ideas and shared cultural understanding (DiMaggio and Powell 1991; Mayer and Scott 1983). In this context, the perception of institutional change comes close to the concept of "implicit constitutional change" elaborated in constitutional economics (Voigt 1999), although the explanation of these processes differs. Constructivist or discursive institutionalism portrays change either as a necessary result of tensions or "frictions" in institutional configurations of ideas and rules (Liebermann 2002) or as evolution resulting from continuous reinterpretation or renegotiation of rules (Hay 2006; Schmidt 2010). In both cases, norms and social practice are regarded as closely connected in ongoing processes of policy-making and reflective communication. In contrast to rational choice approaches, sociological and discursive versions of institutionalism emphasize the need to legitimize rules either by reconciling them with social norms or by communicative discourses (Schmidt 2010: 3) aiming at finding a consensus on rules. While indicating the relevance of processes, these approaches fall short of analyzing which characteristics of processes promise change and which features tend towards continuity. The general thrust of the argument is that institutions evolve only gradually.

The character of constitutions as fundamental principles has been addressed by scholars interested in the role of ideas. There are good reasons to assume that ideas reflecting the collective perceptions and values of a community tend to persist over time. In a long-term perspective, "paradigmatic" shifts may occur, as has been argued by scholars working on organizations and policy-making (Benz 1984; Hall 1993). Yet it remains to be explained which conditions produce such a significant change in ideas and how this affects constitutional rules and practices. As regards the first question, the "multiple stream approach" evokes the argument that interfering developments in politics and policy-making together with an intensification of perceived problems may generate a situation that opens a "window of opportunity" for change (Kingdon 1984; Zahariadis 2007). But like the concept of critical junctures, this view takes significant change as a contingent result of development. Moreover, whereas this theory may explain the setting of an agenda, it does not tell us what makes actors agree on new institutions or constitutional principles, rules or norms. Regarding the effects of changes in ideas, scholars have indicated that they may, first and foremost, result in conflicts between principles and rules or standard operation procedures which create a driving force of institutional dynamics on their own (Lieberman 2002). Although this assumption is convincing, this theory does not give account of the particular causes and conditions that turn conflicts into dynamics.

When looking at the literature on constitutions we also find different suggestions for explaining constitutional change. To a certain extent, the assumptions made in these contexts resemble those inherent in institutionalist theories or theories of institutional policy-making outlined in the preceding paragraphs. Theories of constitutional economics have to deal with the basic problem that rational actors may come to an agreement on a constitution if they act in a "state of nature," but that a renegotiation of rules determining the allocation of rights, powers or resources is much more difficult. The first case conforms to a positive-sum game, while actors are in a zero-sum game when amending a constitution. Nonetheless, constitutional change occurs. To solve this puzzle, some scholars refer to the fact that constitutional decisions are made behind a "veil of uncertainty" on the positions which participants can achieve (Buchanan and Tullock 1965: 78). Consequently, actors can not only pursue individual interests on a redistribution of powers, but also have to come to a common understanding about the consequences of rules, which they develop in discourses (Vanberg and Buchanan 1989). Another explanation emphasizes processes of implicit change, i.e. a revision of shared interpretations, dominant doctrines or "constitutional conventions,"[4] in view of the fact that explicit change of the written text of a constitution is difficult to achieve (Voigt 1999). However, neither of these theories tells us which assumptions, interpretations or doctrines prevail and which factors can explain a particular outcome, not to mention the question of how to qualify outcomes regarding the balance of power that should be stabilized or restored. The distinction between implicit and explicit constitutional change is important, as the following reasoning will make obvious, but the decisive question is how both types of constitutional change interact. Recently, Adrienne Héritier (2007) extended this theory by showing that institutions evolve in various sequences of informal and formal change. But in consequence of her focus on the EU, neither does she tell us which sequences can be expected under varying conditions, nor does she analyze processes of formal change in greater detail and in a comparative perspective. Overall, these theories have their limits and do not provide sufficient insight into the conditions surrounding success or failure of constitutional policy.

Other theories explain the content of constitutional law as determined by economic interests and power structures in a particular society, a reasoning which can be traced back to Charles A. Beard's (1913) interpretation of constitution-making during the American Revolution. Later research following

[4] There is no consensus on what the concept of "constitutional conventions" exactly implies. Without going into the details of the disputes, we can define conventions "as the rules of behavior that ought to be regarded as binding by those concerned in working the constitution when they have correctly interpreted the precedents and the relevant constitutional principles" (Marshall 1985: 39).

this approach has declared a strict economic determinism obsolete and stressed that societal developments have an indirect impact by influencing constitutional ideas (e.g. Galligan and Versteeg 2013). In the 1950s, William A. Livingston elaborated his society-centered theory of federalism along this line of theorizing. He assumed that federal constitutions respond to developments in social structures and evolve accordingly (Erk 2008; Livingston 1956; for a similar theory Friedrich 1968), yet without clearly explaining the causal relation between societal and constitutional change. To overcome these deficits, as mentioned above, theories of institutional change and policy-making should include society-centered explanations. One possible way has been suggested by scholars, who have looked for constitutional moments, following Bruce Ackerman's influential work on the history of the US constitution (Ackerman 1991). Yet, like critical junctures, this concept has more descriptive than explanatory value. Neither does it reveal why and under which conditions constitutional moments occur, nor does it spell out how the existence of such a situation influences constitutional policy or constitutional change. Finally, all these theories do not take into account the particular problems caused by the multilevel character of constitutional policy in federal or regionalized governments.

To conclude: Although the rich literature on institutional and constitutional change provides a wide range of theoretical reasoning and suggests different conceptualizations and explanations of change, there is no single approach that gives us a compelling idea of how constitutional policy can contribute to balance power and to solve problems of performance or integration, and how it can avoid running into the dilemma of instability or rigidity. This practical problem for government and governance in multilevel polities still remains a puzzle for political science. By emphasizing continuity, we cannot understand what drives change in these configurations of a political system. We also cannot understand the conditions favoring significant amendments of constitutions by reform or innovation instead of incremental adjustment. Theories emphasizing societal pressure underestimate that social change tends to increase instability, and that external shocks either lead political actors to avoid change and defend the status quo or to respond with replacing rather than amending a constitution. To avoid the trap of causing either rigidity or instability, non-intentional evolution or adjustment are certainly relevant, but processes of constitutional policy addressing the need for deliberate reform or innovation are no less essential (Benz and Colino 2011: 389; Ginsburg et al. 2009). At least in the longer term, necessary flexibility can be achieved in processes of constitutional evolution. Yet without being legitimized in a policy aiming at deliberate amendment of a constitution and conforming to accepted procedures, it may not achieve a stable balance of power. Evolution driven by actors interested in extending their authority will threaten rather than restore the balance of a multilevel government. Hence, instead of focusing our attention on either incremental adjustment or comprehensive reforms, we need a broader analytical framework covering different patterns of constitutional dynamics, including different mechanisms.

The framework should cover the dynamics of particular multilevel systems. In this regard, it should highlight processes which cause an imbalance of structures and which set off processes of constitutional policy determined to restore balance. Moreover, the framework must aim at explaining how constitutional change can occur despite significant institutional constraints. Thus, it should identify mechanisms of change and outcomes to be expected due to the operation of these mechanisms. The following sections outline such a framework. It is based on theoretical and empirical research. It evolved during the research process, which started with assumptions derived from theories and a confrontation of these assumptions with results from case studies on constitutional change. In this process of shifting back and forth between theory and empirical work, the final framework took shape as presented here. As we aim at explaining change in multilevel government, we do not pretend to provide a general theory of constitutional change. However, we believe that our theoretical reasoning points out some important aspects which are significant to explaining why constitutional reform can go beyond incremental evolution, aspects which are neglected by available theories. In any case, we believe that our framework can provide insights into how governments in multilevel polities may succeed in keeping an appropriate balance of power or why they fail to cope with the fundamental challenge they are always confronted with.

2.2.2 *Mechanisms: Constitutional Policy as Joint Decision-making*

Regardless of the particular expression of problems of governance and integration, federal and regionalized governments need to cope with the outlined challenge by deliberately changing their constitution in case power structures become imbalanced or instable. Therefore, constitutional policy, which more often than not requires a formal amendment of the constitution, has to be regarded as a basic mechanism of keeping the balance. The study summarized in this book focuses on this particular aspect of dynamics, without ignoring the wider context of historical evolution or state–society relations and the related causal mechanisms and outcomes (Benz and Broschek 2013c). Therefore, the core of our analytical framework aims at understanding and explaining the mechanism of constitutional policy.

In federal or multilevel governments, constitutional policy cuts across boundaries of jurisdictions or institutions, in particular when governments from different levels have to find an agreement or coordinate decisions on a reallocation of powers. This is why we labeled the basic mechanism of dynamics as "inter-institutional" policy in interlocked arenas (Benz and Broschek 2013c: 379–83). Regarding constitutional reform, the institutional context of policy-making conforms to the model of "joint decision-making," described and analyzed by Fritz W. Scharpf (Scharpf 1988; see also: Benz 2011), either due to constitutional rules or constitutional conventions. Joint decisions require that actors representing the whole nation and those representing regions find an agreement in multilateral negotiations. Regardless of particular amendment rules or procedures, change of multilevel constitutions must, in the end, be supported either explicitly or implicitly, by all governments representing the *demos* or regional *demoi* in order to find a legitimized and stable constitutional order (see also: Elkins et al. 2009). Therefore, taken as an analytical model (Scharpf 2011), the concept of joint decision-making provides a point of departure to identify mechanisms of effective constitutional reform and to discover conditions of success and failure of constitutional policy in federal systems.

In contrast to veto-player theory, the model of joint decision-making puts emphasis on the process of negotiation rather than on a final decision. Although Scharpf regards veto-players, i.e. those actors who have the power to prevent a decision, as decisive actors, his theorizing addresses the ways these actors find a policy which all can accept. In this context, the distinction between negotiation and final decision (here referred to as "ratification") is important. Tsebelis (2002) has pointed out this distinction by indicating the relevance of "agenda setting," i.e. the process of defining the decision proposal. Scholars applying veto-player theory have mostly ignored this aspect of policy-making when they have examined preferences and power of policymakers. Yet veto-players decide on policy proposals usually resulting from negotiations. The distinction between negotiations and ratification is particularly important when both processes occur in different institutional settings with different actor constellations (arenas). What applies to legislation in general is even more significant in constitutional reform processes.

As we can conclude from empirical research, rules of constitutional amendment hardly make a difference (for a summary, see Closa 2012a) regarding the frequency or scope of change. Accordingly, we have good reasons to assume that institutions allocating formal veto powers alone cannot explain the outcome of constitutional policy. At least they do not have direct effects. Therefore, and in line with Scharpf's model of multilevel governance, constitutional negotiations obviously matter. In principle, all participants in a negotiation are in a position to veto a decision, and in so far as it might make sense to refer to the veto-player concept. However, negotiations proceed in the shadow of decision-making usually occurring in a different arena, and the arenas of negotiation and of decision-making may be more or less congruent or connected.

At a glance, a theory based on the joint-decision model explains why policy-making in multilevel settings likely ends in deadlock. Yet Scharpf's approach to multilevel governance allows for a more differentiated analysis. It implies that actors pursue selfish goals and try to maximize their benefits, but that they are also interested in coming to decisions. These mixed motives particularly drive the behavior of responsible governments or members of parliaments who follow divergent interests, e.g. party political or institutional interests, but who are also highly motivated in proving their ability to govern. As strategic veto-players, they tend to avoid deadlock, if a policy is on the agenda and they have to make a decision on it. As regards normal policy-making, Scharpf himself (Scharpf et al. 1976, 1978) and later other scholars (Benz 2000a; Falkner 2011; Héritier 1999; Painter 1991) uncovered a number of ways how actors avoid the trap inherent in this policy game or found additional conditions which need to be included in an explanation. However, according to Scharpf's theory, deadlock is not to be expected in normal policy-making. The real trap is caused by constitutional rigidity. While compromises on issues in specific policy fields are feasible for incremental modifications of the status quo, the results achieved under the particular constraints of shared powers often frustrate policy-makers and prevent them from solving problems effectively. In order to improve this unsatisfactory situation, actors might decide to initiate institutional or constitutional policy, last but not least if changes in societal conditions make established patterns of agreement on the lowest common denominator no longer appropriate or acceptable. However, whereas in normal policy-making representatives in democratic governments, who want to be re-elected, usually tend to avoid deadlock situations, are motivated to make decisions and thus have an incentive to find a compromise, they prefer the status quo compared to a change if they expect to lose power by an amendment of constitutional rules. As any change in the balance of power necessarily ends with winners and losers, constitutional reforms of a multilevel government where affected actors hold veto-positions are quite difficult to accomplish. Even if all actors acknowledge the functional need for constitutional reform, they rather tend to stick to their existing positions instead of conceding their power base (Scharpf 1988). When it comes to amending the constitution, the mixed-motive game in normal policy-making turns into an "antagonistic cooperation" under the institutional conditions of joint decision-making. This theoretical proposition has hardly been challenged so far.

The joint decision-model is based on an actor-centered institutionalism (Scharpf 1997). It assumes rational actors who pursue their own preferences, but it takes into account that decisions are influenced by actors' strategic behavior and their normative orientations, both of them being influenced by institutions. When agents of governments or parliaments directly affected by a reallocation of powers dominate constitutional negotiations, we might find that a constitutional reform of a multilevel political system is likely blocked due to a confrontation of these actors interested in maintaining or extending power. Given these conditions, at best incremental adjustment of norms guiding practices or of interpretations of rules in a process of implicit change can be expected. However, we might also discover that actors are willing to negotiate a compromise or a package deal on a reallocation of powers or resources. This can occur if negotiators realize that they represent citizens or groups in society and thus are motivated to solve problems of governance. Moreover, considering that responsible politicians seek to legitimize their behavior or decisions by reasons referring to principles or ideas, we cannot rule out the possibility that bargaining turns into arguing and ends with a consensus based on new legitimizing ideas for an amended constitution (see Table 2.2; for details of this model of negotiation: Benz 1994: 118–34).[5] Such an extended framework of joint decision-making requires researchers to look for conditions which have an impact on strategic and normative action orientations and, as a consequence, on different modes of negotiation. They

Table 2.2. Modes of constitutional negotiations

Conditions		Action orientation focusing on		Prevailing mode of negotiation		Probable outcomes
Problems structures and		individual interests	→	confrontation	→	deadlock
Processes of constitutional policy	→	individual interests and joint problems	→	bargaining	→	compromise/ package deal
Situations		general reasons or principles	→	arguing	→	consensus

[5] Confrontation is defined as a mode of negotiation among participants who tend to defend their policy position against other actors' claims and who threaten to react with unilateral action if others do not accept their position. In bargaining, negotiators aiming at an agreement make propositions. In distributive bargaining, they try to get what they want by offering package deals; in integrative bargaining, they make concessions in order to achieve a compromise. Arguing processes are characterized by actors' willingness to justify their propositions by reasons acceptable for all participants and to search for a policy which all can approve due to convincing reasons.

determine the quality of probable outcomes to a considerable extent. In reality, we regularly find all three modes in combinations constituting variable patterns of negotiations. What therefore is relevant to explain is the tendency towards one or another. In any case, this concept of negotiations implies that the joint-decision trap in constitutional policy can be avoided if actors do not run into confrontation and if bargaining on redistributive issues (reallocation of power) is turned into or modified by arguing about reasons and principles.

The assumption that arguing can occur in practical policy-making does not contradict a realistic theory of rational choice, as Vanberg and Buchanan (1989) convincingly explained. Under particular conditions, it is rational for policy-makers to refer to reasons and principles seriously in order to achieve a consensus. When it comes to redistributive issues, compromises and package deals cannot solve the problems at stake, and actors find themselves in a collective choice dilemma. In view of the issues at stake, constitutional policy is likely to cause this situation, which rational actors want to avoid. Yet there is no guarantee that actors refrain from exploiting their bargaining power and maximizing their individual benefits. Therefore, we have to search for conditions which facilitate arguing behavior allowing actors to escape this dilemma.

As can be concluded from the literature review in the precious section, and as Richard Simeon has compellingly shown in a summary of research, a broad range of conditions can have an impact on constitutional policy, like the historical, societal and institutional background, starting points and situations (e.g. constitutional moments) and specific features of processes (Simeon 2009). Leaving aside the varieties of multilevel governments for the moment, we focus on those procedural and structural factors influencing constitutional negotiations, which policy-makers can manipulate, i.e. which are of practical relevance. Therefore, at this point of the analysis, we will not take into account structures and developments in society, regardless of whether they find expression in economic structures, cultural values and group loyalties or party politics. When asking which factors make constitutional policy in multilevel setting effective, the way constitutional negotiations are organized is most important, in particular considering our knowledge on the limited effects of amendment rules. By testing alternative explanations in our empirical study (see Chapter 7), we could support the appropriateness of this approach. Moreover, in contrast to rules entrenched in constitutions which have to be taken as given, other institutional or procedural conditions of constitutional negotiations can be modified without revising the constitutional law, i.e. without policy-makers running into another quandary of constitutional change. Consequently, we have to inquire into those features of constitutional negotiations, which induce actors to deviate from a confrontation or bargaining mode of collective action and switch, at least partly, to the arguing mode.

The benefits of the suggested analytical distinction of modes of negotiation have been confirmed by empirical studies in different policy fields (see, e.g., Bächtiger and Wyss 2013; Holzinger 2001; Landwehr 2009). Its particular relevance for studying constitutional negotiations can be derived from the concept of a constitution introduced above and from theories of institutional change. Interested in legitimizing constitutional rules, policy-makers should be aware that amendments not only need to result from particular procedures, but have to be justified by principles shared in a respective political community. Like every rule conceived as law has to conform to norms which citizens or officials applying the law acknowledge (Hart 1994: 90), constitutional rules have to be based on accepted reasons or principles in order to gain legitimacy. Accordingly, constitutional change in multilevel systems affects the rule for allocating powers and the basic normative concept of a political order justifying a particular rule. It goes without saying that this concept of a constitution does not mean that actors in constitutional negotiations always refer to reasons. Such an idealistic understanding of politics does not bear much relevance for empirical research. Instead, this concept of constitution clarifies the dual nature characteristic for the substance of constitutional policy. Constitutional policy is, implicitly or explicitly, about both principles and rules, and it inevitably affects general and specific interests at the same time.

Yet these substantial dimensions can have a different weight in practice. Depending on the framing of issues as principles or rules, conflicts and modes of negotiations differ. Rules of federal constitutions directly affect the allocation of powers or resources, whereas principles are not an issue of distributive conflicts among institutions or governments, but raise questions of justification. In the first case, negotiations often proceed as bargaining about details of rules and of who should get what kind of rights, powers or resources. When constitutional policy is about conflicting principles, there is no room for compromises or package deals, with the consequence that negotiating actors either run into a confrontation or enter into an arguing process. Hence, the framing of the constitutional problem has a significant effect on constitutional policy. Consequently, we need to find out which conditions affect this framing and in which way they affect frames.

Beyond that, structures of constitutional negotiations, often determined by existing institutions or established practices, set conditions that are decisive for the success or failure of an attempt to reform federal systems. More often than not scholars and experts discuss the pros and cons of committees or conventions. Based on accounts in the literature on constitutional policy (e.g. Elster 1995; Ginsburg et al. 2009; McWhinney 1981: 27–36) and information from available case studies, at least four basic forms of constitutional negotiations, relevant for changing constitutions in multilevel governments, should be distinguished (Benz and Knüpling 2012b: 397–8):

- *Committees* are established either by parliaments or by the executives. In the first instance, they include members selected by parties in parliament, usually in proportionality to the number of seats occupied by a party; in the second case civil servants and experts delegated by central and regional governments negotiate.
- *Commissions* include members from both parliament and the central and regional executives. Their structure of membership usually mirrors the lines of conflicts in the legislature and in the multilevel system, and the members are considered agents of their institution or party.
- *Conferences* are meetings of members of governments. Thus this category stands for an intergovernmental mode of negotiations that we often find in federal systems.
- *Conventions* constitute more inclusive negotiations. In addition to representatives of parliaments and governments from the different levels, civil society organizations are invited to participate. While usually recommended for constitution-making, conventions are rare when it comes to a constitutional amendment. They not only extend the number of actors with different interests involved in negotiations, but also raise expectations as to the scope and impact of a reform.

In reforms of a multilevel constitution in a federal or regionalized government, we can expect that executives and parties tend towards distributive bargaining, whereas experts from the executive or from the academic sector and representatives of civil society organizations are more likely to search for compromises or negotiate in the arguing mode. This would mean that commissions and conferences likely foster distributive bargaining, while committees and conventions support integrative bargaining or arguing. However, constitutional negotiations rarely take place only in plenary meetings of the different types. As is confirmed by the case studies presented below, structures are usually more complex and combine different arenas of negotiations (Ginsburg et al. 2009: 224–6). Moreover, modes of negotiations also depend on how these different arenas are embedded in a wider institutional setting including normal policy-making and ratification. Theoretical reasoning points out the relevance of this additional structural differentiation. Five dimensions seem particularly important:

1. A first structural condition for successful constitutional negotiations refers to the relation between constitutional and normal policy-making. As

argued above, these processes interact and drive multilevel dynamics by reform, by implicit constitutional change or by unintended authority migration. In theory, these types of policy are distinct, with constitutional policy-making aiming explicitly at a reform or formal amendment of rules, whereas implicit or unintended change occurs in normal policy-making. In practice, the latter have effects on the constitution, while the former can actually proceed like normal policy-making, influenced or predominated by actors interested in their particular tasks, resources and power. As regards the fundamental constitutional problem of multilevel governments, both instability and rigidity are highly probable if interests and conflicts related to particular policy issues predominate in negotiations on constitutional change. Instability can set in if policy specialists exploit situations, for instance, an economic crisis or a natural disaster, to introduce their particular policy issues in constitutional negotiations and manage to turn their issue-specific position into extended power. Rigidity results if policy specialists introduce their particular aims into a process of constitutional negotiations with the effect that power conflicts are reinforced by policy conflicts. To avoid these outcomes, an *institutional differentiation of normal and constitutional policy* is necessary. It can both prevent too much flexibility with the risk of instability and too much rigidity, the first by ruling out a "normalization" of constitutional policy undermining the stabilizing function of a constitution, the second by shielding constitutional negotiations against detailed interests and conflicts.

While this argument relates to the quality of constitutional policy, a second reason for separating both types of policy into different arenas can be drawn from Elinor Ostrom's theory of public choice, which she elaborated in her studies on common pool problems (Ostrom 1990; also Elster 1995: 395). Starting from an analytical distinction between constitutional choice and collective choice, Ostrom demonstrated in many case studies that actors, who tend to maximize their individual profits in a policy, may be willing to agree on rules constraining an exploitation of limited public goods. They reframe the problem by "level shifting" (Ostrom 2005: 62–4), i.e. by setting out a process of constitutional policy in a specific arena separated from the arena where collective action occurs. In such a setting, actors, instead of maximizing their profits, have to think about constitutional rules guiding and coordinating their individual action. By dealing with rules, they have to consider their future interest. Moreover, the framing of the problem to be solved compels them to refer to the common good and joint interests when making claims, while merely pursuing their distributive interests would disqualify them as participants (see also: Vanberg and Buchanan 1989). Applied to constitutional policy in multilevel government, we can assume that arguing has a chance to impact on negotiations if the arena of constitutional policy is dissociated from arenas of normal intergovernmental competition or cooperation. In this way, the former process can be protected against particular policy interests and claims for power from specific administrations.

2. A second condition relates to the temporal organization of the process of negotiations. In view of the predominating practice of bargaining, it is often recommended that "nothing should be settled until everything is settled," in order to extend the opportunities for finding package deals. Yet things look different if the aim is to alter the mode of negotiation from confrontation or bargaining to arguing. The relevance of a sequential organization of negotiations can be derived from the concept of constitution introduced above. If constitutions in multilevel governance not only set rules allocating powers and establishing institutions or procedures of intergovernmental relations, but also imply written or unwritten norms, principles and ideas justifying the structure of a multilevel polity, it is possible to deal with both aspects separately. Arguing behavior of negotiators is likely to materialize as long as norms and principles are concerned, which in the second stage can guide bargaining on who will get what in a redistribution of powers. Theories of negotiations on distributive issues support this assumption (Scharpf 1992: 75–84). An agreement can be achieved if negotiations on norms of distributive justice are separated from decisions on the application of these norms. There are no obvious reasons why this idea should not apply to attempts to restore the balance of power in multilevel governments. Therefore, a decisive condition for success is set by an appropriate *sequential structure of negotiation*. If procedures are designed so that negotiations on ideas or principles are separated from and precede negotiations on rules determined to implement ideas or principles, confrontation is unlikely, provided that an ideological controversy can be avoided. While all participants are committed in this way to a general normative frame, bargaining behavior is confined to the second stage, where its impact is constrained by this frame.

3. The third condition concerns actor constellations and power structures. These aspects usually are touched upon when scholars compare inclusive with exclusive procedures, public with private meetings or constitutional conventions with legislative negotiations (Elster 1995; Kincaid 2005; Simeon 2009). However, to contain confrontation and bargaining, a *horizontal differentiation of negotiation arenas* seems to be an essential prerequisite (Goodin 2008: 186–203). It allows for the reduction of complexity by dividing different negotiation tasks and fulfilling them with special knowledge, to avoid particular conflicts mutually reinforcing each other, but also to mobilize information and commitment of different kinds of actors. If negotiations are concentrated in one arena, as implied in the joint-decision model, the number of participants needs to be limited. If many participants are included, negotiations often are

organized or linked as "nested games" (Tsebelis 1990) in a vertical structure. Such a structure emerges since powerful speakers of coalitions or committees necessarily control these negotiations. It not only favors bargaining or confrontation, since speakers tend to defend the interests of their supporting group, it also reduces the range of issues and alternatives, which are selected inside the coalitions or committees. In contrast, if different groups convene in distinct arenas, which are connected on an equal basis ("connected games"; Scharpf 1991), they can express a plurality of opinions and proposals and are induced to reflect on proposals suggested in other arenas. As a consequence, "coordinative discourses" inside arenas have to be translated into "communicative discourses" between arenas (for these concepts, Schmidt 2010: 3). Lacking the hierarchy between speakers and their groups, bargaining is unlikely to prevail. In a horizontal relation between arenas, actors cannot rely on bargaining power to gain influence. Instead, in order to transfer their proposals to another arena, they have to provide convincing reasons whereas bargaining positions may simply be ignored. In such differentiated and connected arenas, even actors without veto power can influence veto-players, and pivotal players, i.e. those who are decisive for reaching a decision or are able to obstruct an agreement, are more likely to be identified and can be addressed and probably convinced in special bilateral negotiations.

Horizontal differentiation can structure negotiations according to functional or social criteria. The first alternative, *functional differentiation*, is regularly applied when conferences, commissions, committees or conventions establish subcommittees to deal with specific issues. More often than not, they include a limited number of experts, and their members meet in private. In order to fulfill the task delegated to them, members of subcommittees prefer arguing and avoid confrontation among groups or bargaining behavior. However, functional differentiation divides the general reform agenda and often has the effect that details of rule formulation take precedence in negotiations over general justification for institutional designs or procedures. This organization of negotiations therefore can promote a "depoliticization" of constitutional policy with the effect that a legalist approach prevails. Therefore, constitutional amendment may turn into detailed formulation of rules, and a constitution may become more rigid.

In the case of *social differentiation*, distinct arenas of negotiations include particular groups. For instance, intergovernmental commissions can be separated from parliamentary committees and from arenas where citizens or representatives from interest groups are involved. This kind of structuring increases the plurality of perspectives and opinions. Which mode of negotiation is likely to predominate in these different arenas is hardly predictable. However, the communication of opinions and proposals across these arenas requires actors to justify negotiation results, which they achieved in a particular arena, by reasons relating to the constitutional problems that are on the agenda. In contrast to functional differentiation, which favors arguing on details, social differentiation supports this mode in the process linking the different arenas of constitutional policy, at a level where fundamental issues are dealt with.

4. Besides these three dimensions of arena differentiation in constitutional negotiations, it needs to be considered *how negotiation and ratification processes are linked*. In contrast to scholars who have studied the immediate effect of ratification procedures and who, as mentioned above, found hardly any impacts of different rules, the argument made here is that the interrelation between the arenas of negotiation and ratification is an essential factor for explaining the success or failure of constitutional policy. It affects the degree of autonomy and the behavioral dispositions of negotiators. Again, a comparison with the negotiation structure assumed in the original model of joint decision-making can serve as a point of departure of the theoretical reasoning.

According to this model, actors negotiating an amendment proposal are conceived as "agents." In order to avoid that an agreement on a proposed amendment is voted down, they anticipate existing preferences of actors who decide on a ratification of the amendment proposal. Agents have a "zone of agreement" which is limited by the predetermined set of preferences of veto-players. However, even in the framework of rational choice we should not take agents as a universally valid model for negotiators. Under different conditions, negotiators may act as "representatives" of affected groups (Czada 1997; Olsen 2013). Claiming to stand for a particular group or veto-players, they are not committed to fixed mandates and are even able to shape preferences of those actors exerting the right to decide on ratification of constitutional amendments.

Which type of actor prevails in constitutional negotiations mainly depends on how this process is linked to the ratification process. By ignoring details, we can identify two types:

- Constitutional negotiations and ratification can proceed in *tightly coupled arenas*. This obviously applies, e.g., if parliaments ratify constitutional amendments which are elaborated in parliamentary or intergovernmental committees. Under these conditions, preferences of parliamentary groups are determined by party politics, and actors negotiating on a constitutional amendment are closely tied to parties. Therefore negotiators are agents and committed to positions of parties, which evolve in a more or less intense competition, if not confrontation. As a consequence, members of committees tend to bargaining behavior. Due to the congruence of preferences of negotiators and veto-players, an agreement resulting from compromises or package deals is likely to be ratified. This is more likely to happen if leaders of parties or of governments participate in negotiations. They also are committed to positions, probably more so than backbenchers or civil servants in committees, as they need the support of their parties in parliaments and in elections. However, as leading members of parties they are usually in a position to control ratification processes in parliament. However, agreements negotiated by these actors reflect the lowest common denominator of party political positions on constitutional amendments.

- We find *loosely coupled arenas* if negotiators profit from a wider autonomy implied in their role as representatives, and if they are not able to control ratification processes. Usually this constellation exists if constitutional amendments have to be ratified in referendums or by regional parliaments. How citizens or coalitions of regional parties decide depends on the formation of political opinions, which can hardly be anticipated. Therefore, actors negotiating constitutional amendments need to justify their proposals in public deliberation. They cannot present results as a triumph in a power game or as success in distributive bargaining. Similar conditions exist if agreements on proposals result from "consociational" negotiations including representatives from interest organizations or civil society, while parliaments have to ratify. In this case, agreements have to be transferred into an arena operating according to the logics of party competition without the latter being able to influence preferences or the behavior of negotiators. Therefore, it is up to the negotiators to engage in public communication and justification in order to win parties' support for the agreement they settled without anticipation of vetoes.

A loosely coupled structure of representation apparently provides a necessary condition for escaping the joint-decision trap of constitutional politics. However, in clear contrast to tightly coupled structures, ratification cannot be guaranteed in institutional settings conforming to this model. Therefore, even if rules of ratification may not explain outcomes, it makes a difference whether agents can anticipate vetoes or whether representatives need to convince veto-players, and whether negotiators can control those who have a vote in ratification or whether they are not in such a position. In the first constellation, agreements on the lowest common denominator are likely to be settled and ratified, but it is uncertain that this results in a robust balance of power. Incremental change or rigidity of a constitution is a more likely outcome under this condition. In the second constellation, proposals for significant change or amendments promising to effectively solve constitutional problems may be voted down in ratification, if decisive veto-players cannot be convinced or if the ratification process reignites conflicts. Apparently, ratification failure is particularly likely if conflicts between deeply divided societies have to be accommodated, which can occur in multinational federations or in regionalized states confronted with strong claims for autonomy of particular regions.

5. The theoretical reasoning in the previous section seems to reveal a dilemma of constitutional policy. On the one hand, those structures, which support arguing processes by linking negotiation arenas in a loose pattern to ratification processes, bear a comparatively high risk of amendment proposals being voted down in ratification, even if these proposals promise to effectively deal with the issues on the agenda. On the other hand, structures which increase the probability that proposals will be ratified are less conducive to productive negotiations and instead make bargaining or confrontation more likely. This conclusion would mean that the skeptical views predominating in the literature are justified. However, not only should we take into account other structural conditions of constitutional negotiations, which may have an impact on the quality of negotiated agreements independent of the shadow of ratification, we also need to consider that multilevel dynamics may foster implicit constitutional change, even if elaborated amendments are not ratified.

In particular, actors who have negotiated a constitutional agreement and therefore are interested in constitutional change can be expected to respond to a negative decision on ratification by searching for ways out of the joint-decision trap. Without neglecting the possibility of a constitutional deadlock, we have to be aware that negotiated agreements are driving forces for "implicit constitutional change" (Voigt 1999: 145–76), i.e. a change of interpretations of principles or norms and patterns of interaction emerging in the context of existing rules, and at least influencing the direction of ongoing change. In normal policy-making, standard operating procedures of interactions are continuously renegotiated (Schmidt 2010). These permanent discourses may result in tacit agreements among policy-makers or find expression in an authoritative interpretation of constitutional rules by courts. Depending on the density of rules, the scope of implicit change of constitutions is more or less limited. These limits arguably can be extended if discourses and agreements are legitimized in public (Bednar 2013: 290–3). If negotiations on a constitutional reform end with a proposal on amendments debated in public or if participants manage to achieve a common understanding of the constitutional imbalance, they can influence a reinterpretation of constitutional rules even if formal amendments are not ratified. Moreover, they can induce a change in practice which may be followed by later reform. Therefore, stability and flexibility can be harmonized if processes of implicit change are linked to negotiations on a constitutional reform. While dynamics of institutions often go through a sequence of implicit and explicit change (Héritier 2007: 46–53), a robust balance of powers can emerge if constitutional evolution is framed by principles, ideas and norms that are explicitly formulated in negotiated agreements and if actors participating in the agreements can convincingly claim to represent all important political groups in a multilevel polity.

The particular structures of constitutional policy do not determine outcomes, but they make success or failure more or less likely. The mode of negotiations induced by structural arrangements has significant effects for the quality of a constitutional reform project and the probability that it passes the formal procedures of legislation, whichever ratification rules are applied. Depending on the arrangement of constitutional negotiations, the failure to ratify an agreement resulting from effective negotiations may not end in an unbalanced multilevel government. Accordingly, in view of their potential to solve the dilemma of rigidity and instability, constitutional policy can generate different outcomes. These can be categorized as outlined in the following section.

2.2.3 *Outcomes: Patterns of Constitutional Dynamics*

If aiming at explicit constitutional change, i.e. an amendment of the written constitution, the final result of constitutional policy depends on the outcome of the ratification process. Yet at this stage, the decision is reduced to the alternative of changing or maintaining the status quo. The substance and the quality of a constitutional amendment are determined in negotiations on amendment proposals. In processes of constitutional reform, we can distinguish negotiations and ratification, not only analytically, but also, more clearly than in "normal" policies, empirically. Therefore, although both processes overlap in reality, each of them has a particular impact on the final result, which the analysis needs to distinguish.

Negotiated proposals can be accepted or rejected in ratification regardless of whether or not they reflect a genuine consensus among negotiators or promise to solve problems of a multilevel political system. If constitutional negotiations end with an effective amendment proposal which is ratified, we can speak of a *successful constitutional reform*. Otherwise, constitutional policy ends in a *constitutional deadlock*, an outcome maintains the status quo by default. This is exactly the situation described as the joint-decision trap (Scharpf 1988). In a third constellation, negotiators agree on a compromise on the "lowest common denominator" of their particular interests without finding solutions to make governance more effective or to stabilize a balance of power. Nevertheless, such proposals can be ratified, but then turn out as an *ineffective reform*. Finally, veto-players can obstruct constitutional amendments in ratification even if negotiators come to an agreement on proposals promising to solve problems. In this case, *ratification failure* occurs.

Empirically, distinguishing the ratification outcomes requires simply looking at the result of voting. It is more difficult to qualify the substance of an outcome of constitutional negotiations and to distinguish between effective and ineffective reforms or reform proposals and determine whether rejection of a negotiated proposal reveals ratification failure with the potential of implicit change or a constitutional deadlock. In view of the complexity of constitutional reforms of multilevel government, only a complicated evaluation seems to allow a judgment, which nevertheless may be disputed as regards the criteria applied, the weighting of the criteria or the effects considered. For the practical purpose of this study, we combined formal and substantive criteria: The first relates to *selectivity* compared to the agenda and the *scope* of the reform. Effective reforms address the issues that are on the agenda to a large extent. Moreover, they reveal a significant revision of constitutional rules rather than merely an incremental adjustment of the status quo. As regards *substance*, a reform can be considered effective as far as it counteracts destabilizing dynamics in a multilevel government, materializing either as performance or integration problems. An effective constitutional change induced by performance problems promises to work against trends towards a concentration of power at the center or in intergovernmental networks and joint decision-making by the executive ("centripetal dynamics"). If integration problems matter, constitutional policy needs to reduce regional disparities, preventing a further fragmentation of power or a threatening secession ("centrifugal dynamics"). Accordingly, we can assess a constitutional policy as ineffective if negotiations leave undone important tasks of the agenda or if they bring about only marginal changes having no significant consequences in the required direction. More problematic are ineffective agreements, which deteriorate the imbalance of power. In this case, a far-reaching reform can cause more damage than one with a strictly limited scope.

The substantive criteria defined above imply that we can only assess the quality of constitutional policy by considering inherent dynamics of multilevel politics. Therefore, processes following a reform also determine outcomes of constitutional reforms. Success and failure can directly induce implicit constitutional change. A successful reform is likely to be implemented according to agreements passed in constitutional legislation, although implementation problems cannot be ruled out. An ineffective reform can be revised in normal policy-making, if policy-makers realize the deficits and have to cope with the governance problems or conflicts. For the same reason, a deadlock situation may be dissolved by political pragmatism. But without a guideline established in constitutional negotiations, significant change becomes less likely. If agreements have been negotiated successfully but ratification has

Table 2.3. Patterns of constitutional change and continuity

	Ratification		No ratification
Effective negotiations	SUCCESSFUL REFORM ↓ implementation		RATIFICATION FAILURE ↓ non-constitutional change
Ineffective negotiations	INEFFECTIVE REFORM ↙ rigidity/revision	 ↘ destabilization	CONSTITUTIONAL DEADLOCK ↓ stagnation

failed, they can be implemented in practice at least to a certain extent and depending on the flexibility of constitutional law. Moreover, if principles of a balanced multilevel government are made explicit in constitutional negotiations, they can serve as guiding ideas for interpretation or application of the persisting constitutional rules. Therefore, implicit change can reduce conflicts or governance deficits by non-constitutional means.

By combining these analytical dimensions and criteria, we can distinguish patterns of constitutional dynamics as summarized in Table 2.3. This analytical scheme implies normative statements on the outcomes of constitutional policy, based on the assumptions regarding the effects of different patterns on multilevel dynamics and the balance of powers. In order to comprehend these effects, a closer understanding of the particular dynamics of different multilevel political systems and the constitutional problems arising in them is essential. This is the subject of the following chapter.

2.3 Research Design and Method

In order to substantiate the assumptions derived from our theoretical framework, we studied cases of constitutional policy in federal and regionalized states. As our research questions aimed to understand the impact of constitutional policy on stability or instability of a balance of power and the flexibility or rigidity of the constitutional order, we considered states with multilevel governments. In these states, we studied particular processes of constitutional reform. As we are interested in the capacities of multilevel governments to maintain and change their constitution by deliberate policy-making, we take

Table 2.4. Institutional variation of selected multilevel governments

	Regional authority (self-rule/shared rule)*	Difficulty to amend constitution**	Party system
Germany	29.3 (20.3/9,0)	6.0	pluralist party system with moderate regional party, vertically integrated
Switzerland	19.5 (15.0/4.5)	7.0	moderate pluralist party system without regional party, vertically differentiated
Austria	18.0 (12.0/6.0)	3.0	moderate pluralist party system without regional parties, vertically integrated
Canada	22.7 (17.7/5.0)	7.0	moderate pluralist party system with regional party, vertically differentiated
Belgium	29.1 (21.1/7.0)	9.5	pluralist party system, regionalized
Spain	22.1 (19.1/3.0)	6.0	dualist party system with regional parties, vertically integrated
Italy	22.7 (21.0/1.7)	4.0	pluralist party system with moderate regional party, vertically integrated
France	16.0 (16.0/0.0)	4.0	moderate pluralist party system without regional parties, vertically integrated
Great Britain	9.5 (9.0/0.5)***	1.0***	dualist party system with regional parties, vertically integrated

* Regional Authority Index (Hooghe, Marks and Schakel 2010: Table B3) data for last period
** Index of constitutional rigidity (Lorenz 2005: 358–9). Range from 1 to 9.5
*** Data for the UK

into account cases of implicit constitutional change affecting the meaning and practice of the constitution as far as a direct connection to processes aiming at explicit constitutional change existed. Moreover, due to the particular challenges for empirical research on implicit change, we went into the details of these processes only in two cases.

The countries included in our comparative case studies represent multilevel governments with different institutional structures and confronted with different constitutional problems. Table 2.4 gives a rough account of these variations based on data on the division of power, rules for amending constitutions and basic features of party systems. Beyond six federal systems, we included France, Italy and the United Kingdom as regionalized states. With the exception of the UK, all states rank high on the regional authority index, which measures the amount of division of power between levels of government. The three regionalized states rank low in the category of shared rule, whereas among the federal states, the extent of power sharing is low only in Spain. Moreover, with the exception of the UK, constitutional amendment in all states requires qualified majorities and poses high institutional hurdles for change. Belgium, Canada and Spain are federations with integration problems, and the same challenge predominates in the UK, as is reflected in the party system. In the other states, party systems indicate no integration problems. As will be portrayed in detail in the next chapter, these multilevel governments have to deal with different kinds of performance problems in constitutional policy.

It goes without saying that many other conditions differ in these multilevel governments. They include unitary states where reforms contributed to a process of regionalization as well as established federal states with more centralized and more decentralized governments, dual and cooperative types of federalism. Moreover, the international context varies, in particular when considering membership in the EU, which does not apply to Switzerland and Canada. Moreover, patterns of democracy vary between consensus democracies and majority democracies (Lijphart 2012). We certainly take these aspects into account in the case studies. Given the state of theory building in comparative research on multilevel governments, we avoided selecting cases according to a limited set of "variables." The diversity of our cases allowed us to take into account as many conditions as possible. Therefore, we applied the comparable cases strategy in a research process iterating between elaboration of a theory and empirical research, following the scientific logic of set theory and the QCA-method (Ragin 2000). However, two sets of conditions justify our case selection: One concerns the particular manifestation of constitutional problems due to societal or institutional developments. The other relates to institutional conditions of constitutional policy-making. In reality, the different institutional constraints give rise to specific procedures. Therefore, the cases allow focusing our empirical research on the causal relations between problems, procedures and outcomes, which are particularly relevant according to our theoretical framework.

In these multilevel governments, we concentrated our empirical research on the following processes of constitutional policy:

- *Austria*: Constitutional Convention (2003–5);
- *Belgium*: Fifth State Reform (1999–2001);
- *Canada*: Charlottetown Accord (1990–2);
- *France*: Decentralization Act II (2000–3);
- *Germany*: Federalism Reform I and II (2003–9);
- *Italy*: Reform of Title V of the Constitution (1997–2001);
- *Switzerland*: Renewal of Fiscal Equalization and Allocation of Power (1994–2008);
- *Great Britain*: Devolution (1989–2006); and
- *Spain:* Third Round of Reform of Autonomy Statutes (2004–10).

What these cases have in common is that they address constitutional problems of a multilevel system, be it an existing or an emerging one. They can be considered attempts to overcome threatening instability of a division of power by changing the federal constitution. While rules of amendment vary in these countries, they all have to cope with the fact that actors at the central and regional level, who are affected by a redistribution of power or resources, have the right or political power to block a decision of a constitutional amendment.

In the case studies, we traced processes of constitutional change by collecting and analyzing documents (reports and records, memoranda or notes of negotiations available online or in archives), by interviews with experts and participants and by gaining additional information and perceptions from written responses of two or three experts to a questionnaire. Most of our partners who provided detailed information in written reports participated in a conference where they presented their findings and assessments for discussion. The results of this conference are published in a volume edited by Arthur Benz and Felix Knüpling (Benz and Knüpling 2012a). For the German case, the author profited from participating in the first Reform Commission (2003–4) as an expert.

Given the amount and diversity of the material, we were not able to use discourse analysis or speech act analysis to discern modes of negotiations. However, we gained sufficient insights into negotiation processes in order to identify whether actors extended or reduced an agenda, whether they operated in the bargaining mode aiming to defend their particular interests and settling compromises or package deals or whether they interacted in the arguing mode and search for new solutions to problems and reasons for defending decisions. Moreover, and most importantly, the negotiation result gives a clear indication about which negotiation mode prevails, with agreements going beyond positions defined at the outset revealing that actors at least at certain stages of the process turned to arguing whereas package deals and compromises at the lowest common denominator of interests result from bargaining behavior. The style of confrontation has been obvious when actors openly stick to their position and refuse to compromise, when they question the legitimacy of demands from other actors or when they fail to come to an agreement.

Research on implicit constitutional change is more demanding and requires a look at the evolution of constitutional discussions, normal legislation and policy-making having effects on the understanding of constitutional rules and court decisions. While we considered the interplay of constitutional reform and the context in politics and policy-making in all nine states, we focused on Canada and Germany in a more detailed study on constitutional evolution covering a longer time span. These cases are particularly interesting since Canadian reform failed in ratification, whereas German reform was ratified despite negotiations which turned out as rather ineffective. The findings on these processes, summarized in Chapter 7, have been gained during a one-year stay in Canada by the author and his particular expertise on German federalism.

The following chapters are based on these case studies. We start by describing the particular constitutional problems, then explain their appearance and evolution as issues of constitutional policy. Chapter 4 portrays the processes of constitutional reform and their outcomes for the different cases. Based on these descriptive chapters, we analyze the impact of amendment rules and implicit constitutional change, before we finally discuss conditions explaining the success or failure of constitutional policy regarding the balance of power.

3

Constitutional Problems and Reform Agendas in Federal and Regionalized States

(*with Andrea Fischer-Hotzel and Bettina Petersohn*)

The analytical distinction of performance and integration introduced in Chapter 2 (section 2.1.2) helps us to understand the particular constitutional problems under scrutiny here. They indicate different imbalances of power in a multilevel government. In reality, the problems related to these two types overlap or coexist and are invoked simultaneously by actors interested in initiating a constitutional reform process. Nevertheless, the categories allow us to determine the agendas of constitutional policy, since usually one type of problem dominates while the other arises as a secondary problem. In this section, we briefly sketch dominant and secondary problems for each of the selected cases. The constitutional reform debates in Austria, Germany and Switzerland addressed problems of performance mainly due to strong interlocking of levels of government, while in France and Italy reforms were initiated to counterbalance centralizing tendencies of the regionalized state. Constitutional problems related to territorial integration predominated in Belgium, Canada, Great Britain and Spain.

3.1 Problems of Performance in Federal States

The three federations in Central Europe are, despite economic imbalances or linguistic divides as in Switzerland, fairly well integrated. Social integration was supported by an early foundation of the welfare state in Germany and Austria, whereas in Switzerland direct democracy fostered a nation of citizens ("*Willensnation*") to develop during the second half of the nineteenth century. In all three countries, although for different reasons, state capacities evolved at the regional level—the *Länder* in Austria and Germany and the Cantons in Switzerland. In the late nineteenth and early twentieth centuries, the central governments of Austria and Germany gained legislative and fiscal power with the expansion of welfare services, which were introduced in order to contain pressure for democratization and to moderate class conflicts. At about the same time, early democratization in Switzerland limited the expansion of central powers and delayed the expansion of the welfare state (Obinger, Leibfried and Castles 2005). In consequence, while decentralized state building in Central Europe, where administrative powers evolved in cities and principalities, prevented these countries from establishing a unitary government—with the exception of the era of dictatorship in Germany and Austria—federalism never revealed a watertight separation of powers. Rather, the functional division of central legislation and decentralized administration and the need for coordination of policies in small territories (in particular in Switzerland) gave rise to sharing of powers and an extensive practice of intergovernmental relations.

This "cooperative federalism" became a matter of dispute when conflicts between governments intensified due to party political divides or increasing redistributive conflicts during periods of economic stagnation in the 1970s and 1990s. In all three countries, federalism as it existed was blamed for causing excessive public spending, inefficient or ineffective policy-making, lack of accountability of governments to parliaments or citizens and limited capacities to reform the welfare state. These debates became more intense when the three countries felt the impacts of globalization and European integration (which affected Switzerland as well, although formal membership never was envisaged) and could no longer rely on growing revenues to stabilize the high level of public services (summarized in Grotz and Poier 2010).

Switzerland has often been characterized as a multinational federation. However, diversity and integration problems were rarely a decisive issue in politics or constitutional reform. Due to the need to adjust the decentralized federal structure to requirements of a modern welfare state and an internationally competitive economy, the allocation of powers to federal and cantonal governments was changed regularly. For similar reasons, a comprehensive revision of the constitution was on the political agenda as of the 1950s. In this context, a reform of the territorial organization of the state was a decisive objective. Although federalism was strongly embedded in the political culture, "creeping centralization" (Kriesi and Trechsel 2008: 35) and interlocking between federal and cantonal politics and policy-making became a matter of disputes, like in Germany or Austria. Leading representatives of the business sector attacked cooperative federalism as inefficient and threatening the competitiveness of Switzerland in the global economy. In the public sector, performance problems of the federal system were expressed in discussion about the fiscal equalization scheme, which appeared nontransparent and counterproductive. In this context, experts also saw a need to revise the allocation of powers and procedures of intergovernmental coordination (Freiburghaus 2009).

A constitutional reform of Swiss federalism was an issue at least as early as 1978 when an old project of a total revision of the federal constitution gained new momentum. However, the federal parliament decided in 1987 to exclude the allocation of power and the fiscal equalization scheme from this project and to address these issues in a separate reform process (Freiburghaus 2005). The federal and the cantonal governments supported this course of action. At the beginning of the 1990s, the fiscal equalization scheme became a central matter in the reform of federalism, when federal and cantonal executives, assisted by experts, discovered that the existing system increased imbalances between Cantons, instead of decreasing them. They also realized that they could only succeed in their aim to restore the federal balance if they dealt with intergovernmental relations, the allocation of power and the fiscal equalization scheme as connected problems. The agenda of the reform therefore included all three issues, so that separating the subjects would not be an option for the actors involved. Negotiations on a constitutional reform started in 1994.

In *Germany*, joint decision-making in the federal system, the particular version of cooperative federalism which compels federal and *Länder* governments to negotiate agreements in legislation or joint tasks, has been critically discussed since the 1970s (Kilper and Lhotta 1996: 143–203). After German unification and the following economic crisis, changes in economic and social policies seemed to become urgent, but institutional conditions of federalism were widely viewed as obstacles to these changes. In these policy fields, federal legislation required the consent of the *Bundesrat*, the second legislative chamber representing the *Länder* governments. As the parties forming the opposition in the federal parliament often supported the majorities of the *Länder* governments, legislation required the agreement of competing parties (Lehmbruch 2000). Under this condition, prospects for significant changes in policies were poor. Although the actual number of laws blocked in the *Bundesrat* remained low, joint decision-making required compromises at the lowest common denominator and impeded significant policy innovation that was deemed necessary (Manow and Burkhart 2007). The reform backlog ("*Reformstau*") became a catchword summarizing the perceived performance problems which federalism was blamed for. The rule of joint legislation came increasingly under attack (Scheller 2008). Moreover, implementation of legislation at the *Länder* level was considered to be ineffective, too, in cases where the federal government had to ensure compliance with European regulations.

The problem of performance due to interlocking of levels appeared as particularly pressing in fiscal policy. As a consequence of revenue sharing concerning the most relevant tax resources, the federal government, but more so the *Länder* governments, were hardly able to raise taxes on their own but instead had to negotiate with the other governments in order to pass a federal law (Renzsch 2008: 112). In addition, the fiscal equalization scheme was criticized for causing inefficient budgetary politics due to the increasing amount of redistributed revenues (Scharpf 2010: 27). Tensions between the federal and the *Länder* governments intensified after German unification, since greater economic imbalances between Eastern and Western *Länder* affected the fiscal equalization system and required increased redistribution of public funds to the East. Governments of the economically strong *Länder* complained that most of the tax surplus they raised went to the weaker *Länder,* leaving no incentive for efficient economic policies. The poor *Länder* likewise were said to rely on financial transfers without being motivated to improve their economic base by their own policies.

As early as the 1990s, the federal government and governments of the economically strong *Länder* called for a constitutional reform in order to reduce joint decision-making, to extend legislative powers of the *Länder* and to revise fiscal federalism. In 2003, they agreed on an initiative to change the federal constitution. The reform agenda included demands for a clearer separation of legislative and administrative powers, for decentralization of legislative powers and for an increase in fiscal autonomy by a revision of tax powers and the equalization scheme. The federal government and governments of the rich *Länder* supported a separation of powers, while the less well-off *Länder* argued for maintaining solidarity horizontally and vertically (Renzsch 2008: 112). The reallocation of power and fiscal federalism were considered the main and closely connected areas of a reform. Nonetheless, two separate and subsequent reform processes were initiated.

In *Austria,* the constitutional problem expressed in these debates even dated back to the 1920s when the founders of the constitution could not come to an agreement on a division of powers, a catalog of human and basic rights and arrangements of fiscal federalism. After World War II, governments of a Grand Coalition closely cooperated with employers' associations and unions in a kind of consensus democracy. This coalition was able to pass legislation with the super-majorities required for a constitutional amendment. Many times, the federal constitution was changed by means of ordinary laws that were declared constitutional. As a consequence, the Austrian Constitution turned into a conglomeration of numerous laws and legal statutes instead of forming a coherent document of basic principles (Bußjäger 2009). This lack of transparency of the constitutional framework was felt as a serious obstacle since problems of coordination between the levels of government intensified with the decline of consensus democracy. Moreover, the *Länder* governments suffered from centralizing tendencies, promoted by the powerful Grand Coalition governments and furthered after Austria became a member of the European Union in 1995. These tendencies led to a clear imbalance of the federal system. With the rise of regionalist tendencies all over Europe, Austrian *Länder* governments increasingly mobilized against centralist trends.

Ambitions for an extensive reform were articulated in the aftermath of the general election of 1999 and the formation of a coalition government of the Christian Democrats (ÖVP) and the Liberals (FPÖ). This change in government ended a long period of Grand Coalition governments, which increasingly proved unable to come to agreements, were compelled to make ineffective compromises and often wound up in gridlock. Since the parties forming the new coalition government did not have a qualified majority in parliament, the consent of Social Democrats was necessary for the planned constitutional reform. Expecting to gain influence and reputation by participating in constitutional policy, or on an equal basis with the majority parties, the Social Democrats agreed to initiate a larger reform and to set up a convention following the then highly esteemed European Convention model (Grotz 2005). Beyond the integration of human and basic rights into the constitution, decentralization of powers, amending fiscal federalism and strengthening of the second chamber of the federal legislature were major topics on the reform agenda (Blümel and Konrath 2009). Thus a revival of Austrian federalism was a central aim of this comprehensive constitutional reform.

3.2 Problems of Integration in Federal States

Canada, Belgium and Spain became federal systems mainly due to linguistic and cultural divides of societies. However, the sequence of institutional and political development needs to be taken into account in order to explain why these federations have been challenged by serious problems of integration. The divides between regions and the conflicts between central and regional governments are rooted in the history of these countries. They surfaced as a constitutional challenge at different times and for different reasons. Processes of democratization and economic developments played a primary role in provoking political conflicts between regional groups and regions and the central government, which at some points threatened the cohesion of the political system.

Canada was founded in 1867 as a federation, when it was still subject to the sovereign power of Great Britain. At the same time, the constitution introduced the Westminster system of a parliamentary democracy at both levels of government. Early democratization had integrative effects, as long as a two-party system prevailed and as long as the state had limited capacities to engage in policies affecting the provinces. Yet right from the beginning, the federal system was shaped by the different histories of Quebec, a province founded as a French colony, on the one side and the English-speaking provinces on the other. After defeating the French colonial power, the British government conquered Quebec, but accepted the use of French as the official language, the role of the Catholic Church and civil law tradition. Consequently, the unification of Canada in 1867 introduced a federal constitution, although the parliamentary system and policies of nation building strengthened the central government. The original constitution, passed as the British North America Act by the parliament in London, conceded powers to the provinces including those concerning public welfare. Accordingly, the Canadian welfare state emerged at the provincial level, and later efforts to introduce a national pension plan for the whole federation failed when Quebec opted out. At about the same time, it became obvious that nation building in Canada did not contribute to the integration of Quebeckers who became self-assertive in the wake of an economic upswing during the 1960s (the so called "quiet revolution").

Since then, integrating Quebec into the federation has been the predominant constitutional problem. Earlier attempts that either increased conflicts or ended with ratification failure (Russell 2004) triggered the reform of 1990–2. Quebec had not accepted the Constitution Act of 1982, which had replaced the British North America Act of 1867, and thus "patriated" the constitution,[1] and introduced the Charter of Rights and Freedoms (Bergeron 1983; Laforest 1991). From Quebec's point of view, this constitution placed individual rights above the rights of communities that the province wanted protected. The formation of the Bloc Québécois as separatist party at the federal level demonstrated the necessity to solve the constitutional question. During the negotiations on the 1982 Constitution Act, another salient integration problem emerged due to the demands of Aboriginal peoples for recognition, autonomy and self-government. The 1982 constitution acknowledged these groups as "First Nations," but their claims had not been met sufficiently despite several First Ministers' Conferences discussing their demands in the 1980s (Hawkes 1985; Watts 1996: 357). These integration conflicts translated into pressure from the Quebec government and organizations of Aboriginal peoples, which aimed at a constitutional recognition of distinct societies, at the establishment

[1] The Constitution Act 1982 introduced a new amending formula which relied only on Canadian institutions. Prior to that date, constitutional reforms required the consent of the British parliament and the signature of the Queen for ratification. The "Patriation" of the constitution and the amending formula had been an issue in Federal–Provincial Conferences for decades.

of certain group rights, at the protection against majority decisions, at the right of Aboriginal self-government as well as at the decentralization of policies and financial resources.

Adding to these dominant problems of integration, the agenda of constitutional policy included the aim to foster the economic union of Canada, which was deemed to reduce inefficient internal trade barriers. Furthermore, intergovernmental conflicts on social policy and the problem of fiscal imbalance were addressed. Particularly the western provinces perceived these performance problems and additionally proposed a better representation of provinces in federal legislation by a reform of the Canadian Senate (Gibbins 1989; Government of Canada 1991).

Belgium was founded as a unitary state in 1830, and would be transformed into a federal state between 1970 and 1993 (Deschouwer 2009: 16–40). Since French had been the only officially recognized language, the Flemish Movement quickly formed after state foundation and fought for recognition, equality and the means to develop their culture and language. With democratization during the late nineteenth and early twentieth centuries, the nature of the community of citizens and political communication became basic issues, and the predominance of the French language was felt as a significant cause for political inequality. The creation of monolingual regions in the 1930s somewhat served to ameliorate the situation for the Dutch-speaking community. However, as discrimination in central institutions continued and the territory of the bilingual region of Brussels expanded into Flanders, the linguistic conflict resurfaced shortly afterwards. The conflict between the two large linguistic communities remained salient after World War II, inflamed by the referendum on the return of King Leopold III and the general strike in 1960 supported mainly in Wallonia (McRae 1986). Unequal economic developments in the North and South as well as the expansion of the welfare state organized at the central level contributed to increasing tensions between the two language communities who realized redistributive effects of social policies not only between individuals, but also between communities. Consequently, the pressure for establishing regional governments and for decentralizing powers increased. The late federalization of Belgium did not follow a coherent design agreed upon at the outset of this process. Therefore, a number of peculiarities compared to conventional federal systems characterize the emergent federal structure (Deschouwer 2009: 69–71). A dual structure of three regions (Flanders, Wallonia and Brussels-Capital) and three communities (Flemish, French and German) has been created, with the small German community situated in the Walloon region and the two large communities overlapping in the Brussels Region without a clear-cut border. These entities received constitutive autonomy (except for the Brussels Region and German Community), various powers and financial autonomy for the regions, leaving only limited competences for the federal level (Hooghe 2004; Swenden et al. 2006).

Despite the transformation of the unitary into a federal state, demands for further constitutional reform, especially regional fiscal autonomy and the regionalization of social security, have not ceased on the Flemish side. Furthermore, the special regulations for the use of languages in the so-called communes with special language provisions at the Brussels periphery have been a thorny issue. However, it was actually problems of inadequate financial resources for the communities that recently triggered a reform of fiscal federalism and the equalization scheme (Sinardet 2010). In addition to the underlying problem of integration and community conflicts, political parties on both sides are aware of the performance problems, fiscal imbalances and an increased number of deadlock situations. Therefore they initiated negotiations for the reallocation of power and resources among the different levels of government in Belgium.

Spain evolved from a unitary to a federal system after the transition to democracy after 1975. For historical reasons, the country is divided into regional communities demanding more legislative or financial autonomy. This divide can be traced back to the period when kingdoms developed in different territories (Moreno 2001: 36–48). Unification started under the Catholic monarchs in the fifteenth century, who united their kingdoms of Aragon and Castilia. This union existed during the area of state formation. Held together under the rule of changing dynasties, it allowed the former kingdoms to maintain their autonomy. Unitary forces prevailed after the reign of the Bourbon kings after 1700 when the state was reformed according to the French model and Spain adopted the Napoleonic state tradition (Loughlin and Peters 1997). Democratization and the welfare state were late developments resulting in a weak integration of the nation state. Under the second republic, statutes of autonomy had been approved for Catalonia, the Basque Country and Galicia creating historical precedents in addition to the recognition of the special fiscal powers, in the so-called *territories forales* of the Basque Country and Navarre. However, the formation of a Spanish nation was enforced under the Franco dictatorship, which suppressed minority languages. Resistance against this regime and demands for language protection and autonomy intensified especially in regions with territorially concentrated minorities. For these regions, democratization and decentralization became inseparable, after Franco's death had ended its authoritarian regime in 1974. During the period of democratic transition, seventeen Autonomous Communities (ACs) were created with legislative powers in a variety of policies.

As for the territorial structure of the state, the compromise on the new Spanish constitution did not establish a definite solution, but set off a process of allocating powers. It granted three communities of the so called "historical nationalities," Catalonia, Basque and Galicia, a higher degree of autonomy and extended powers compared to the other ACs. Distinct identities, languages and history were the foundation for this special recognition, but the economic strength of the Basque and Catalan regions also played a role for certain demands (Moreno 2001: 208–10). For the other ACs, the constitution stated that they might, with the consent of the central legislature, adopt additional powers and obtain the same level of autonomy (Guibernau 2000: 60–2; Keating 1993: 218–20).

The Spanish central government refused to create a fully-fledged federal state, trying to limit decentralization to what was at least necessary and to introducing measures aimed at a symmetric allocation of power within a period of five years (Art. 148 of the Spanish Constitution). In catching up with the historical nationalities and their high level of autonomy as early as 1980, Andalusia set the example for further decentralization and induced a process eventually leading to symmetrical power arrangements for all ACs (see Maiz et al. 2010). This step instigated a process driven by a kind of competition for powers, since ACs with historical nationalities were eager to reinstall asymmetric federalism so that their distinctiveness would be more clearly reflected in the institutional settings and the distribution of power (Moreno and Colino 2010: 292). After the conservative *Partido Popular* had refused to decentralize or allow for further piecemeal accommodation of regional demands during their second term in office (2000–4), nationalist parties participating in coalition governments in Catalonia and the Basque Country radicalized their demands and pushed for constitutional change. When the socialist PSOE won the general election in 2004, the new central government initiated a new round of territorial constitutional reform, announcing that it would be favorable to any reform proposal coming from the regional parliaments (Keating and Wilson 2009; Nagel 2005: 460–1).

3.3 Problems of Performance in Regionalized States

France and Italy constitute unitary states. Both unite strong regions and are often categorized as regional states. However, in both cases regions never achieved real autonomy and are integrated into different systems of interlocking politics. Therefore, demands for decentralization had less to do with regionalist movements or divided nations but rather with perceived problems of performance. In France, decentralization for a long time was implemented by administrative reforms, until it became a matter of constitutional policy in the mid-1980s. In Italy, demands for autonomy of northern Regions emerged as a major issue during the 1970s, and the territorial integration of the country has remained a challenge into the present. Nonetheless, the last reforms mainly aimed at problems of performance.

In *France*, regionalization has its roots in administrative decentralization under the *Ancien Régime*, which survived the unitary forces initiated with the French Revolution and the state reform under Napoleon. Yet the French monarchy was able to consolidate a territorial state long before the era of democratization. The revolution turned the former catholic state into a secularized republic, which was highly integrated by a uniform linguistic and cultural fundament of society, and created a nation of equal citizens. As a consequence, political structuring of society never gave way for regionalist parties. The evolution of the welfare state reinforced this integration.

After World War II, divergent economic developments in the central region and the rural peripheries induced debates about the limits of French centralism. However, performance problems arose from relations between the central and local government, which were linked by local elites, who participated in the national legislature and in national government, and powerful prefects who managed conflicts between central and local policies. This system proved nontransparent, elitist, inflexible and ineffective when it came to revising policies.

Despite several steps towards decentralization, these problems remained on the agenda of state reforms. On the contrary, the decentralization reforms of the 1980s, the so-called "lois Deferre" or "*Acte I de la decentralization,*" increased problems resulting from the interlocking of administrative levels (Hoffmann-Martinot 2005: 335; Pasquier 2009: 1). They ended with many competences shared between central ministries and local authorities. Moreover, horizontally and vertically intertwined administrative and financial structures between municipalities, *départements* and *régions* emerged, leading to "a myriad of competing and non-coordinated initiatives within the same territory by unlimited use of co-financing operations" (Hoffmann-Martinot 2003: 158). Consequently, the system resulting from decentralization of a formerly unitary state was perceived as inefficient and as lacking transparency and accountability (Hoffmann-Martinot 2003: 158; 2005: 336; Négrier 2000: 123; Schmidt 1990: 137). In fiscal policies, centralizing tendencies prevailed and reduced capacities of regional and local governments to apply their powers effectively. Since the early 1990s, the French government has tended to replaced local taxes by central grants, a process which local representatives perceived as an assault to local fiscal autonomy.

At the turn of the twenty-first century, French local politicians reacted to this situation by submitting a legislative proposal to the Senate. It defined four principles for a reform: first, subnational tax autonomy, second, subnational autonomy in spending, third, the assignment of taxes according to the devolution of new policy powers, and fourth, veto power for the Senate on legislation concerning decentralization (legislative proposal no. 432, 22 June 2000). Observers and participants in the reform process identified this legislative initiative as the agenda for the 2002–4 constitutional reform (Le Lidec 2005: 86).

Like Germany, *Italy* was divided into cities and territories until the late nineteenth century. But unlike in Germany, the unification of Italy ended with a unitary state, in spite of a strong federalist tradition. In both countries, the creation of the nation state, supported by powerful national movements, succeeded under the leadership by a predominating state government—the Prussian government in Germany and the government of Sardinia-Piedmont in Italy. However, whereas the Prussian government had to negotiate a federal constitution with rulers of well-established and powerful states, the counterparts of the government of Sardinia-Piedmont represented kingdoms with limited state capacities and weakened by wars (Ziblatt 2006). This constellation explains the emergence of a unitary state, which, however, was characterized by fundamental asymmetries.

When after World War II Italy introduced a democratic republic, the federalist model resurfaced, but the parties agreed on a compromise and introduced a regionalized state. The constitution distinguishes between ordinary Regions and Regions with a special status. It took until 1970 for these Regions to become fully established. Reforms in the 1970s and the 1990s extended administrative powers, but did not introduce effective regional autonomy or a federal system. In addition to the asymmetry of the territorial state organization, the Italian state was confronted with serious economic disparities between the north and the south. Nonetheless, integration problems played a limited role in state reforms. Regionalist movements emerging in some regions did not find persistent support in the population. Since the 1990s, an integration problem has been perceived in the north, which has aggravated the economic and political north–south divide. Here, politicians as well as the population became increasingly reluctant to support the—as it was perceived—inefficient central state (Fedele 2010). The voters in the north expressed their discontent with the existing political system by supporting the populist *Lega Nord*, a party that advocated regionalization or federalization as the only proper solution for the performance problems of the central level (Albertazzi and McDonnell 2005; Gomez-Reino Cachafeiro 2000). In the south, alienation from the political system has not found expression in a regionalist movement, but reinforced identity with families and favored political populism. However, deficits of governance were perceived as principal problems. After state reforms of the late 1980s and early 1990s failed, a political crisis surfaced which led to a collapse of the established party system of the First Republic (Donovan 1995). As a consequence, the country saw the rise of Berlusconi's populist movement (Bull and Pasquino 2007; Fusaro 1998), the decay of communism and the electoral success of the *Lega Nord*.

The decentralization reform of 2001 responded to the performance problems, although it also aimed at reducing regional disparities and attempted to appease growing dissatisfaction in the northern Regions with the central state. The governance problems of the Italian state resulted from territorially based clientelism (Di Giovacchino 2005) as well as interlocked decision-making, which substantially constrained the constitutional power of the Regions. Furthermore, regional and local administration in the south increasingly failed to produce a sufficient quality of public goods necessary for economic development (Putnam 1994), while financial transfers to southern Regions added to already excessive spending of the central government and increased public debt. In the Italian unitary system, these deficits inevitably were attributed to the central level. The pressure for reform increased with rising fiscal deficits and corruption scandals ("*Tangentopoli*"). The crisis of the "blocked democracy" (Fix 1999) opened a window of opportunity for political and institutional change. A fundamental reform of the political system and proposals to strengthen the Regions dominated the political agenda. Both parliamentary chambers established several joint commissions designed to find a consensus between the two major political camps.

3.4 Problems of Integration in a Regionalizing State

Integration problems are typical for so-called multinational federations, where they are tamed but never really solved by a constitutional division of powers, by granting autonomy to regions in policy fields relevant for preserving the distinct identity of community or by protecting fundamental regional interests through legislative procedures. In unitary states, problems with integrating territorially concentrated communities are even more difficult to manage. In Eastern and South-Eastern Europe, they led to a separation of states, often in the wake of wars against the central government, after the autocratic communist regimes had collapsed. In democratic nations, violent confrontations may occur but central governments usually are willing to concede rights and powers to particular regions. In the UK, Northern Ireland saw a civil war until the Good Friday Agreement was settled with the support of the US government. In this study, the focus is on integration problems in *Great Britain,* where Scotland and Wales long strove for devolution of powers, if not independence.

Great Britain has been labelled a "union state" composed of three formerly independent kingdoms. While Wales was integrated early into the English state, the unification with Scotland started with the Acts of Union of 1707. Cultural differences and economic imbalances between the three parts of Great Britain created continuous tensions in an increasingly centralized state.

Political structuring in the parliamentary system, which developed in the area of industrialization, emerged from the dualism of majority and opposition in the House of Commons. With the beginning of the twentieth century it reflected the class conflict in British society which predominated regional divides for a long time. The creation of a liberal welfare state after World War II reduced this conflict and supported social integration. However, tensions between the central government in London and the "Celtic Fringe" loomed under the surface of unitary politics.

The constitutional problem triggering devolution for Scotland and Wales (Tierney 2009) became manifest when centralizing policies of the era of a Conservative government lasting from 1979 to 1997 (Wright 1997: 137–43) caused increasing resistance. In Scotland, this was more salient than in Wales because the Scottish people had always been a distinct group within the UK with their own national identity and even specific institutions such as the legal system or the Church (Keating 2004). Wales had been incorporated into the UK before it could develop its own Welsh institutions (Hechter 1975; Rawlings 2003: 2; Van Morgan 2006: 256). Accordingly, its national identity has been less pronounced than the Scottish one, in particular since the Conservative government had met the most pressing nationalist demands by introducing Welsh language TV and a Welsh Language Act in 1993 (McLean and McMillan 2005: 173). Nevertheless, during the era of the Thatcher government, the Scottish and the Welsh felt increasingly marginalized, both economically and politically. Economically, the decline of the coal and steel industry during the 1980s, the market-oriented economic policy of industrial restructuring implemented by the Thatcher government, and the parallel decline of welfare benefits were felt hard in the "Celtic periphery" (Bradbury 2010: 2; Mitchell 2009a; Morgan and Mungham 2000: 45–54; Rawlings 2003: 30). In Scotland, the economic profits from oil production in the North Sea raised expectations for an autonomous economic recovery.

In political terms, the integration problem in Great Britain found expression in a conflict between the central government and regions. It was intensified by administrative reforms of the Thatcher government, which in both regions were perceived as an encroachment of the central state. In the unitary state of Great Britain, Scotland profited from guaranteed representation at the center beyond the Westminster parliament and a certain degree of autonomy via local intermediate bodies such as health boards or school boards and quasi-corporatist bodies established around the Scottish Office (Paterson et al. 1992: 94; Wright 1997: 140). Although applying to Great Britain as a whole and not aiming at particular regions, Conservative administrative reforms were nevertheless perceived as anti-Scottish since they weakened or abolished these bodies (Stolz 1999: 224). In Wales, the government appointed technocrats dominating the many quangos (quasi-autonomous, non-governmental organizations). Moreover, the legitimacy of the central state was called into question since representation in the Westminster parliament seemed unsuitable to making regional interests heard. Both Scotland and Wales repeatedly turned out Labour majorities but were in the end governed by a Conservative majority in London (Bradbury 1998; Brand et al. 1994: 216; Jones and Jones 2000: 259; Rawlings 2003: 29–30; Trench 2008).

The immediate trigger for the reform in Scotland was the introduction of the poll tax in the region one year earlier than in the rest of the UK (McLean and McMillan 2005: 172). Thus, devolution was increasingly seen as a defense mechanism against Thatcherism as such (Miller 1998: 187). In this situation a group of activists, the Campaign for a Scottish Assembly, established the Scottish Constitutional Convention (SCC), a forum bringing together all Scottish political parties apart from the SNP and the Conservatives, local government, trade unions, churches and other civil society organizations. The mandate of the SCC was simply to draw up a concept for an elected Scottish Assembly and to ensure its implementation (Scottish Constitutional Convention 1990). In Wales, a resolution calling for the establishment of a Welsh parliament passed at the 1987 annual conference of the Welsh Trade Union Congress, and the formation of a Campaign for a Welsh Assembly in the same year led the Welsh Labour Party to reconsider its initially negative opinion on devolution. The party included a proposal for an elected Assembly for Wales in their manifesto for the 1992 general election, based on an internal report from 1989 (Wales Labour Party 1989), which can be seen as the original agenda of the 1997 devolution program (Bradbury et al. 1996: 690, 97).

3.5 Constitutional Problems and Political Dynamics

In the cases outlined in this chapter, reform agendas do not exclusively focus either on performance aspects or on group conflicts and cultural issues, but also include a number of issues attributed to problems that are more specific. Moreover, the consequences of these problems for an agenda of constitutional policy differ in federal and regionalized states. Nevertheless, the reform processes are framed by actors according to one basic constitutional problem. Therefore, a distinction of the two types of constitutional problems makes sense from an empirical point of view. For our analysis, it not only allows us to clarify the particular agendas in the different cases, as summarized in Table 3.1. It also sheds light on the types of crucial conflict to be dealt with in constitutional policy.

The short descriptions of sequences of historical development should not explain the particular constitutional problems. They are meant to point out

Table 3.1. Varieties of constitutional problems in selected multilevel governments

		Vertical dimension	
		regionalized political system	federal political system
Horizontal dimension	integrated	**performance problems**	
		Italy: over-centralization, inefficient overlap of powers, economic imbalance	*Austria*: over-centralization, nontransparent allocation of powers
		France: interlocking of levels, fiscal over-centralization	*Germany*: joint decision problems
			Switzerland: joint decision problems; deficit of fiscal equalization
	disintegrated	**integration problems**	
		Great Britain: over-centralization in face of demands for regional autonomy	*Canada:* divided society, secessionist parties
			Belgium: divided society, regionalist parties, economic imbalance
			Spain divided society, secessionist parties, economic imbalance

durable historical trajectories of territorial constitutional problems. Performance problems as well as those of territorial integration reflect particular imbalances of territorial structures that persist over time. Therefore, they may resurface after a previously terminated reform. In consequence, negotiating a new balance of power and finding at least temporary solutions for these lasting problems gain even more importance for the long-term territorial development and policy performance of a multilevel political system.

The analytical distinction between these types of constitutional problems is also important, as performance and integration problems arise due to different driving forces of federal dynamics influencing processes of explicit and implicit constitutional change. Performance problems are debated in public, often with associations from different societal sectors being engaged in discussions. They also may become a matter of party politics. These debates trigger reform processes. However, at least in integrated federal systems, a reform agenda is usually defined by the executive. In unitary states, the general direction of change seems to be obvious with decentralization or regionalization appearing as framing concepts. Moreover, the pressure for change is high as problems are ascribed to the central government, in particular if a political crisis weakens the government. In integrated federal systems, there is not such an obvious connection between the debated performance problems and particular structures of government. Therefore, a widespread perception of performance deficits does not immediately translate into a reform agenda.

While they are expressed in public debates, it is established in internal discussion in government whether, to what extent, and which way these deficits are caused by institutions or constitutional law or whether they merely reflect conflicts in normal policy-making. As a consequence, performance problems mostly relate to internal dynamics of power structures.

Furthermore, if performance problems predominate, concerns about fiscal imbalances or inadequate fiscal equalization schemes often accompany demands for a reallocation of legislative powers. Centralizing dynamics due to greater financial resources of the center are regarded as an essential factor of the constitutional problem from the perspective of substate entities fearing encroachment by the central government into their jurisdiction. Arguments for change focus on aspects of fiscal imbalances, accountability and transparency as well as on accommodating regional disparities, sometimes appealing to distinctive regional identities, which, however, have more symbolical functions and never mobilize societal groups. Proposals for a change affect power and resources of governments and actors often formulate reasons for them in a legalistic or expert terminology.

In contrast, integration problems concern society, even if they often are expressed by political leaders. Citizens affected in their identity and feeling alienated or excluded from a nation mobilize easily. Accordingly, parties regularly become drivers of constitutional policy, in particular those aspiring for secession. Governments cannot control dynamics set off under these society-centered conditions. At the same time, conflicts relate to basic values rather than to powers or resources. Package deals and compromises hardly seem capable of solving the fundamental divides existing between different conceptions of a political order in an integration conflict.

Therefore, with regard to constitutional negotiations and reform results, we expect two types of territorial constitutional problems to have different effects. Reform processes concerned with performance problems tend to unfold within existing political institutions and are initiated by political elites, either from the central or regional level. We therefore assume that these processes tend to be embedded in everyday politics and to be noticeably influenced by party politics and competition either between economically stronger and weaker regions or between local or regional and the central government. Regional identities will be much less important, and we expect a lower level of participation or dedication of societal actors. Accordingly, an appropriate design of the reform process must counterbalance the tendencies towards exclusive party politics or intergovernmental politics, since both are prone to bargaining processes. Reform processes concerned with problems of territorial integration are triggered within society in a bottom-up direction and require a certain level of participation of the groups concerned in order to find a compromise on their demands. Inclusiveness, participation and access to the process are considered necessary for a reform result to be regarded as legitimate (Banting and Simeon 1985b: 8–9, 15; Tully 2001). At any rate, the process must be designed to make conflicts manageable and to avoid confrontation among participating actors.

For these reasons, we assume that the type of problems framing constitutional policy is an important condition to be considered when explaining constitutional change in federal and federalizing systems. However, as the following case studies demonstrate, success or failure is caused by additional factors. In any case, the intense conflicts due to integration problems do not necessarily make it more likely that the constitutional policy in multilevel systems is caught in the joint-decision trap. Moreover, regionalized unitary states are not in a better position to change their territorial structures compared to federal states, where we find failed as well as successful reforms. We need to analyze in detail how constitutional policy evolves and proceeds in different multilevel governments in order to understand how they manage to balance their power or why they fail to do so.

4

Patterns of Constitutional Policy in Multilevel Government: Case Studies

(with Dominic Heinz, Eike-Christian Hornig, Andrea Fischer-Hotzel, and Bettina Petersohn)

As empirical research on federal and regionalized states has revealed (Banting and Simeon 1985a; Behnke 2010; Behnke and Benz 2009; Benz and Knüpling 2012a; Lorenz 2008), constitutions are more often amended in multilevel governments than predicted by theories of institutional change. Moreover, compared to unitary states, institutional conditions of constitutional policy in states dividing powers between territories do not differ as much as it is often assumed (Kaltenborn 2012). Therefore, the effective structures and proceedings in constitutional negotiations should be considered when searching for an explanation of the outcome of reforms and constitutional change. In these processes, which reveal a significant variety across cases, the substance of constitutional reforms is determined.

The outcomes to be explained can be categorized, according to the criteria defined above, as indicated in Table 4.1. Details justifying the categorization will be provided in the following case studies and are summarized in Table 4.2 and in the summary near the end of this chapter. It goes without saying that outcomes as defined for the purpose of this study cannot be measured by quantitative indicators. We try to describe tendencies in the political development of multilevel states independent of particular policy fields. Even the criteria of scope and selectivity cannot be quantified, as we are interested in the substance of constitutional policy. More difficult to operationalize is the criterion "balance of power." We are aware of these problems and have tried to provide, as precisely as possible, reasons for our assessment of the different aspects of outcomes, which we checked through opinions from our experts. However, what is relevant for answering our research question are historical

Table 4.1. Outcomes of constitutional policy in the selected cases

	Ratification		No or vetoed ratification
Effective negotiations	SUCCESSFUL REFORM		RATIFICATION FAILURE
	Switzerland		**Canada**
	implementation of significant change		non-constitutional change
↓ Federal dynamics			
Ineffective negotiations	INEFFECTIVE REFORM		CONSTITUTIONAL DEADLOCK
	Germany	**Belgium**	**Austria**
	France	**Great Britain**	
	Italy	**Spain**	
↓ Federal dynamics	rigidity	destabilization	stagnation

Table 4.2. Outcomes of constitutional negotiations

Country	Scope		Balance	
	scope of intended reform (+: large; –: limited)	selectivity (+: low; –: high, 0: medium)	balance of power (+: more balanced; –: less balanced, 0: no improvement)	rigidity/flexibility (+: flexible, –: rigidity)
Switzerland	+	+	+	+
Canada	+	+	+	+
Germany	+	–	+	–
Italy	+	+	+	–
France	–	+	+	–
Belgium	–	+	–	–
GB	+	0	–	+
Austria	+	–	0	0
Spain	+	0	–	+

accounts of constitutional policies, which we studied for selected but decisive periods in the nine countries.

As Table 4.1 shows, both successful reforms and utter failure are rare outcomes. Only the Austrian Convention ended without any agreement in constitutional negotiations, and, even in this case, later processes of expert negotiations produced some modification of the legal framework. We find, on the other hand, a clear case of a successful reform in Switzerland. Also rare

are cases of a constitutional reform process which did not end with ratification of constitutional amendments. Besides Austria, we find this result in Canada, where fairly successful negotiations produced an agreement on a framework for constitutional change, which failed to get ratified. Ratification failure at the last resort results from amendment rules, but they do not determine the effective outcome, if we take into account the consequences of the reform endeavor. Both the result of negotiations and the ensuing constitutional dynamics we observe particularly in Canada require a different explanation. In Spain, which is in many respects a specific case, the last round of constitutional reform was partially blocked by the Constitutional Court, after the regional population and the majority of the Spanish parliament had ratified an agreement between the Autonomous Community of Catalonia despite strong resistance from the opposition party. As a consequence, after formal ratifications of a number of regional statute reforms, the incremental change from below came to its limits. In most other cases, outcomes have to be categorized as ineffective reform. In the Scottish case, the evaluation of devolution is still discussed controversially. Compared to the aims defined in the agenda and the pressing problems of integration, one can consider this case a success story. However, this assessment applies only to the reform of the Scottish government. The British state is still confronted with continuous pressure for secession caused by the insufficient solution of integration problems. Besides Scottish devolution, the reform attempts turned out less effective in other parts of Great Britain. For Wales, the reform had more limited effects, and it was blocked right from the outset in most regions of England. Overall, not the least due to a segmentation of devolution, serious constitutional problems of the British territorial order prevail. The same holds true for Belgium where the newly created federation became more and more instable and unable to solve conflicts. It was only in 2012 that pragmatic politicians overcame a decade of deadlock and parties agreed on a modest institutional reform probably countervailing disintegration. Yet the previous reform attempt analyzed in our study turned out as less successful. In Germany, France and Italy, more or less significant constitutional amendments had been ratified, but decisive problems of performance of multilevel governance had not been solved.

This finding, which will be exposed in detail in the following case studies, seems to conform to theories of institutional change. In a way, the outcomes also seem to reveal the typical effects of patterns of joint decision-making. However, by underrating the probability of institutional change, the model of the joint-decision trap does not take into account the dual incrementalism characteristic of both ordinary policy-making and constitutional policies. If we find ineffective outcomes in both dimensions, the political system may suffer from deficient flexibility or become instable. Therefore, we have all reasons to search for ways out of these fatal dynamics. Theories of historical institutionalism focus on the scope of change and can only explain the incremental nature of constitutional evolution in the respective countries. What they do not explain are variations in the scope of change or effects regarding stability or flexibility of a balance of power in multilevel systems. Therefore, a closer look at the processes of constitutional policy and the causes and consequences of the outcomes in the particular cases is required.

The case studies are presented in the same order as in the previous section. Nonetheless, as the brief account of outcomes demonstrates, neither the dominant constitutional problem nor the distinction between regionalized unitary or federal states can explain different outcomes of reforms, attempted reforms or implicit constitutional change following a reform. As will be revealed in the case studies, effectiveness or ineffectiveness can be traced back to different structures of constitutional negotiations. Implicit constitutional change in the aftermath of reforms apparently varies depending on whether integration problems are at stake or whether interlocking politics causes performance problems, but the direction of evolution of these processes are to a considerable extent determined in constitutional negotiations during reform processes.

4.1 Integrated Federal States Addressing Performance Problems

In the three integrated federations, we observe contrasting outcomes of constitutional reforms addressing performance deficits. Interestingly, the most successful reform occurred in Switzerland, where a rather ambitious project had been launched and where ratification rules set the highest institutional constraints compared to the Austrian and German case. Even taking into account that other constitutional reform processes in Switzerland had ended with less success or even utter failure, the case study summarized in the ensuing section challenges common assumptions in theories of constitutional or institutional change. It also sheds light on the need to study the structures and processes of constitutional negotiations carefully.

4.1.1 *Switzerland: The Renewal of Fiscal Equalization and Allocation of Powers (1994–2008)*

In the context of ongoing debates about Swiss federalism outlined above (Chapter 3), a reform of the federal system was initiated in the 1990s. At that time, the Federal Department of Finance published an alarming report, charging the system of financial transfers from the federal government to the

Cantons as inefficient and counterproductive. The results revealed not only a bewildering variety of grants, but also, against all intentions, a widening fiscal gap between poor and rich Cantons (Rey 1994). In order to come to a more effective federation, governments agreed that fiscal relations had to be revised. They also realized that a reallocation of grants between Cantons had to be linked to a revision of competences of the federal and the cantonal governments. Moreover, there was widespread agreement on the need to strengthen the autonomy of the Cantons against creeping centralization and blurring of powers (Freiburghaus 2005: 507).

Constitutional negotiations started in 1994. Nine years later, in October 2003, the Swiss parliament passed a proposal for a comprehensive constitutional reform—the *Renewal of Fiscal Equalization and Allocation of Powers* (also known as NFA), which was ratified by the required popular referendum in November 2004. In order to achieve a positive vote in a referendum, governments, political parties and interest groups had to come to an agreement and then support the proposal publicly. While parliaments and the people were the final decision makers, many actors had de facto power to intervene and threaten the success of the reform. Ultimately, the necessary agreement on a new fiscal equalization scheme was achieved, against all odds. The federal government hoped that a more efficient fiscal federalism could reduce costs of government and thus avoid redistributive effects, so that no Canton or the federal government would lose money. However, this positive effect was not certain, and in relative terms, some Cantons could be perceived as net losers. Therefore, the reform gave rise to conflicts on the reallocation of powers and finances. Nonetheless, it was completed along the lines defined in the agenda, and has meanwhile been implemented. Despite disputes on details, it is widely praised as successful (Freiburghaus 2009).

The new fiscal equalization scheme operates on clear criteria related to the fiscal capacities and the fiscal needs of Cantons. Although the final compromise acknowledged additional long-term compensations for those Cantons rendered net losers by the reform, this scheme still managed to improve fiscal relations in Switzerland significantly. The transfers are no longer allocated as specific grants, but as general grants in order to equalize fiscal resources and to compensate for particular burdens of Cantons (EFD 2004). Thus, fiscal equalization addresses imbalances, concerning both revenues and expenditures, in a coherent system. Regarding the revision of legislative and administrative powers, some were decentralized and others centralized, while the number of shared powers was reduced. Certainly, the protagonists of a far-reaching reform had to accept compromises. During the negotiation process, the number of powers revised decreased. Originally, no less than fifty areas of joint decision-making were scrutinized. After several sequences of negotiations, six of the previously shared powers were assigned to the federal government and ten to Cantonal governments. Nine competences are now fulfilled in horizontal cooperation among Cantons and seventeen are left for joint federal–Cantonal decision-making. "In the end, the separation of powers turned out to be much less extreme than it had been hoped for at the beginning" (Freiburghaus 2012: 72). Compared to other constitutional reforms in federal systems, the extent of change in the allocation of power achieved in Switzerland is nevertheless remarkable. Critics also have complained that the new rules of intercantonal cooperation interfere with procedures of direct democracy. But horizontal cooperation allows for decentralized policy-making despite external effects produced in small territories. Moreover, the federal government can now enforce intercantonal contracts in order to prevent "free riding" behavior by Cantons. This shadow of hierarchy makes intergovernmental policy-making more effective compared to the previous voluntary contracting.

Forgoing a long story of the reform process in all its particulars (for a more detailed analysis see Fischer 2012), only the most important steps shall be recapitulated. Negotiations started with an initiative within the executive branch. Officially, it was the Federal Department of Finance and the Conference of Ministers of Finance of the Cantons which launched the reform project. They set the agenda including the issues referred to above. Actually, experts in the Federal Department of Finance triggered the reform process.

Right from the beginning, the structure of the negotiations process was a matter of dispute (Wettstein 2012: 82). Among the alternatives of an expert-based approach and a political approach, governments decided for a combination of both. Negotiations did not follow an explicitly determined design. Their structures rather emerged under the impact of standard operation procedures in Swiss government and politics, of institutional rules, and of pragmatic decisions adapted to situations in an open temporal framework that removed pressure to meet deadlines. In retrospect, the process proved effective.

In 1994, governments set up a project organization responsible for analyzing the problems of Swiss federalism and for drafting the framework of the reform. It included delegates from the federal financial administration and the Cantonal administration with both levels represented on equal terms. This project team guided specialized working groups and summed up their contribution in reports. The results were submitted to the Ministers of Finance and, subsequently, to the Conference of Federal and Cantonal Governments. As a first step, the executive elaborated a framework for the reform—the "guidelines" defining the general approach and basic principles. In view of the professional background of civil servants and participating experts, it was not surprising that theories of fiscal federalism and new public management had a strong impact on the framework. Yet this was not a theoretical concept, but a pragmatic scheme for a comprehensive and coherent revision of federalism.

The report on the "guidelines" of the reform was discussed and accepted by the federal government and the Conference of Cantonal Governments. It was then subject to public consultation, in order to test the feasibility of the reform project. Cantonal governments, political parties and civil society organizations were invited to participate, and more organizations than those officially addressed submitted opinions. As the consultation proved, there was widespread support for a reform and agreement on the principles defined in the "guidelines" (Interview CH, 12 June 2006).[1]

Following this consultation, a project organization adjusted to the new task was set up and committed to transform these guidelines into proposals for detailed revisions of the constitution. This second phase of the reform started in 1997. The team coordinating the project presented its final report to the federal and cantonal governments. When the governments had approved this report, it was published for a second round of consultation. In this process, some groups raised a number of objections related to their particular interests. After settling the disputes, the drafts for a constitutional amendment bill and ordinary bills on fiscal equalization were elaborated. In November 2001, the government introduced the drafts in the legislature. This was the first time that the federal parliament officially had a say in the process. However, members of parliaments from all jurisdictions certainly had ample opportunities to get involved either in public consultation or in informal contacts to the executive (Wettstein 2002).

Finally, after the draft proposal had passed the federal legislature, it was subject to the required constitutional referendum, which took place in November 2004. Governments and parties succeeded in convincing a clear majority of Swiss citizens in the referendum campaign. When the constitutional amendment was in force, the reform was implemented in legislative and administrative decisions.

That the reallocation of powers, the fiscal equalization system and the coordination of decentralized policies could be renovated in a coherent reform, is an astonishing result not only compared to similar attempts in other countries but also under the difficult institutional conditions of Swiss federalism and democracy. Certainly, governments acted without the pressure of elections in Swiss consensus democracy, where the positions in government are distributed among parties according to proportional rule. Therefore, the executive had all the time to elaborate a reform proposal and to manage conflicts. Moreover, party competition on constitutional issues was not ignited during election campaigns. The political culture facilitated a consensus among all political and societal groups (Freiburghaus 2012: 76). However,

[1] The interviews are cited with a country code and the date of the interview.

these particular institutional conditions alone cannot explain the outcome of an ambitious constitutional reform project. In view of a far-reaching redistribution of powers and fiscal resources between territories—an issue which in other federal states has regularly blocked reforms—other conditions need to be considered. What is striking in this case is the differentiated structure of constitutional negotiations, which went through expert-dominated, intergovernmental, parliamentary and consociational processes (Wettstein 2009).

Upon closer inspection, this process, apart from its long duration, is particularly characterized by its organizational features. While constitutional politics and normal politics are hardly distinct in the consensus democracy of Switzerland, the NFA-process differentiated them. This was achieved by the decision to deal with constitutional issues sequentially. The first sequence of the reform focused on aims and general principles guiding the renovation of federalism. It ended with the agreement on the "guidelines," elaborated by a group of experts and accepted in intergovernmental conferences, in parliament and in consultation with interest organizations. After the aims and principles had been fixed, details of constitutional amendments were elaborated in the second sequence. Finally, having been ratified, the new rules were implemented in laws and executive decisions. This sequential process implied that constitutional policy took place in a distinct arena. It provided conditions which favored an integrated approach to deal with fiscal equalization, the allocation of powers and intergovernmental relations (Braun 2009).

Such an integrative approach runs the risk of failing because of its complexity. By affecting a variety of interests of powerful actors, it tends to induce bargaining on package deals. Yet the sequential process implied a temporal as well as a substantial differentiation of the constitutional negotiations. By separating decisions on principles from decisions on particular powers and rules of financial transfers, the process avoided these problems. In negotiations on the "guidelines," all actors developed a shared understanding of the general premises and the normative framework justifying the reform. This differentiation of constitutional principles and rules created a "veil of ignorance" (Freiburghaus 2009) on redistributive consequences in the first phase, which favored arguing behavior of all actors involved and made it possible to find a basic consensus. In the following phases, this consensus on a normative framework significantly reduced the scope for distributive bargaining on particular issues.

A second particular feature of the Swiss reform process was a differentiation between the administrative and the political tier of the executive, and between executive, parliamentary and consociational arenas. The federal government set up a project team responsible for managing and coordinating the process. Moreover, committees and subcommittees of the federal–cantonal Conference of Directors of Finance worked on specific aspects of the reform.

Thus, from the very beginning, civil servants from the federal and the cantonal ministries of finance cooperated closely, supported by experts who provided the theoretical basis for the reform program (Interview CH, 12 June 2006). These actors shared the mission to achieve a significant reform of Swiss federalism and, as a team, promoted the reform. Executive committees and working groups submitted the results of their consultation to intergovernmental conferences of the Ministers of Finance and heads of government, where negotiations on the proposals continued, now among political actors legitimized to make decisions on a draft proposal for constitutional amendments. In a further step, the reform concept and, in the second stage, the legislative package elaborated in the executive was discussed with representatives from interest groups. Finally, the Swiss legislature debated and voted on the reform. Both the decision on principles (the "guidelines") and the decision on detailed amendment proposals passed these four arenas.

This structure of constitutional negotiations was set up by deliberate decisions of the federal government but also emerged due to the particular institutions of Swiss democracy. It combined a functional and a social division of arenas. They were linked in such a way that the number of actors and the range of interests were incrementally opened up. Thus complexity became manageable in a process that comes close to the model of "negative coordination" (Wettstein 2012: 86–7), but actually combined positive coordination between federal and cantonal representatives in the executive with negative coordination in parliamentary and consociational arenas, which—according to tests in simulation—appears to be most effective for dealing with complex issues (Scharpf and Mohr 1994).

Certainly, this multidimensional differentiation of arenas and processes did not rule out bargaining processes and strategic moves of actors determined to promote their interests. Governments of the rich Cantons, which feared being disadvantaged under the new fiscal equalization scheme, accepted the reform only after the federal Social Democrats threatened to introduce a bill on tax harmonization. This motion was deemed likely to pass if the constitutional reform had failed, with the consequence that those Cantons would have lost not only power but also money. Furthermore, the Federal Department of Finance had promised to compensate financial burdens on Cantons facing reduced transfers (Cappelletti et al. 2014). Finally, new rules for intercantonal cooperation protected small Cantons against being dissolved by territorial reorganization, which some experts had suggested as a more efficient and democratic solution (Rhinow 2003). In the second phase of consultation with interest groups, conflicts with the association for disabled persons arose, a well-organized group both on the federal and at the Cantonal level controlling a considerable mobilization power in a referendum campaign. Since efficiency of governance was one of the basic goals of the reform, this association feared that the quality of social services could be reduced if they were provided in competition between Cantons (Interview CH, 13 June 2006). To settle the conflict, responsibility for disabled persons remained a joint task of federal and cantonal governments. Another matter of conflict was road construction that had been jointly financed by federal and cantonal governments. Due to resistance mobilized at the cantonal and local levels against centralization in this policy field, the federal government only transferred responsibility for national routes (Bundesrat 2001: 2422–6). A compromise also ended disputes on environmental protection, for which special grants were continued (Bundesrat 2001: 2449–52). Education was turned into a joint task as the result of a compromise between federal and cantonal governments (Bundesrat 2001: 2418–20). As regards public schools, a definite solution was postponed, and a further constitutional reform passed in 2006 establishing particular procedures for joint decision-making in this field.

However, intergovernmental bargaining and the resulting compromises never undermined the framework of principles and reasons justifying the reform. Only a few matters were removed from the agenda of the reform. The basic goals, the guidelines and the coherence of the project could be maintained. In the different arenas, governments found increasing support for the reform project. By moving from one arena to another, the proposal has to be justified repeatedly, and this was made possible by a media campaign of the executive and due to the basic consensus on reform principles.

The proposal for a new fiscal equalization scheme and a reallocation of powers in the federal system elaborated in constitutional negotiations was ratified by the federal legislature and in a referendum. Sixty-four percent of citizens casting their vote, including a majority in three of the six Cantons burdened as net payers by the reform approved the amendment. The low turnout (35.5 percent) signified that citizens accepted the reform and no important group or party mobilized opposition (Freiburghaus 2012: 75). The arenas of negotiation and ratification are loosely coupled in Switzerland. Constitutional amendments have to pass formal legislation procedure in the national parliament and the second chamber, the Council of Cantons (*Ständerat*). After that, they have to be adopted in a referendum. In order to become constitutional law, a majority of Swiss citizens both at the level of the federation and in a majority of the Cantons have to approve the proposed amendments. In both houses of the legislature, majorities are not determined by governmental coalitions but by fluid, issue-specific coalitions in parliament (Linder 2010). Therefore, governments cannot anticipate vetoes in legislature when negotiating an amendment bill or make deals to form majorities. The impact of party competition on constitutional negotiation is limited for the same reason. Despite consultation with interest organizations, which can mobilize their members, it is difficult to anticipate how people feel affected by a constitutional amendment and will vote in a referendum. Therefore, all that promoters of a reform can do is to provide compelling reasons in the legislative process. At the same time, governments, parties and civil society organizations supporting the reform have to convince citizens in public discussion by explaining the rationale of the reform rather than declaring what they may gain or lose.

The need for persuasive deliberation in parliamentary proceedings and in referendum campaigns was well known among political actors in Switzerland elaborating the NFA project. This had consequences for the mode of negotiations on a draft proposal. Therefore, actors negotiating on a constitutional reform had to search for the presumed general will of the people; they could not behave like agents of veto-players. Experts, civil servants and representatives of governments at all levels acted accordingly. If this is a feature of a particular political culture, it is a culture generated and reconfirmed in institutions and political practice of the political system. In the case of the federal constitutional reform, the particular organization of constitutional negotiations supported the effects of these institutions in a decisive way.

Given the high number of incohesive veto-players in Swiss federalism and the redistributive effects of the reform, the simultaneous reallocation of powers and resources in the vertical and horizontal dimensions was a remarkable outcome. The reform changed the constitutional status quo significantly. The positive evaluation in public and the unproblematic implementation process indicated a successful amendment process. The constitutional reform contributed to stabilizing Swiss federalism against tendencies towards centralization and fiscal imbalances.

4.1.2 *Germany: Reform of Federalism I and II (2003–9)*

Since the Basic Law came into force in 1949, Germany has seen a number of reforms of the federal constitution, most of them ending with a limited reallocation of powers (Busch 1999). After 1989, German unification triggered a debate as to whether the enlarged Federal Republic required a new constitution or whether a revision of the existing Basic Law would be sufficient. As a compromise, the two houses of the federal legislature convened to set up a joint committee responsible for reviewing the constitution. After fourteen meetings and nine hearings of experts and interest groups between 1992 and 1993, the committee submitted proposals for constitutional amendments, which in September 1994 found the required two-thirds majority in both houses, the *Bundestag* and the *Bundesrat*. The discussions mainly reflected the well-known critiques regarding joint decision-making and centralization, but the allocation of powers and resources between levels of government was not a major issue of this reform (Batt 1996; Benz 1993; Bremers 2001;

Jeffery 1995). An additional constitutional amendment passed in 1992 related to the role of *Länder* governments in European integration. A new article entrenched the practice of intergovernmental cooperation in EU affairs into constitutional law and made the definition of the German position in EU policy a matter of joint decision-making, as far as the powers of the *Länder* are affected. Part of the 1994 amendment was a revision of the conditions for federal legislation in areas of concurrent competences and a new procedure, which obliged the Constitutional Court to decide on conflicts between the federal and the *Länder* governments when the application of this constitutional rule is a matter of dispute. By giving the Court the power to limit federal legislation, it had effects on the reform of the federal system, which is the subject of this case study.

In the mid-1990s, problems of German federalism became an issue of intense public debates (Scheller 2008: 470). Increased economic disparities and the challenges of Europeanization induced these processes. On the one hand, economic disparities between East and West Germany made it difficult to maintain the high degree of uniformity of public welfare provisions and the redistribution of finances was increasingly disputed. On the other hand, cooperation between federal and *Länder* governments required by the constitution in important areas of legislation was hampered by a growing divergence of interests. This was particularly a problem in policies where Germany had to transpose European law. Moreover, the *Länder* governments tried to compensate their veto rights, which they lost with the delegation of powers to the EU by rights to participate in European policies, while the federal government argued that the *Länder* would tie its hands in European negotiations.

In response to these debates, legislation to amend the constitution was started in 2003, when the *Bundestag* and the *Bundesrat* set up a bicameral committee determined to draft a reform of the federal system. In 2006, the federal legislature passed the reform, which political leaders praised as the most significant change of the constitution since the foundation of the Federal Republic in 1949. Yet matters of tax powers and fiscal equalization were postponed. Therefore, the *Bundestag* with the consent of the *Bundesrat* initiated a second reform in 2007, which ended with another constitutional amendment in 2009. While the first reform aimed at a clearer separation of powers in order to increase the autonomy of governments and a decentralization of powers in order to restore the federal balance in favor of the *Länder* governments, the second reform focused on fiscal federalism and administrative powers. The division of these issues and the sequence of the reform were not planned, but resulted from the limited effectiveness of the first reform negotiations (Interview D, 8 May 2009). In both cases, many of the issues originally on the agenda were left unresolved.

When evaluating the outcome of both reforms, the result appears less impressive than how it was presented in official statements (Moore and

Jacoby 2009; Scharpf 2009). Worth noting is that the first step of reforming federalism ended a trend of extending legislative powers of the federal government which prevailed during most of the first five decades since 1949. With the 2006 constitutional amendment, twelve legislative matters were reassigned to the *Länder*, among them legislation on universities and on remunerations for civil servants of the *Länder* (Lachmuth et al. 2006). This is indeed an important achievement. But the reform left existing modes of joint decision-making in place, at least in those matters where risks of policy deadlocks were rather high due to conflicts on fiscal or budgetary facets of decisions. Neither had the reform significantly diminished the need for intergovernmental cooperation, nor had it improved the effectiveness of decision-making. What is even more problematic is the increasing constitutional regulation of the federal system (Benz 2008). A more detailed definition of competences and the altered regulations of federal grants are meant to prevent the federal government from extending its powers. On the other hand, aside from the legislative competences assigned to them, the constitutional amendment hardly changed the fiscal capacities of the *Länder* governments for decentralized policy-making. Moreover, the drift of power from parliaments to the executive was not corrected and will certainly continue. Although the reform proved that constitutional rigidity of German federalism is not as high as it is often assumed, these changes certainly reduce flexibility in policy-making. Consequently, political practice will likely entail increasing clashes with constitutional rules constraining political decisions. There are already initial indications for this. When the federal government, with the support of *Länder* governments, decided to invest in day care for children under the age of three years, it established a special fund in order to circumvent the constitutional limitation of its powers now in force. If such an evasion of constitutional rules unfolds, it may set a precedent for further circumvention and even undermining of the constitution.

As mentioned above, the second reform mainly dealt with fiscal federalism. It ended with the introduction of a new rule to limit public debts and procedures to implement this rule. In principle, federal and *Länder* governments are committed to balance their budgets. However, a number of exceptions relax this general rule. Deficits are allowed if natural disasters or certain crises occur, or if they are deemed necessary for fighting a recession. For the federal government, the budget is considered balanced if the annual deficit is below 0.35 percent of the GDP. To compensate for their particular burdens, five *Länder* have received financial grants to assist consolidation until 2020 (Deubel 2009; Oettinger 2009). While the new budget regime was praised as a success, both a reallocation of tax powers and a revision of the disputed fiscal equalization were again postponed. In contrast to the original goal to reduce joint decision-making, the second reform gave federal–*Länder* cooperation in budgeting an increased relevance (Heinz 2014; Niechoj 2010), while it also introduced new joint tasks in public administration. So far, these patterns of multilevel governance have not proved particularly effective.

What needs to be explained in this case is an ineffective reform, which was nevertheless ratified. Compared to the Swiss case, the German process reveals less differentiated structures of constitutional policy-making. In particular, a joint committee of the two houses of the legislature elaborated the reform proposal. Moreover, since constitutional amendments have to be ratified in parliament with the assent of the *Bundesrat*, arenas of negotiation and ratification were closely linked.

The joint committee established in 2003 to prepare the reform to modernize the federal system actually was a commission according to the typology introduced above (Chapter 2), and it was thus called in official terms. It included sixteen members of the federal parliament, the *Bundestag*, and sixteen members of the *Bundesrat*, actually the Prime Ministers of the *Länder* or their deputies. Members representing the federal government, the parliaments of the *Länder* and the local governments had no voting rights. In addition, twelve experts participated in the consultations. Most of the meetings of the Commission were held in public, but the response of the media or citizens was limited. Citizens or interest groups could submit written proposals, an opportunity which was used by some groups and a few individuals. The Commission's secretary summarized these statements, but they had no real impact on the negotiations (Benz 2005). Civil servants of ministries, who prepared materials and analyses for their governments, had much more influence on negotiations (Interview D, 8 May 2009). While the *Länder* governments mainly relied on generalists, specialists from different departments were involved at the federal level.

In the first meeting of the Joint Commission, the representatives of the *Bundestag* and of the *Länder* governments declared effective governance and accountability through a clear separation of powers to be the primary goals. These should be achieved by reducing the number of federal bills requiring the consent of the *Bundesrat* to become law. Moreover, legislative competences should be transferred from the federal level to the *Länder* parliaments. The participation of *Länder* governments in European affairs and the sharing of burdens caused by European laws were issues on the agenda as well. Moreover, decision rules in the *Bundesrat*, the allocation of tax competences and federal grants to *Länder* or local governments were discussed. However, the scope of the reform was restricted from the outset by the unanimous decision on a fundamental premise: By anticipating potential vetoes in ratification, members of the Commission explicitly stated not to alter the relative resource base of each government.

During the first meetings, an open discussion on alternative proposals for a reform of German federalism unfolded. This deliberation was essentially influenced by contributions of experts. They presented their opinions not only in two hearings, but also during the ensuing plenary meetings of the Commission. However, members of parliament and *Länder* representatives increasingly proved unwilling to lose control over the process. In a second stage, they divided the Commission work in two subcommittees and later set up seven working groups, with the latter excluding most of the experts. This reorganization clearly changed the mode of negotiation from arguing to bargaining, at a stage when conflicts on particular issues had to be dealt with.

Although it included members of parliament, the Commission actually turned constitutional negotiations into intergovernmental bargaining. Right from the beginning, discussions aimed at finding a package deal, in order to avoid redistributive outcomes. The federal government should profit from reduced veto power of the *Länder* governments in federal legislation, and the *Länder* should gain from a decentralization of legislative competences. However, this deal was doomed to fail for two reasons. First, while the parliaments of the *Länder* fought for extended legislative rights, their governments wanted to have a say if a federal law placed burdens on their fiscal and administrative capacities. Second, the *Länder* were divided in their demand for legislative powers. While the rich and large West German *Länder* pleaded for far-reaching decentralization, the economically depressed East German *Länder* feared the fiscal burden of new responsibilities and disadvantages in competition among jurisdictions (Auel 2008: 432; Interview D, 8 May 2009). Finally, the Commission agreed on rules defining the veto rights of the *Bundesrat*, which hardly met the expectations of the federal government. On the other hand, legislative powers assigned to the *Länder* concerned a number of less important matters, the exception being secondary education and remuneration for civil servants. Compared to earlier attempts to decentralize, this was a substantial degree of progress. But the compromise on competences included a differentiation of types of legislative competences and more detailed definitions of federal legislative powers. With the same effect of constraining future options for flexible adjustment of intergovernmental policy to particular situations, constitutional rules concerning European affairs were changed by a compromise on the lowest common denominator. Although they have been applied in a number of cases (Schneider 2013: 176–80), the new constitutional rules had hardly any visible effect in practice.

At the end, the Commission achieved compromises on a number of issues, by excluding matters like the decision rules of the *Bundesrat* and, much more importantly, most issues relating to fiscal federalism. Nevertheless, negotiations ended without a final decision. The first Reform Commission was not able to agree on a proposal for constitutional amendments to be submitted to the federal legislature. The obvious reason for this deadlock was a conflict between federal and the *Länder* governments on federal powers in education.

But beyond this, there was discontent among the rich Western *Länder* on the suggested scope of decentralization (Scharpf 2009: 101–7), while the Eastern *Länder* viewed the reform package as a gateway into competitive federalism. Committed to a consensus, the *Länder* representatives blocked the final session of the Commission, and the two chairpersons could only declare failure.

Nevertheless, German constitutional reform did not end in a deadlock. In the course of forming a Grand Coalition government after the 2005 general elections, a small group of high-level politicians of the federal and *Länder* governments resumed negotiations and finally clarified the remaining open questions. After a dispute in the federal parliament on powers in education and research had been settled by a compromise, the bill to amend the constitution passed both houses of the federal legislature with the necessary two-thirds majority. The package for a constitutional reform prepared in intergovernmental bargaining reflected more the interests of governments and administrations to maintain their powers and resources than ambitions to renew the federal balance. However, under the amendment rules of the German constitution, explicit constitutional change nevertheless was possible. As mentioned above, the price of this bargaining process was that federalism became more regulated by detailed constitutional provisions (Benz 2008).

While the competence for framework legislation was abolished, the issues falling under this category are now subject to a particular version of concurrent federal competence. If the federal government uses this power, the *Länder* parliaments are allowed to pass acts deviating from a federal law. The problem of this provision is not the ensuing diversity of regulation but the probability of competence conflicts. They are likely to arise in those matters, for which laws of the *Länder* are not allowed to deviate from basic principles of a federal law. Depending on future practice, these constitutional rules will maintain the status quo of framework legislation, if the federal government accepts the existing *Länder* laws, or they will cause disputes when politically salient issues are at stake.

The 2006 amendment rendered rules on legislative competences even more complicated. Before, a federal law was allowed in matters of concurrent competences "if and to the extent that the establishment of equal living conditions throughout the federal territory or the maintenance of legal or economic unity renders federal regulation necessary in the national interest" (Article 72 Paragraph 2 Basic Law).[2] The amended version of the Basic Law exempts a number of concurrent competences from this provision. Since in all these matters the federal government has already used the competence, there is actually no room left for deciding whether federal legislation is necessary or not.

[2] Cited according to the official translation: http://www.bundestag.de/htdocs_e/parliament/function/legal/germanbasiclaw.pdf.

This regulation reducing political discretion on the subsidiarity principle followed decisions of the Federal Constitutional Court in favor of the *Länder*.[3] In order to counteract unexpected decisions of the Court, which has to decide according to the new rules introduced by the 1994 amendment, the federal and *Länder* governments decided to confine the application of the subsidiarity clause (Stünker 2007).

The reformulation of Article 84, Paragraph 1 concerning the regulation of administrative organization and procedures by federal law seems to have opened up new room for manoeuver for the federal and *Länder* governments. The federal government can now avoid the veto power of the *Bundesrat* if the respective law allows the *Länder* governments to deviate from provisions on their administration (Röttgen and Boehl 2007). Nevertheless, if the government deems necessary, the federal law can set binding rules. Again, some additional rules qualify and constrain the political leeway. First, the federal law can make legal rules on procedures binding for the *Länder* governments, but not those on organization, and only if there is need for uniformity. Second, federal legislation is no longer allowed to delegate tasks to local governments. As a consequence, in significant policy fields the federal government lost influence on how its law is implemented. Options for federal policy-making are further reduced by a corresponding rule. Under the old constitutional provisions, the federal government could avoid the *Bundesrat* veto simply by defining regulation of administrative organization and procedures as non-binding. This escape route is no longer available if a federal law obliges the *Länder* governments to provide grants or benefits in kind equivalent to grants or services. Since federal government's right to provide grants have been also restricted, laws triggering conflicts among governments with regard to burden of implementation will be subject to the veto power of the *Bundesrat*, without the federal government being able to evade it by package deals (Manow and Burkhart 2006).

The same ambivalence applies to the amended rules for federal grants. They are now generally subject to term limits. This makes sense, as it requires regular reviews as to whether grants are still effective and needed. What makes less sense, however, is the rule forbidding federal grants in matters under the exclusive legislative competence of the *Länder*. It prevents the federal government from participating in areas such as education. This constitutional amendment ignited intense disputes among federal and *Länder* governments as also among experts, which continued after the ratification

[3] Geriatric Nursing Act case (2BvF 1/10 on 24 October 2002), Fighting Dogs case (1 BvR 1778/01 on 16 March 2004), Shop Closing Hours case (1 BvR 636/02 on 9 June 2004), Junior Professor case (2 BvF 2/02 on 27 July 2004), and Student Fees case (2 BvF 1/03 on 26 January 2005). Decisions are accessible at http://www.bundesverfassungsgericht.de/EN/Homepage/home_node.html.

of the reform. Moreover, in view of the exclusion of taxation power from the reform, the existing constitution drastically worsens the prospects for further decentralization as long as the *Länder* are not compensated by their own revenue sources. The amendments pertaining to European affairs follow the same trend of constitutional over-regulation. The constitution now sets forth a form of burden sharing in case the Federal Republic is fined for infringement of European law. But instead of defining a principle of distributive justice, the constitution fixes the exact percentage for dividing the amount, which then has to be applied under all circumstances.

With the 2006 decision on the constitutional amendment, the federal parliament initiated a further step of constitutional reform, to which the *Länder* governments agreed. In March 2007, a new Joint Commission of the *Bundestag* and the *Bundesrat* started to work on an agenda, which focused on fiscal federalism and administrative issues (Baus et al. 2008; Margedant 2008; Heinz 2012). Still, the structure of constitutional negotiations had the effect that intergovernmental bargaining prevailed, in particular since fiscal issues regularly were discussed in private meetings instead of public deliberation. A change in the structure of the Joint Commission contributed to this effect. Now representatives of the federal government were full members and had a right to vote in the Commission, whereas independent experts participated only in two public hearings, but had no access to negotiations. With the exception of the hearings, the Commission met in private. Although proposals for significant changes of fiscal federalism had been submitted to the Commission, negotiations soon concentrated on technical aspects of the new debt rule and administrative powers. Accordingly, the influence of experts from special administrations had increased (Interview D, 8 May 2009).

This second Commission intended to deal with fiscal federalism in general and fiscal equalization in particular. In fact, it extended its arena by starting with an open collection of issues to be dealt with. The final list included an extensive account of policy issues defined by administrations, and many had nothing to do with constitutional law. Nonetheless, induced by a ruling of the Federal Constitutional Court that denied the debt ridden *Land Berlin* a right to being bailed out by the federal government, the discussion shifted towards budgetary policy before the negotiation started (Ebert et al. 2010b: 143). Again bargaining processes led to an exclusion of important matters from the Commission's agenda. While it focused on regulating public debts of *Länder* governments, negotiations on a reallocation of powers to raise taxes and tax administration produced no result. As the chairpersons of the Commission declared in a paper summarizing the state of discussions, an agreement on these matters was not achievable due to conflicts among the *Länder* governments (Struck and Oettinger 2008). Interestingly this paper also stated that the existing fiscal equalization scheme should not be touched, and thus postponed an important matter. As regards the matters on which a consensus was found, it is worth noting that most if not all intended effects would have been achievable under the existing constitutional law. The second reform of federalism, more than the first one, dealt mainly with normal policy issues and worked with a clear orientation towards politics of the day. In view of the fiscal crisis that broke out in 2008, the Commission even established expert discourses (*Fachdiskurse*) and a working group to evaluate the budgetary situation in the four weakest *Länder*. Though these negotiations allowed shifting to an arguing mode, the effect of this procedural modification for the federal system remained limited. As a consequence, the reform process likewise ended with an agreement, which the legisature ratified. But again the amended constitutional rules brought about more constitutional constraits for policy-making than is neccesary in a democratic polity.

This outcome can be explained by the particular organization of constitutional policy. More or less, the whole process followed the procedures of ordinary legislation. At a glance, the Joint Commissions of both houses of the legislature established to draft the constitutional amendments looked like an extra-ordinary institution. Yet, although established for a special purpose, this institution did not constitute an arena separating normal and constitutional negotiations. Moreover, its full members, selected according to the parity principle to balance the influence of governments and parties, acted as agents of the veto-players, i.e. those actors who in the final legislative decision had to agree in order to achieve the required two-third majorities in the *Bundesrat* and the federal parliament. Thus, constitutional negotiations reproduced the power games and bargaining in ordinary intergovernmental politics.

Constitutional negotiations in German federalism were also closely linked to ordinary party politics. Although most conflicts divided federal and *Länder* governments and not political parties, elections changing majorities in the federal parliament and in the *Bundesrat* had an impact, and members of the Commission anticipated the shifts in veto powers. Moreover, while the Christian Democrats had no interest in avoiding a blockade while they were in opposition until 2005, they had interest in an agreement and in ratification when they participated in a Grand Coalition government as of 2005. Therefore, the reform project was revived although it did not change in substance. The package deal elaborated in the Commission had been hardly modified, the exception being a guarantee for the Eastern *Länder* that financial support according to the fiscal equalization scheme would be continued until 2019. The overlap of normal and constitutional policy was even more obvious in the second reform. Although most governments aimed at a balanced budget and were willing to revise the constitutional debt rule, the meetings of the Commission had been canceled in fall 2008 under the impact of the fiscal crisis. To improve the economic situation, governments launched fiscal stimulus packages. This measure caused the highest annual rise of public debts since German unification and stood in sharp contrast to the primary aim of the second Reform Commission. To avoid the impression of a constitutional debt limit being no more than pure symbolic politics, the Commission invented the Stability Council and an early warning system to prevent future budgetary crises in federal and *Länder* governments (Ebert et al. 2010a).

The internal organization of the Commissions revealed a functional differentiation. Its members met regularly once a month in plenary sessions, but compromises actually were carved out in subcommittees, working groups, informal negotiations or, finally, in a small circle of leaders of each group. Here, policy-specialists of ministries and legal experts of *Länder* governments gained access. In contrast, interest groups and civil society organizations did not participate in constitutional negotiations and could only provide opinions in hearings. Accordingly, negotiations tended to deal with details, whereas ideas on how to make German federalism more effective or explicit definitions of principles guiding the reform hardly played a role. This increasing closure of negotiations prevented confrontation but fostered bargaining. During the ratification process, debates resumed in the federal parliament and its committees or in hearings of experts. But they led to only marginal changes of the proposal in the first reform and no change at all in the second. These conditions proved all but favorable for substantively amending the structures of the federal system.

However, disputes on federalism have continued since. Debates about a revision of constitutional amendments in education policy and about fiscal equalization have intensified. In childcare and education, the federal government found ways to circumvent the new constitutional constraints for funding *Länder* and local governments. Nonetheless, the constraints for the federal government to stimulate policy innovation by grants have been criticized, and the so-called "ban on cooperation" with *Länder* governments has been alleviated for labor-market policy and higher education by constitutional amendments. The consequence of the new debt rule for *Länder* governments is still an open issue. While budget coordination works smoothly, confrontation surfaced on the future redistribution of revenues among federal and *Länder* governments. At the end of 2013, the *Land* governments of Bavaria and Hesse submitted fiscal equalization, a still unresolved problem, to the Federal Constitutional Court for review. These are indications of a deficient reform. Performance problems hardly have been reduced and the federal system is meanwhile more rigid than ever.

4.1.3 *Austria: The Austrian Convention (2003–5)*

Between 2003 and 2005, Austria saw a major attempt to revise its constitution. It followed previous failures of a state reform and long discussions on the problems of federalism. Determined to come to a significant change, parties and governments agreed to set up a "convention" (*"Österreich-Konvent"*), modeled after the EU conventions (Lienbacher 2005). In contrast to the European role model, the Austrian Convention failed. It never came to an agreement on constitutional amendments and the reform process as a whole ended in a constitutional deadlock (Bußjäger 2012).

The idea to establish a constitutional convention was expressed in the program of the new Conservative government, which came to power after the general elections in 2003. The government set up a founding committee including the heads of the federal governments, the presidents of each house of the federal legislature, leaders of the parties in parliament, the chairs of the Conference of *Länder* Governments and *Länder* Parliaments and the chairs of the Association of Local Governments. This committee was to decide on the structure and the agenda of the Austrian Convention, which convened between June 2003 and January 2005.[4]

The agenda of the Convention was rather broad, with the reform project coming close to a comprehensive revision of the constitution (Bußjäger 2003). Although governments and parties avoided officially declaring the process a total revision, which would have required a compulsory constitutional referendum, the reform went beyond modifying federalism in a narrower sense. As an endeavor to consolidate the dispersed body of constitutional statutes, it was in particular to introduce a catalog of fundamental rights into the constitution. Regarding the territorial organization of the state, the reform aimed at a revision of the existing allocation of powers between the federal and the *Länder* governments and an overhaul of fiscal federalism. Moreover, constitutional conditions for public administration were to be improved in order to avoid an overlap and over-regulation of competences, for example in education and health care, and in order to pave the way for a modernization of administration. Governments, the political parties in parliament, and the groups represented in the Convention agreed on the urgent need to renovate Austrian federalism, which was deemed overly centralized and lacking a transparent allocation of powers and fiscal relations. However, they could not find a consensus on how these problems should be solved. The final report prepared by the steering committee of the Convention was not passed by the plenary. Accordingly, a draft of a constitutional amendment submitted by the chair of the Convention was regarded as a private opinion (Fiedler 2005).

At the end, negotiations failed not only compared to high ambitions, but also regarding more modest claims (Hörtenhuber and Steiner 2004). The

[4] Österreich-Konvent, Sitzung des Gründungskomitees des Österreich-Konvents. Die Grundsätze zur Staatsreform (http://www.konvent.gv.at/K/ZD/grundsaetze.pdf, last access 22 October 2015).

Convention did not achieve any substantial result on a new balance of power between federal and *Länder* governments. While the members of the Convention unanimously supported the idea of an incorporation of constitutional law in one document and endorsed a committee proposal to improve legal protection of citizens against public administration, the final report amounted to no more than a minimal agreement to maintain the status quo of the federal system.

Following the European model, the Austrian Convention assembled all major political forces of Austrian politics (Grotz 2005). In view of the aim to revitalize the centralized federalism, the *Länder* governments demanded to be represented by the heads of their governments and by members of their parliaments. After some debates, the federal government accepted. In addition, representatives from parliaments, courts and local governments as well as major interest groups and civil society organizations were invited to participate. Nominated by the different groups, a number of experts took part in negotiations, with full rights of membership. Decisions were to be based on a consensus, so that all members had veto power.

At first glance, this Convention seemed to separate constitutional and normal politics, as had been the case in the EU. However, as a closer inspection reveals, negotiations in the Convention actually did not significantly deviate from the normal patterns of politics and policy-making indicative of Austrian corporatist democracy (Bußjäger 2012). In the course of its work, it evolved into a kind of committee of the houses of the federal legislature where constitutional amendments had to be ratified, with the members of the Convention acting as agents of parties.

The Convention was supposed to provide a forum for public deliberation on constitutional problems and on alternative proposals for their solution (Interview AUT, 9 February 2010). The plenary sessions were open to the public, the results documented on a webpage, and private actors were invited to submit their opinions. But with seventy-one members in total, the Convention had to adopt practical proceedings of a parliamentary institution. With the exception of two public hearings, allowing representatives of civil society to speak to the Convention, plenary debates regularly started with statements of the representatives of the political parties, which were followed by a presentation of the chairs of committees. Actually, these statements mainly repeated well-known propositions and did not stimulate a lively discussion. Sessions hardly lasted longer than two hours, although they were scheduled for a whole day. Accordingly, the plenary lost its significance as a forum of constitutional deliberation. Instead, it turned into an arena where political parties exposed their differences instead of trying to overcome them (Bußjäger 2012: 99).

More intense negotiation took place in ten subcommittees established to settle disputes and elaborate proposals. Their tasks were defined by the steering committee headed by the chair of the Convention, which also coordinated their work. Although the committees were set up for providing expertise, for settling conflicts and for elaborating proposals, most of them proved unable to find agreements. The functional differentiation of the Convention did not prevent negotiations from being increasingly burdened by confrontation from political parties. Involved in the political game, experts had no chance to modify this negotiation mode, and representatives of civil society had no access to these negotiations (Hämmerle 2005).

While the committees were increasingly drawn into party politics, the Convention lost political support. Heads of the *Länder* governments reduced their engagement, and other members sent their deputies instead of participating on their own (Interview AUT, 9 February 2010). As a consequence, actors that could have influenced public discussion and debates in parliaments remained absent, and actors that participated had to behave as agents of parties and governments. Therefore, it is understandable that they tended to block all negotiations beyond a confrontation of positions. Lacking political support, the Convention failed to integrate the contributions of subcommittees into a reform package.

The Convention was scheduled to work for a limited time, which was extended at a point when negotiations already were in a deadlock situation. Although this schedule was independent of election periods, the close overlap between regular party politics and constitutional negotiations had the effect that election campaigns influenced the work of the Convention and increased confrontation. In particular the Social Democrats, then the opposition party in federal parliament, saw a chance to exploit the Convention as a platform for electoral success. One of their delegates in the Convention ran for the federal presidency and successfully used his position to attract public attention (Ulram and Plasser 2005). But for this purpose he had to stick to party-political positions in order to gain support of the Social-Democratic voters.

The overlap of normal and constitutional politics also had the effect of weakening the involvement of the heads of *Länder* governments. During the Convention process, they were engaged in intergovernmental negotiations on a financial framework of the public budget. These negotiations including federal, *Länder* and municipal governments sidelined the Convention committee working on finances. At the same time, *Länder* governments elaborated reforms of the police, military, railway and postal services in intergovernmental negotiations. Although these issues were of fundamental relevance regarding the position of the *Länder* in Austrian federalism, the governments of the *Länder* did not pursue them inside the Convention (Blümel and Konrath 2009). Also institutional reforms in the energy sector were underway and of central interest for those *Länder* governments which produced and distributed electricity by their own public corporations (Brauner 2004).

These different arenas were clearly separated since the *Länder* governments considered them as more appropriate venues for coordinating their policies than the Convention. While dealing with these policies in normal intergovernmental venues, the *Länder* governments only took care that bargaining in the Convention would not harm their interests (Interview AUT, 9 February 2010). Playing such a passive role, *Länder* representatives were hardly able to mediate party political conflicts in the Convention, where they felt to be less at stake in view of their current tasks. While these political processes in ordinary intergovernmental policy-making interfered by coincidence with constitutional negotiations, their impact on the Convention remained limited due to the separation of the respective arenas of policy-making. Yet this constellation did not help to differentiate constitutional and normal policy-making, it only had the effect that normal party politics predominated in the Convention.

The structure and practical work of the Convention also ruled out a separation of negotiations on principles and negotiations on rules. The document defining the mission of the Convention determined five general principles of the Austrian Constitution that should not be changed (Konrath 2005: 353). Actually, these principles never were a matter of negotiations but were simply taken as given. They were never meant as a normative frame for constitutional amendment. The design of the negotiation process also revealed no sequential structure. According to the original work plan, the process should start with reformulating constitutional principles, continue with identifying disputes on different matters and finally focus on settling the disputes. However, real negotiations never conformed to this order of issues and proceedings. As mentioned, principles were never discussed in order to establish a guideline for the reform. Committees were able to identify disputes, but when the steering committee demanded proposals, they were not able to reach agreements since committee members resumed bargaining and confrontation of positions (Bußjäger 2005).

Challenged to reallocate power in the federal system, the Convention was doomed to end in the joint-decision trap. With the confrontation mode prevailing in negotiations, even compromises on particular issues were impossible to achieve. For instance, committee 10 responsible for fiscal federalism proposed only marginal constitutional amendments. In this case, a clear redistributive conflict between levels of government led to a deadlock. While the federal government showed no willingness to abandon its residual power to decide which level was allowed to raise taxes, the *Länder* governments hesitated to fight for more fiscal autonomy. As Peter Bußjäger reported, debates focused on more marginal issues like the decentralization of minor tax sources from the federal to the *Länder* level (Bußjäger 2012: 114). This outcome stands in sharp contrast to the significance of fiscal federalism according to the agenda of the Convention.

Committee 5, which was established to discuss the allocation of legislative powers and the participation of *Länder* governments in federal and European policy-making, could not settle federal–*Länder* conflicts. In a promising first step, the committee discussed a three-pillar model as a frame of reference. With exclusive powers of the federal government and the *Länder* governments falling under the first two pillars, the third one should include shared powers to legislate. Instead of defining criteria to determine which power should be assigned to which category, the committee debated on variations of the framework, with its members arguing from ideological positions, and failed to come to a consensus. Without an agreement on the framework, no compromise on a change of the existing constitutional rules was possible. At the end, the three-pillar model was abandoned, and disputes focused on particular competences. Parties presented their catalogs of powers to be reallocated but did not find a common ground (Konrath 2005). Finally, the draft elaborated by the chair of the convention proposed a particular allocation of powers. By declaring health care, education and economic policy as matters of exclusive powers of the federal government, this proposal would only have petrified the centralized structure of Austrian federalism. Thus, it did not meet expectations in public and confirmed the skepticism of Convention members (Interview AUT, 8 February 2010).

The status and legitimacy of the drafted constitutional amendments provided by the chair did not indicate an agreement. Many members of the Convention took it as a private opinion rather than an official document. The federal government passed on the Convention report to the parliament. However, lacking an explicit decision of the Convention supporting the document and considering the many issues still under debate, parties in parliament ignored the proposals and did not initiate ratification procedures.

After the Convention failed, the federal parliament set up a special committee for constitutional reform, inviting only two members from the *Länder* governments (Lienbacher 2008). Again, confrontation of political parties blocked the negotiations. In 2007, the federal government called an expert commission to prepare a reform of state and administrative law and a working group for administrative reform. Thus the process continued, but the outcomes remained limited (Konrath 2012). The work of these committees led to a consolidation of legal documents forming the constitution, but did not induce any change of the federal system. Considering the problems of effectiveness of an over-centralized federalism (Braun 2011: 43) and the ambitions of the Convention, constitutional policy in Austria appeared as a clear failure, ending in the joint-decision trap.

4.2 Federal States Confronted by Integration Problems

In divided societies, constitutional reform seems to be doomed to failure, and incremental change appears as the only way out of deadlock (Lerner 2011). Our case study supports this assumption to a certain extent, but nonetheless points out the relevance of the institutional design structuring politics of constitutional change. In the three federations confronted with integration problems, we find successful, ineffective and failed constitutional reforms aiming at a balanced structure, like in the previous three case studies. Again, constitutional policy in the most differentiated setting stands out when regarding results of negotiations, as is revealed by the Canadian case. However, it also proved that ratification by citizens in a state-wide referendum apparently bears greater risks in multinational than in integrated federations (Tierney 2014: 242–9). Conflicts also emerged after ratification of constitutional amendments, if not all political groups were included in an agreement, as is exemplified by the Spanish case. In Belgium, traditional patterns of negotiations among executives and party leaders ended with problematic package deals, which did not contribute to stabilizing the federal balance.

4.2.1 *Canada: The Charlottetown Process (1990–2)*

The Charlottetown Agreement of August 1992 concluded between the Prime Minister, the Premiers of the ten provinces, representatives of the Territories, and leaders of Aboriginal organizations marked the final episode of negotiating constitutional reforms in Canada. The process leading to this agreement, the so-called *Canada Round* of constitutional policy, was closely connected to previous reforms or reform attempts that, as in 1982, failed to gain the consent of Quebec or could not meet the requirements necessary for ratification as happened with the Meech Lake Accord elaborated between 1987 and 1990. The Charlottetown process displays several new features compared to previous reform rounds, introduced in order to remedy former deficits and separating the process clearly from ordinary politics. Nonetheless, the program for a constitutional amendment was voted down in ratification. The reasons for this failure and its consequences have been disputed among scholars in Canada (contrasting positions are exemplified by Lusztig and Knox 1999 and Stein 1997). But in a comparative view, the constitutional negotiation during the Charlottetown process proved in many respects rather effective, although the proposal was rejected by a majority of voters in a referendum. The consensus found among governments after extensive participation of parliaments and civil society at all levels of the Canadian federal system eventually paved the way for a "non-constitutional renewal" (Lazar 1998) after the negative result of ratification. As Michael D. Behiels concluded:

"Charlottetown, placed in this larger perspective, was both a necessary and positive experience for all Canadians" (Behiels 2002: 69).

The agreement finally signed in the city of Charlottetown was often characterized as diffuse, overloaded or incomprehensible. There are good reasons for such an assessment. In fact, in a number of its sections the Accord documented a compromise at the lowest common denominator. Examples were the rather complicated "Canada clause," which was an attempt to accommodate unity and diversity. Moreover, the Accord did not include a proposal on how the reformed Senate should be elected, thus leaving open an important constitutional question. In other parts, for example the suggestions for a social and economic union, it remained imprecise. Also heavily criticized was the guarantee of at least 25 percent of seats for Quebec in the House of Commons that should compensate the province for its loss of seats in a reformed Senate. However, for quite a number of important issues, the Accord at least paved the way to solving the enduring constitutional conflicts, for example concerning the allocation of powers, the spending power of the federation, the internal market, the amendment rule and in particular Aboriginal issues. Instead of formulating precise constitutional rules, most proposals defined principles or goals for further negotiations. Detailed regulations were proposed for a few issues like the representation of Quebec in the Supreme Court and in the national parliament as well as for procedures of legislation. Competence allocation between the federal and provincial governments should be determined in a rather flexible way, in particular by allowing intergovernmental cooperation instead of federal policy-making if requested by provinces. Overall, the Accord drafted a decentralized and cooperative federalism. It combined the principles of proportional representation of provincial populations in parliament, equal representation of provinces in the Senate, and acknowledgment of distinctiveness of provinces in policy-making. It also included elements of a "societal federalism" (Hueglin 1999) for Aboriginal peoples. Finally, it emphasized the coherence of the federation by rules for an economic and social union. As a framework for constitutional politics, the proposed changes could have framed a process to be continued in the legislative and intergovernmental arenas (Cook 1994: 6). Actually, this is what the Charlottetown Accord did, although not in the way intended, because its ratification failed.

When in 1990 the federal government initiated a further round of constitutional negotiations after the defeat of the Meech Lake Accord—in this case because two provincial parliaments did not ratify—it was well aware that a new practice of constitutional negotiations was to be introduced. However, the different components of the process were not designed at the beginning or orchestrated during the process by one institution (Brown and Young 1992: 5). Rather, they emerged from the dynamics of an open process stimulating consultations and negotiations in a variety of arenas.

Compared to previous rounds of constitutional reform in Canada, but also compared to the other cases studied in our comparative research, the Charlottetown process stands out with regard to arena differentiation. Moreover, we can also observe a particular sequence of negotiations, differing from the Swiss case. The consultation and negotiation process can be divided into four phases (Bakvis and Hryciuk 1993: 122) differing by the levels of government they were organized at, the leading actors, participants or opportunities for participation, and the style of negotiation. The multitude of issues on the constitutional agenda attracted different actors, which formed negotiation coalitions on certain topics while they were divided on others. The variety of arenas blurred the conflict lines and complicated the search for package deals among the negotiating partners, but also prevented them from fixing bargains in early phases. After intensive public consultation provided venues for open deliberation, but also revealed processes shifting between confrontation and arguing, traditional modes of intergovernmental negotiations prevailed at the end.

The first sequence started immediately after the ratification of the Meech Lake Accord had failed in June 1990 and lasted until spring 1991. In an attempt to revitalize the reform process, governments tried to define their position in internal discussions at the federal level and, in separate processes, in Quebec. At this stage, consultations and negotiations in commissions were open to civil society, but in a rather unstructured manner. While this sequence mainly was about defining interest, questions of procedures were raised, too. Overall, the agenda was still in flux.

At this stage, the government of Quebec again emphasized the minimum condition to sign the *Constitution Act 1982*, which had already defined the agenda of the Meech Lake process (Government of Québec 1985). They included the constitutional recognition of Quebec as a distinct society, a veto in constitutional reforms for the province or full financial compensation in case of opting out of an amendment, a limitation of the federal spending power binding it to provincial consent in case it is applied in fields of provincial jurisdiction, and participation of the province in appointing Supreme Court judges combined with a constitutional guarantee that three out of nine judges were chosen from Quebec. With regard to the allocation of powers, Quebec's demands focused on the recognition of existing autonomous jurisdictions of the province and the extension of jurisdiction in the fields of communication and family law (Government of Québec 1985).

The federal government included these issues in its agenda for constitutional negotiations. But although the reform process aimed at integrating Quebec in a constitutional consensus and at reducing pressure for secession in the province, the agenda was not limited to these demands. Apart from the already known grievances of the Aboriginal peoples and their demand for an inherent right of self-government, the federal government sought to reform federal institutions and to extend central powers in order to strengthen the economic and social union. The newly elected Premier of Ontario, Bob Rae, was not only supportive of enshrining Aboriginal rights into the constitution, but also suggested including a Social Charter thus establishing nationwide standards of social policy (Brown and Young 1992: 7; Russell 2004: 176).

However, even at this point of the process, there was by no means a fixed reform agenda. Instead, the federal government attempted to grasp public opinion and to identify which parts of Canadian federalism the population deemed in need of reform. For this purpose, the "Citizen's Forum on Canada's Future" (the so-called *Spicer Commission*) was established with a broad mandate to collect opinions of Canadian citizens on the necessity of reforms and to organize a dialog between citizens. Eventually this commission managed to get no less than 400,000 citizens involved (Hurley 1996: 114–25). Although the unstructured consultations attracted criticism and although the impact of the final report of June 1991 on subsequent commissions and negotiations remained limited, the Spicer Commission significantly reduced the gap between citizens and political elites in constitutional policy which had opened up after the Meech Lake Accord (Peach 2007: 91–2). In parallel, the "Joint Parliamentary Committee on the Process of Amending the Constitution of Canada" (or *Beaudoin–Edwards Committee*) discussed the rules for constitutional amendment and the possible introduction of a veto for Quebec in future constitutional reforms. It recommended a national constitutional referendum and an amendment formula without dealing with Quebec's demand for a constitutional veto (Brown and Young 1992: 6).

Within the province of Quebec, separate debates about the future of the province were initiated simultaneously. The "Constitutional Committee of the Quebec Liberal Party" chaired by Jean Allaire focused on political autonomy of the province and on the reallocation of powers, which was deemed necessary in order to preserve and promote the distinct character and identity of the province. In its final report, the committee demanded first and foremost that the federal government stop applying its spending power in twenty-two policy fields which already fell under exclusive provincial jurisdiction (Québec Liberal Party 1991: 38). The parliamentary "Commission on the Constitutional and Political Future" (*Bélanger–Campeau Commission*) established in September 1990 focused on the procedures to be applied in order to obtain the autonomy Quebec considered necessary. It gathered parliamentarians from different parties, those of the Québec parliament, the *Assemblé Nationale,* and those representing the province in the federal parliament, and included representatives from business and cultural organizations, the municipalities and the education sector. This commission agreed on a legislative initiative introduced in the provincial parliament in May 1991. It set a deadline for the constitutional reform process for 26 October 1992. On that day, the citizens of Quebec would be called to vote in a referendum either on the proposition for major constitutional reform elaborated at the federal level or on Quebec's secession from Canada, if the reform failed to meet Quebec's demands by this date (Québec 1991). With this Bill 150, Quebec not only put pressure on the negotiating partners in the so-called "rest-of-Canada" to come to an agreement, but also decided to wait for an offer before becoming officially engaged in the negotiations. It also made clear that the substance of the Meech Lake Accord was the minimum Quebec would find acceptable.

During the second sequence, which overlapped with the first, the federal government formulated its reform proposals and presented them in fall 1991. Before making them public, representatives from the federal and several provincial governments met to discuss existing conflicts and options for consensus in the *Cabinet Committee on Canadian Unity and Constitutional Negotiations* that convened from April until August 1991. Quebec also sent delegates. But due to the adopted "wait-and-see" attitude of the province, their positions often remained unclear. Despite several contacts with members of the Quebec government and an informal exchange of information, direct talks with Quebec took place only when the Committee entered its final stage in August 1991. During the sessions of the Committee, executives and civil servants from the federal and provincial levels gained strong influence by preparing sessions and drafting papers. The public or civil society organizations played no role during this sequence, aside from a few efforts of the Committee to meet with local representatives across the country in order to gather opinions (Bakvis and Hryciuk 1993: 130–1, 137–43).

Following the publication of the government's proposals in September 1991, major efforts for public consultation were made in the third sequence. The paper titled "Shaping Canada's Future Together" contained a variety of topics and aimed at nothing less than the reformulation of the social contract and major reforms of federal institutions "to build a better federation for the 21st century" (Canada 1991: vii). Quebec's distinct character was recognized but so was the existence of linguistic minorities outside and inside the province. The demands of the Aboriginal peoples were also met with the proposal of enshrining "a general justifiable right to aboriginal self-government" (Canada 1991: 7) in the constitution. In order to avoid problems of implementing this right, all governments were to commit to negotiating the terms of self-government with the Aboriginal organizations. A reform of the Senate sought to make the representation of provinces at the federal level more effective and more legitimate, and a new Council of the Federation was suggested in order to facilitate federal–provincial coordination. Furthermore, the federal proposals included provisions for strengthening the economic union, increasing the effectiveness of governing and reducing the duplication of services.

This framework for the reform laid out for public consultation did not prevent more issues from being added during the following deliberations, which broadened the agenda of the reform. Consultation was organized by the "Special Joint Parliamentary Committee on a Renewed Canada" (or *Castonguay–Dobbie/Beaudoin–Dobbie Committee*), established by orders of the House of Commons and the Senate in June 1991. It held public hearings across the country and invited representatives from interest groups, minorities, parties, legislative assemblies and individual citizens to discuss the federal proposals. The Committee also invited Canadians to present their opinions on the proposals and received around 3,000 submissions (Canada, Senate and House of Commons 1992). Simultaneously with the parliamentary hearings of the "Special Joint Committee," the provinces established different kinds of commissions, parliamentary committees or executive task forces in order to discuss the federal proposals within each province. Representatives of the provinces fed their positions and opinions into the federal consultation process by appearing in sessions of the federal committee (Russell 2004: 168).

After experiencing difficulties in its initial set of hearings which were ill-prepared, took place in empty halls or provided a platform for comments damaging to national unity, the *Special Joint Committee* had run into a deadlock after holding hearings in Manitoba and there was doubt that it could meet the deadline of February 28. The idea of holding televised constitutional conferences paved a way out of this deadlock. The five ensuing conferences on a *Renewal of Canada* were organized by independent, non-governmental agencies in order to re-establish trust and to save the constitutional consultation process. They took place in different cities between January and March 1992, each dealing with one of the major topics of the federal proposals. During the concluding conference in Vancouver, the progress and preliminary consensus were reviewed and participants had a last opportunity to express their views. These conferences were not only a new consultative device intended to stimulate debate and to identify areas of broad agreement on principles. They also broke new ground with the invitation of randomly selected citizens participating in addition to delegated leaders of interest groups, representatives of parties and governments, a number of constitutional experts and members of the *Joint Committee*. The conferences discussed in plenum, but also in smaller workshops focused on selected topics. In all venues, politicians were in a minority among the participants, listening and questioning those making statements or presenting alternatives in a public deliberative process before retiring to their own negotiations (Milne 1992: 28–38).

These conferences set in motion an unexpected dynamic of intense debate. They revealed the common desire to find an agreement. Sometimes participants emphasized topics that did not enjoy the utmost priority within the federal proposals or even attacked the federal package. Compared to the symmetric decentralization proposed by the federal government, delegates and participants of the conference in Halifax were much more open to asymmetrical arrangements in favor of Quebec. Similarly, the proposed Council of the Federation was openly rejected at the conference in Calgary. While an elected, effective and equitable Senate generally was approved, the participants emphasized the need to represent the social diversity of Canadians—multiculturalism, native peoples, gender equality—in addition to territorial representation. The conference on economic union in Montreal also expressed severe criticism regarding the constitutional proposal, but participating social interest groups and unions successfully placed the Social Charter on the agenda, which so far had not been part of the federal proposals at all (Milne 1992: 40). Women's organizations raised attention to women's and equality rights and achieved their inclusion into the reform of federal institutions (Interview CA, 11 June 2010), whereas social interest groups attacked the economic agenda of the federal package. Through these conferences, Aboriginals were also able to participate fully and more visibly in the constitutional discussions and promoted their demands for an inherent right to self-government. Skeptical at the beginning, they later accepted the offer of a special conference devoted to Aboriginal issues. The Premiers of Ontario and Prince Edward Island supported their demands, but tensions increased with the government of Quebec, when Aboriginal leaders argued that they had a stronger claim for demanding a distinct society status and for self-determination than the province of Quebec did (Brown and Young 1992: 8).

Thus, in clear contrast to the negotiations behind closed doors characterizing the Meech Lake process, this sequence was marked by multiple opportunities for citizen participation and inclusion of civil society organizations. It stimulated a broad public deliberation over constitutional issues and influenced the negotiation mode in the parliamentary arenas. Public opinion changed towards a more accommodative mood and the conferences demonstrated that people were supporting an active federal government especially with regard to social standards. In its final report at the beginning of March, the *Beaudoin–Dobbie Committee* managed to overcome some conflicts over the federal proposals and followed the directions of the conference discussions on several issues. In its report, the Committee removed the unpopular Council of the Federation, supported the Social Charter and the Aboriginals' inherent right of self-government, presented alternatives for a Senate reform and, compared to the government's proposal, cut back the economic powers of the federal level. The Committee was more willing to include a veto for Quebec in constitutional reforms, but it recommended an asymmetric allocation of powers only with regard to culture and broadcasting, while otherwise supporting symmetric federalism (Canada, Senate and House of Commons 1992). Although partisan considerations could not be ignored entirely and lurked in the background, the *Beaudoin–Dobbie Committee* helped to establish a consensus among the major political parties on most of the issues through extensive arguing.

In the fourth sequence of the reform process, lasting from March to August 1992, ministers of governments, supported by their experts, negotiated the final draft of the constitutional reform. In this arena, arguing turned into bargaining, but results of public deliberations continued to influence negotiations. At first, these negotiations were held in multilateral settings between delegates of the federal level, the provinces—except Quebec—the two Territories and the four Aboriginal organizations. Although the latter had been part of intergovernmental negotiations since the mid-1980s, they had never before participated in discussions on constitutional issues (Brown and Young 1992: 8). In order to prepare for negotiations, four working groups discussed and prepared the major topics. These working groups took account of different reform options and prepared drafts of constitutional amendments. Afterwards they were presented to the deputy ministers' meetings and fed into the "Continuing Committee on the Constitution," where they were prepared for the multilateral meetings on the constitution. Overall, a chain of communication had been established from the working groups and their subgroups to the deputy ministers meetings up to the ministerial level of provincial and federal government negotiating in the multilateral meetings on the constitution.

Now, the interconnectedness of numerous aspects of the reform that had been divided in the separate televised conferences became obvious again and could be tackled in this manner.[5] Moreover, negotiations were complicated because of Quebec's still valid position that it would only enter into negotiations after the substance of the Meech Lake Accord had been restored (Brown and Young 1992: 9). The government of Quebec once again sent observers but refused to fully participate in these working group meetings (Interview, CA 23 June 2010). Although the interests of Quebec were always included by means of observers attending intergovernmental meetings or of back channel phone calls, Quebec's positions were not clearly defined. The influence of the representatives of the province on the negotiations remained limited compared to the other Premiers (Interviews CA, 29 September 2008 and 16 June 2010; Russell 2004: 198). The deadline for presenting an accord was postponed several times due to the difficulties in finding an agreement on every topic

[5] For the back and forth of drafts and reports between working groups, multilateral meetings on the constitution and the First Ministers Conferences see for example: Continuing Committee on the Constitution, Working Group I, Issues Tracking Report as of 5 May 1992. Document: 840-636/012 Peter Meekison Archive: Box 76 File 1396, University of Alberta, Edmonton.

on the agenda. Severe conflicts resurfaced over the Senate reform, with the discussion shifting again towards preserving equality of the provinces and questions of territorial representation while aspects of social representation were dropped entirely or left for each province to determine later.

In late June 1992, negotiations continued as First Ministers Conferences between the federal level and the nine provinces, which followed established patterns of intergovernmental meetings behind closed doors, with results being reported in press conferences but with no opportunities for public participation. These negotiations aimed at breaking the impasse on the Senate reform and eventually ended on 7 July with an agreement, the "Pearson Accord." It was then officially presented to Quebec as an offer for reforming Canadian federalism (Russell 2004: 193). This report on the constitution deviated from the idea of an asymmetric allocation of powers recommended by the *Beaudoin–Dobbie Committee*. Compared to the federal proposals, economic powers of the federal level were limited. The Social Charter promoted by Ontario's Premier continued to be a prominent part of the negotiated package, whereas the distinct society provisions for Quebec were reduced to binding the interpretation and application of the Charter of Rights, but not of the entire constitution. The discussed options for reforming the Senate also included the equal representation of the provinces thereby reducing the relative weight of Quebec in that chamber significantly (Canada 1992).

By that time, all participants were willing to defend the compromise against changes, especially the provinces that had managed successfully to change the original federal proposals. The day following the presentation of the Pearson Accord, Quebec's Premier Bourassa recognized it as an offer containing the substance of the Meech Lake Accord. But by announcing that it had to be studied in more detail by his cabinet and the caucus of the Quebec Liberal Party, he left the position of the province in ambiguity (Laforest 1992: 53). When Bourassa finally joined the negotiations on 10 August, it became clear that changes with regard to the distinct society clause and the Senate would be necessary in order to gain his consent. As compensation, Quebec should be guaranteed to elect 25 percent of the members of the House of Commons, regardless of demographic developments. On 28 August 1992, after another four days of negotiations, the federal government, the provincial Premiers and the leaders of territorial governments and Aboriginal organizations managed to bridge remaining conflicts and agreed on the "Charlottetown Accord Consensus Report."

The Accord was the result of successful combination of arguing and bargaining in different arenas. It reflected compromises and benefits for office holders and the major groups, balanced regional interests and economic cleavages, so that in the end everyone could find some benefits and acceptable trade-offs (Stein 1993: 96). At the same time, numerous political accords were envisaged in the final consensus report in which details were still left to be worked out in the future. Although Quebec's Premier gave his consent to the final reform package, it was not received with enthusiasm in the province. Moreover, it was at best regarded as the beginning of a process of constitutional amendment (Boismenu 1993: 56). It certainly did not sell well to Quebec nationalists and proponents of sovereignty (Gagnon and Rocher 1992). Compared to the options discussed during the different sequences, the publicly debated issues and the consensus reached on several topics during the consultation process, it also did not meet expectations regarding women's and equality rights and the inherent right of self-government of Aboriginal peoples. Yet, the general public seemed in favor of the Accord. Immediately after the end of constitutional negotiations, opinion polls indicated that a majority of citizens supported the agreement (Johnston et al. 1996).

However, when it came to ratifying the negotiated Accord and governments agreed to ask citizens in a consultative referendum, the public campaign accentuated the conflict between a federalist and a confederalist vision of the Canadian state, which was not really settled in the constitutional negotiations. Moreover, the final package deal between Quebec and the other governments, which was bargained in closed-door negotiations, raised the most criticism and eventually backfired when the federal government and provincial leaders tried to rally public support for the negotiated Accord. As it turned out, parliamentary and societal consultations and intergovernmental negotiations were not linked in an appropriate way, not the least as the latter focused on the Quebec–Canada conflict (Stein 1997). Finally, a majority of voters in Canada and in six provinces rejected the Accord. The successful negotiations were followed by ratification failure.

After the 1992 referendum, an accommodation of diversity between the federation and Quebec seemed impossible, since the nationalist *Parti Québécois* (PQ) benefited from the crisis and won the majority in the provincial parliament. However, in 1995, the PQ's strategy for secession failed as well, when citizens rejected this option in a referendum by a very narrow margin, thus revealing a divide within the provincial citizenry. Eventually, two referendums petrified the constitutional status. But the double negative vote contradicted all interests of the different groups participating in constitutional policy, including citizens and their representatives. Therefore, after a period of "constitutional fatigue" in the wake of the Charlottetown referendum, political elites searched in collaboration with experts for ways to overcome the deadlock by implicit change. As J. Peter Meekison, both a scholar and participant in constitutional negotiations as member of the government of Alberta, argued: "Canadians have spent so much time, energy and emotion on constitutional reform that we have ignored other means of solving our problems" (Meekison 1993: 81).

As will be explained later in detail (Chapter 6), implicit adjustments of the Canadian federal system, pursued after the failed ratification of the constitutional reform, followed the guidelines defined in the Charlottetown Accord and led to the solution of a number of constitutional problems, with the Senate reform being the most important exception. The substantial outcome of successful constitutional negotiations legitimized governments' efforts to overcome the constitutional deadlock. Given agreements on important principles, actors in the Canadian federal system became committed to a certain path of development from which they could not depart without risking reaction from other actors. While parliamentary, intergovernmental and Court resolutions confirmed principles, decisions to implement them were made in normal politics. While the deep conflict about the nature of the federation was left in abeyance, the division and sharing of power between the different governments of the Canadian federation, including self-governments of Aboriginal peoples, have been better balanced and the integration of the federation increased.

4.2.2 *Belgium: The Fifth State Reform (1999–2001)*

The transformation of Belgium from a unitary into a federal state was a necessary and essential precondition for coping with the deep societal divide of the country. As outlined above (Chapter 3), this development started with the first state reform in 1970 and continued with reforms in 1980, 1988 and 1993. The case study summarized in this section concerns the Fifth State Reform. It started in 1999 and ended in 2001 with a number of constitutional statutes, so-called "special majority laws" which implemented political agreements. As in previous reforms, the drafts of the amendment laws were negotiated in a parliamentary-executive committee. De facto, they resulted from bargaining among party leaders (Sinardet 2012). The structure of constitutional negotiations has many features in common with the German case. In contrast to German attempts to modernize the federal system, constitutional reform in Belgium brought about some significant changes including fiscal powers, but was followed by a decade of stagnation. Like previous reforms, it advanced the process of decentralization. Thus, it reinforced centrifugal dynamics of an evolving federal state confronted by serious problems of integration in a divided society.

The discussion on a new reform started when, in 1999, the Flemish parliament adopted five resolutions meant to serve as a guideline for further constitutional reforms. Based on a vision of a Belgian federal system, with the Regions of Flanders and Wallonia constituting the basic parts and Brussels and the German Community being specific entities, the parliament suggested a reform of Brussels institutions to better reflect the duality of this city-region, a more coherent allocation of powers, an increase in fiscal autonomy for the Regions, and a transfer of the power to supervise provinces and municipalities to the Regions (Pagano 2000). Although these resolutions served as reference point for the Flemish parties in the later reform (Jacques and Boromée 2001: 9), they did not express a unanimous position of all Flemish parties. The Flemish Socialists and Greens regarded them as too radical and partly abstained from voting. The impact of the resolutions on the later negotiations therefore remained ambiguous (Sinardet 2012: 140), but they certainly inflamed the public debate on a new state reform.

While the Flemish parties demanded a wider reform of the allocation of powers and resources, Francophone parties preferred a limited reform particularly addressing the structural financial problems of the Francophone education system. In the end, Francophone parties succeeded in limiting the declaration initiating a constitutional reform on the harmonization of human rights with regulations in the European Union and the reform of the police and justice system (Jacques and Boromée 2001: 13–14).

As regards the reform process, the formal amendment procedures were avoided. Amending the wording of the Belgian Constitution requires an agreement between those political parties that form a majority in parliament. This agreement has to enumerate the articles of the constitution which are affected by the envisaged revision. Then parliament is dissolved and elections are held in order to create a constituent parliament which can then alter the constitution with a two-thirds majority of votes provided that two-thirds of all parliamentarians are present and an additional simple majority in each linguistic group in parliament is reached. As the allocation of powers to levels of governments and regulations of fiscal federalism are not enshrined in the constitution but formulated in special majority laws, changes can be achieved without a dissolution and re-election of the Belgian parliament. But these laws have to be passed according to decision rules similar to a formal constitutional amendment and requiring a double majority.[6]

The Fifth State Reform resulted in several agreements, which reflected a compromise on almost all topics of the agenda, although not all of them met the expectations of participants. The federal legislature voted on most modifications of the respective special majority laws on 13 July 2001. The amendments included a transfer of power to supervise municipalities and provinces to the Regions with the exemption of the so-called "Communities with linguistic facilities." Moreover, the Regions achieved extended powers in agriculture (now completely in their hands) and international trade. The transfer of developmental cooperation was envisaged, beginning in 2004,

[6] Given the hybrid character of the agenda of the state reform in 2000/01, it was contested under which category the reform fell.

but implementation was delayed. The reform revised special majority law regulating fiscal federalism as well, but it accomplished only some advances towards increasing fiscal autonomy for the federated entities. Fiscal powers of the Regions were extended due to a transfer of several smaller tax resources (television and radio tax, tax on automobile licensing, euro vignette) as well as an increase in the rate of the total federal income tax imposed by Regions and constituting part of their revenues. The new rules allowed tax variation in the range of ± 3.25 percent between 2001 and 2003 and ± 6.75 from 2004 onwards.[7] For the institutions in the Brussels Region the principle of absolute majority in each linguistic group was modified. An elevation of the fixed number of Flemish representatives to seventeen out of eighty-nine members met the demands to change the representation of Dutch speakers in the parliament of the Brussels Region.

The constitutional negotiations producing these outcomes were concentrated in parliamentary commissions and informal meetings of party leaders. After the elections in June 1999, the newly formed government of Liberals, Socialists and Greens spelled out the overall purpose of the state reform in their coalition agreement, but did not clearly define particular topics or directions of change (Lagasse 2009). Lacking a two-thirds majority, the government had to rely on opposition parties in order to ratify changes of the federal constitution. Under these conditions they slightly modified the usual structure of constitutional negotiations in Belgium among party leaders and members of the federal executive. The government instituted a commission for state reform, the "Intergovernmental and Interparliamentary Conference for Institutional Renewal" (COSTA/COREE).[8] It comprised representatives of federal, regional and community governments and parliaments,[9] with the selection of members guaranteeing linguistic parity. Decisions in the Conference were to be taken by a majority of votes within each linguistic group. The establishment of this commission set the agenda for the broad task of evaluating the current state of the federal system and the drafting of proposals for amendments. It included the regionalization of power to supervise municipalities and provinces, an increase of constitutive autonomy for Regions and Communities, regionalization of agriculture, foreign trade and development cooperation, a revision of the special finance law and other more technical matters recommended by the Senate Commission for Institutional Affairs of the previous legislature.

[7] *Loi spéciale portant refinancement des communautés et extension des compétences fiscales des régions*, published in *Moniteur belge—Belgisch Staatsblad*, 3 August 2001: 26646–58.

[8] *"Conferentie voor de Staatshervorming"* (COSTA)/*"Conférénce pour la réforme de l'Etat"* (COREE).

[9] Only the *Vlaams Blok* was exempted from participating in the COSTA/COREE.

An additional commission was created for the evaluation and modification of the Brussels institutions. The so-called mini-COSTA/COREE focused on an agenda agreed upon by the government of the Brussels Region. It suggested increasing the numbers and visibility of the Dutch-speaking minority in the regional parliament, in order to prevent deadlocks to which the decision-making rules at the time were prone due to the rise of the right-wing extremist *Vlaams Blok*, and in order to improve the fiscal basis of the Community Commission burdened with structural deficits.

Due to the fact that changes of the allocation of power were combined with a revision of fiscal federalism and the reform of Brussels institutions, the agenda of the entire reform appeared rather complex. The establishment of a different commission for dealing with the Brussels Region reduced this complexity only slightly. Members of both conferences were in contact throughout the process since the topics were interrelated, and each commission depended on the outcome of negotiations in the other arena for achieving a reform.

By setting up the mentioned commissions, the government apparently attempted to separate discussion and negotiation on federal changes from everyday politics. However, the chosen form of negotiations did not deviate from the traditional Belgian patterns of consociational democracy and strengthened the impact of parties. The second effect turned out as particularly relevant, since party politics in Belgium had been a strong driving force for decentralization. Not only had state-wide parties dissolved in the course of the federalization process, the competition between left and right parties had also long since centered on regionalization. While the Flemish Christian Democrats and the Francophone Socialists often formed a coalition at the federal level, they jointly supported a decentralization of power to the Regions and Communities, where they had a greater chance of governing alone (Sinardet 2012: 138; Deschouwer 1999). Due to the establishment of the commissions negotiating the Fifth State Reform, these political forces became the decisive players and had all opportunities to pursue their particular policy goals by constitutional means. Accordingly, there actually was no clear separation of constitutional and normal policies.

Sessions of the COSTA/COREE took place between October 1999 and June 2000, but only the first session was open for the participation of the media and the public. At the beginning, discussions centered on formulating a definite agenda and on organizing working groups for the different issues. Already at this stage, negotiations were burdened with a confrontation between the parties of the two linguistic Communities reflecting the divide of the country. Due to the regional fragmentation of the party system, disputes also arose among parties within the same Community. The mutual building up of claims and counter-claims clearly indicated the bargaining mode predominating in these constitutional negotiations, as long as it did not turn into a confrontation. Bargaining usually ended with package deals favoring both the Francophone and the Dutch-speaking part of the country at the cost of the federal government. More often than not, decisions on issues related to the constitution were linked to decisions on non-constitutional matters.

A first accord on an increase of financial transfers for the education sector—the *Saint-Éloi* Accord—was agreed upon in December 1999. The necessity of refinancing the Francophone Community responsible for education was exploited by the Flemish Nationalist Party, the *Volksunie*, to demand further fiscal autonomy for Flanders. The commission dealing with the issue could not settle the conflict, and negotiations transferred to a conciliation committee of members of the federal executive, the Communities and the Regions. The Flemish Nationalists finally signalled their assent to this agreement in exchange for concessions related to fiscal autonomy (Delwit and Hellings 2002: 100; Jacques and Boromée 2001: 41, 45–7).

Negotiations turned then towards regionalization of agriculture and international trade policies. Again, the COSTA/COREE did not turn out to be the arena where the main aspects of the reform were decided. Instead, negotiations took place in a two-day meeting of the Prime Minister, the two federal ministers responsible for negotiating the reform and the two chairmen of the commission while the governing parties and the opposing *Volksunie* endorsed the reform proposal subsequently (Jacques and Boromée 2001: 56–7). Although the opposition parties protested against this proceeding, not least because of its limiting their influence, the chairpersons of the commission accepted it. The commission continued to hold sessions, but even the draft bill resulting from the Accord was negotiated by ministers of the federal level and the two chairpersons of COSTA/COREE, and not by the working groups of the conference. The draft bill was presented to the commission, where it were discussed and accepted with amendments by the governing parties and the *Volksunie*.

Conflicts between the parties of the two linguistic Communities and among parties within the same Community erupted again when further regionalization of policy fields was negotiated. As in previous processes, these conflicts were settled in small circles of leaders of parties and governments representing the veto-players. The *Hermes* Accord included the regionalization of agriculture and foreign trade (Jacobs and Swyngedouw 2003). In October 2000, in an overnight meeting initiated by the Prime Ministers the negotiators agreed upon the *Lambermont* Accord (or *Accord de la Sainte Thérèse*) with the consent of the governing parties and the *Volksunie*. Representatives of the governments of Regions and Communities also participated in these negotiations, but crucial decisions were made in smaller circles of the parties in federal government (Sinardet 2012: 145). The accord contained the main aspects of the fiscal reform: an increase in fiscal autonomy for the Regions as mentioned above, the right of Communities and Regions to enter into development cooperation as far as their jurisdiction is concerned, and the regionalization of the power to supervise municipalities. Compared to the COSTA/COREE—which had again not been the loci of negotiations—the "*Lambermont*-Group" was more dominated by members of executives and involved fewer parliamentarians (Bourgaux 2003: 22–3; Delwit and Hellings 2002: 100–1).

Specifying and translating the accord into legal texts involved mostly legal experts of the parties. However, a number of political issues had to be dealt with by party leaders. They had to anticipate vetoes of party groups in legislation, when conflicts resurfaced during this phase of constitutional negotiations despite the agreements having been reached between the members of the governing parties and the *Volksunie*. Parts of the *Volksunie* were not satisfied with the transferred legislative powers, which they regarded as too limited. When it became apparent that only four of the party's eight members of parliament might vote in favor of the amendment bill, the ratification of the entire reform was at risk. Moreover, the Brussels Liberals (FDF), who participated in the governing coalition at the federal level and in the Brussels Capital-Region, announced their unwillingness to sign the special majority law on the regionalization of supervision of the local level. Therefore, the governing coalition was forced to make further concessions in order to appease the *Volksunie* and the FDF.

The FDF feared the consequences of this part of the reform for bilingual municipalities in the Brussels periphery, which benefited from protection under federal supervision. The votes of the party's representatives in parliament were secured by several exceptions in the regionalization of powers in this field. In order to gain the support of the *Volksunie*, adjustments in the Brussels institutions were agreed upon, especially an increase in the numbers of guaranteed seats for Dutch-speaking members of the regional parliament. Nevertheless, the main task of the mini-COSTA/COREE was a change in decision-making rules. Previous constitutional reforms had established linguistic parity in the Brussels institutions as well as the requirement that—in specified policy areas and in decisions on institutional change—the majority in each linguistic group of the regional parliament was required. With the rise of the *Vlaams Blok*, a majority had to include this right-wing extremist party. Since none of the other parties were inclined to cooperate with this party, the double majority rule was replaced. If a proposal received the absolute majority in the Brussels Regional Council but failed to gain the majority in each linguistic group, a second vote was supposed to be held one month later, when again the overall majority was necessary but only one-third of the votes of each linguistic group had to give its assent (Nassaux 2001: 41–4).

Nevertheless, this so called *Lombard* Accord (signed on 29 April 2001) was insufficient in order to gain the consent of the *Volksunie* to the original

Lambermont Accord. The governing coalition under Guy Verhofstadt therefore turned towards the Francophone Christian Democrats that were in opposition at the federal and regional level. In order to let the reform pass, an abstention from the Francophone Christian Democrats was sufficient. The inclusion of an opposition party changed negotiations slightly and Francophone Liberals still thought further negotiations with the *Volksunie* were the more promising way to succeed in concluding the deal. But the Christian Democrats proved to be reliable and their abstention was achieved with a couple of further concessions regarding the financing of the Francophone Community in the so-called *Accord de la Saint Boniface* (Sinardet 2012: 147–8).

During these additional negotiations aimed at gaining the required majority, parliamentary debates on the draft bills specifying the state reform had already started. In March 2001 the proposals were discussed in the Senate's special committee on institutional affairs before being transferred to the Chamber of Representatives in May 2001. Again the *Volksunie* proposed numerous modifications to the agreements, emphasizing the remaining discriminations against Flemish people and the need to give the linguistic Communities more autonomy.[10] More severe debates arose on a statement of the State Council delivered in February and May to the Senate. The Council confirmed previous criticism that the regionalization of the powers to supervise local governments required a formal constitutional amendment. But it had not been part of the declaration of constitutional revision prior to the elections of 1999.[11] This intervention was basically ignored by leading politicians. Since a second statement of the Council regarding the refinancing of the Communities was positive, parliamentary discussions on the reform bills continued despite doubts on the constitutionality of some parts of the reform (Delwit and Hellings 2002: 103). The reform finally passed the legislature and thus was ratified.

Overall, the negotiations of the Fifth State Reform included several different but linked elements. The first *Saint-Éloi-Accord* spelled out the basic goal of increasing financial transfers to the Communities for the education sector. The following *Lambermont* Agreement included regionalization of legislative powers and powers to supervise municipalities. The *Lombard* Accord, related to the institutions of the Region of Brussels-Capital, and the *Accord de la St. Boniface* was basically negotiated between the governing parties and opposition parties in order to secure the ratification of the reform. Thus, actors were aware of the ratification requirements and additional parties were included in negotiations in order to meet the necessary threshold of agreement. At no point were negotiations opened to societal actors or the public to any

[10] Sénat, Doc. parl., no. 2-709/3 (2000–1).
[11] Sénat, Doc.parl., no. 2-709/1; n° 2-709/6 (2000–1).

meaningful extent. In all these sequences, parties (especially party leaders) and members of the federal and regional executives dominated the negotiations. After reaching an accord among party leaders, the respective committees in both chambers of parliament started to work out the details, transferring the agreements into legal texts. When conflicts resurfaced, party leaders resumed negotiations.

The leading actors in negotiations had one goal in common, which was the extension of powers and resources for Regions and Communities. Yet the negotiations demonstrated that the Flemish and the Francophone side did not form two utterly internally homogenous groups. Some conflicts arose within the respective regional camps and even inside parties. These conflicts required compromises, but the general package deal meeting the demands of the Flemish side for more fiscal autonomy and powers and the needs of the Francophone Community for fiscal transfers remained in place. The outcome was achieved in a pure bargaining mode, typical for an overlap of intergovernmental politics and party politics. This stems from the fact that constitutional negotiations mainly proceeded in one arena. Since principles of constitutional and federal reforms were discussed in the negotiations on coalition formation after an election, a separation of the arenas of ordinary policy-making and federal constitutional reform was made difficult by institutional constraints. But it was not achieved in practice, as the fate of the COSTA/COREE revealed. Like previous reforms, the traditional way of elite accommodation with a strong position of party presidents predominated in the process of the Fifth State Reform.

In line with previous reforms, the outcome of this reform process was not appropriate to reduce the integration problems in Belgian federalism. On the contrary, it reinforced a centrifugal process of decentralization. Bargaining and deals between Regions were reached at the cost of the federal government and those forces holding together the federation. Moreover, due to the increasing fiscal disparities between the Regions, the established pattern of constitutional reform had reached its limits. For a long time, decentralization had been the common ground for the regional governments and parties of all parts of the country and made agreements feasible despite bargaining processes. But decentralized policy-making reinforced fiscal imbalances between the Regions. They became an issue as of the mid-1990s. As a consequence, redistributive conflicts have changed the former "positive sum-game" of decentralization into an asymmetric constellation, with Flanders being more interested in additional powers and a confederal structure of Belgium, while for Wallonia fiscal equalization, maintaining the central social system and remaining part of a federation became a primary concern (Popelier and Cantillon 2013: 7). For more than a whole decade, the federal system was in gridlock. Flemish parties have proposed to decentralize the Belgian welfare system, but no result has been achieved so far. To decentralize such a system implies complicated redistributive issues between individuals and territories (Béland and Lecours 2007). In view of the divergent developments of regional economy and society, there is good reason to doubt that Belgium would separate, regardless of the wicked problems confronting the country's federal order. However, a policy of further integration appears equally improbable.

Hence constitutional policy in Belgium with its patterns of joint decision-making has not succeeded in changing the dynamics of the federal system which, driven by ineffective constitutional reform, ran deeper into the joint-decision trap. The agreement on the Sixth State Reform of December 2011, negotiated after a political deadlock lasting over 541 days, revealed all features described in our case study, in regard to processes as well as outcomes. Negotiated in the usual patterns of constitutional politics described here for the previous reform, it hardly solved the real problems. The fact that the deadlock was dissolved by an agreement may give reason for an optimistic assessment: "In a so-called 'postmodern federation' such as Belgium, characterized by decentralization, linguistic protection, and regionally based nationalist political parties, the process of accommodating demands for greater autonomy will continue indefinitely, despite concessions by central governments" (Popelier and Cantillon 2013: 7). The risk of this process of accommodation, however, is an ongoing imbalance of power and disintegration, although a dissolution may appear unrealistic. In summarizing studies on different aspects of the reform, Wilfried Swenden concludes, "that the deal on constitutional reform does not fundamentally change the nature of the Belgian federation; if anything, it continues the gradual hollowing of the Belgian centre, with the transfer of some powers to the Communities and Regions, most notably in taxation, welfare (child allowances) and labour market regulation" (Swenden 2013: 369).

4.2.3 *Spain: The Third Round of Reform of Autonomy Statutes (2004–10)*

Like Belgium, Spain represents a case of a late federation in a multinational state. After the fall of the Franco regime, historical regions like Catalonia or the Basque Country quickly demanded the restoration of their statutes of autonomy approved during the Second Republic. Apart from accommodating aspirations from different regions for more autonomy, efficient public management and making decisions closer to the people had been expressed as further reasons for granting self-government to regions in general, not only to the so-called historic nationalities. The process of democratization induced pressure to review the territorial organization of the state. The 1978 Spanish Constitution postponed the settlement of the emerging conflict between the central government and the newly constituted Autonomous Communities

(ACs). It avoided a final definition of powers of the latter and merely fixed exclusive powers of the central government. The balance of power should be found in a process of regionalization initiated "from below," by a revision of individual Autonomy Statutes (the constitutions of the ACs). To become constitutional law of the Spanish state, both houses of the Spanish legislature had to approve such reforms at the lower level by passing an organic law with an absolute majority. In contrast to regular constitutional amendments, a national referendum was not required. Thus, the conflicts caused by a rising regionalism were transformed into a process of decentralization "a la carte," whereby asymmetries in the allocation of power were supposed to be of transitory character. This strategy to accommodate diversity set out a competition of regions seeking extended autonomy (Hombrado 2011). Confronted with strong regionalist parties, the central government had to make concessions in bargaining on the distribution of powers and consequently on redistributing revenues, which it could not deny ACs in less developed regions. Consequently, the territorial organization of the Spanish state changed indeed significantly, but this result was achieved without a coherent revision of the national constitution (Magone 2009: 194–216).

The character of the Spanish state is still disputed and ambiguities in the constitution indeed allow for different readings. According to the text of the constitution and the prevailing view of constitutional lawyers, it is a "State of Autonomous Communities," but not a federal state (Aja 2003). While this denomination may be taken as a matter of wording, since according to all definitions Spain must be categorized as federal (Sala 2014; Watts 2008: 41–2), it only reveals the tensions inherent in the existing constitutional order. In practice, pacts at the central level between the two main state-wide parties, the PSOE and PP, as well as repeated changes of the ACs' powers by amendments of their statutes have driven the process of federalization, turning Spain into "one of the most decentralized countries in Europe" (Watts 2008: 42). This interplay of central and regional politics led to decentralization in several rounds of statute reforms, resulting from party strategies, intergovernmental competition and bargaining. It was driven by economic developments generating divergent effects from region to region, and in particular by linguistic and cultural divides. These dynamics caused serious imbalances of power and resources between regions and levels of government. Therefore, need for a constitutional reform of the Spanish federation has increased during the last decade. However, the federal government was not willing to initiate such a reform and instead tended to react to pressure from below. For this reason, constitutional change in Spain reveals a unique pattern and does not easily fit into the categories defining outcomes (Colino 2009a: 263).

Party competition and party constellations at the different levels of government play an important role in the processes of federalization and constitutional reform in Spain. The party system has changed significantly with the rise of distinct regional party systems in several ACs or the creation of new regionalist parties even in Communities without distinct nationalities. At the same time, state-wide parties lost their territorial pervasiveness and changed their internal organization accordingly, giving certain regional branches more autonomy than others (Fabre 2008; van Houten 2009). These changes in the party system significantly affected the negotiations on constitutional reform (Orte and Wilson 2009). On the whole, they intensified the pressure for change at the regional level but obstructed agreements at the central level.

Overall, these political changes did not contribute to stabilizing the federal system already confronted by serious problems of integration. As in Belgium, constitutional change has caused more instability than stability. In contrast to Belgium, this outcome was not the result of ineffective constitutional reform, but rather was due to the lack of a state-wide reform appropriately responding to dynamics of regional statute amendments. The consequences became obvious when the last round of statute reforms ended de facto with a deadlock after an intervention by the Spanish Constitutional Court, which declared significant parts of the changed statute of Catalonia and accordingly the agreement between the Catalonian and the central government unconstitutional.

This third round of reform of the ACs started in 2004, initiated by proposals to amend statutes in a number of ACs. Some of the regional reforms failed (e.g. in the Basque Country), but others succeeded. For the constitutional change in Spain, the reforms passed in the parliaments of Andalusia and Catalonia in 2006 turned out as crucial. Negotiations with the central government ended with agreements. In 2006, the Andalusian statute reform was approved by the Spanish parliament and the Congress of Deputies and in 2007, it found a majority in the regional referendum. However, the 2006 central-regional agreement on the Catalan statue passed parliament with a majority vote, and opposition parties and other ACs challenged this decision. They took recourse to the Constitutional Court, where the statute reform was dismissed. In its final decision, the Court declared significant parts of the agreement invalid. Although it passed formal ratification procedures at the central level and although a clear majority in a regional referendum supported it, the new statue of the AC of Catalonia could not come into force as intended. The Court's decision triggered intense debates and confusion regarding its consequences for Catalonia, for other reforms and for the Spanish constitution at large. It "has caused political turmoil and citizen frustration in Catalonia. It also has led to some legal uncertainty in other ACs, alongside a general feeling of a stalemate in the reform and adaptation capacity of the system, now also under financial and efficiency pressures due to the economic crisis" (Colino and Olmeda 2012: 193). In Catalonia, a new secessionist movement has meanwhile developed and threatens the Spanish federation

(Guibernau 2013). This is a clear indication of destabilization due to an ineffective reform, which generated ongoing efforts to implicit change of the federal order.

The process ending with this outcome followed a period of stagnation between 1996 and 2004, when the government of the conservative PP had rejected further decentralization. This led to increased frustration in several Autonomous Communities prompting regionalist parties to radicalize their positions and demand further autonomy or secession. Reorganizing the statutes of Autonomies became part of the election campaigns first in Catalonia—especially of the radical nationalists (ERC), the nationalist electoral alliance CiU, but also of the Catalan Socialists (PSC)—and then in the general elections of 2004.

Regionalization gained new momentum when the Socialist Party won the general elections and formed the central government (González and López Nieto 2008: 124). This government was much more in favor of further regionalization than the previous one. The newly elected Spanish Prime Minister Zapatero proposed a constitutional reform of the Spanish state, when he presented the program of his government in 2004. However, in view of the confrontation between party political camps after the elections, which even seemed to threaten a modest reform, the government did not risk initiating a political project doomed to failure. As a consequence, change was sought and achieved to a certain extent by a "multilevel bilateral reform" approach (Colino and Olmeda 2012: 193). Premier Zapatero called on the ACs to reform their statutes and attempted to coordinate the process by establishing a conference of regional Prime Ministers.

In the situation resulting from the 2004 general elections, ACs indeed took the lead. In particular the Catalonian government supported by a coalition of left and nationalist parties saw an opportunity to make a bold step towards more autonomy, when the Socialist Party came into power at the central level and controlled the absolute majority in the legislature. As will be explained below, the vertical linkage between parties and the congruence of majorities at the central and regional level proved more favorable for statute reform in Andalusia, the second AC leading the reform process. As the regional processes occurred almost simultaneously, negotiations in both pioneering ACs mutually influenced each other in terms of issues and agendas.

In accordance with the rules for amending Autonomy Statutes, the reform process went through two sequences. It started at the regional level, where ACs used different procedures to negotiate and decide on amendments to their statutes. In the second sequence, the national legislature negotiated and finally ratified agreements settled by the ACs and the central government. Particularly this second process is interesting in a comparative perspective. However, in order to understand the different outcomes of the negotiation process at the central level, the conditions set by regional constitutional policy ought to be considered as well.

Statute reform in Andalusia, a region without strong secessionist parties or ambitions to become independent but interested in self-government, aimed at making government more effective. Therefore, the proposed amendments, initiated by the regional government in 2003, were mainly targeted at better coordination with the central government, fiscal decentralization, increasing powers in justice administration, social rights for citizens and renovating institutions of the AC. Moreover, in response to claims in Catalonia, Andalusia demanded symbolic recognition as a nation. While not intended to promote a nationalist project, the AC aimed at maintaining an equal status with other ACs in order to avoid falling behind in the decentralization process (Hombrado 2011: 489–95).

The regional government defined the agenda of the statute reform in a document submitted to parliament in December 2003. Titled "Basis for Reform of the Statute of Autonomy for Andalusia," it set out the scope of the intended changes. Overall, the ten chapters concerned nearly all parts of the regional statue, but mainly intended to strengthen self-government capacities and institutions of the AC. Moreover, they clearly spelled out the commitment of Andalusia to solidarity with other parts of the country and its willingness to be a cooperative partner in the Spanish federation and in the EU (Olmeda 2009: 7–9). To elaborate these amendments, the parliament set up a special committee (Commission for Statute of Autonomy Reform), where all parties in parliament were represented. It invited experts and representatives of civil society to participate in hearings. Thus intra-regional negotiations were concentrated in the parliamentary arena, but were more open to societal groups than, for instance, constitutional negotiations in Belgium. But while in Catalonia representatives of civil society effectively participated in the dialog, negotiating actors in Andalusia widely neglected to include the public (Colino 2009b: 7). Afterward, the regional parliament debated the proposal of the committee and a second hearing took place on the final draft of an amended statute. Again, bargaining among party representatives prevailed, and party competition had a much stronger effect than opinions submitted by experts, consultative bodies or interest groups. In state reform, regionalist parties in Spain—like in Belgium—have favored decentralization of powers and party competition has stimulated outbidding of parties with corresponding proposals. This could also be observed in Andalusia, although to a limited extent since the Socialist Party had to find support of the conservative Peoples' Party (*Partito Popular, PP*), a party preferring more centralization than the Socialists do. The parliament discussed the statute reform in plenary session and passed the law with the required three-fifths majority in May 2006.

The dynamics of party politics were more intense in Catalonia, where the statute reform was negotiated in a similar setting to the one described for Andalusia. The agenda and the general goals were, however, different. Here, the recognition of the uniqueness of Catalonia, autonomy in governing the affairs of the region without intervention of the central government, and an extension of powers were the primary claims, and thus expressed by the Catalan Minister for Institutional Relations in 2005 (Colino, 2009b: 3). In clear contrast to Andalusia, Catalonia aimed at separating powers and at protecting its jurisdiction against the central government. Moreover, the reform was framed more in a nationalist ideology and put emphasis on the distinctiveness of the AC—with the consequence of an asymmetrical allocation of power in the Spanish federation, while Andalusia was among those defending symmetrical federalism.

In February 2004, the reform process started in the parliament of Catalonia, which elaborated a first proposal for amendments of the existing statute. This draft was then discussed in an expert commission appointed by the regional government. The government also invited lawyers to write reports. Organizations of civil society, experts and members of the executive could provide their opinion in public hearings. The draft of a revised statute was prepared by an academic institution run by the government and finally refined in a parliamentary committee. After these intense negotiations in different arenas, serious conflicts between parties remained unsettled. They related to fundamental issues like the definition of Catalonia as a nation, language policy or the representation of the region in the European Parliament. This situation led the Prime Minister of Spain to intervene in the regional process and to press the leaders of the majority party and the main opposition party to negotiate a compromise. In September 2005, the Catalan parliament passed the reform with the votes of all parties except the PP.

At the national level, the Constitutional Committee of the Spanish parliament was responsible for elaborating the document. According to rules, this Committee negotiates in joint session with representatives from the parliament of the respective AC. Actually, meetings of party leaders from the regional and national level turned out to be decisive. The Andalusian reform succeeded. In this case, an agreement between both levels was favored by the congruence of Socialist governments at the center and in the region as well as the stronger bonds within the Socialist Party between its central and its Andalusian branch. At the time of negotiations, the President of Andalusia was simultaneously leader of the Spanish Socialist Party. Beyond party linkages in the majority camp, the support by the regional PP for a reform, which in general tended to strengthen a cooperative federalism in Spain, helped to produce a consensus among the parties in the Congress of Deputies, after negotiating on a number of amendment proposals submitted by the party groups. In November 2006, the Congress and the Senate passed the statute with an overwhelming majority. After the regional parliament had endorsed the modifications, the statute reform was ratified in a regional referendum with a clear majority.

The Catalonian statute reform was introduced in the Congress of Deputies on October 2005. The extensive claims for powers and autonomy of the AC instigated more intense disputes with central parties and the government than the Andalusian proposal had caused. The party constellation at the two levels was not as congruent as in the Andalusian reform, due to the role of nationalists in the region. The opposition parties at the center strongly opposed the new statute presented by Catalonia, but the National Committee of the Socialist Party also requested to revise the draft regarding the allocation of powers, the language regime and regulations that affected the single market in Spain and Europe. The government passed the reform proposal of the AC to a group of experts who regarded many provisions in the amended statute as incompatible with the Spanish constitution. Representatives of the Spanish Socialists and Catalonian parties openly discussed their conflicts in the media, while the Prime Minister negotiated with leaders of the regional parties in private meetings. The Spanish PP was excluded after the Prime Minister had rejected an offer to cooperate with the opposition party in parliament. The conflict was related to a number of issues, but the designation of Catalonia as a nation in the statute was the most debated topic.

Parallel to these negotiations led by the Prime Minister, the Spanish Minister of Finance worked towards an agreement with Catalan parties on fiscal resources and funding of the AC. Again, both sides at the table adhered to their positions over the course of several meetings. The central government offered to turn personal income tax into a shared revenue source with 50 percent to be allocated to the ACs. Catalan parties rejected the proposal, while the central government persisted. After further meetings, it tried to split up the front of Catalonian parties in bilateral negotiations. Finally, in February 2006, a package deal was settled. To put the main points briefly, the AC accepted the financial offer of the central government, which made concessions in the allocation of powers.

The parliament, where legislative proceedings began in November 2005, started its negotiations in February in the responsible subcommittee and in March in the Standing Committee for Constitutional Affairs. According to constitutional rules, reforms of the statutes of ACs required an absolute majority in the Spanish parliament and the Senate. After the majority party found an internal agreement, the Congress voted in favor of the Catalan statute in May 2006. The concentration on exclusive negotiations of the central government with regional parties, excluding the opposition parties, turned out to be inappropriate for finding the necessary consent for a reform, which, according to the opposition and experts, affected crucial elements of the federal constitution of Spain. Defeated by a majority decision in the legislative institutions, opposition parties and governments of other ACs appealed to the Constitutional Court.

In its 2010 decision (for details see Colino 2011), the Court declared unconstitutional a number of provisions of the new statute of Catalonia, four years after it was approved in a popular referendum and entered into force in August 2006. The Court accepted some rules with central relevance for the AC, in particular the concept of a Catalan nation or the bill of rights. However, it subdued them to interpretation in accordance with the Spanish Constitution. In this context, the Court emphasized the prevalence of sovereignty of the Spanish people and of fundamental rights of individual citizens in the constitution. Accordingly, it rejected claims for sovereignty of regional nations and constrained the rights of ACs to extend their powers if this contradicted the Spanish constitutional law as interpreted by the Court. It also discarded the right of ACs to shield their powers against the central government or legislature. With this decision, the Court invalidated basic parts of the new Catalonian statute, with significant consequences for the constitutional framework of the Spanish federation.

Thus, ratification of an important statute reform was declared partially invalid. Therefore, the constitutional process in Spain ended not in an overall deadlock, but in an ineffective outcome and merely a gradual change of the federal constitution, although the amendment rules provided for a flexible process for redistributing powers between central and regional governments. The processes of reform at the regional level proved quite successful from the point of view of ACs. This can be explained due to a rather differentiated structure of constitutional policy-making, combining negotiations in parliament and consultation with civil society. Nonetheless, we observe a clear predominance of political parties. Dynamics of the reform process were clearly driven by competition among parties to outbid claims for decentralization or autonomy against the central government. In a way, this process resembled party political dynamics in the Belgian case. In Spain, bilateral negotiation between ACs and the central government can counterbalance this centrifugal mechanism. However, the competition of ACs weakened the bargaining power of the center. In exclusive negotiations among party representatives, the issue of federal integration hardly played any role. Thus the process of constitutional negotiations failed to consolidate the multinational federation and to stop decentralist processes from going beyond a sustainable balance. As with Belgium, the predominance of bargaining among party agents in informal procedures and exclusive committees led to this result. For this reason, the Spanish Constitutional Court stepped in and adopted the position of an institution holding together the federation. In doing so, it simultaneously blocked constitutional dynamics and thus the flexibility of the Spanish federation.

4.3 Regionalized States Addressing Performance Problems

Italy and France are among the unitary states in Europe which have been going through processes of decentralization since the 1970s. Although the central government seems to be in a strong position in these states and can take the lead in constitutional policy, and although performance problems have not raised deep conflicts over accommodation of nations, a number of changes have evolved incrementally in both cases. The outcomes of the constitutional reforms proved more or less ineffective in processes of constitutional policy, which hardly differed from normal policy-making.

4.3.1 *Italy: The Reform of Title V of the Constitution (1997–2001)*

The constitutional reform of the Italian territorial order of 2001 directly built upon earlier processes and reform attempts and profited from them. Therefore, the history of constitutional policy needs to be taken into account in this case study. This path of constitutional policy was redefined in 1997. Before this date, it was a widely shared understanding among the political elite that constitutional issues should be decided in a consensual way. Given the experience of fascism and war and later the segmentation of the country during decades of confrontation between Christian Democrats and the Communist Party, this consensus served to mutually secure each side its proper rights and created a kind of consociational politics until the 1980s (Bogaards 2005). The establishment of a joint Reform Commission of both parliamentary chambers conformed to this political culture. The so-called *"Bicamerale"* constituted a particular arena of constitutional negotiation in order to produce consensus on major constitutional issues among the political parties.

In the late 1980s and early 1990s, the first two Joint Commissions failed to achieve the expected consensus. Nonetheless, the established patterns of constitutional negotiations initially survived the transition to the Second Republic. Due to the widely felt need for institutional reforms, a law was passed in 1997 providing for the appointment of a third Joint Commission of both parliamentary chambers committed to preparing a constitutional reform (*"Commissione parlamentare per le riforme costituzionale"*), which was headed by Prime Minister Massimo D'Alema. The reform project included a change of the territorial organization of the state. With his personal engagement and leadership, D'Alema underlined the ambitions of the reform project. However, conforming to the established path of consensual constitutional negotiations, the representatives of the major parties in the Commission were in a position to apply their veto power.

The Commission was organized along sectoral lines into four different committees, each dedicated to one specific reform area: (1) The structure of the national parliament, (2) the form of the government, (3) the judiciary system and (4) the nature of the state ("*Forma di stato*"). The head of the committee for the nature of the state, Senator and Professor of constitutional law Francesco D'Onofrio, initially presented a first draft of amendments to the committee, according to which the national level and the Regions were supposed to bilaterally negotiate on the allocation of powers in an asymmetrical federal structure. Yet the committee preferred a symmetric constellation while maintaining the Regions with a special status. The constitution also should acknowledge the state, the Regions, the provinces and the municipalities as constitutive parts of the Republic. The allocation of powers between the levels was to be defined by constitutional law, based on the principle of subsidiarity, with responsibilities for international policies, for the organization of the state and for minimum standards of social and economic rights remaining with the central government. The amendment proposal also included a right of the Regions to establish their own political systems, including electoral laws, by regional statutes. As to fiscal resources, the proposal did not go beyond mentioning that the distribution of the fiscal revenues must conform to the subsidiarity principle (D'Onofrio 1997).

Together with the suggestions of the other three subcommittees, the work of the "nature of state"-committee was compiled to form a general proposal for constitutional reform. A broad majority of the Commission agreed to the final decision taken in June 1997. Only the four members of the new communist party PRC (*Partito della Rifondazione Comunista*) opposed the draft and presented their own version. Despite this almost unanimous approval in the Joint Commission, the political support of the entire project within the center-right coalition parties faded suddenly (Bull and Pasquino 2007: 673) and it vanished from the parliamentary agenda one year later. Especially, Silvio Berlusconi and his party were no longer interested in a major reform, which in their view might be credited to the center-left government. Thus, the center-right coalition left the path of consensual constitutional change and obstructed the reform. However, the proposals on the vertical allocation of powers developed and approved by the commission were later introduced again by the center-left majority.

Shortly after the failure of the constitutional Reform Commission, the center-left majority in parliament led by Romano Prodi unilaterally passed a set of decentralization laws named after Minister Franco Bassanini. The drafts of these laws were discussed in the cabinet, but de facto legal experts in the ministry elaborated them. Besides a reform of public administration, these laws, especially the first one of 1997, prepared the ground for various steps of decentralization, implementing the existing constitution, but actually changing it. They made effective a constitutional provision already introduced with the establishment of the Regions in the early 1970s. It stated that the

Regions could exercise legislative powers on specific matters within basic principles defined by national law. But these principles had been missing so far, and Italy had remained a decentralized unitary state (Fabbrini and Brunazzo 2003: 104) until the Bassanini laws entered into force. They introduced principles such as subsidiarity, efficiency or responsibility (law no. 50, Art. 4), and enabled the Regions to exercise their legislative rights in the areas enumerated in the constitution. In addition, the law transferred administrative powers to the Regions and local governments in all areas not exclusively reserved for the national level. As a result, Regions hold administrative powers to an extent comparable to German *Länder* (Bassanini 2012: 237).

The transfer of legislative and administrative powers to the Regions and the rationalization of intergovernmental relations were inspired by EU programs. A number of institutional changes led to the application of procedures copied from the European regional policies. In contrast to major institutional reforms, the procedural changes were easily implemented (Fabbrini and Brunazzo 2003: 114). To make effective the transfers of administrative and legislative competencies, the Bassanini laws also introduced institutional monitoring, provided assistance and consultation for regional parliaments, and transferred staff and resources within the public administration. A joint committee of both parliamentary chambers was established to monitor and report regularly on the progress of decentralization. Another committee including representatives of the national, regional, provincial and local governments was designed to coordinate decentralization policies, yet without having veto power.

These laws set the stage for a next attempt to reform the territorial organization of the Italian state, the reform of Title V of the Constitution. In March 1999, the government of Prime Minister Massimo D'Alema presented a constitutional amendment proposal in the Chamber of Deputies, under the title of "Federal Order of the Republic" ("*Ordinamento federale della Repubblica*"). In his initial declaration, D'Alema referred to the failed bicameral commission of 1997 and underlined that institutional reforms were still an important issue on the agenda of his government. With the center-left government acting unilaterally at this time, the consensual mode of constitutional negotiation undoubtedly ended. The proposal only dealt with one of the four major reform issues previously discussed in the *Bicamerale,* the transfer of powers from the national government to the Regions. This selectivity was due to party political interests. Similar to the negotiations in the *Bicamerale,* the center-left coalition viewed regionalization of the country as an appropriate issue for garnering electoral support given its broad support in the public (Bull and Pasquino 2007; Roux 2008). To put it in another way: the center-left government picked one issue from the whole package of major constitutional reforms which promised to raise attention and be acknowledged in the public and within the political class. Yet, as Mazzoleni pointed out, a profound policy change within the center-left camp made federalism one of the main items on the agenda of government (Mazzoleni 2009: 142).

The finally approved constitutional law No. 3 of 18 October 2001 mainly built on the steps taken through the Bassanini laws. It amended Title V of the second part of the constitution concerning the institutional order of the political system (*"Ordinamento della Repubblica"*). Altogether, ten articles of the constitution were changed and five were eliminated in the new version. The amendments can be categorized according to the type of powers (either legislative or administrative) and to the involved level of the political system, with the explicit assignment of powers to a level being the main innovation. Whereas the new article 114 introduces the metropolitan cities as a constitutive unit of the Republic and generally guarantees autonomy of each of the territorial units, including the right to decide on appropriate statutes, article 117 determines the distribution of authority.

Powers exclusively reserved to the national level resemble the list in the Bassanini laws, but, in contrast to the proposal of the *Bicamerale*, they were clarified during parliamentary negotiations. Given the economic disparity between the north and the south, the national government still holds the basic responsibility for public welfare by determining social living standards for all parts of the country. Article 117 also makes clear that the national level is responsible for the institutions and functioning of local government (provinces, cities and communes), and thus constrains their autonomy. Regional autonomy is guaranteed, and according to article 127, each Region may call upon the national Constitutional Court in cases of a potential violation of regional rights by a national law.

Shared powers, the so-called concurrent legislation, actually constitute a kind of framework legislation (Palermo 2004: 7). In the areas enumerated in article 117, the Regions can legislate according to main principles determined by central legislation. Therefore, these regional powers may be hollowed out if no principles exist in the respective areas. Article 116 confirms the special status of the Regions with ethnic or linguistic minorities. They can gain further powers by bilateral agreements with the central government. The initial proposal of the *Bicamerale* extended this possibility of authority transfer to ordinary Regions, which the negotiations in parliament limited to matters of concurrent legislation (Senato della Repubblica—Servizio Studi 2001: 10).

Deviating from the previous rule that Regions only can legislate in matters of enumerated powers, the amended constitution assigns reserved powers to them. Moreover, the ex-ante control of regional laws by the central government now was turned into an ex-post control (Cento Bull 2002: 207). However, this rule has limits for three reasons: First, beyond the catalog of article 117, the constitution allocates exclusive legislative powers to the central level in other articles, which remained unchanged, e.g. concerning education and universities (article 33). Some matters enumerated are not clearly allocated to one level, like legislation on strikes (Senato della Repubblica—Servizio Studi 2001: 37). Second, under certain circumstances, the central government may replace decisions of Regions, provinces or local governments. Such replacement used to be justified in case of violations of international contracts, threats to the public order or in order to protect the legal and economic unity of the country. Moreover, not all Regions, particularly those in the south, had been ready to exert the new competencies on their own, and meanwhile the central government remains in charge. Accordingly, the implementation of the constitutional reform has resulted in a "*geometria variabile*" (Cento Bull 2002: 209). Third, the Regions are still dependent on fiscal resources determined by the central government. According to the amended constitution, each territorial unit has autonomous resources coming from proper revenues in accordance with the tax system. However, centralized tax-raising powers deprive the Regions of any institutional means to influence decisions. It took until 2009 for the first law implementing the constitutional rules on allocation of fiscal resources to be passed, and the process of developing fiscal federalism is still under way.

Overall, the amendment of Title V of the Italian Constitution is significant as regards the scope of the reform. However, a closer look reveals that the many detailed new rules on the allocation of powers amount to a federal structure, which is both complicated and open to interpretation. In fact, the central government has exploited its discretionary power and has continued to rule from above as it has done before the reform (Baldini and Baldi 2014: 99). In addition, fiscal federalism still does not meet the requirements of regionalization of powers. Although Italy came closer to a real federal balance, the outcome of the 2001 constitutional reform hardly solved all problems of governance and maybe produced new ones. In any case the reform of the Italian territorial organization is "far from complete" (Bassanini 2012: 248, see also: Baldini and Baldi 2014; Lippi 2011).

This outcome was the result of constitutional negotiations, which mainly took place in the parliamentary arena and, accordingly, were clearly influenced by bargaining between parties. The draft introduced in legislation was based on previous works of the bicameral committees and the intergovernmental committee. Thus, parliamentary and intergovernmental arenas can be distinguished, but the latter had limited impact. In the process of legislation, representatives of territorial government provided opinions. However, they had no significant influence on negotiations, in particular compared to the centralized parties. Regional, provincial and local actors spoke with many voices and could not come to a common vision, concept or strategy for designing a federal system. Even if their support for the reform finally was important for gaining a majority in ratification, they played a minor role in negotiations on the substance of the reform (Bassanini 2012: 244).

As mentioned above, the consensual mode of constitutional policy could not be restored after the collapse of the *Bicamerale* in 1998. Although the reform proposal presented by Prime Minister D'Alema in 1999 built on the work of the bicameral committee and hardly diverged from the consensus found among party representatives, it immediately became part of the bipolar party competition. The center-right opposition stood against the proposal in the Constitutional Affairs Committee and in the final votes in the assemblies. In the run-up to the general election of June 2001, the constitutional reform became an issue of competition for votes. Particularly the Democratic Left (*Democratici di Sinistra*) appealed to the moderate voters of the *Lega Nord* to secure the electoral victory. "The political temptation for the coalition to secure a reform of Title V of the Constitution (relating to Regions, provinces and communes)—taking the wind out of the Northern League's sails in advance of national elections—was perhaps too strong" (Bull and Pasquino 2007: 673). Even though this process began in spring 1999, the major losses of the center-left parties in the regional elections of April 2000 eliminated the last doubts within the coalition about the necessity of the reform. For these parties, "[the] goal was clearly to limit the electoral support of the center-right in northern regions" (Roux 2008: 332). Yet this plan did not work out in the end, since the center-left government was not able to profit from its reform record (Newell and Bull 2002) and eventually lost power to Berlusconi's coalition.

The reform immediately surfaced as a bill in parliament. Prime Minister Massimo D'Alema presented the constitutional law proposal (Act no. 5830 Camera dei Deputati) in the Chamber of Deputies on 18 March 1999. It was then up to the responsible committee to start the examination and to finally make a recommendation to the Assembly. After ratification in the Chamber, the same process of examination of the proposal started in the Senate. The committees always decided by majority. External experts were invited to the hearings, but the draft of the constitutional reform was never presented or deliberated in some other institution or forum.

In the Constitutional Affairs Committee of the Chamber of Deputies, the amendment proposal sparked various additional suggestions for constitutional amendment, which were negotiated together. For this purpose, a special subcommittee of only nine members was installed (*"Comitato dei nove"*) in order to present an approved version of the amendment bill at short notice. The Presidency of the Chamber and the conference of party group presidents set a strict and narrow time limit for committee negotiations. Given the importance of the project, even members of the government coalition expressed their concerns and discontent about the hastiness with which the reform was pushed through the parliamentary committee of the Chamber.

In contrast, the plenum needed almost a year to approve the bill in first reading before it was passed to the Senate. A similar process evolved in the Senate. The responsible committee only had one month to examine the proposal, since the Presidency of the Senate had scheduled the issue for the debate in the plenum on 10 November 2000. Seven days later the Senate approved the bill without any single amendment. After passing the second reading in both houses, the constitutional amendment bill was ratified with the required absolute majority.

Thus, the arena of negotiation on the constitutional amendment was absolutely identical with the arena of everyday politics in parliament and followed its logic, which was bargaining and confrontation between the opposition parties and the parties forming the government majority. The opposition parties demonstrated their rejection of the proposal by boycotting the process of parliamentary deliberation (Interview I, 29 September 2010). Nonetheless, the parliamentary process brought some changes to the initial proposal negotiated within the center-left coalition. Compared to the government's draft, the constitutional affairs committee was more reluctant in granting the Regions autonomy. Accordingly, it inserted various clarifications and limitations of regional power, for example, the right of the central government to intervene in order to secure the uniformity of living conditions in the country.

The Italian Constitution prescribes a binding referendum as an additional step of approval of constitutional amendments in cases where one-fifth of the members of one Chamber, 500,000 voters or five Regional Councils demand it. With the reform of Title V of the Constitution, a project of the center-left government, the members of the center-right opposition in parliament requested this step. On 7 October 2001, the first constitutional referendum according to article 138 of the constitution was held. The entire campaign was dominated by partisan rivalry. Whereas the center-right coalition won the election in June of the same year, the center-left coalition's reform was approved in the referendum by 64.2 percent of the votes. Yet the turnout was low with an overall participation of only 34.1 percent of the electorate.

It is hardly surprising in a country so profoundly dominated by political parties like Italy that the process of regionalization is "a story of partisan logics" (Mazzoleni 2009). However, the reform of 2001 profited from previous work of the *Bicamerale* and the Bassanini reform of 1997/98. In both processes, party politics were pushed back by negotiations among legal experts. Thus, the outcome must be explained by a sequence of technocratic politics and majority decisions in parliament and in the referendum. This sequence explains the scope of the reform. Regarding substance, the outcome was less significant. Although the reform brought the Italian state closer to a federal system, it left many problems of effective governance unresolved.

Accordingly, it was criticized both for being too superficial and leaving many issues untouched or to be clarified through subsequent legislation. Furthermore, the question of whether Italy has become a federal state has not been decided. "To be sure, the reform has a federalizing thrust, in the sense that is pushing the Italian once unitary state (1948–70), then decentralized unitary state (1970 onwards) in the direction of 'something more' than a regional state. [...]. In sum, the constitutional article set in motion a federalizing tendency, but they did not create a federal state" (Fabbrini and Brunazzo 2003: 116f.). Still the Regions do not exercise sovereign power. They are authorized by the central government to fulfill specific tasks. Moreover, a representation of Regions on the national level is still missing, while the newly institutionalized intergovernmental conferences lack any formal powers. According to Keating and Wilson, the political elite adhered to the unitary state model with the regionalization being only a strategic response to the pressures from regionalist movements (Keating and Wilson 2010: 1).

Lacking a broad support among parties and citizens, the new constitution suffers from a legitimacy deficit. This became obvious after the 2001 general elections, when the new center-right government of *Forza Italia*, *Lega Nord* and *Alleanza Nazionale* introduced their own constitutional reform of the political system. Besides the introduction of a semi-presidential system, the federalization of the country was one of their aims. The parliament passed the reform in 2005, but the amendment bill failed in a constitutional referendum in 2006. The evolution and consolidation of the federal path in Italy continues nonetheless via different implementation laws. The most important one, the Parliamentary Law 42 passed in 2009, delegated execution and negotiation of details of the *"federalismo fiscale"* to the national government, which already released two respective decrees in 2009. Observers characterized this act as "one of the farthest-reaching reforms of Italy's fiscal framework" (Blöchliger and Vammalle 2012: 102) resulting from a sequence of various reforms. However, the reform has not introduced significant fiscal autonomy of the Regions, and its implementation has been delayed. Still, the distribution of fiscal competences is a central issue of the debates on the territorial organization of the state in Italy.

4.3.2 *France: Decentralization Act II (2000–4)*

After the first decentralization under the socialist government (1982–5), France saw a second step to reform the territorial organization of the state under a Conservative government. The first decentralization laws delegated powers to local governments, upgraded Regions as territorial units and constrained the supervisory power of the central government. The second reform, considered here, aimed at adjusting the constitutional framework to developments after the first decentralization, at renovating inter-local cooperation in order to improve governance in territorially fragmented structures, and at solving deficits caused by a fiscal imbalance between levels that constrained capacities of Regions and local governments and created a serious obstacle to effective decentralization.

The reform addressed most of these issues, but experts have evaluated its effects as disappointing. The problem-solving capacity of the 2002/2004 constitutional reform has been considered severely limited (Le Lidec 2012; Pasquier 2005: 116). Substantial improvements were not achieved. Compared to the previous decentralization reform of the 1980s, only incremental changes were codified (Rémond 2007: 449). The problems of suboptimal institutional performance and the lack of transparency and accountability could not be alleviated (Zimmermann-Steinhart 2004: 219). Instead, some powers were redistributed, and the only innovative element worth mentioning was the local referendum (Hoffmann-Martinot 2005: 339). The reform has not improved the balance of power, but actually weakened the local level. "The reforms of 2004 and 2010[12] considerably upset the balance of power within state territorial networks: the regional level has become stronger to the detriment of the départemental level and regional prefects have finally become the hierarchical superiors of *département* prefects" (Le Lidec 2012: 264). Even Prime Minister Raffarin himself was unsatisfied with his reform in hindsight, deploring the ongoing inefficiency and intransparency (Raffarin and Séguillon 2007: 57ff.). Thus, although the constitutional amendment was finally passed, negotiations have to be regarded as inefficient since they did not contribute to solving the problems on the agenda.

Overall, the reform process in France lasted from 2000 to 2004. It was characterized by separate negotiations on the constitutional amendment law and on laws implementing the constitutional reform (Gaudin 2004: 55). Whereas the constitutional reform proceeded relatively smoothly, implementation turned out to be slow and cumbersome (Zimmermann-Steinhart 2006: 365). The turning point between these phases was marked by the regional and departmental elections of March 2004. They ended with majorities of the Socialist Party in many councils of the *départements* and Regions, with the consequence that the opposition party in the national parliament became stronger in constitutional negotiations. Yet problems emerging during the implementation phase also resulted from the incoherence of the governing party UMP, which became more salient when details of the reform had to be

[12] The 2010 reform, not considered here, aimed at strengthening the *Métropoles* as territorial units to govern city regions. However, against the resistance of the Senate, the proposals of a commission to establish a single level of local government in these areas was watered down. The metropolitan government remained an additional intermunicipal level to the local governments.

clarified. The two phases also differed in the substance of the outcome: In the first phase, the Senate's proposal set a starting point, and the Senators had to make more concessions to the government than vice versa. However, in the second phase, the government made concessions to the Senators and to external actors. In both phases, the strong group of small local governments represented in the Senate was able to block a significant territorial reform.

The constitutional reform was negotiated in the parliamentary arena according to the established rules of legislation. In contrast, negotiations of the implementation laws formally took place in two separate arenas: in parliamentary committees and in forums of public consultation, organized as the *Assises des libertés locales*. The main actors interested and participating in the reform process were the central administration, both houses of the national legislature and French politicians holding multiple local and national mandates, the so-called *élus*. For the broader public, decentralization did not play any particular role (Thoenig 2005: 706). Regarding party politics, the conservatives had a strong position due to their majority in both houses of parliament, and the President as well belonged to the Conservative camp. In reality, however, parties are generally weak in France, and the governing party UMP (see Haegel 2002 for details) proved particularly incoherent. Thus, policy was in practice mainly determined by the executive (Costa and Kerrouche 2009: 328), even in cases of constitutional amendments where the instruments of the so-called "rationalized parliamentarism" do not apply and members of parliament have more power than in ordinary legislation. In decentralization reforms, the Senators have a particular stake. Moreover, as *élus* they had a broad power base through their constituencies and thus exerted considerable influence.

The formalization of negotiations within parliamentary procedures suggests that the mode of negotiation was bargaining, and that the relevant actors played a game with complete information on all sides, with only a small degree of uncertainty generated by the unpredictable impact of the *Assises*. Under these conditions, the veto-players' interests could at least to some extent be anticipated from the outset. However, Prime Minister Raffarin underestimated his own party's internal divisions. Moreover, subnational elections of March 2004 changed the Senate's preferences unexpectedly. In addition, the government had to respond to the demands both of lobbyists from the subnational units and of citizens expressed in the course of massive public protest against the reform. Accordingly, actors who had no veto power, whose participation in the process was not formally envisaged and whose preferences could not be sufficiently anticipated, also managed to modify the reform result. Certainly, preferences of the citizen associations were satisfied to a lesser extent than those of the well-known subnational lobbyists (Fischer-Hotzel 2013: 115–18).

Nonetheless, the constitutional amendment can largely be understood as a compromise between the Senate and the government. Raffarin had been one of the signatories of the Senate's proposal when he was a member of the Senate. But as Prime Minister he changed his preferences to some extent, partly because he was now able to act according to his personal agenda and partly because he had to take interests of the central administration into consideration. Thus, the government's initial bill, the *Projet de loi constitutionnelle relatif à l'organisation décentralisée de la République no. 24* from 16 October 2002, deviated considerably from the Senate's proposal. It was more detailed, included additional matters, toned down some of the Senate's initial demands and ignored others completely. Length and the degree of details are not surprising, as a government bill elaborated by civil servants is usually more detailed than a Senators' bill. The aspects that were left out or watered down indicated which concessions the Senators (and Raffarin) had to make to the central administration and how the agenda changed when it went through the institutions of the government.

Matters of dispute were the local referendum, principles of distribution of powers (subsidiarity clause, the principle determining a leading unit in case of cooperation among local governments, the transfer of competences to individual subnational units on an experimental basis), the status of overseas territories, and the character of the French state. The first two issues seemed inevitable in a decentralization reform addressing the perceived deficit of democratic governance and the confusion of responsibilities, which for a long time had been criticized. With regard to the overseas territories, the reform process simply provided a window of opportunity to pass long overdue adjustment of constitutional law. The amendment of Article 1 of the Constitution defining the character of the state was of a rather symbolic nature. The first section now reads: "*La France est une République indivisible, laïque, démocratique et sociale.... Son organisation est décentralisée.*" The Senate's demand for a veto right for all legislation concerning the French subnational units was likewise attenuated. In the government bill, this was reduced to a right of a first reading of such bills, which is, however, of high symbolic importance (Le Lidec 2005: 86). Fiscal autonomy on the other hand was dropped from the agenda. The *élus'* claimed that the tax share of local budgets should be "dominant" (*préponderante*) compared to other sources of revenue which were changed to "important" (*déterminante*). This was a concession of Raffarin to the ministry of finance (Pasquier 2009: 7), which supported decentralization as an opportunity to cut spending but opposed extended financial resources and greater fiscal discretion of the subnational units (Interview F, 31 May 2010).

The final constitutional law differed in two important matters from the government bill. The final law explicitly prohibited the *tutelle,* supervision over a lower level subnational government by a higher one, thus ruling out a hierarchy of territorial units of the French state. Moreover, in contrast to the original version of the bill, the final law explicitly mentioned financial autonomy of regional and local governments. Both modifications resulted from the first reading in the Senate, and were elaborated in a committee hearing of regional and local government associations, the *élus'* lobby groups (Garrec 2002: 211ff.).

Prior to parliamentary scrutiny of the implementing legislation and parallel to the ratification of the constitutional law, the Ministry of the Interior organized the *Assises* as a separate arena for public discussion on the implementation laws (Gaudin 2004: 55; Marzelier 2004: 17). The distribution of powers, both the enumerated powers and those to be assigned on an experimental basis, was a particular topic to be addressed (Ministère de l'Intérieur, de l'Outre-Mer et des Collectivités Territoriales 2009). Altogether, twenty-six *Assises* were held, and additionally 123 thematic workshops were organized. In these discussions, all subnational executives including representatives from their elected assemblies participated, as did members of parliament, experts and representatives of civil society (Marzelier 2004: 17). However, the impact of the *Assises* on the reform legislation was minimal. Even Patrick Devedijan, one of the organizers, pointed out in an interview that the procedure was of purely consultative nature and that the effects of the *Assises* are not clearly visible in the legal texts (Interview F, 16 July 2010). Observers agree that the publicity aspect was actually much more relevant than substantial policy input. Even opinions expressed by the *élus* did not change much (Interview F, 31 May 2010). Both the existence of a separate arena and the plurality of participants suggest that the mode of negotiation was probably closer to deliberation than to bargaining. Nevertheless, as the agenda of deliberation was constrained to detailed aspects, the usual actors in intergovernmental relations and experts dominated the process. Therefore, it could not have any significant effects counteracting the prevailing bargaining mode in executive and parliamentary processes.

The actual negotiation of the implementing legislation, which related to three organic laws and one ordinary law, took place in the parliamentary arena. The laws finally passed show characteristics of compromises at the lowest common denominator while there is no evidence that package deals have been made among the houses of the legislature or the parties. The first implementing law was the *loi organique no. 2003–705* du 1er août 2003 *relative au référendum local*. The local referendum was rather unpopular with the *élus* so that the bill was amended considerably in the Senate (Zimmermann-Steinhart 2004: 321). The second law, the *loi organique no. 2003–704* du 1er août 2003 *relative à l'expérimentation par les collectivités territoriales*, regulated procedures for transferring competences on an experimental basis. By leaving open which powers might be affected, it excluded all potential matters of conflict. The *loi organique no. 2004–758 du 29 juillet 2004 prise en application de l'article 72.2 de la Constitution relative à l'autonomie financière des collectivités territoriales* was introduced in parliament in October 2003. Due to the uncertain development of costs related to the newly transferred competences, the bill needed two readings in both the *Assemblée Nationale* and the Senate and was again considerably amended by the Senate (Zimmermann-Steinhart 2004: 366).

By far the most controversial implementation law was the ordinary law *no. 2004–809 relative aux libertés et responsabilités locales* of 13 August 2004 (Gontcharoff 2004: 12–14) regulating the new allocation of powers (Zimmermann-Steinhart 2004: 267–8). It took over a year to get the initiated bill through parliament, after it had been controversially discussed within the government. At one point, Raffarin had to interrupt parliamentary scrutiny in order to settle conflicts within his own party. In the final vote, forced by the Prime Minister with a "guillotine motion," twenty-two members of his party nevertheless voted against the bill. In addition, Raffarin had to make important concessions to the Senate. The government proposal aimed for instance at transferring responsibility for tourism to the Regions, but the majority of the Senate succeeded in maintaining the status quo of local powers. In matters of economy, Regions achieved considerably fewer powers than originally anticipated. Apparently, the conservative Senate majority became unwilling to grant too much power once a majority of Regions came to be governed by the Socialists after the subnational elections of March 2004 (Interview F, 31 May 2010). Moreover, finally the *départements* managed to receive more powers at the expense of the Regions due to successful lobbying of their representatives in the Senate (Pasquier 2004: 17).

The bill also had to be amended considerably due to pressure from outside the parliament. The original government bill had included provisions to decentralize the responsibility for non-pedagogic educational staff. By massive strikes and demonstrations (see e.g. Davidenkoff 2003), the trade unions of the educational sector forced the government to retract this provision. Interestingly, unions had already protested against decentralization in the *Assises*, but were ignored then, which demonstrated the actual irrelevance of this procedure.

The reform process in France reveals a formal division between constitutional and normal policy. However, the actual differentiation remained limited since both policies overlapped in the predominating parliamentary procedure. Therefore, negotiations on constitutional principles always related to particular matters dealt with in legislation implementing these principles. The attempt to open the process to the public had limited effects since the *Assises* came closer to intergovernmental processes than to arenas of public deliberation. Therefore, it is not surprising that unions or civil society organizations only attracted attention by acts of protest. Under these conditions, compromises had to be found among the negotiating actors, who excluded important issues of fiscal powers and resources, although they had been on the agenda of constitutional reform. Thus, many problems that the reform addressed remained unresolved.

Since *Acte II de la decentralisation* took effect, the process of a territorial reconfiguration of the French state has continued. Between 2010 and 2015, the government took two further steps towards upgrading the regional level. In 2010, it introduced metropolitan regions, and the *Acte III de la decentralisation* passed by the legislative in December 2014 will reduce the number of Regions from twenty-two to thirteen by the beginning of 2016. These territorially consolidated Regions will gain additional responsibilities formally fulfilled by the *départments*. Thus, the French central state still responds to the pressure of regionalization, driven by cultural, social and political mobilization as well as functional imperatives of multilevel and regional governance (Pasquier 2015). Whether these reforms have come closer to a robust balance of power is still a controversial issue among experts.

4.4 A Regionalized State Confronted by Integration Problems

Integration problems in Great Britain arose during the early twentieth century, when Scottish and Welsh parties demanded more autonomy of the regions from central government in London. They turned into a critical issue of British Politics in the early 1970s and induced the first reforms changing Great Britain from a highly centralized unitary state towards a regionalized state. The problem became more pressing when the nationalist party, demanding secession of Scotland, gained votes. With the reforms analyzed in this case study, Great Britain made wide strides towards a federal territorial order (Hueglin and Fenna 2006: 22; Laffin and Thomas 1999), although with clearly asymmetrical structures. However, the term federal has been precluded from political discussions. Federalism is still a disputed or even denied concept in the UK (Laffin and Thomas 1999) and therefore not appropriate for selling a reform. Moreover, the terms devolution and federalization must be distinguished. In contrast to allocation of powers in a federation, devolution does not constitute institutional autonomy (or statehood) of subcentral governments. Devolved powers are granted (or delegated) by a government of a unitary state, which, in principle, maintains its sovereignty. In the defined areas, devolved powers can be exerted independent of central supervision or control. Additionally, devolution can indicate a transitory stage in a process of federalization or be regarded as a "slippery slope towards federalization" (Hueglin and Fenna 2006: 22). For these reasons, the case of Great Britain, as a regionalized state, fits into our comparative research design covering multilevel processes of constitutional policy.

4.4.1 *Great Britain: Devolution (1989–2006)*

In order to understand constitutional amendments concerning the territorial organization of Great Britain (Bogdanor 1999; Bulpitt 1983; Gamble 2006), two particular features need to be taken into account. One is the absence of a written document entrenching constitutional rules. The system of government is constituted by conventions or by-laws which de facto have a constitutional character. Therefore, speaking of constitutional change may be problematic, not the least due to the lack of a particular amendment procedure. Any law passed by parliament with a simple majority can amend the constitution. However, the definition problem—i.e. which decisions represent constitutional-type as opposed to regular policy-making—can be solved in the British case by focusing on those issues of constitutional reform that have also been identified in other countries. Moreover, regarding devolution, the main rules have been defined in a number of basic laws, among them the Scotland Act 1998, the Government of Wales Act 1998, the Northern Ireland Act 1998, and the Greater London Authority Act 1998 (Bogdanor 2005), all of which were clearly constitutional in nature.

The second unique aspect of the British case affects procedures of constitutional reform. The United Kingdom of Great Britain and Northern Ireland is peculiar in its asymmetrical territorial organization. Whereas England evolved as a highly centralized and unitary state, Scotland, Wales and Northern Ireland were integrated to different degrees and governed from the center in various ways. Therefore, territorial problems of these parts of the union have been dealt with in different processes. They combined in the reform project of devolution, which the Labour Party implemented after it had gained a parliamentary majority in the 1997 election. Although the constitutional reform was not designed to federalize the United Kingdom, it aimed at a new balance of power between the center, the regions and local governments. Nevertheless, it resulted from distinct processes that were not held together by any overarching concept (Flinders 2010; Mitchell 2009a).[13] The Northern Ireland Act based on the Belfast Agreement ended decades of violent conflicts. The different parts of this Agreement included an international accord of the UK with the Republic of Ireland. As this process went beyond constitutional

[13] One impetus for a constitutional reform came from Charter 88, a kind of social movement supporting a constitutional reform of the UK. Among the requests formulated in a list of basic principles was a constitutional guarantee of an equitable distribution of power between the nations of the UK and between local, regional and central government. The Charter 88 movement did not succeed in convincing the Labour Party to initiate a national constitutional reform (Erdos 2009).

policy within a multilevel government, we excluded it from this study. The other processes aiming at a reconfiguration of the territorial order of Great Britain constituted part of one reform project, but evolved separately, too, and each revealed its particular patterns.

Since the late 1980s, constitutional reform in the UK has emerged onto the agenda of politics. However, it was mainly a project of the Labour Party and the LibDems, while the Conservatives showed no interest and did not participate. In order to gain legitimacy, Labour decided to hold referendums on all major reform acts. Therefore, it had to include other parties and civil society associations in negotiations on a constitutional agreement at the regional level. Moreover, parties had to settle conflicts between their central and regional organizations. Given the different political structures in England, Scotland and Wales, and due to different pressures for reform, the whole devolution project, although meant to renovate the British territorial order, was divided into three segments.

In England, the Labour Party had intended to introduce elected regional assemblies. In line with the general approach of devolution policy, this was designed to address each region as a distinct unit. The party intended to ask "the people, region by region, to decide in a referendum whether they want directly elected regional government. Only where popular consent is established will arrangements be made for elected regional assemblies" (quoted in Mitchell 2012: 224). When in 2004 a referendum failed in the North-East region with 78 percent of citizens voting no, the process came to a halt. Only in the capital city region did the reform project of the Labour government pass a referendum, with a low turnout of 34 percent. As a consequence, the Greater London Authority is now governed by a directly elected Assembly and a directly elected mayor. The failure of devolution in the rest of England certainly shows that the "British voter remains obstinately concerned with substance rather than procedure and remains profoundly indifferent to constitutional issues" (Bogdanor 2005: 80). But it also proves that preparing a reform proposal in a party and then submitting it to a referendum is apparently a high-risk strategy. In the end, devolution in England turned into an administrative reform with the establishment of Regional Development Authorities.

Devolution in Scotland and Wales ended with significant institutional changes for these regions and, as a consequence, for the constitution of the UK. The two cases need to be analyzed separately due to their different structures, processes, dynamics and outcomes. Nonetheless, they are part of a process of constitutional change in Britain, and their outcomes have to be evaluated in relation to the stability or instability and flexibility or rigidity of its territorial order. It needs to be emphasized that devolution in Scotland and Wales has involved multilevel processes of constitutional change right from the beginning. This is a distinctive feature compared to the reforms of Statutes of the Autonomous Communities in Spain, which did not turn into multilevel processes until the regional parliaments had decided on the amendment bills. This had the inevitable effect that regional processes contributed to intensifying the integration problem, which then had to be dealt with in intergovernmental negotiations and in the Spanish parliament. In contrast, negotiation processes on devolution in Scotland and Wales addressed the integration problem of the British state immediately in relations between regional and central party organizations, although a particular regional perspective prevailed from the outset.

Despite significant changes, the British constitution is still confronted by severe problems. "Devolution has been successful as a response to particular problems of legitimacy in components of the UK. However, the unintended consequences and spillover effects of devolution were paid scant attention. Again, issues of finance and intergovernmental relations, especially financial IGR, are evidence of an absence of coherent thinking" (Mitchell 2012: 225). This summarizing assessment by James Mitchell captures the ambivalence of constitutional change in Great Britain. Notwithstanding considerable improvements and promising approaches to meet the integration problem, the reform has left significant issues unresolved. For sure, the financial dependence of Scotland on the central government and the limited powers of the Welsh Assembly constrain regionalization, and the asymmetry of the territorial organization has remained on the political agenda in London. An indication of the remaining imbalance of the territorial order is the new debate on secession in Scotland. The failed Scottish independence referendum of September 2014 did not end these debates on the "Scottish Question" (Mitchell 2014) and again made devolution a central issue of British politics.

4.4.2 *Devolution in Scotland*

The process in Scotland was in many respects different from the other devolution processes. It resulted in significant changes of the constitution, which were wider in scope and less selective despite a more ambitious agenda than devolution in other parts of Great Britain. First, Scotland is now governed by a parliament elected according to proportional rule, and an executive responsible to parliament. Legislative powers have been regionalized in a number of important areas. Yet not unlike in other reforms, the allocation of fiscal resources remained a problem, which was postponed and has still not been appropriately solved.

The reform process in Scotland lasted for eight years from 1989 to 1997[14] and passed different arenas: First, the Scottish Constitutional Convention

[14] In fact, the first Scottish Parliament was elected only in 1999 and commenced its work immediately thereafter. However, most relevant decisions were made by 1997.

(SCC) working between 1989 and 1995 constituted the focal arena, before debates moved to party politics during the election campaign and the referendum campaign (1995–7). The SCC was set up in 1989 by a pressure group of "eminent Scots" (Campaign for a Scottish Assembly 1988). It published two reports, a preliminary one in the run-up to the 1992 general election (Scottish Constitutional Convention 1990) and a final report in 1995 (Scottish Constitutional Convention 1995). The 1992 general election marked a turning point in the way the SCC worked, so that the two periods have to be considered separately (see also Mitchell 2014: 218–51).

Initially, reform discussions were restricted to the SCC. The standing orders of the Convention did not include any particular rules of negotiation. But when the members agreed on decision-making by consensus, they implicitly meant that negotiations were supposed to be deliberative (see for example reports of McFadden 1995; Wright 1997). Actually, the mode of negotiating apparently varied. Members report a much less confrontational atmosphere than they were used to from the parliament in Westminster or from local government councils (Interview GB, 18 November 2009; see also McFadden 1995). However, there is also evidence of bargaining, and the LibDems used exit threats to pursue their aims (Scottish Liberal Democrats 1990: 9–10). Most of the work was done in five committees ("working groups") focusing on the main matters of conflict. At an early stage, the SCC's working group on constitutional issues also held two public consultations based on questionnaires (Wright 1997: 125–32). The first one was sent to civil society organizations only, while in the second consultation, citizens could take part as well. Yet opinions submitted did not have any particular impact on the result.

As ambiguous as the negotiation mode was, the SCC demonstrated inclusiveness regarding issues and actors, but did not succeed in attracting all political parties. Although it intended to include all relevant groups of society and to represent a broad spectrum of opinions, it rejected from the outset a referendum on independence, which prompted the Scottish National Party (SNP) to leave the Convention. There was some debate among scholars whether all other members of the SCC were intrinsically opposed to such a referendum (Wright 1997: 42–4) or whether this was a strategic move by the Labour Party to keep the SNP out (Mitchell 2009b: 17). As a consequence, the chance for an agreement increased at the cost of legitimacy of the outcome. The Conservatives had no interest in participating right from the beginning. In contrast, organizations of employers and unions, the churches and civil society organizations sent representatives. Nonetheless, of the numerous participants, the Labour Party and the LibDems turned out to be the key actors (Lynch 1996; Mitchell 2009b: 18). In the end, the final Scotland Act (1998) shows a compromise between these parties.

Although the mission of the SCC was to find consensus on a Scottish Parliament among a wide range of Scottish opinions, an underlying purpose was to commit the only prospective pivotal player, the Labour Party, to legislate on devolution (Interviews GB, 11 November and 20 November 2009). However, rather than influencing the party through arguments, for most of the time the SCC members seemed to have anticipated the particular interests of the Scottish Labour Party, which they assumed to conform to official Labour policy at the national level. Yet on this point, they seem to have miscalculated party politics. Whereas the central party leaders Neil Kinnock and John Smith had granted the Scottish Labour Party considerable freedom (Jones 1997b: 4–5; Mitchell 2007: 485), the advent of Tony Blair as party leader changed the situation and the central Labour Party became much more involved in regional constitutional negotiations (Bradbury 2010: 2; Gamble 2006: 28), partly even overriding Scottish Labour positions. Accordingly, strategic behavior of party representatives increasingly superseded the arguing mode in negotiations.

The broad agenda confronted the participants with a number of problems and controversial issues. One set of issues was of a constitutional nature, like the entrenchment of the Scottish Parliament, the powers of the parliament, financial resources and women's rights. Others were neither of constitutional nature nor controversial, and therefore need not to be considered here. On most issues, Labour and the LibDems disagreed, with matters related to the Scottish Parliament causing the most intense disputes. The first problem was constitutional entrenchment, i.e. a guarantee that the Scottish Parliament could not be abolished by a simple majority decision of the Westminster parliament despite the undisputed UK constitutional principle of parliamentary sovereignty. Labour originally had not envisaged any entrenchment mechanisms at all, whereas the LibDems preferred legal provisions that would essentially foreclose weakening or abolishing the Scottish Parliament. Another dispute concerned the so-called "West Lothian Question,"[15] a constitutional problem resulting from the asymmetric nature of regionalization. This meant that in a nominally unitary state with a devolved Scottish (or other regional) parliament, non-Scottish MPs in the House of Commons would no longer be able to decide on devolved matters in Scotland, while Scottish MPs would still be able to decide on the same matters for the rest of the UK. On this issue, the LibDems proposed the reduction of the number of Scottish MPs in Westminster; Labour initially preferred the status quo. With regard to the future of the Secretary of State for Scotland, the LibDems argued that this

[15] The problem is named after the constituency of the Scottish (Labour) MP Tam Dalyell, who had already outlined the respective problem in the course of the failed devolution reform of the 1970s.

post would become superfluous and should be abolished; Labour, on the other hand, proposed a somewhat weaker parliament under the legislative and budgetary oversight of the Secretary of State. As to financing Scottish expenditure, Labour preferred the status quo, i.e. a block grant, plus a power to vary the rate of income tax; the LibDems, in contrast, demanded assigned revenues. Concerning legislative powers, Labour had originally proposed lists of enumerated powers for both the national and the Scottish level, leaving the question of the residual power open. The LibDems demanded a residual power for the Scottish Parliament and a conclusive list defining powers for the national level ("retained competences").

By far the most controversial issues were the voting system and, in conjunction with this, problems of gender balance, as well as the number of members of the Scottish Parliament (MSPs). Initially, Labour officially wanted to apply the majority system used for elections in the House of Commons (first past the post). However, the party soon realized that this position was both untenable and imprudent (Brand et al. 1994: 225). The LibDems strongly argued for proportional representation, and especially for the Single Transferable Vote. With the Additional Member System, under which a certain number of candidates would be elected according to the majority system and a certain number from regional lists, the parties found a compromise quite early. In contrast, the issues of gender equality and the number of seats remained unresolved and controversial for a long time. With regard to the former, Labour came to support statutory provisions (Wright 1997: 214). The LibDems strongly opposed these as undemocratic. With regard to the number of seats, Labour preferred 144 whereas the LibDems proposed 175. Gender balance and local government reform were examples of issues pushed onto the agenda by lobby groups within and outside the Labour Party (Mitchell 2009b: 19). Local councils and their umbrella organization COSLA successfully tried to secure extensive autonomy for local government. Compared to gender balance, this issue did not appear particularly controversial.

The Convention did not find an agreement between Labour and the LibDems. The first report, published in 1990 (Scottish Constitutional Convention 1990), only contained rather vague provisions. The Scottish Parliament was to be entrenched in a way so that changing the new status quo would require the consent of both levels of government. The report also contained lists of competences for both levels but avoided addressing the question of residual power. With regard to finance, the parliament was to receive assigned revenues and a narrow but not yet defined power to vary the income tax rate. In its section on the voting system, the report only formulated a number of principles, but made clear that the majority system would not be (at least not exclusively) applied. Gender equality was proclaimed as a goal. All other controversial issues outlined above were not even mentioned. In the wake of the publication, the SCC continued without producing further results, waiting for the next election to come.

The role of the SCC changed after the general election of 1992. The SCC members had expected Labour to win (McFadden 1995: 220; Mitchell 2009b: 23). When this did not occur, the party's position still provided a point of reference for the Convention, but the party's organization ceased to be an effective negotiation arena. Instead, the SCC set up an independent Constitutional Commission of non-partisan members to find a solution for the open questions outlined above. This commission met twelve times during the years 1993 to 1994, with sessions devoted to gaining oral and written opinions and to deliberating disputed issues. Since the members had no primary partisan interests, they tended towards arguing rather than bargaining. Nevertheless, the Commission's report was not fully endorsed by the SCC members, most of whom could not agree to the proposals on gender equality, on the size of the Scottish Parliament and details of the voting system (Mitchell 2009b: 23).

Arguably, against the backdrop of the next general election, the regional process turned into a nested game (Tsebelis 1990) with the electoral campaign and parties on the national level, in particular Labour, constituting a second arena. Both Labour and the LibDems now had an incentive to compromise. The British Labour Party took a much greater interest in the proceedings in Scotland and even altered negotiation results unilaterally. With increasing involvement of their respective national organizations, the two parties finally reached compromises in bilateral negotiations on the issues of gender balance and the size of the Scottish Parliament. As regards the former, they signed a self-binding "electoral contract" according to which they would distribute male and female candidates equally to winnable seats and recommend that the other parties act accordingly. Concerning the size of the parliament, they finally agreed on 129 seats (MacWhirter 1995: 25).

The financial scheme for the Scottish Parliament was defined after a unilateral decision initiated and pushed through by Tony Blair, the leader of the British Labour Party. He wanted his party to shed its traditional tax-and-spend image at a time when the Conservatives campaigned against devolution, arguing that the establishment of a Scottish Parliament would inevitably lead to rising taxes (Denver 2002: 828). Hence, Blair pushed through his party's original proposal, i.e. a block grant plus a power to vary the rate on income tax of up to three percent. It was also a unilateral decision of the Labour Party to solve the entrenchment problem by passing a "declaration of intent" of the Westminster parliament before deciding on the Scotland Act, and not to include respective provisions in the Act (Wright 1997: 220).

In the course of 1995, all controversial issues were to be be resolved so that the SCC's final report could be published on 17 October 1995. Like the first one, this report spelled out the main principles and basic rules for devolution in Scotland and left the elaboration of precise legal provisions to the central government. After the publication of the SCC's final report and in the run-up to the 1997 general election, Tony Blair decided to hold a pre-legislative referendum. It was agreed that the referendum campaign should be organized across party lines. There was even a consensus between Labour and the LibDems that the SNP should join. In order to facilitate cooperation, a separate organization, Scotland Forward, was established as a neutral arena for the campaign (Jones 1997a: 5). In the course of the referendum campaign, the White Paper "Scotland's Parliament" (Secretary of State for Scotland 1997) was published. It was mainly based on the SCC final report (Gay 1998: 13), but provided further details. Several of these ran counter to some of the SCC members' initial preferences. The LibDems for instance had explicitly demanded that abortion legislation should be devolved as part of health policy (Scottish Liberal Democrats 1990: 13), but the White Paper explicitly stated that the national government would retain this power. It also included a rather vague section on intergovernmental relations, an issue hitherto not figured prominently and retrospectively considered the weakest point of the devolution settlement (Jeffery and Wincott 2006: 8).

In the referendum, 74.3 percent of voters supported the reform, with turnout of 60.4 percent. The British parliament then enacted the devolution package thus overwhelmingly approved into law. At this last stage, the parliamentary procedure took place without any noteworthy impediments. In the following years, the Scottish Parliament developed into an effective legislative institution (Bradbury and Mitchell 2002: 300). However, fiscal powers have remained a matter of dispute, as have the precise interpretation of powers of the Scottish Parliament and intergovernmental relations. In particular, the frustration in Scotland on fiscal dependence from the government in London in spite of a strong regional economic base and the still predominating unitary conception of the state in England gave rise to new demands for independence (Keating 2009).

4.4.3 *Devolution in Wales*

Devolution in Wales had fewer effects than the Scottish process, and it has not met expectations in the region. The Welsh process started with negotiations on the original Government of Wales Act (1998), which was revised in 2006. The elected assembly introduced by a referendum holds administrative powers, and can legislate only in matters explicitly delegated by the central government. The powers of regional institutions have been extended, but are still considerably limited compared to those decentralized to the Scottish Parliament and executive.

At the outset of the reform process in the late 1980s, the Welsh Labour Party had no detailed plan for setting up an elected Assembly. The sealed-off nature of the negotiations made it neither possible nor necessary for the participants to develop a comprehensive constitutional agenda and detailed proposals (Commission on the Powers and Electoral Arrangements of the National Assembly for Wales 2004; Interview GB, 3 December 2009). Thus, discussion was restricted to four issues with constitutional implications: finance, legislative powers, the mode of election and the structure of the Welsh Assembly.

With regard to finance, the participants settled on a block grant at an early stage. Proposals for the powers of the Assembly varied between a transfer of secondary legislative powers that the Welsh Office had acquired over several decades, or primary legislative powers. However, the concept of primary legislative powers remained somewhat vague, as the question of the residual power never arose. The discussion on the electoral system was similarly vague with opponents of devolution arguing for the traditional first-past-the-post system and supporters for some form of proportional representation. As to the Assembly, supporters of devolution favored a parliament with legislative functions separated from the executive, while opponents proposed a kind of local council without formal separation of legislative and executive functions.

The most powerful political actor in Wales at that time, the Welsh Labour Party, managed to contain negotiations within its lines. This way, it could control controversial debates, which split and damaged the party during a previous devolution attempt in the 1970s (Rawlings 2003: 28–32; Stolz 1999: 227). Within the party, a special "Policy Commission" was set up to draft plans for an elected Assembly for Wales. The Commission's official mandate was to collect evidence from the Welsh public (Interview GB, 10 November 2009), but retrospective reports from Commission members suggest that the true aim was to keep the process within the party (Interviews GB, 2 and 3 December 2009). It collected opinions by sending out a questionnaire and by holding public meetings, which were rather poorly organized and attracted limited participation (Osmond 1995: 35). The consultation procedure had hardly any impact on the first report of the Commission, titled "Shaping the Vision" (Wales Labour Party 1995). Interventions from the national level of the party were frequent and supported opponents of a far-reaching devolution. Negotiations took place in the bargaining mode and were rather tense (Bradbury 2010: 9; Morgan and Mungham 2000: 99–100; Interview GB, 3 December 2009). The Commission finally suggested an assembly based on the local government model, elected according to majority rule, financed by a block grant and responsible for secondary legislative powers, which so far had been fulfilled by the Welsh Office.

Those members of the WLP who were in favor of a much stronger Assembly saw an opportunity to revise this proposal, when Tony Blair announced the consultative, pre-legislative referendum for the Scottish Parliament. The Shadow Secretary of State for Wales, Ron Davies, an ardent supporter of devolution, convinced Blair to also hold a referendum for Wales. Davis assumed that the referendum would only have a positive result, if voters perceived the Assembly as a significant and legitimate institution, with genuine legislative powers and proportional representation. He deemed these elements essential in order to achieve a cross-party referendum campaign including Plaid Cymru. To this end, Davies held informal contacts to this second biggest party in Wales (Bradbury 2010: 11–12; Interview GB, 3 December 2009).

At the same time, the Labour Party and the LibDems were negotiating on a coalition government at the central level of government, which they deemed a likely outcome of the forthcoming elections. The prospective cross-party referendum campaign made devolution an issue on the agenda of these negotiations. Thus, Davies could now negotiate in London and effectively sideline devolution opponents in Wales. When the Policy Commission was reconvened in order to reconsider the electoral provisions (Bradbury 1998: 138), Labour's actual proposal (Wales Labour Party 1997) was a compromise between Labour and the LibDems on the central level. Labour's devolution proposal finally included legislative powers for the prospective assembly to alter or repeal acts of the national parliament if they include a respective provision. These powers resulted from a compromise between Davies and his opponents in the Welsh Labour Party and, more importantly, Tony Blair. In the course of the preparation of the devolution legislation, Ron Davies made various attempts to improve the institutional structure, all focusing on separating the legislative and the executive powers. The effect, however, was minimal, as at this stage only details could be changed (Jones 2000: 190–2; Thomas 1999: 299; Trench 2008: 12).

The Government of Wales Act (1998) came into effect after a narrow majority of 50.3 percent had voted for the assembly in the referendum, with a turnout of 50.1 percent, and after the parliament had passed the bill. However, the established structures turned out to be almost unworkable (see for example Bradbury and Mitchell 2002; McAllister 2000; Rawlings 2003; Trench 2008: 12–13). In sum, there was a great deal of uncertainty on all sides regarding the exact responsibilities and powers of the Assembly. Instead of constituting an effective and democratic institution, the Government of Wales Act established the smallest common denominator of preferences expressed by Labour devolution supporters and sceptics (Rawlings 1998: 473).

While limited in its immediate results, the reform induced further efforts to remedy its deficits. The first explicit attempt to revise the devolution settlement was undertaken after the first Labour minority government broke down in Wales and the Welsh Labour Party formed a coalition with the Welsh Liberal Democrats. The coalition established an independent commission to elaborate recommendations for the electoral system and the legislative competences of the Assembly (McAllister 1999, 2005a, 2005b). The Commission, which came to be known as the "Richard Commission" after its chair Lord Richard, consisted of ten members. The chair was appointed by the First Minister, four more members were nominated by all four parties in the Assembly, and another five were selected in a public recruitment procedure. The Commission held a number of seminar style meetings as well as public hearings, through which it gathered opinions from about 150 participants. The negotiations within the Commission have been described as deliberative. They resulted in recommendations including a clear separation of the executive and the legislative functions, primary legislative powers like in Scotland (i.e. with reserved matters for the British parliament and a residual power for the regional parliament), an extension of the Assembly by twenty seats, and the use of the Single Transferable Vote procedure for elections.

The immediate impact of the Commission's work was limited once the governing coalition, which had set it up, lost power in 2004. The 2003 general Assembly election had led to a Labour government, which was no longer interested in the Commission's report. However, the deficits of the original Government of Wales Act (1998) were obvious and the report of the Richard Commission was well received by the interested public and by academic observers, which revived internal debates in the Welsh Labour Party. These renewed discussions culminated in a revised Government of Wales Act in 2006. The bill was largely drafted in the Welsh Office in London, but with a certain amount of consultation of the Welsh Assembly (Trench 2008: 19–20). The most important points of this Act were a separation of executive and legislative functions, a complex reorganization of the Assembly's legislative powers, and an announcement of a referendum on the question of the transfer of primary legislative powers for twenty specific matters from the central level to Wales. In the referendum held in March 2011 a majority of voters adopted the reform extending legislative powers to all devolved matters. In 2014, the House of Commons passed another Wales Act delegating limited fiscal powers and, subject to approval by referendum, the power to vary income tax rates.

4.4.4 *Patterns of Devolution*

Considering the process of constitutional policy, devolution in Great Britain revealed a variety of facets. Like constitutional change in Spain, different processes combined to create the outcome, a redistribution of power and institutional reforms differing between regions. The variety of these processes was even greater than in the Spanish case. Nonetheless, some basic features can be highlighted as those mainly having influenced the overall outcome.

First, constitutional policy in the UK is procedurally identical with normal policy. Constitutional negotiations were never clearly separated from party politics, and they could not be protected from being influenced by electoral campaigns. This applies even for the Scottish Constitutional Convention. Not unlike the Austrian Convention, it became dominated by the leading parties. While the quality of deliberations in this arena should not be underrated, not the least after an independent committee had been established, these processes only had impacts on peripheral issues (Fischer-Hotzel 2013: 71–5), while in general the participants always had to take into account the position of the Labour Party. Therefore, all attempts to differentiate arenas and to change from party political bargaining to arguing turned out futile.

Second, in all devolution processes, the extensive use of consultation with citizens and civil society is noteworthy. However, a genuine consociational arena, where constitutional issues could have been deliberated in public and which initiated a momentum for the negotiation process, never existed. The negotiating parties took written opinions or statements in hearings as information. Furthermore, limited to the regional level, these consultations could hardly influence party political communications across levels, which proved essential for determining the outcome.

Third, what is particularly striking in this case, not unlike in Spain, is the lack of public debates at the central level. The parliament in London served as the legislator like in normal policies. Members of parliament debated the constitutional project of the Labour government, but they never considered it as an integrative reform and instead dealt with the different devolution acts related to the parts of the country separately.

Fourth, party politics clearly shaped negotiation processes, with bargaining and compromising between competing parties and British and regional party levels determining the agreements. The overlap of negotiations and party politics was particularly obvious in the reform processes concerning Wales and England, where in public devolution evidently was perceived as a Labour project. In consequence, election campaigns and elections significantly affected constitutional negotiations.

Fifth, despite ending with majorities, the referendums did not necessarily demonstrate a broad consensus for the reform, given the comparatively low turnout rates. Moreover, campaigns intensified party politics, instead of fostering deliberation. Voters arguably decided according to their party political preferences rather than according to their evaluation of the constitutional reform (Hornig 2011: 142). More than substantive reform proposals, the willingness for political change in the country after eighteen years of conservative hegemony might explain the positive results of the pre-legislative referendums in 1997. It is therefore unsurprising that the legitimacy of devolution continues to be disputed (Mitchell 2012: 226).

Lacking a state-wide constitutional process, reforms responded to particular demands from regions, but could not effectively cope with the integration problems of the British state. At no point in the process were the consequences of an asymmetric devolution of powers really addressed, apart from debates in the central parliament and discussions among experts. Devolution never became an integral part of constitutional reform at the central level. It ended as a fragmented and unfinished project.

4.5 Summary

The nine reform processes illustrated above arrived at widely different results. As outlined in Chapter 2, the results of the constitutional negotiations can be evaluated according to the scope of a reform and their effects on the balance of power in a multilevel government. For purpose of the operationalization of these evaluation standards, we defined the following criteria to distinguish outcomes: (1) the scope of the intended reform according to the significance and number of issues under revision; (2) the content of agreements compared to the original agenda, indicating the selectivity in dealing with issues at stake; and (3) the direction of change in relation to destabilizing dynamics of multilevel structures, indicating whether a reform promises to have stabilizing effects or whether it threatens to bring about more instability. Moreover, considering the robustness of an achieved or maintained balance of power, we assess (4) whether a reform increases or decreases the rigidity of a constitution. We indicate an increase of rigidity, if deadlock situations in constitutional policy become more likely or if constitutional rules become more detailed.

As regards the scope of reforms, most projects of constitutional amendment had been launched with high ambitions. They aimed at a significant revision and reorganization of territorial structures of government. As somewhat of an exception, in Belgium and France a limited number of powers and a modest change of the fiscal relations between central, regional and local governments were on the reform agenda when the constitutional negotiations started. In all other cases, though to different degrees, the primary matters of negotiation were the extension of rights of regional governments to decide autonomously on their affairs, the appropriate representation of regional governments at the central level, the decentralization of legislative and administrative powers, and constitutional provisions for a redistribution of fiscal resources.

Given the limited agendas observed in Belgium and in France, the final results that had been achieved revealed that matters were dealt with in a comprehensive way in both cases. In Germany, the reform also amounted to rather modest changes, but there was a considerably higher selectivity compared to the wider agenda. The same applies to Austria, even with regard to the discussion in the Convention. In contrast, the negotiated agreements elicited significant changes in Switzerland, Canada and Italy, where the negotiated agreements covered most issues raised in a rather wide-ranging agenda. In Spain, regional reforms resulted in far-reaching and comprehensive changes, but only part of them had been transformed into an amendment of the Spanish constitution due to the deep conflict between parties. In Great Britain, only devolution in Scotland brought about significant changes along the lines defined in the agenda, while changes in Wales remained more selective and exceptionally limited in England.

In Canada, Great Britain, Austria, Germany and Italy, institutional reforms to enhance representation of citizens or regions appeared on the agenda, but corresponding changes only prevailed in Scotland and Wales, where devolution laws introduced elected regional assemblies. The Canadian Charlottetown Accord included a proposal for a reformed Senate, while the reforms of second chambers representing regions did not rank high on the agenda in the other three countries and eventually were excluded from reform proposals. Procedures of intergovernmental relations were explicitly discussed in Switzerland, Canada and Italy, and, as a minor issue, in Great Britain and in Spain (in particular in Andalusia).

The reallocation of legislative powers was a central matter of constitutional negotiations in all cases. Compared to intentions, negotiations in Germany and Austria again ended with rather moderate and selective changes. In Switzerland and Italy, not all powers originally dealt with were reallocated, but the outcomes nevertheless showed more than incremental adjustments. In Canada, France and Belgium, all powers under review were changed. In Great Britain, there were again variations between the different devolution processes, and in Spain, far-reaching demands for decentralization were curtailed in intergovernmental and parliamentary negotiations at the central level.

Most, though not all, reforms dealt with fiscal federalism (fiscal powers, vertical fiscal balance and horizontal equalization). In Switzerland, this constituted the primary topic. It was also an important issue in Germany, Belgium, France, Italy and—as a topic with lower priority—in Austria, Great Britain and Spain. Only in Canada did negotiations hardly address fiscal aspects of federalism beyond the specific issue of federal spending power. Here, fiscal imbalance had been a matter of continuous debate between the federal and provincial governments (Lecours and Beland 2013). Not surprisingly, all these cases demonstrated that fiscal federalism appeared to be the most difficult reform subject. This is illustrated by the fact that many amendments envisaged in constitutional negotiations were either excluded or postponed in the final agreements, if not already in negotiation processes. Switzerland's NFA is a clear exception in this regard. In Austria, the *Länder*

In Belgium and Spain, changes increased the powers of regional governments and undermined the integrative policies at the center. In both countries, constitutional reform processes favored centrifugal dynamics, instead of strengthening forces that hold the federation together. Governments in both countries also proved unable to solve the constitutional problems on the agenda, although the government of Belgium in 2011 ended a decade of deadlock with a further state reform. Yet basic problems of the federation remained unresolved (Deschouwer and Reuchamps 2013). The Spanish federation slipped into an impasse when the Constitutional Court strengthened the central constitution against the ever-increasing claims of the ACs to extend their powers. Meanwhile, the situation has become more difficult, in particular due to the serious fiscal problems and imbalances of the country, which remained despite the 2009 reform. Disintegrative forces, driven by distinct cultures, have been invigorated due to economic disparities. Yet the Spanish federal system is still in flux and thus flexible with integrative forces (the central government, integrated parties, the Spanish Constitutional Court) counterbalancing centrifugal tendencies. In Belgium, the latter have evolved nearly unfettered, with only the social partners at the central level constituting an integrative force. Here constitutional rigidity due to political structures compensates to a certain extent disintegration.

Table 4.2 (see p. 68) summarizes our evaluation of the outcomes of constitutional negotiations. The qualifications refer to the effects of the negotiation results in the constitutional policy processes covered in the case studies. Although the tentative assessments of stability or instability and flexibility or rigidity/deadlock take into account the dynamics of the territorial structures in the countries, they are not meant to give a complete view of the state of the federal or regionalized political systems. Instability in states with integration problems does not mean that secession is always imminent.

A systematic explanation of these outcomes will be provided in Chapter 7. However, by summarizing the case studies, we shall draw some tentative comparative interpretations at this point.

Obviously, the two successful constitutional negotiation processes in Switzerland and in Canada stand out due to their differentiated structure.

- In both cases, constitutional policy was clearly separated from normal policy. Whereas in Canada, this had to do with the relevance of the constitutional conflict in politics and society, which the process reflected, in Switzerland it was achieved by a particular organization of the process.
- Even more remarkable, compared to the other cases, was the differentiation of arenas and sequences. Intergovernmental negotiations in the executive, parliamentary negotiations and consociational negotiations took place in distinct institutional contexts, linked by processes in

which results of the negotiations in individual arenas were communicated into other arenas, either by written reports or by overlapping memberships. In Canada, these arenas worked more or less simultaneously, and the sequence that can be observed here led to an increasing closure of the process towards intergovernmental negotiations. In Switzerland, the sequence opened the process, which started in the executive, to consultation with civil society groups, to parliament and to the public. This way, the executive was able to control the agenda in order to maintain the coherence of the reform project. In Canada, consultation with civil society extended the agenda, thus giving new impulses for innovation, but also raising new conflicts.

- Both reform processes were also unique in that they dealt with constitutional principles and constitutional rules. In Canada, they appeared as issues in all arenas of negotiations, but the distinction between principles and institutional rules was obvious. In Switzerland, the organization of the negotiation process in two phases clearly separated negotiations on principles from negotiation on rules.
- Finally, the ratification procedures ruled out that actors in negotiations followed positions of veto-players. Therefore, negotiations were hardly influenced by party competition or election campaigns. Ratification in a referendum (or in all parliaments, as would have been necessary in Canada, had the consultative referendum ended with a majority for the Accord) could only be influenced by selling the amendment proposal with good reasons. In this regard, Canadian politics failed in the referendum campaign, while the process proved successful in Switzerland.

Processes in all other cases turned out less differentiated compared to those observed in Canada and Switzerland. The establishment of conventions or commissions aimed at a distinction between normal and constitutional policy. However, in the actual negotiations, this institutional setting never had the intended effects, albeit for different reasons.

Conventions were set up in two cases: in Austria and at the regional level in Scotland. These forums allowed representatives of civil society and experts to participate in the process. Both examples, however, reveal that parties exploited this particular constitutional arena, arguably because conventions symbolize the salience of constitutional policy. The Scottish Constitutional Convention managed to shield negotiations against party politics when it set up an independent committee. However, in doing so, it reduced the participation of other actors at once. Moreover, party conflicts from the beginning provoked the Scottish nationalists to leave the Convention and the Conservatives to refrain outright from participating. In Austria, the Convention turned from the intended arena of deliberation among a plurality of representatives into a venue for party politics. The dualist party system in both cases may have contributed to this development, and the confrontation in Austria was certainly an extreme consequence. However, in view of the other cases, it is unlikely that a convention favors arguing instead of party political bargaining.[16] Without differentiation of the institutional setting, representatives of civil society can hardly change the negotiation modes of party politics.

The concentration of constitutional negotiations in commissions or parliamentary committees no less reduces the chances for arguing processes. In Germany and France, intergovernmental bargaining explains the outcome of rather ineffective negotiations. They mostly resembled the usual patterns of policy-making in both countries, though with some differences such as the establishment of the Joint Commission of the *Bundestag* and the *Bundesrat* in Germany and the organization of the *Assises* in France, which instituted a venue for interest organizations to participate in consultation. Nevertheless, in both cases these institutions only formalized intergovernmental bargaining, which normally occurs in informal circles. In Germany and France, constitutional negotiations gave way to bureaucratic politics, as the manner in which they were organized provided plenty of opportunities for special administrations to influence the negotiations. This was in particular the case in Germany.

The Italian reform was negotiated according to the usual legislative practice. However, it built on the work of an earlier bicameral committee, an institution that in many aspects resembled the German Joint Commission. This sequential development of the decentralization reform explains the scope of the reform. But compromises in bargaining processes produced the same result as in Germany; a rather detailed and inflexible allocation of powers without an appropriated amendment of fiscal relations between central government and the regions. The role of subnational governments and, accordingly, intergovernmental bargaining, was less visible in Italy than in Germany or France, but the party system reflected similar conflicts. A parliamentary ratification according to the rules in Germany would probably have failed in Italy, where the referendum saved the reform.

In Belgium, Great Britain and Spain, party politics was the main arena of constitutional negotiations. Accordingly, constitutional and normal politics were blended. Parties controlled the agenda and formulated positions; they made deals and settled compromises in bargaining; finally, they organized majorities for ratification in parliaments. In all three countries, regional

[16] The Conventions of the European Union apparently are exceptional (Closa 2004; Göler 2006; Magnette and Nicolaïdis 2004). This can be explained by the limited impact of parties at the European level and the highly pluralist party system that has evolved.

governments introduced agendas and reform proposals in processes which more or less included civil society, but again were clearly dominated by parties. These initiatives from below, typical for federal or regionalized states with integration problems, put pressure on the central government and generated intense conflicts on the distribution of decision-making or participation rights and on the reallocation of powers and resources between levels of government. These conflicts translated into party conflicts, in Great Britain and Spain between the parties of the center-left and the conservative camp, in Belgium between the different parties of the regions. In Great Britain and Spain, the governing party or coalition could pass the reform with its majority in parliament, while in Belgium regional parties concluded package deals at the cost of the central government. In all three cases, the outcome of bargaining processes reflected power relations in party politics. Under these conditions, neither was it possible to achieve a consensus on the reform, nor did the reform contribute to a territorial reintegration of the political system.

Regarding the structure of constitutional negotiations, we find no distinctive pattern typical for either states with integration problems or states with performance problems. This is not surprising, considering the impact of the existing institutional framework of political systems and the complexity of agendas. Nonetheless, the case studies call attention to two important aspects.

First, processes including civil society in a meaningful way can set innovative impulses and counter the trend towards incremental changes caused by intergovernmental bargaining or by confrontation in party politics. In divided societies, participation of special interests groups can also increase the intensity of conflicts and tensions, if consultation lacks proper management, as can be observed in the Canadian case. In integrated societies, this risk is low. Here, consultation and consociational patterns of constitutional policy allow reform actors to convince societal groups to support a reform. Likewise, these procedures or forums express conflicts, which then can be managed in negotiations. These findings confirm the assumptions that arena differentiation is an important condition for effective constitutional negotiations, since it contributes to conflict containment, preventing disputes from accumulating.

Second, redistributive conflicts apparently can be solved if actors differentiate between principles and rules, and decide on principles under a "veil of ignorance" (Rawls 1999) before they determine rules on the allocation of powers and resources. However, in cases of value conflicts arising in divided societies, it is unlikely that actors come to an agreement on principles, which here regularly express different concepts of a political system, different weighting of individual and group rights, or diverging visions of ways of life to be supported by government. In this case, the separation of negotiations on principles and negotiations on rules is no less relevant, in particular since constitutional policy in multilevel governments is always framed as a process of redistribution. However, as the Canadian case indicates, it might be necessary to acknowledge the divergent opinions on values or principles and leave the conflict in abeyance in order to search for pragmatic ways on how to implement a constitutional *modus vivendi* in practical policy-making. This was one of the results the Charlottetown process has brought about in Canada, and this is one of the reasons why it can be categorized as fairly effective.

5

Ratification and Ratification Failure: The Impact of Amendment Rules

(*with Jörg Kemmerzell and Bettina Petersohn*)

Successful negotiations on constitutional reforms result in an agreement among negotiating partners reflecting their interests in one way or the other. Such agreements can express compromises or package deals as well as decisions by consensus. As illustrated in the previous chapter, not every negotiating partner feels committed to supporting an agreement on amendment proposals and not every member of a political party or interest group rallies behind an accord. Even in cases of successful negotiations, conflicts may resurface during ratification processes, which are to translate outcomes of constitutional negotiations into law. Formal procedures of constitutional amendment in legislatures often require qualified majorities, which have to include members from the parliamentary opposition. Moreover, ratification procedures may span over different levels of government or include a regional or state-wide referendum. In parliamentary debates or in referendum campaigns, new disputes can arise, although the proposal for a constitutional amendment cannot be revised to a substantive extent.

The fate of ratification is affected by the number and type of effective veto-players, which can be derived from the formal constitutional amendment rules. However, according to the theoretical approach outlined in Chapter 2, these actors having the right to ratify a constitutional amendment or reject it decide under particular institutional conditions. Therefore, beyond the number, preferences and internal coherence of veto-players, their effective impact on constitutional policy has to be considered too. It is the coupling between the arenas of negotiation and ratification that also influences the probability that negotiated amendment proposals will be ratified, either because negotiators can anticipate vetoes or because they control the ratification process. Bearing these assumptions in mind, we will subsequently adopt central concepts of the veto-player theory in order to distinguish between varying rules of ratification and to theorize about the consequences of different degrees of arena coupling.

Subsequently, ratification results in our selected cases are analyzed with regard to the formal ratification procedures, the types of veto-players and the coupling of negotiation and ratification during a reform process. As indicated in the previous chapter, it is less the immediate effect of amendment rules on ratification decisions that explains the outcome of constitutional reform, but the indirect impact of these rules on constitutional negotiations. Actors consider ratification requirements during negotiations on amendment proposals. This becomes obvious, when they compromise on contested issues and change or drop aspects of a reform agenda in anticipation of expected vetoes in formal decision-making. Thus, formal hurdles of ratification also have an impact on the negotiations of constitutional reforms, and due to the higher number and different types of veto-players rather in federal systems than in unitary states. We will examine this impact in this chapter before drawing conclusions on the relevance of the ratification for the results of federal constitutional reform.

5.1 Rules of Constitutional Amendment and Veto-players

As a rule, changing the constitution requires higher thresholds of consent than changes to ordinary laws. These hurdles are established to protect the constitution from being exploited for short-term political interests of incumbent governments and thus to increase constitutional stability. Under the label of "constitutional rigidity," several authors have constructed indices measuring the difficulty of constitutional amendment in democracies based on these hurdles (see also Lijphart 2012: 206–11; Lorenz 2005; Lutz 1994). If only a parliamentary vote with simple majority is required, for example, constitutional rigidity is considered low, then changes of a significant scope can be expected. Other rules requiring qualified majorities, votes in two legislative chambers or regional parliaments, a re-election of parliament, or a popular referendum increase the rigidity according to these indices.

The procedures of ratifying a constitutional reform constitute certain actors as veto-players, thereby determining whose consent is required for a draft of an amendment to become part of the constitutional law. With regard to Tsebelis' veto-player approach, we can distinguish between institutional and partisan veto-players (Tsebelis 2002: 19). The power of institutional veto-players is vested in formal requirements while partisan veto-players' power depends on specific political situations, e.g. the actual distribution of votes and a party's ability to control decisions. Rules of constitutional amendment usually require cross-party agreement and give individual parties a particularly strong position. In case of contested reform agendas, an increase in the number of veto-players can raise the complexity of the reform process and potentially cause deadlock situations during the negotiation phases or in ratification of amendment proposals. According to Tsebelis, the "winset of the status quo" regularly decreases with the number of veto-players, and, consequently, the possibility of meaningful institutional reform should diminish. Moreover, since parties forming the opposition in a majority democracy regularly need to support a constitutional amendment, ideological distance between veto-players tends to be high. If second chambers represent regional interest, we find a strong institutional veto-player with a low degree of internal cohesion. These additional conditions should reduce the probability of change. However, empirical studies have convincingly demonstrated that a high number of veto-players does not generally reduce the likelihood of constitutional reforms (Lorenz 2004, 2011), but that institutional constraints due to ratification rules may pose obstacles for the reform success if matters are contested among negotiating partners.

We assume that rules of amendment affect political actors' opportunities to shape the outcome of territorial constitutional reforms. While those participating in constitutional negotiations play a constructive role, veto-players in the ratification process can only respond to an amendment proposal by endorsing or rejecting it. This veto power is basically negative. Consequently, negotiators try to include veto-players and opponents of the reform in order to find a compromise prior to ratification, or they anticipate potential vetoes. On the other hand, veto-players' decision is reduced to a choice between two alternatives, i.e. adopting a proposal or maintaining the status quo. Political actors with veto power are aware of the possible political damages that may result from a failure to ratify a constitutional reform. Under this condition, a limited change is often regarded as better than no change at all. If reactions of veto-players are evident or if their preferences can be influenced, the probability of successful ratification can be increased by adjusting the proposal or by communicating convincing reasons for a reform. By this, amendment rules do not only determine the procedures of ratification but also have an impact on negotiating constitutional reforms and processes of consultation.

Ratification rules can be categorized according to the institutions and levels of government involved in the passage of constitutional law. The least complex formal-institutional setting for ratification is a single-chamber parliamentary system. If a governing party attains the majority required to approve a reform bill, it represents the only effective partisan veto-player. This is likely to occur in the rare cases of a democracy where a simple majority is sufficient to pass a constitutional amendment. Accordingly, constitutional negotiations usually take place in the appropriate policy-making bodies of the governing party, as we described for devolution in Great Britain. In most countries, the number of veto-players rises with additional institutional or partisan actors entitled to participate in decision-making processes. If a coalition government is in charge or if the assent of opposition parties is necessary to achieve qualified majorities, the number of partisan veto-players increases according to the number of partners required to pass the amendment law, while there is still just one institutional veto-player. In a two-chamber parliamentary system, with the second chamber holding equal power, reform bills regularly have to meet similar majorities in both chambers. While two institutional veto-players exist in this case, it may be possible that the same party or majority controls both chambers. Consequently, one partisan veto-player may absorb the two institutional veto-players if a vertically integrated party system exists (Thorlakson 2009). If a party system remains vertically disintegrated, parties of the same camp may nevertheless emphasize different territorial interests in a reallocation of powers, and the institutional veto-player is not absorbed under these conditions.

Similarly, the complexity of the ratification process intensifies with additional institutional veto-players. For example, a president in a presidential system may hold a veto power with regard to constitutional amendments. More common, and intensely debated in the literature, is the inclusion of the people in constituent assemblies or by means of popular referendums (Elster 1998; Tierney 2014). A popular, state-wide referendum makes ratification of a constitutional reform less predictable, but adds legitimacy to a reform project. Additionally, the number of veto-players further increases if legislative assemblies of subnational units have to agree to a reform in addition to the federal or central parliament. Like in the case of the two-chamber parliamentary system described above, congruent majorities in all parliaments involved in ratification can absorb those additional institutional veto-players, yet this is less likely than in a two-chamber system. Approval by regional referendums can form an additional hurdle based on special provisions in the constitutions of subnational entities. As this short categorization of ratification procedures already indicates, each of these options has its advantages as well as pitfalls with regard to legitimacy of the result or the probability of passing a reform bill.

5.2 Coupling of Constitutional Negotiation and Ratification

As explained above, the fate of constitutional reform not only depends on amendment rules but also on the way the two stages of negotiation and ratification are linked. In order to distinguish between different degrees of coupling we can refer to the relative dependence or autonomy of veto-players at the ratification stage. Apart from the common distinction between partisan and institutional veto-players, we can specify them further as *controlled* or *independent* veto-players. We define those veto-players as controlled whose behavior can be anticipated during the negotiations and who likely support their representatives in negotiations. In contrast, decisions of independent veto-players can be influenced, but not anticipated. Based on this distinction, we assume that the higher the number of controlled veto-players, the more entangled the negotiations will be in the ratification stage. Including these veto-players in the negotiations and adapting proposals to their needs or interests can ensure their approval and ratification. While the success of the overall reform process is supposed to be higher, the veto-players also gain stronger influence on negotiation results.

Initially, we can identify two factors accounting for the predominance of either controlled or independent veto-players. First, popular referendums constitute the "people" as an independent veto-player which is per se not entirely controlled or absorbed by partisan veto-players. A popular referendum adds to the legitimacy of a constitutional reform according to the idea that a constitution depends on the will of the sovereign people (Tierney 2014; Tully 1995). Usually, a government and its majority in parliament initiate a referendum with the explicit claim to hear the voice of the people and accept a majority vote even in case of a legally non-binding, consultative referendum. Studies of referendum results have demonstrated that the more parties are supportive of a reform and campaign in favor of it, the more likely a referendum will pass (Hornig 2011). Nevertheless, there is no guarantee for a majority in a popular vote even if the majority of parties campaigns in favor of a reform. Second, characteristics of the party system provide crucial elements of control. This becomes particularly relevant if second chambers representing subnational territories or subnational parliaments take part in ratification. Congruence of government coalitions at the different levels or a strong vertical integration of state-wide parties and party systems offer more opportunities for parties at the center to keep their regional branches under control. In the absence of vertically integrated parties, an agreement among party elites of the central level does not automatically result in an approval of the negotiated proposal at the ratification stage.

The distinction between controlled and independent veto-players points to the concept of *arena coupling*, which integrates the stages of negotiation and ratification of constitutional reform (see Chapter 2). If parliaments ratify constitutional amendments negotiated in parliamentary committees or intergovernmental conferences, the constitutional reform unfolds in *tightly coupled* arenas. Negotiators can easily anticipate positions of parliamentary parties responsible for final decisions and try to find an agreement including the preferences of those actors who control the required majority. In analytical terms, partisan veto-players represented in the negotiation arena control the institutional veto-players in the ratifying bodies. Consequently, ratification of an agreement within the win-set of the relevant players will be guaranteed, unless majorities in parliaments change in the wake of elections or due to unpredictable incidents. Furthermore, agenda setters have a powerful position and control over the reform processes if negotiation and ratification are tightly coupled. We expect that reform results resemble the initial proposals of the agenda setters in these cases especially if amendment rules do not constitute many veto-players. High hurdles of constitutional reform may, however, prolong negotiations and increase the opportunities for each veto-player to use bargaining tactics and force others into renegotiations until their interests are satisfied.

If veto-players independently decide on ratification of a constitutional reform, the two stages of a reform process—negotiation and ratification—are only *loosely coupled*. This indicates, on the one hand, that negotiators do not necessarily adopt positions of institutional veto-players. On the other hand, partisan veto-players do not completely absorb these institutional players. The stages are loosely coupled if proposals have to be approved by referendums, since voting by citizens is in general hardly predictable, or in regional parliaments, where different parties are in a majority position or where changes in government constellations may occur after an agreement has been negotiated. Similar challenges may occur due to the absence of a vertically integrated party system if ratification needs approval in second chambers representing subnational governments. If central policy-making bodies do not tightly bind parties, they can hardly act as cohesive partisan veto-players who are able to take definite and reliable positions. In this case, the success of the reform process depends more on the quality of the result and the consensus among negotiating partners and societal interests, both of which can be transformed into convincing reasoning in public communication. Therefore, actors negotiating constitutional change cannot entirely resort to bargaining tactics determined to find a common denominator among existing positions, which is characteristic for reform processes taking place in tightly coupled stages. Instead, the reform proposal must appeal to the "common good" apart from satisfying particular interests. Whether a reform enjoys wide acceptance may also depend on the inclusiveness and openness of the negotiations themselves (see Table 5.1).

In the following section, the cases of constitutional reform in federal or regionalized states are analyzed based on the following distinctions: We define such actors as institutional veto-players whose commitment to constitutional reform proposals are unconditionally necessary. Formal rules constitute institutional veto-players. Partisan veto-players are those actors who control the institutional veto-players. A combination of formal rules (for example special majority requirements), the respective power constellation and characteristics

Table 5.1. Constitutional veto-players and arena coupling

		Coupling of constitutional negotiations and ratification	
		tight	loose
Number of veto-players	high	ratification most likely, if veto-players are generally interested in formal reform success; post-negotiation bargaining possible until compromise is achieved	ratification success uncertain, because negotiators cannot entirely anticipate developments and dynamics at the ratification stage
		ratified reform reflects a solution on the least common denominator; ineffective reform is likely	ratified reform depends on inclusion of governmental, partisan and civil society actors; therefore, the reform proposal must appeal to generalized interests and the "common good"
	low	ratification highly probable, independent of effectiveness of negotiations	ratification likely but not guaranteed; successful ratification depends on communication of amendment proposal to ratifying actors

of a party system determine whether partisan veto-players exist or not in a certain situation. Finally, we will examine the degree of coupling between negotiation and ratification. Based on these definitions we can formulate three guiding hypotheses about the relation between ratification and negotiation and their impact on ratification success:

a) High hurdles of ratification cause an increase in the number of (effective) partisan veto-players independent of the actual number of institutional veto-players. Under these conditions, reforms of a limited scope are more likely because of the decrease of the win-set. But we expect no impact on formal success of ratification, which depends on the mode of arena coupling.

b) A tight coupling of the negotiation and ratification stages almost certainly guarantees successful ratification of negotiation agreements, because bargaining tactics can be used in the course of negotiations to solve interest conflicts. However, the number of partisan veto-players reduces the win-set (the common denominator of interests). For this reason, reforms that are ratified tend to be limited in scope and insufficient to solve the constitutional problems.

c) With loosely coupled stages, there is a greater need to present reform proposals as conforming to general public reason and the common good. Nonetheless, the ratification of negotiation results is less secure due to incomplete control of institutional veto-players or insufficient cohesiveness of partisan veto-players. Consequently, effective reform proposals may fail.

5.3 Ratification Processes in Selected Cases of Reform

As Astrid Lorenz (2005: 358–9) has paid special attention to systematically include veto-players, referendums and voting rules in bicameral legislatures in her "rigidity index," we can take her measures (on a scale from 1.0 to a maximum of 9.5) as a basis for comparisons. Accordingly, constitutional reforms in the regionalized states of France (4.0), Italy (4.0) and the United Kingdom (1.0), as well as in federal Austria (3.0) face relatively low institutional constraints, while the federal constitutions of Germany (6.0), Belgium (9.5), Switzerland (7.0), Canada (7.0) and Spain (6.0) set higher barriers for amendments. With only a majority vote in the House of Commons as a formal requirement and given the dominance of single party governments, constitutional change in the UK is confronted with the lowest number of veto-players. Upon closer inspection of the devolution processes, however, we can identify deviations from this formal procedure such as regional referendums as additional ratification requirements. This has to be taken into account in some other cases, too. The constitutional rigidity index has its value as a starting point since the ratification followed formal procedures in the majority of our cases. However, we will pay special attention to deviations in practice and the applied rule for ratification (summarized in Table 5.2). For instance, we consider the people as an institutional veto-player regardless of whether referendums are obligatory or consultative. Actually, even non-binding referendums compel governments to comply with the will of the people as expressed in a majority vote. We also consider the Constitutional Courts in Germany and Spain as (conditional) institutional veto-players since they can annul a constitutional amendment in total or in parts. With these detailed descriptions, we are better equipped to identify independent veto-players and can include actual power constellations into our analysis of the conditions for successful ratification.

In many instances, formal procedures define the chambers of parliament as institutional veto-players. Yet, due to electoral rules or power constellations, partisan veto-players absorb most of the second chambers. Coalition governments or the requirement of supermajorities give smaller parties more weight in the ratification process and turn them into strong partisan veto-players. Distinguishing institutional and partisan veto-players during each ratification process gives us a clearer picture of the power different actors can apply to prevent a reform from passing. However, their effect depends on negotiators' ability to anticipate vetoes and influence ratification.

In *Germany*, the federal parliament (*Bundestag*) and the federal council of *Länder* governments (*Bundesrat*) have to pass a constitutional amendment with a two-thirds majority in both houses. The specific composition of the *Bundesrat*, where *Länder* premiers and ministers represent individual *Länder*,

Table 5.2. Veto-players in constitutional reforms

Case	Central/Federal level		Regional level	
	institutional veto-player	partisan veto-player	institutional veto-player	partisan veto-player
Switzerland	*Nationalrat* *Ständerat* majority of voters in referendum	majority parties	majority of cantonal voters in referendum in majority of the Cantons	–
Germany	*Bundestag* *Bundesrat* *Constitutional Court*	parties (more than one-third of votes)	–	–
Austria	*Nationalrat* *Bundesrat*	parties (more than one-third of votes)	–	–
Canada	House of Commons Senate	majority party	provincial parliaments consultative referendum	majority parties in provincial parliaments
Belgium	*Chambre des Représentants/Kamer van Volksvertegen-woordigers Sénat/ Senaat*	parties (more than one-third of votes or majority of each linguistic community)	–	regional parties
Spain	*Cortes Generales (Congreso de los Diputados, Senado)* *Tribunal Constitucional*	majority parties	parliaments of ACs referendum	regional parties
Italy	*Camera dei deputati* *Senato* referendum (if required by one-fifth of votes in one chamber, 500,000 voters or 5 regional assemblies)	majority parties	–	–
France	*Congrès* (joint session of *Assemblée nationale* and *Sénat)* referendum (if initiated by President)	parties (more than 40 percent of votes)	–	–
Great Britain	Parliament	majority party	consultative referendum	–

but also pursue policies of state-wide parties, has made this institution particularly vulnerable to strategies of party politics and a prevailing interaction mode of competition (Lehmbruch 2000: 27–13). Both the Federalism Reforms I and II shed light on the importance of partisan veto-players. Even though negotiating partners had agreed to exclude many controversial topics right from the beginning, the first reform was not adopted until the Grand Coalition on the federal level moderated party competition in negotiations

(Burkhart 2009). In consequence, the involvement of the second chamber in the ratification process worked similarly to the requirement of supermajorities in a parliamentary decision, and cross-party consensus and cooperation within a Grand Coalition or between parties in government and opposition are necessary. In the course of the second reform of federalism, the Grand Coalition of Christian and Social Democrats lost the two-thirds majority in the second chamber with the regional election in Bremen of 13 May 2007, when a minor party, the Liberal Democratic Party (FDP), became a decisive actor and partisan veto-player due to the party's participation in *Länder* governments. Effectively, constitutional reform depended on three institutional veto-players, with the Constitutional Court as a potential final arbitrator (which was called after the 2009 amendment by the parliament of Schleswig-Holstein to decide on the new debt rule), and four partisan veto-players, the Christian Democratic Parties (CDU together with its Bavarian sister party CSU), the Social Democrats, the Green Party and the FDP.

Belgium displays a similar pattern, although both chambers are composed almost equally, effectively establishing one institutional veto-player. By the time of the Fifth State Reform of 2001, the governing coalition of Liberals, Socialists and Flemish Christian Democrats lacked the two-thirds majorities and depended on support from the opposition. Negotiations were held with the Flemish nationalists (*Volksunie*) thereby turning them into a crucial partisan veto-player. Due to defections among the ranks of Brussels Liberals (FDF—then part of the governing Francophone Liberals MR) and internal cleavages in the *Volksunie*, the success of ratification was still in abeyance despite concessions made to both parties. As explained in section 4.2.2, constitutional policy-making in Belgium was dominated by party politics and largely followed the procedures of ordinary legislation. Sinardet points to the fact that the negotiations of constitutional amentments "not only illustrate the dominance of parties, but also that of party leadership" (Sinardet 2012: 142). Moreover, in both cases we can detect a tight coupling between the stages of negotiation and ratification, which means that the negotiators usually acted as agents of the partisan veto-players at the ratification stage. The success of ratification depended on the support of smaller parties in opposition and on a non-state-wide nationalist party.

According to Lorenz, *Austria* is the federal state with the lowest constraints against constitutional amendments. In the constitutional reform analyzed in our case study, political parties aimed at a total revision that would have required special majorities and a referendum. However, the character of the reform and the amendment rules were left in limbo. With regard to the broad alliance of parties at the federal and *Länder* level, which launched the Austrian Convention for constitutional reform, meeting the two-thirds requirement in parliament and in the *Bundesrat* would have been reasonably attainable. The federal government tried to separate constitutional policy-making from ordinary politics in that it opened up the Convention to important interest groups and civil society organizations. This institutional setting could have separated constitutional negotiation from ratification in the federal legislature and thereby limiting the effects of party competition. Unfortunately, the approach did not succeed, because in the run-up to presidential and parliamentary elections party politics were immediately superimposed upon the Convention (Bußjäger 2012). In reality, negotiations and ratification became tightly coupled and followed the same logics of collective action.

A tight coupling of negotiation and ratification also is characteristic for the reform process in *France*. Here, institutional barriers to constitutional change are slightly lower in comparison to Germany and Belgium, because a three-fifths majority in the Congress, the joint session of both legislative chambers, is sufficient for passing a constitutional amendment (provided that the President does not initiate a referendum, which he did not in the case under review here). The French decentralization reform nevertheless remained doubtful, because Conservatives committed to the local level and critical towards the envisioned strengthening of the Regions controlled the Senate (Le Lidec 2012). Obviously, the weak internal integration of the French parties enabled the Conservative "*notables*" to mobilize against the government's reform project. Regional and departmental elections in March 2004 helped to reinforce Conservative opposition in the Senate. After the socialists had gained majorities in all but one Region and in a majority of departments, the Conservative majority in the Senate rejected provisions in the drafted bill on subnational responsibilities and liberties, which would have strengthened the Regions. The Senate acted as an effective veto-player and attained the devolution of several matters to the local and departmental instead of the regional bodies (Fischer-Hotzel 2013).

Ratification and negotiations are only loosely coupled if veto-players escape the control of governing parties and can act independently from those negotiating a reform proposal. We find a combination of high institutional hurdles and loose coupling in Switzerland as well as in Canada, moreover in Spain at the level of the ACs. Independent institutional veto-players are either the legislative assemblies of the central government and the regions, as in the Canadian and Spanish cases, or national or regional referendums as in Switzerland, in the Charlottetown process, in Canada and in Spain, where statute reforms in Catalonia and Andalusia had to pass a referendum. A closer review of these cases, however, reveals differences in the way negotiation and ratification are connected despite the independence of veto-players.

In *Switzerland*, we find formally loosely coupled stages of negotiation and ratification, because parties in parliament do not form a stable coalition supporting the government and citizens always have the last say in a constitutional referendum. Besides this, ratification hurdles are remarkably high with the need for double majorities in the legislature and in the referendum (a federal at-large majority and in a majority of the Cantons). However, the actual practice of direct democracy opened up some ways for executives negotiating a constitutional amendment to reduce the uncertainty of the ratification process. First, the long-term horizon of the constitutional reform project allowed for communicating proposals to the public via the media and thus actually influencing the ratification process. Second, powerful groups, which may have led a No-campaign at the ratification stage, could be included early during the consultation process. Third, as already mentioned, elections in the Swiss consensus democracy do not change the government constellation at the federal level and partisan veto-players do not actually exist.

Formal amendment rules in *Canada* and *Spain* establish strong institutional and independent veto-players at the regional level. However, if we consider the particular party systems, we discover greater variation in the potential for controlling the ratification processes in these cases. In Spain, the legislative assemblies of ACs can be absorbed in cases of congruent coalitions at the regional and central level, while the low vertical integration of parties in Canada (Thorlakson 2009) renders provincial governments more independent from government constellations at the center. The rules requiring compulsory regional referendums in Catalonia and Andalusia, however, each constitute one independent veto-player and loosen the coupling of ratification and negotiation. In the Charlottetown process, the provincial assemblies did not vote on the reform agreement but were replaced by a consultative referendum, which actually introduced an additional independent veto-player. In the end, the negotiated agreement failed to gain the support of the people in October 1992. Although majority and opposition parties as well as the majority of provinces and aboriginal organizations had rallied behind the negotiated agreement, the lost referendum terminated both the ratification process and any further attempts at significant constitutional reform afterwards.

Ratification processes in Spain followed the formal rules for amending AC statutes. They required a compromise between parties at the regional level before negotiations started with the central government, which during the period under consideration was led by the Spanish Socialist Party (PSOE). In the cases of Catalonia and Andalusia, the regional branches of the Socialist Party governed both communities. The Catalan Socialists, PSC, however, enjoyed significant autonomy from the state-wide party PSOE (Roller and Van Houten 2003) while Andalusian PSOE-A maintains stronger ties with the party at the central level. As a consequence, the congruence in governments had differing implications for the two regions. Furthermore, the minority government under PSOE needed the votes of the Catalan nationalists, CiU—in opposition in Catalonia and the center—in order to meet the threshold in the Congress. This partisan veto-player, however, could be controlled by including it in the negotiations. Zapatero met with CiU leader Artur Mas, leading to the Zapatero–Mas Agreement on January 22 in 2006 and thereby bypassing PSC with which it had been difficult to come to an agreement (Colino 2009b). In Andalusia, the Socialists governed alone but required the consent of opposition parties in order to meet the necessary three-fifths threshold at the regional level. In this case, CiU lent the governing PSOE its votes in the regional and central parliament, while additional support came from the conservative PP for ratification at the central level (Orte and Wilson 2009). The regional referendums passed successfully in both cases, although the turnout was very low in Andalusia. Due to characteristics of the party system and in contrast to Canada, the regional parliaments as institutional veto-players could be more easily absorbed and controlled in the Spanish cases.

Another difference between ratification of constitutional amendments in Spain and in Canada lies in the temporal order of different sequences affecting the coupling of negotiation and ratification. The legislative assemblies of the Catalan and Andalusian Autonomous Communities initiated a reform of their statutes by voting on a draft bill and sending it to the central parliament. In these cases, negotiations were divided into a first phase that took place within the legislative Assembly in the region followed by a first vote that formed part of the ratification requirement. The second sequence started with negotiations between parties at the center and the ACs and allowed for renegotiations before the final vote in the two legislative chambers and before the regional referendums, which concluded ratification (Colino 2009b). In contrast, the reform process in Canada reveals an opposite order. Here, the legislative assemblies of the provinces have to approve federal constitutional reforms, but their vote is supposed to take place after the federal parliament and the Senate have decided and within a certain period starting with the first provincial vote. While the procedures in Spain lead to a tighter coupling between the parliamentary arenas of the ACs and of the central state, the regional referendums still constitute an independent veto-player, which is difficult to control.

Furthermore, the bilateral mode of federal reform in Spain allows for differentiated action among the parties and voting across the regions as well as across levels of government. The requirement of supermajorities in the regional parliaments—two-thirds in Catalonia and three-fifths in Andalusia—called for a consensus between majority and opposition parties, including nationalist parties at the regional as well as at the central level in the Catalan case. In the end, PP opposed the reform proposals in Catalonia and Andalusia at the regional level, but consented to the Andalusian reform later in the Congress after modifications had been negotiated (Keating and Wilson 2009). Despite the similar substance of the two statute reforms, supporting the Andalusian statute reform did not prevent PP from invoking the Supreme Court to review the constitutionality of the Catalan reform. This way an additional independent veto-player decided the fate of the constitutional reform, when the Court eventually declared significant parts of the Catalan Statues unconstitutional (Colino and Olmeda 2012).

Finally, loosely coupled reform stages go hand in hand with a low constitutional rigidity in the decentralization reform in Italy and in devolution of *Great Britain*. In the latter case, constitutional amendment in principle does not deviate from ordinary legislation, and usually one partisan veto-player, the single governing party, absorbs the only institutional veto-player, the Westminster parliament. However, in the case of the devolution laws, consultative regional referendums formed part of the ratification process prior to the final parliamentary decision on reform of multilevel government. Although not compulsory, the regional referendums weakened the coupling between ratification and negotiation. This had significant consequences for ratification. First, constitutional reformers were compelled to cover the "median voter's" position in their proposal, and, second, they had to be aware of the spoiling potential of parties or interest groups, who were able to launch a No-campaign. In Scotland, the Constitutional Convention as agenda-setter in the devolution process partly followed a consociational approach in order to avoid such an unforeseeable development (Mitchell 2012). The overwhelming support for devolution in Scotland was to some extent grounded in the work of the Convention. In Wales, the devolution proposal essentially became the product of Labour's internal policy-making without significant public involvement. Support for the proposal at the polls led to a narrow majority (50.3 percent) at a moderate turnout (50.1 percent), which could particularly be explained by the lack of feedback with society in the run-up to the referendum and, consequentially, the weak inclination of the voters to attend the referendum (Bradbury 2010). In England, the ratification failed in the first region, and, with the exception of the region of Greater London, the government gave up further devolution plans.

Ratification in *Italy* is difficult to categorize. In the legislative arena, the power of several veto-players in multi-party coalitions and the requirement of two approval votes in each chamber of the legislature make ratification difficult. Moreover, a referendum is not a compulsory part of constitutional reform, but the hurdles to its initiation are rather low, requiring just 20 percent of the members of one chamber, 500,000 voter signatures, or a referendum request by five regional councils. In the particular case analyzed in our study, a majority of senators called for a referendum. Parliament can circumvent a referendum if it adopts amendments by two-thirds majorities, which overrules the call for a referendum. Therefore, coupling of constitutional

Table 5.3. Ratification rules in the cases of constitutional reform

		Coupling of constitutional negotiations and ratification	
		tight	loose
Number of veto-players	high	Germany Belgium	Switzerland Canada Spain
	low	Austria France	Great Britain Italy

negotiation and ratification in Italy depends on particular circumstances. Stages were loosely coupled in the reform of Title V of the Italian Constitution, because the parliamentary vote fell short of the required majority, so that a group of center-right senators was able to initiate a referendum. Without procedures of mobilizing a consensus among powerful groups in society, the outcome of a referendum was not predictable for policy-makers.

Table 5.3 sums up the categorization of ratification procedures in the nine countries compared in our research.

5.4 Impact of Ratification Rules

As clearly illustrated, our research project confirms results of recent quantitative studies on the impact of formal rules of amendment. These studies use different indicators to measure the institutional conditions for constitutional amendments, but overall they focus on rules for passing constitutional amendments in legislative institutions or in referendums, i.e. rules of ratification. When testing the effects of amendment rules on the frequency of constitutional amendments, scholars have not found significant correlations (Rasch and Congleton 2006; Closa 2012a, 2012b; Lorenz 2005; Lutz 1994). Carlos Closa also considered the actual application of rules, but the result of his research was similar (Closa 2012a): Variations in ratification do not make a difference regarding the outcome of constitutional policy.

Our case studies confirm this conclusion. The two cases where the ratification of a constitutional amendment failed (Austria and Canada) show quite different ratification rules. The same holds true for the cases where reform proposals passed the ratification processes. Neither the number or type of veto-players nor the coupling of negotiation and ratification arenas explain whether an explicit constitutional change is likely or not. Regarding arena coupling, studies including more cases would be necessary to prove this statement, since theoretical reasoning speaks for a causal relationship between tight coupling and probability of ratification. However, under the condition of loose coupling, additional procedures can reduce the uncertainty of independent veto-players, as can be observed in Switzerland or in the Scottish devolution process.

Therefore, amendment rules established in a constitution cannot tell us much about the success or failure of ratification. But this does not mean that these rules and the corresponding constraints are irrelevant. Those actors negotiating a draft of a constitutional amendment do not formulate ideal proposals. As responsible policy-makers, they must search for a feasible solution, and amendment rules are one factor influencing feasibility of constitutional change. Therefore, participants in constitutional negotiations account for them. Consequently, although conditions for ratification do not determine the probability of constitutional reform, they have an impact on negotiations by providing constraining and enabling structures, which political actors consider when deciding on their strategies in politics determining the modes of negotiations. In this indirect way, they affect the substance of an amendment proposal and the success or failure of constitutional policy.

As outlined above, the formal rules of constitutional amendment effectively constitute certain political actors as veto-players. Their power, however, does not rest upon their ability to affect the content of constitutional reform; they merely can accept or reject an already negotiated proposal. In negotiations on the substance of change, participants have to anticipate preferences of those actors with veto power and include their demands in order to propose amendments that, in the end, are acceptable to them. However, veto anticipation is not always possible, and, only if it is possible, it clearly has an impact on negotiation results. Otherwise the mode of negotiation prevailing during the processes may be adapted to reduce the uncertainty of ratification.

If the reform process is mainly located in the parliamentary arena, political parties regularly dominate negotiations and ratification. They constitute the decisive linkage between both processes. Veto-players' decisions can be anticipated and negotiators representing parties in parliament have strong control over ratification, as long as elections do not lead to a swing in parliamentary majority. Even if political constellations in the legislature change, a reopening of the negotiation results and the renegotiation of some parts of an agreement provides a feasible strategy to secure successful ratification. Such strategies have been applied repeatedly in our cases, particularly when elections modified the party political composition of the required majority. More often than not, they contributed to advancing a ratification of reform proposals, though they proved counterproductive in Austria.

Regarding the outcome of constitutional policy, the four cases featuring tight coupling of constitutional negotiations and ratification clearly reveal repercussions from ratification rules on the negotiations and negotiation results. In Germany, the specific ratification requirement of two-thirds majorities in both chambers already influenced the agenda of both commissions on the modernization of the federal order. It excluded matters where an agreement seemed impossible, like amendments causing a redistribution of fiscal resources or a revision of *Länder* territories. Members of the commission with a right to vote actually acted as agents of the veto-players, the parties in the federal parliament and the Länder representatives in the *Bundesrat,* who had to decide on the proposal. Right from the beginning negotiations prevailed in a bargaining mode and aimed at package deals (Benz 2008: 446–7), while the mutual protection of interests between federal and *Länder* governments on the one hand and between well-off and rather poor *Länder* on the other hand became a crucial commitment. During negotiations, the anticipation of vetoes led to a further exclusion of important matters and an agreement at the lowest common denominator.

While party competition in Germany merely appeared as a menacing background condition, the political parties and the logics of the segmented Belgian party system immediately dominated the Fifth Belgian State Reform. The requirement of two-thirds majorities in both chambers demanded the inclusion of seven parties. Particularly the regionalist VU and FDF gained disproportional influence on the negotiations but without being able to enforce all their demands. The party dominance gained further relevance after crucial negotiations were repeatedly relocated from the parliamentary commission to a closed circle of party elites where bargaining prevailed (Jacques and Boromée 2001; Sinardet 2012). Under the conditions of the Belgian party state, the ratification procedure not only had an impact on the negotiations but also distinctively shaped the negotiation results. Regional parties successfully used their veto power to negotiate concessions according to their demands—an increase in fiscal autonomy for the Regions as well as higher financial transfers to the Francophone Community (Delwit and Hellings 2002; Jacques and Boromée 2001). The conflicting objectives of the different federal units were achieved at the expense of the federal level.

France represents another example of tightly coupled stages, but the weak vertical (and horizontal) integration of the French parties generated a distinct pattern. Due to the wide absence of partisan veto-players, the central government was able to act autonomously in agenda setting and policy formulation. However, the government saw itself confronted with the veto-power of the Senate, which prevented the significant strengthening of the regions at the expense of the municipalities and the *départements* intended by the reform initiative (Le Lidec 2012). Therefore, the inclusion of civil society in a consultative process had no visible impact on the process of bargaining between central and local governments.

As reported above, the Austrian Convention ended without an agreement. After negotiation failed, the parliament did not initiate ratification procedures. Therefore, it seems rather superfluous to ask to what extent ratification procedures had an impact on the negotiation results. Some scholars argue that the main purpose of the Convention was to demonstrate reform willingness on the part of the political elite and not to ratify a substantial constitutional reform (Bußjäger 2005). According to another opinion, a "small" coalition of ÖVP and FPÖ initiated the Convention since they needed the approval of the Social Democrats in order to achieve the required two-thirds majorities in both chambers, which would not have been achievable by the governing coalition alone. Yet if the intention was to form a grand constitutional reform coalition in order to secure ratification, the Convention could not work as an institution for setting apart constitutional from normal politics. In any case, party politics remained the bond between negotiations in the Convention and ratification in the legislature. The Austrian political system, traditionally affected by party dominance, countered the idea of a cross-partisan Convention, which in reality turned it into a strange mixture of public arena and joint committee of the legislature. In the shadow of party competition in parliament, the influence of representatives from associations remained limited. Since parties realized the impact of a significant reform of the Austrian Constitution in public, they feared that their respective opponents would profit from the convention process. In consequence, they turned the Convention into an arena of political confrontation.

As these case studies demonstrate, a tight coupling of the stages tends to facilitate ratification of reform proposals, but prevents effective problem solving and fosters negotiation results located within prevailing path dependencies: This meant in Germany a package deal that avoided tackling effectiveness problems of cooperative federalism. In Belgium, the Fifth State Reform confirmed the path development of "hollowing the center" (Hooghe 2004; see also Petersohn 2011) to the advantage of the subnational entities. The French Senate eventually played its role as a conservative power in that it prevented the *old* subnational entities of municipalities and departments from losing too much ground to the *new* Regions. In Austria, we observed a reform running into a deadlock in constitutional negotiations.

In those cases where independent veto-players exist, and negotiations and ratification are only loosely coupled, particular mechanisms are required to bridge the gap between the stages. Political structures like an integrated multilevel party system may provide these bridging mechanisms. Yet if a referendum is required, parties may influence but cannot control the ratification process, at least not in constitutional reforms affecting multilevel government. Within the cases displaying loosely coupled stages, we must distinguish between reform processes focusing on the regional and those developing on the central level. Of course, the former similarly affect the territorial structure of the state, but only need approval by regional referendums (British and Spanish cases), while the latter need approval in national referendums (Switzerland, Canada and Italy). However, in both instances voting in referendums seems to be more or less unpredictable. Therefore, the negotiating actors themselves must try to influence ratification processes by opening the negotiations and broadening opportunities of participation to those who might oppose a reform. In case of loosely coupled stages, exclusive bargaining within closed circles is a risky strategy as it is not conducive to discovering potential resistance.

We explained the ratification of a far-reaching constitutional reform in Switzerland by emphasizing the specific culture of consensus and direct democracy: If political elites want to secure the ratification of a proposal, it is imperative to reach a broad consensus between parliamentary and non-parliamentary actors. In order to meet the demanding requirement of a "double majority" in the referendum, politicians had to explain the reasons of a reform and resort to broad principles and the common good. Those requirements forced the political elite to frame the reform project as a joint endeavor aiming at the public interest (Freiburghaus 2012; Grotz and Poier 2010; Wettstein 2012). However, in order to achieve a consensus, negotiations had to produce convincing results and effective solutions of the debated problems. Well aware that they needed to respond to opposition groups in society with the power to mobilize against the reform project, governments opened negotiations to public discussion. Insofar as the ratification procedure kept the political elite from resorting to pure distributive bargaining, it compelled them to resort to arguing and to concentrate on problem solving (Braun 2009).

In contrast to Switzerland, Canada had almost no experience with a popular vote and political actors decided very late in the negotiation process to hold a state-wide referendum after the provinces of Alberta and Quebec had announced their intention to use this instrument for ratification at the provincial level. One could argue that Canada recognized the necessity of opening the process for public involvement by initiating an extensive consultative process and holding televised national conferences on constitutional change. Yet they did this in view of the high risks of ratification failure in the provincial parliaments where opposition groups succeeded at mobilizing resistance in previous reforms. Looking closer at the different steps of the process reveals that governments searched for agreement in public consultation and negotiations in different arenas in order to meet the challenges in ratification (Milne 1992; Stein 1993). Accordingly, not the referendum but ratification in provincial parliaments motivated negotiators to find a broad consensus. Nevertheless, the referendum proved to be a failure despite the fairly successful negotiations. Due to the different federal visions existing in

Canada as well as the numerous reform aspects included in the final agreement, several organizations, parties and individuals found something they did not agree with. After a short but intense campaign on both sides, final ratification failed on 26 October 1992 in almost every province (Johnston et al. 1993). Communicating the agreement in negotiations to veto-players in ratification, which turned out to be decisive in the Swiss reform process, was insufficient in Canada where the referendum campaign was characterized by a mobilization against the project. In fact, the ratification process was decoupled from the negotiations.

In Spain, different ratification rules are applied at the regional and central levels in the case of federal reform by amendments of AC Statutes. As a consequence, effects on negotiations varied. In the cases of Andalusia and Catalonia, passing the reform in the regional referendums was not a great concern for negotiating partners. During the negotiations in Catalonia, governing parties reached out to regional civil society and initiated discussions or received written contributions, while no similar effort was made in Andalusia to broaden the reform debate. Here, the process remained purely elite driven and representatives of civil society only appeared in the parliamentary hearings (Colino 2009a; Olmeda 2009). The reform in Catalonia raised public interest to a higher degree in comparison to Andalusia, where the issue remained one of mere governmental reorganization. Accordingly turnout in the referendum was significantly lower in Andalusia in contrast to the high mobilization of voters in Catalonia.

At the central level, party politics and intergovernmental bargaining predominated. A reallocation of power was usually achieved by an agreement between the Socialists and Conservatives in order to secure the thresholds of absolute majorities in Congress (Orte and Wilson 2009). In the case of the statute reforms analyzed above, the governing PSOE had to reach out to ethno-regionalist parties, because the PP particularly rejected the far-reaching demands of the Catalans. Therefore, negotiations displayed a stronger character of intergovernmental bargaining and included governing parties of lower levels. However, the congruence in governments between the regional and the central level worked better in Andalusia and facilitated compromises. The greater autonomy of the Catalan Socialists (PSC) as well as the potential threat of several ethno-regionalist parties in Catalonia increased conflicts between PSOE and PSC during the negotiations. Therefore, PSOE turned towards the oppositional Catalan nationalists, CiU, in order to reach the "Zapatero–Mas Agreement." In the end, both referendums passed, but the overall approval rate was significantly lower in Andalusia (Colino 2009b: 11; Olmeda 2009: 14).

In the British cases, ratification also went through regional and central processes. Although there are usually no other veto-players challenging the single party majority in the Westminster parliament, the referendums forced Labour to pursue a broad coalition, reflecting also policy positions that lay at best at the periphery of Labour's spectrum of preferences. Apparently, the party saw different potentials for conflict and opposition in the regions affected by devolution. Therefore, the reform process was divided. Constitutional negotiations took a different course in Scotland and Wales—not to speak of the particularities of devolution in English regions—although Labour headed the process in both regions (Jeffery 2009). Following the varying intensity of regional identity, the strength of ethno-regionalist parties and pressure for autonomy, the negotiation processes differed in terms of inclusiveness and outreach to civil society. In Scotland, the cross-party and consociational Constitutional Convention dominated debates about devolution at the beginning of the 1990s and framed general matters (Mitchell 2009b), which later could not be ignored by Labour's policy-makers in the run up to the referendum. Although not all parties participated, the support from civil society organizations ensured the silent consent of the strong Scottish National Party (SNP) to the devolution proposal, and this was crucial in the referendum campaign. The extent of public involvement and public concern reached in Scotland was not matched in Wales, where negotiations essentially took place within the Labour Party, and the average preferences of the citizens remained rather vague. Since policy-makers should try to convince voters when it comes to a referendum, it seems clear why the proposal on Scottish devolution exceeded Labour's proposed concept, which particularly aimed at administrative decentralization. The (hidden) influence of the SNP, together with a more vibrant and concerned civil society, put pressure on the negotiations, which eventually resulted in a significantly larger scope of devolution proposals in Scotland than in Wales.

Regarding the impact of a referendum, Italy constitutes a deviant case. Here, decentralization reform took place within the narrow governmental sphere dominated by political parties. Feedback with civil society was widely absent. Moreover, according to Mazzoleni, the logics of party competition always eclipse territorial politics at the expense of integrative bargaining or arguing (Mazzoleni 2009). Policy-making merely unfolded within the center-left coalition after the consensual-oriented bicameral committee dissolved in June 1998 (Palermo and Nicolini 2010). Additionally, one could argue that ratification by popular referendum initiated by members of parliament released the political parties from the necessity to find a broad consensus and did not alter the usual style of policy-making. Instead, negotiators could resort to the adversarial style of party politics. Usually applied as an instrument of party politics, the constitutional referendum had hardly any impact on the negotiation process and bears high risks of ratification failure. Considering the fact that center-right governments in the northern Regions supported the reform, the center-left coalition had nothing to fear and eventually 64.2 percent voted in favor of the reform, albeit on a low turnout of 34 percent. However, in the later reform of the Senate initiated by the second Berlusconi government, the instrumental use of the referendum in 2006 met the same fate as in the Canadian case and resulted in rejection.

5.5 Summary

Our analysis confirms results of previous studies contradicting a direct causal relationship between ratification rules and the probability or scope of a constitutional reform. Yet it provides evidence of an indirect effect of these rules on constitutional negotiations and thus the substance of constitutional change. Formal rules of passing a constitutional law or veto-players cannot explain the success or failure of constitutional policy. Although most of the cases of constitutional reform in federal or regionalized states had to be passed with qualified majorities and/or in different legislative bodies or procedures, i.e. they had to gain approval by many veto-players, only in Canada did ratification fail outright, though in the Austrian case, the reform process did not even reach this stage. Rules aiming at high constitutional stability did not automatically prevent constitutional change by formal amendment. The NFA in Switzerland yields the most astonishing result: Despite the demanding requirements for ratification, a far-reaching reform of the federal constitution succeeded.

In line with the theory outlined in Chapter 2, constitutional negotiations have to be regarded as decisive in order to explain success or failure of constitutional policy in multilevel governments. However, ratification must be taken into account as one condition affecting negotiations. From this point of view, we discussed the impact of different types of veto-players and their potential to influence or jeopardize the entire reform process. In most reform processes covered by this study, representatives of veto-players were included formally or informally in the discussion of a reform proposal. The effects on negotiations differed: In some cases, we find an extension of the topics on the agenda due to demands of a partisan or institutional veto-player (like in Switzerland or in Scotland). In other cases, the scope of the reform was reduced due to the limited win-set of those actors voting on the final reform bill (like in Germany, France or Belgium). Usually, negotiators know that they have to anticipate opposition by veto-players and they try to structure processes and the substance of a proposal accordingly. When it comes to ratification, no further substantial modification of package deals, compromises or a consensus is possible. Only processes of parliamentary ratification at the central level offer the opportunity to reopen the deal and renegotiate an agreement, but the core elements of a draft bill can hardly be revised at this stage.

However, under these institutional conditions renegotiations usually affect only marginal aspects. Parliamentary ratification usually causes a tight coupling of negotiation and ratification, with negotiators acting as agents of partisan veto-players they can rely on. This condition favors the anticipation of veto power in negotiation processes and makes ratification less risky. Yet exactly under this institutional condition, negotiators tend to be bound to positions of external actors, which they need to consider but cannot change. Hence, negotiations tend towards the bargaining mode ending regularly with compromises and ineffective reforms.

As demonstrated, independent veto-players weaken the coupling of negotiation and ratification, thereby reducing the control of negotiators over the passage of a reform. The requirement of regional or state-wide referendums forms the most challenging mode of ratification since results may be predictable by public opinion surveys during negotiations, but still difficult to control or change in political practice. Moreover, referendums compel political actors to table a definite proposal without offering the opportunity for "post-negotiation negotiations" as is possible in processes of parliamentary ratification. Bridging the gap between negotiation and ratification will then rely only on the quality of the proposal as perceived by the public and the efforts made by political elites to convince the citizens of the benefits of a Yes-vote. Widespread agreement among negotiating partners might improve the prospects for successful ratification while disagreement might intensify political competition and deteriorate reform perspectives even after successfully completed negotiations. Referendums, therefore, add a momentum of uncertainty, especially in those cases where negotiated deals could not entirely overcome existing differences. In this respect, the success of regional referendums in Andalusia, Catalonia, Scotland and Wales may be less surprising as disputes concentrated on details of the reform while almost all negotiating partners agreed on a fundamental aim and direction of change, the increase of regional autonomy. A state-wide referendum, in contrast, is vulnerable to divergent ideas and interests regarding the reallocation of power or resources or the different conceptions of a federation that exist throughout a multilevel government. The failure of the referendum in Canada aptly demonstrates the difficulties of ratifying a comprehensive reform of the allocation of power as well as recognition of distinct groups by putting it to popular vote.

Yet if constitutional amendments have to be ratified in referendums or if other independent veto-players are involved, negotiations show a stronger tendency towards the arguing mode. At least they are not entirely constrained by determined positions or influenced by party competition. The effects of referendums on constitutional negotiations may be limited as in the Italian case, but as our comparative research indicates, negotiators need not to behave like agents of parties. Therefore, incentive structures of actors in constitutional negotiations differ from a constellation where their hands are more or less tied by veto-players.

6

Constitutional Reform and Implicit Change

As illustrated in the previous chapter, ratification rules and veto-player theory cannot explain the probability of constitutional amendments. They tell us nothing about the quality of amendments which passed legislative procedures, nor do they provide any indications as to whether changes of a constitution stabilize the balance of power and maintain flexibility or whether they go in the opposite direction. For this reason, an analysis of processes of constitutional policy needs to look beyond formal procedures of amendment. As revealed in our case studies, it is not unlikely that effective amendments can be voted down in ratification and that ineffective, destabilizing reforms can pass. In both cases, instability persists or even worsens and rigidity of a multilevel government can increase. Yet regardless of which kind of decision is taken, this is not a necessary outcome.

As summarized above (Chapter 2), most theories of institutional change put emphasis on gradual change accumulating to an ongoing evolution. Yet this evolution can go through periods of continuity and discontinuous developments, depending on the particular sources and conditions of change. This reasoning has inspired the concept of federal dynamics and the proposal for a dynamic institutionalism (Benz and Broschek 2013c). Following a number of influential contributions to the theory of institutional or constitutional change, this conceptualization assumes that effective change results from a continuous interplay of reform and evolution or explicit and implicit constitutional change (Voigt 1999).

The distinction between explicit and implicit change has attracted criticism. Some scholars have refuted such a dichotomy because "it can be problematic and obscure more than it reveals, especially with regard to written federal constitutions" (Kincaid 2012: 38). Implicit change is said to be difficult to identify on account of its ambivalence, permitting different and even conflicting interpretations, and as it confuses the distinction between constitutional and ordinary laws, rules and norms. These arguments have to be considered with care. Indeed, it is rather difficult to clearly draw the lines between matters of constitution from other policy-making issues or to discern interpretations, statues, decisions or agreements, which are acknowledged as shaping the effective constitution and those that only pretend to do so. The best way to define implicit change is to refer to norms, which are not written down in constitutional law but nonetheless enable and regulate politics and policy-making. These norms can be found in normal law (such as electoral rules) or in agreements among political actors. They must be evident in political practice and should not be disputed over a significant time span. Of course, like explicit amendments of constitutional law, implicitly established constitutional norms can always be revised. But in contrast to an amendment to constitutional law that is valid after the formal act of ratification, implicit change needs to develop in ongoing practice in order to find lasting acceptance. This equally applies to court decisions interpreting constitutional law, which can only be regarded as effective if they turn into a prevailing view in jurisprudence.

We cannot rule out that a political system emerges and develops exclusively in processes of implicit constitutional change. History of course provides countless examples for this. Moreover, the concept of federal dynamics points out driving forces that continuously or discontinuously affect a constitutional structure without explicit constitutional amendment according to formal procedures or by deliberate decisions. However, we are interested not in change as such but in constitutional change contributing to a robust balance of powers. Robustness cannot be determined according to any objective standard, but signifies that a particular order is capable of withstanding various pressures and that its division of powers is accepted as legitimate. Legitimacy can be assumed to be given as long as citizens or office holders do not openly dispute a balance of power. In cases of open dispute, politics shifts from collective action to constitutional policy and aims at revising conditions for policy-making (Ostrom 2005: 62–4). This is the reason why constitutional policy is decisive for maintaining or restoring stability. And for this very reason, implicit constitutional change alone cannot provide for stability. It must be linked to policies aiming at explicit constitutional change, i.e. to processes allowing the relevant actors to express their agreement or disagreement with constitutional change.

As Adrienne Héritier convincingly showed, institutional change can be explained by sequences of informal and formal change (Héritier 2007), or, in the terminology applied here, implicit and explicit change. Our case studies provide ample evidence for this. Reforms regularly aim at revising imbalances of power caused by an actual "migration of authority" in legislation and policy-making, or they adjust constitutional rules to accepted norms or standards that have evolved in political practice. Reform projects in Austria, France and Germany most clearly illustrate the first development. They mainly intended to correct centralist trends or a tendency towards joint decision-making. In Canada, adjustment of constitutional rules to changed norms is particularly obvious, and constitutional rules for intercantonal cooperation in Switzerland responded to an emerging practice. On the other hand, all reforms in one way or another have been followed by processes of implicit change, which will be analyzed in more detail in this chapter. Beyond these sequences of implicit and explicit constitutional change, our case studies also indicate that simultaneous processes of both types of change can influence reform processes. A most instructive example is federalism reform in Germany. Here, negotiations on the allocation of legislative powers gained fresh impetus when governments realized that the Federal Constitutional Court has reinterpreted the subsidiarity clause of the constitution.

The interplay of implicit and explicit constitutional change contributes to the dynamics of development and can explain the scope of change. Yet much depends on the kind of linkage of these processes. Moreover, the arenas of informal constitutional policy-making also need to be taken into account: Constitutional courts can clarify disputed issues or can set issues on the agenda of a reform process. They are legitimized to intervene in constitutional debates and political processes and their decisions usually have effective impacts. Parliaments can modify the balance of power and decide on how constitutional rules should be applied. These decisions can appease constitutional conflicts if a large majority in parliament supports them, while they can ignite conflicts if a simple majority decides against a strong opposition. Executives modify constitutional rules by interpreting their meaning or by the way they apply the distribution of powers. Effective implicit change occurs if they achieve intergovernmental agreements. These agreements can stabilize a federal balance, if they are accepted by parliaments; otherwise, they contribute to the ongoing migration of power, which usually causes imbalances.

Our research focused on constitutional reform processes. Therefore, we cannot report processes of implicit change for all selected cases. This chapter reviews these two particular cases of federal reform which are most interesting in order to understand the dynamics of power in multilevel governments. Implicit changes are most relevant if constitutional negotiations end with an agreement but fail in ratification. This outcome can petrify an imbalanced federation, but it can also induce processes of constitutional evolution based on a consensus achieved in negotiations. In cases of unsuccessful reforms which are ratified, implicit change can increase the federal balance or revise the deficits of the constitutional amendments. Moreover, implicit constitutional change can also induce dynamics of constitutional negotiations, albeit they proceed under unfavorable conditions, which usually bring about bargaining processes. The first process is illustrated by the Canadian case, while German federalism exhibits the second one.

6.1 Constitutional Change Following Ratification Failure: The Case of Canada

In 1992, after the "mega-constitutional" reforms finally had failed with the negative vote on the Charlottetown Accord, Canadian federalism entered a serious crisis. Constitutional policy was in a deadlock, seemingly condemning the federal system to further disintegration. Already in 1990, a violent confrontation between the Mohawks, a group of Aborigines living in Quebec, and the Canadian government had revealed increasing conflicts with the First Nations. After the 1992 referendum, an accommodation of diversity between the federation and Quebec seemed impossible, not the least since the nationalist *Parti Québécois* (PQ) profited from the crisis and won the majority in the provincial parliament. This situation did not improve when, in 1995, the government of Quebec called for a secession referendum, which failed as well.

The situation of Canadian politics after the Charlottetown Accord has often been characterized as "constitutional fatigue," and most politicians and experts regarded the Charlottetown process as a debacle that should not be repeated. Scholars tended to categorize Canadian constitutional policy as failure. In the country, it has been argued that implicit change, by adjusting constitutional conventions or by intergovernmental agreements, proves more appropriate for the Canadian multinational federation (Meekison 1993: 81). However, one should not underrate the impact the constitutional accord had on politics and policy-making, since this agreement had been reached among the federal and the provincial governments following intense constitutional negotiations in parliaments and no less intense consultations with interest groups and citizens. As the referendums on the Charlottetown Accord and Quebec's secession had expressed no clear opinion of citizens on the future of the federation, revealing the ambivalence of the public in this matter, governments and parliaments continued constitutional policy-making by "other means." Instead of a constitutional reform, they implemented the basic guidelines defined in the Meech Lake Accord and in the Charlottetown Accord. This way Canadians were able to solve a number of constitutional problems, at least those that did not require an explicit amendment of constitutional law (Behiels 2002).

Important adjustments have been achieved by intergovernmental agreements (Poirier 2004), serving as an "*ersatz* à des réformes constitutionnelles" (Poirier 2008: 10). With the "Agreement on Internal Trade" concluded in 1995, the federal and provincial governments defined a regulatory framework for a free market in Canada, including a dispute settlement mechanism. Without shifting formal powers to the central level, the agreement acknowledges that economic regulations and interprovincial commerce are matters of the federation. In a similar way, the "Social Union Framework Agreement"

(1999) confirmed the guiding role of the federal government in social affairs. In addition, it introduced rules for constraining the federal spending power and a new mode of intergovernmental coordination based on monitoring and benchmarking of provincial performance according to approved standards. Although the Quebec government opted out of this agreement, it participated in its implementation. In 2004, the federal and provincial governments, this time including Quebec, signed an agreement on health services. It included a bilateral contract between the federal government and Quebec allowing the province a more flexible use of federal funds. All three intergovernmental agreements, while acknowledging the distinctiveness of Quebec's welfare state, signalled the preference for cooperation and negotiated settlements. Although real policy changes and their impact in both fields were debatable (for example Cameron and Simeon 2002; Jeffrey 2006) and varied depending on the party in power at the federal level, the agreements set the rules for cooperative federalism, which several years earlier had been stated in the Charlottetown Accord.

Negotiations and agreements also brought about significant progress in dealing with claims of Aboriginal people (Papillon 2008). The "Nunavut Land Claims Agreement" signed in 1992 led to one of the few formal constitutional amendments since the Charlottetown process, the establishment of Inuit self-government in the new Nunavut territory as of 1999. Moreover, Aboriginal organizations gained access to various intergovernmental organizations although the federal and provincial governments never accepted them as a third order of government as suggested by the Charlottetown Accord. With various organizations of Aboriginal self-government emerging, powers for administering federal grants to these groups were decentralized. So far, the effects of these developments are to be considered as mixed. But without formal constitutional amendment, relationships between Aboriginal people and federal and provincial governments had been changing significantly, pointing in the direction of a community-based federalism. The evolution of diversified multilevel governance now proves a more successful way to cope with the remaining problems and conflicts (Alcantara 2008; Papillon 2008: 308).

The installation of the Council of the Federation in 2003 by an agreement among the provincial governments signified a further change in intergovernmental policy-making. Promoted by Quebec, this institution put horizontal relations between all provinces on a more regular basis. Under the conditions of a multinational federation and the increasing economic divergence between regions, such an institutionalized mechanism of coordination, which is unique among multinational federations, added a stabilizing element to the federal order (Courchene 2005). It was designed to counterbalance the power of the federal government, which since the late 1990s has tended to cooperate with the provinces on specific programs through contacts by ministers or civil servants rather than by meetings of the Canadian prime minister and provincial first ministers (Papillon and Simeon 2004: 123).

Beyond these intergovernmental agreements, the federal parliament passed resolutions in 1995 and 2006, and all provinces and territories except Quebec signed the "Calgary Declaration" in 1997. These documents officially acknowledged Canada as a multinational federation. However, Quebec regards declarations as insufficient and insists that the distinctness of the province must be entrenched in constitutional law. In fact, the precise degree of sovereignty granted to Quebec or to self-government of Aboriginal people is still an open question. However, the explicit declarations are considered a second best solution and turned the "distinct society clause" of the Charlottetown Accord into a constitutional convention. Due to the substantial flexibility and formal rigidity of the federal system, the question of which theory justifies Canadian federalism came to be held in constitutional "abeyance" (Foley 1989; Thomas 2003). The ideological confrontation thus gave way to a pragmatic policy of settling compromises when specific issues arise. In 2006, the federal government led by the Conservative Party defined an "Open Federalism" as a concept guiding the future development of federal–provincial relations. Although interpreted in different ways by scholars (Bickerton 2010; Caron and Laforest 2009; Institute of Intergovernmental Relations 2006), it emphasized the multinational and decentralized character of Canada and paved the way for a more balanced and flexible federalism. This concept conformed to political debates among Quebecers. They prefer more autonomy for their province, but at the same time call for collaborative federal–provincial relationships in Canada (Mendelson et al. 2005: 43). Cooperative federalism under the premise of recognized distinctiveness made it easier for Quebec to remain in the Canadian federation and to maintain its established welfare system (Courchene 2005: 230). Pragmatic cooperation also prevails in relations between the federal government and Aboriginal self-government, which has evolved in an ongoing process of negotiations.

Secession of Quebec has been debated from time to time, but the issue is no longer imminent in political processes and less salient in elections than during the 1980s and 1990s. In principle, even the Canadian government has accepted secession as an option, but only under precisely defined conditions. Following an opinion of the Supreme Court, the federal parliament passed the "Clarity Act." It states that legitimacy of secession requires a clear majority of citizens in a province voting in favor of a clearly formulated question before negotiations with the federal government start. As a consequence, the power of Quebec to threaten to leave the Canadian federation has diminished. The province protested, but was to some extent compensated by the Constitutional Amendment Act 1996 (Act C-110), which introduced a veto right for five provinces against any constitutional amendment that affects crucial parts of the constitution. Both acts further protected the core of the constitution against changes. Senate reform continues to be discussed, and some changes have occurred by legislation on term limits and practices of nomination of Senators. Legislation introduced by the Harper government proved that this approach reaches its limits when the election of senators is concerned. This does not rule out that, meanwhile, provincial affiliations have greater relevance on the appointment of Senators and will influence their behavior. Accordingly, the Senate revealed a capacity to adapt within the current political system (Smith 2003: 177).

All these changes have been achieved, while the constitutional law determining the distribution of powers between the federal government and provinces has persisted, and while the formal rigidity of the constitution has even increased due to the provincial veto. Moreover, different ideas about what the federation should be, whether multi-nationality requires symmetry or asymmetry in powers or whether the federal constitution expresses a fundamental law of citizens or a contract among governments or communities, continue to set high hurdles for any significant constitutional reform. Formal constitutional amendments therefore have been avoided in the past two decades and are not to be expected in the near future. Yet since the agreement settled at Charlottetown was never rejected by parliaments, i.e. those institutions which have the power to ratify, it could serve as an informal consensus on what holds the federation together. This way Canadians found a rather stable constitutional "modus vivendi."

Certainly, this depiction of constitutional developments should not suggest a harmonious picture of Canadian federalism. The flexibility of the constitution comes at a price: As can be exemplified by federal politics under liberal and conservative leadership, governing parties can exploit it to pursue their political agenda. Since 1995, the Liberal government under Premier Jean Chretien and Paul Martin, Minister of Finance between 1993 and 2002, responded to growing public deficits by unilaterally cutting transfer payments to provinces and reducing spending on social programs. The governments of the provinces protested against what they saw as an unfair sharing of the burden, and their mistrust against the federal government persisted until the fiscal balance was restored around the turn of the century (Brown 2012: 81). Under the Conservative Harper government (2006–15), the agenda of an Open Federalism favoring decentralization and diversity has turned into a politics of dismantling the Canadian government (Jeffrey 2014). Rather than acknowledging the provinces in line with the Charlottetown Agreement, the federal government has ignored them and abandoned cooperation in First Minister Conferences since 2009. Since Prime Minister Harper failed with his plan to give the provinces an effective representation in the Senate, Canadian federalism has revealed increasing indications of a divide and even distrust between federal and provincial governments (Laforest 2014: 184–7). These developments seem to indicate a lack of effective safeguards against authority migration. However, since they are caused by politics of a party government, elections can revise those tendencies. It cannot be ruled out that an increasing ideological divide in Canadian politics undermines the principles of federalism, which resulted from constitutional negotiations. However, under those circumstances, calls for explicit constitutional change should grow, and this is currently not the case.

In sum, while explicit constitutional change of Canadian federalism failed, implicit change has resulted from intergovernmental cooperation, parliamentary resolutions and court decisions. As unintended result, procedural rigidity of the constitution sustained its substantial flexibility. Moreover, constitutional negotiations generated guidelines for implicit change, in particular after the extensive public discussions leading to the Charlottetown Accord. On this basis, ongoing dynamics of centripetal and centrifugal processes, which are still mainly driven by the federal fiscal power and economic regulation of a common market on the one hand and by Quebec's nationalism, economic regionalism and the rise of self-government of Aboriginal peoples on the other, have been kept in a balance by a flexible management of conflicts and adjustment. As Thomas J. Courchene put it: "Canadians and their governments have shown themselves to be masters of the art of managing a federal system in that most of the above accomplishments have been achieved without much, if any alteration in the written constitutional word" (Courchene 2008: 3).

The dynamics of intergovernmental relations enabled this far-reaching implicit constitutional change. Cooperative federalism in Canada is not required by the constitution, but results from the need to manage interdependences in a highly decentralized polity (Bickerton 2010). Conflicts emerging within the federation reflect a plurality of societal, territorial, party political and institutional interests with each government having to weigh them up according to the needs of its own jurisdiction. This complex pattern of cross-cutting conflicts opens up space for manoeuver in negotiations. Moreover, the possibility for individual provinces to opt out of constitutional requirements or intergovernmental agreements and the opportunity of the federal government to arrange with individual provincial governments enables decisions, even when a comprehensive consensus cannot be reached (Hueglin 2008). Cooperative federalism based on voluntary negotiations has reduced the risk of intergovernmental policy-making ending in the joint-decision trap (Painter 1991). Ongoing communication among federal and provincial executives and standard operation procedures of pragmatic bargaining contribute to the effectiveness of coordination (Simeon 2006: 228–55). However, voluntary intergovernmental negotiations cannot stop the competitive dynamics resulting from unilateral actions. Each sovereign parliament at the federal or provincial level can reject or defect from intergovernmental agreements. Hence, politics in the federal system is always subject to a tension between cooperative and unilateral action of governments. This combination causes conflicts, but also drives innovation and change (Broschek 2009).

It has often been argued that constitutional reforms have caused instability while stability has been achieved by constitutional evolution or "non-constitutional change" (Lazar 1998). Others have pointed out that the democratization of constitutional reform blocked changes and gave way to impenetrable intergovernmental policy-making or unilateral decisions by the federal parliament or the Supreme Court, two processes which lack any safeguard for sufficiently considering the claims of minorities (Adam and Fournier 2012). However, not only did implicit constitutional change remain the only way out of the deadlock when reforms of the federal system failed, but also effective constitutional negotiations and agreements became a necessary precondition for keeping the federal balance, if, as in Canada, serious problems of integration have to be solved. Without guiding constitutional ideas developed in constitutional negotiations and legitimized by public consultation and intergovernmental agreements, implicit constitutional change could have proceeded as a pure intergovernmental power game. Constitutional negotiations in arenas distinct from normal intergovernmental politics render these ideas relevant for policy-making following the failed ratification. For this reason, the interplay of implicit and explicit constitutional change contributed to stabilizing Canadian federalism. The extensive parliamentary and societal constitutional negotiations legitimized guidelines for intergovernmental politics. The accord signed by federal and provincial governments provided standards for determining the federal balance.

6.2 Ineffective Constitutional Negotiations and Implicit Change: The Case of Germany

How a constitution evolves in processes of implicit constitutional change when no guiding norms or principles have been negotiated can be observed in Germany. As described above, the federal constitution in Germany became more rigid due to amendments negotiated in a parliament–executive commission. Bargaining in this commission proved inadequate for solving the problems addressed (see Chapter 4). Moreover, although it was established to make proposals for a "modernization of federalism," the commission focused on detailed constitutional rules, whereas negotiations at no point aimed at defining what modern federalism should mean. The close connections between arenas of constitutional and normal politics have caused this process to end with many amendments but failed to achieve the intended renovation of federalism.

On the surface, the sheer number of amendments in the allocation of powers and the introduction of a new debt rule may contradict the characterization of constitutional negotiations as ineffective. However, these changes were less induced by negotiations in the commission but by another mechanism, which revealed the close coupling of the constitutional and normal policy-making arenas. In fact, implicit change preceding constitutional negotiations or occurring from simultaneous processes triggered dynamics of federal change that would have been unlikely in the institutional setting of Federal–*Länder* joint decision-making. Yet whereas in Canada we observed implicit change largely resulting from political processes in parliaments and intergovernmental relations, in Germany it was the Federal Constitutional Court which became the driving force of change. As a matter of fact, constitutional reform is always linked to implicit change of a constitution, and in German federalism, as elsewhere, the Court has been an important actor in influencing this evolution. But given the intensity of constitutional regulations and the deficits in Federal–*Länder* cooperation, it has become a central player in matters of primary importance (Benz 2016; Blair 1981; Blair and Cullen 1999; Dörfer 2010; Kisker 1989).

Until German unification, the functional division of powers and fiscal intergovernmental relations provided room for flexibly adjusting the federal constitution to changing conditions resulting from the expansion and later the consolidation of the welfare state as well as from globalization and regionalization of the economy. Since the 1970s, the *Länder* governments used their administrative powers to engage in regional economic and social policy, and vertical fiscal imbalances had been corrected by modifying the federal and *Länder* governments' shares of the Value Added Tax or by increasing federal grants (Hesse and Benz 1990: 152–8). According to the rules of cooperative federalism, these adjustments required federal and *Länder* governments to agree on the direction of change, with unilateral action having been constrained to administrative reform. After German unification, increasing divergence of interests among the *Länder* governments obstructed joint decision-making on redistributive policies. At the same time intergovernmental conflicts intensified and reduced the potentials of flexibility. Since at that time discussions on federalism increasingly focused on demands to separate powers, governments no longer considered adjustments in cooperative federalism a viable option.

As a consequence, German federalism was doomed to ossify in times of significant changes in the political and social context. Moreover, as experience after German unification has shown, constitutional policy in patterns of joint decision-making that hardly differ from normal intergovernmental politics did not promise to bring about innovation of federalism. Significant amendments of the federal order could only be expected by shifting issues to a different institutional arena with different actors deliberating and making binding decisions. The Federal Constitutional Court proved its relevance as such an arena, when, since the late 1990s, *Länder* governments increasingly resorted to the Court in their efforts to revise the distribution of concurrent legislative powers and fiscal equalization. Notably, constitutional change did not consist simply of a reinterpretation of law by the judges when governments initiated legal proceedings. More often than not, the Court provided no final solutions but rather set an agenda for constitutional policy, or its decisions were interpreted by governments as indicating problems which require amendments of the constitution. Therefore it was the interplay between dispute settlement by the Court and constitutional policy which drove the dynamics of federalism.

Although judicial review processes had been shaping German federalism for a long time, they gained increasing momentum after unification. During the 1990s, those *Länder* governments which felt burdened by payments for fiscal equalization initiated legal proceedings in order to alter the equalization scheme. Given the clear constitutional rules in this matter, the court had little leeway to question the existing law. In its 1999 decision it still supported the concept of "unitary federalism" and the principle of solidarity among the *Länder*. Moreover, in legal disputes on the application of the right for equal treatment in social policy and taxation, the Court, following its decisions on earlier cases, requested harmonized public policies in all territories. The demand for uniform solutions stated reasons for federal legislation in matters of concurrent competences, but also required that all *Länder* governments have appropriate financial resources. Against all attempts by governments of more prosperous *Länder*, the Court affirmed fiscal equalization regulations.

In this case, faced with already precise constitutional rules, the Court was not able to change the constitution implicitly. Nevertheless, it reacted to public debates on fiscal federalism. In its 1999 decision, it demanded a more explicit and precise definition of norms of distributive justice. While it required a law stating these norms, it de facto induced discussions on how the level of equalization can be justified. Thus the issue was turned back into a matter of constitutional politics.

The outcome of constitutional politics by the Court was different in matters of legislative powers. In this case, the Court modified its opinion on federalism and supported those *Länder* governments arguing for decentralization. After the turn of the century, a number of decisions revealed this significant change.

According to the Basic Law, the rules on concurrent and framework competences allowed the federal government to make laws in order to achieve or preserve equal living conditions in all regions. This clause permitted diverse interpretation, even after it had been specified by a constitutional amendment in 1994. In the West German federal republic, the federal government had made extensive use of this opportunity, exploited the clause to justify federal legislation, and left the *Länder* parliaments hardly any room for additional legislation in the policy fields concerned. The Court had accepted this practice, because it considered the allocation of legislative powers a matter of politics and not of legal reasoning. When in 1994 the constitution was amended in order to prescribe the conditions for federal legislation more precicely, a new rule was introduced which obliges the Court to decide on disputes in this matter. Following this change, several *Länder* governments and the CDU, when it was in opposition in the federal parliament, denied federal competence for a number of laws and instituted legal proceedings. In all cases, the Court revised its former opinion on this issue and took a more restricted interpretation of the conditions allowing a federal law. As a consequence, the *Länder* governments actually gained power to prevent federal legislation, but they could only achieve decentralization through a complicated procedure without any guarantee of success. On the other hand, the federal government had to accept that even its power to change existing law can be constrained by Court decisions. This being an extremely problematic situation for both sides, governments had all reason to pursue a constitutional amendment. But since the Court had altered the status quo to the benefit of the *Länder* governments, the balance of power in constitutional negotiations shifted as well (Scharpf 2006).

In this situation, the implicit constitutional change was turned into explicit change. In November 2004, after another decision of the Constitutional Court on legislative competences was published, the federal government became aware of the consequences and made a significant move in the "Commission on the Modernization of Federalism." It delivered a catalog of legislative competences which should be transferred to the *Länder* level. With only two meetings scheduled, the commission was not able to deal with all aspects of this proposal, not the least since the concession of the federal government divided the *Länder* representatives. Therefore the negotiations ended as described above (section 4.1.2). But the changed status quo compelled the federal government to continue efforts to revise the constitution. At the same time the *Länder* governments supporting decentralization exploited this situation, accepted the offer and compensated the East German *Länder* by a constitutional guarantee to maintain existing fiscal equalization agreements of the so called Solidarity Pact II (Article 143c, Section 3 Basic Law).

A similar interplay between governments and the Court influenced the agenda of the second reform process, ending with the Federalism Reform II. It was prompted by the Berlin government's attempt to compel the federal government to bail out the debt-ridden city-state. Deviating from an earlier judgment emphasizing solidarity and cooperation, the Federal Constitutional Court ruled against Berlin. In their reasoning, the judges unambiguously confirmed the constitutional principles holding *Länder* governments responsible for their budget, and they declared the extisting fiscal equalization law compatible with the constitution. However, they called for an improved constitutional regulation to prevent excessive public debts of individual governments. The commission, which started to work on a reform of fiscal federalism soon after this decision, reacted to this "clear order of the Federal Constitutional Court" (Struck and Oettinger 2008: 3; translated A.B.) by making the issue a matter of high priority. It was obvious from the beginning of negotiations that a new rule limiting public debt was a principle task of the commission.[1]

The back-and-forth between implicit and explicit constitutional change had quite different effects in Germany compared to those observable in Canada. Constitutional negotiations were framed in legal terms and became influenced by jurisprudential reasoning of the Court, which members of the commissions took as instructions. Whereas intergovernmental politics in structures of joint decision-making tended to circumvent political conflicts, the demarcation of problems or tasks in legal terms reinforced depoliticization both in normal politics and constitutional politics, with the latter being converted into a matter of fine-tuning the law rather than opening leeway for substantial change. Specification of constitutional law at least was made possible in these structures, but with the effect of an over-regulation of the Basic Law described above.

In contrast to decisions of the Federal Constitutional Court, implicit constitutional change by intergovernmental agreements has not proved very effective in Germany. Several examples illustrate this. For instance, federal and *Länder* governments did not come to an agreement on decentralization of concurrent competences, an opportunity which had been opened by the 1994 constitutional amendment and which was expected to be taken adavantage of at that time. Moreover, when the federal government cut its share in funding the Joint Tasks, those *Länder* governments which could afford it stepped in by increasing their contribution. Nevertheless, the

[1] It is worth mentioning that the parties forming the Grand Coalition formed in December 2013 at federal level agreed to set up a new commission committed to dealing mainly with fiscal equalization. This commission was never established. Negotiations have proceeded in usual meetings of civil servants and Ministers of Finance, as well as in this particular case in meetings of heads of government. Again, the negotiations take place in the shadow of a court decision, which can be expected after the *Länder* Bavaria and Hesse instituted proceedings against the existing fiscal equalization scheme. After the court declared this law compatible with the constitution in 1999 and in view of the fact that the existing law will expire at the end of 2019, this move by the *Länder* can only serve to set the terms for the intergovernmental negotiations.

institutional framework of the Joint Tasks was not adjusted to the new conditions of German unification and Europeanization (Benz, Detemple and Heinz 2016). This stagnation is unsurprising in view of the structural conditions for intergovernmental negotiations, which are basically the same as those for formal constitutional change. Intergovernmental agreements require the participation of all governments, due to constitutional norms, law or conventions. Even if decisions can be made with a qualified majority of the *Länder* governments, provided that the federal government or, in legislation the federal parliament votes accordingly, they are often difficult to achieve. As a rule, the federal government is confronted by *Länder* governments with divergent interests, and agreements require de facto unanimity of all governments. For these reasons, an important mechanism to avoid vertical fiscal imbalance in German federalism, the modification of the federal and *Länder* shares of the Value Added Tax, has also become more complicated, not the least as the different fiscal needs of individual *Länder* are not considered in this mechanism of vertical redistribution.

Disputes in intergovernmental policy-making have been reinforced rather than mitigated by party politics, with the consequence that a significant change of the existing power structure or allocation of resources is not possible without formal constitutional amendments. Despite trends towards regionalization of parties and party constellations, the multilevel party system in Germany is, in a comparative perspective, considerably integrated and congruent (Grande 2002; Thorlakson 2005). Therefore, if governments are supported by the same party, they have strong incentives to avoid open conflicts, but if they adhere to different parties, they tend to refrain from cooperation and favor competitive behavior. In both cases, decisions with redistributive effects and changes of power structures are avoided. Thus in contrast to theories of federalism, which praise a vertically integrated party system as guarantee of stability (Filippov et al. 2004; Riker 1964: 111–36), in Germany it has turned into a burden for Federal–*Länder* negotiations.

Given the limited potential for implicit change in ongoing intergovernmental relations, a shift of issues from normal policy-making to the constitutional level is often used to evade the obstacles of cooperation. To reframe policies in constitutional terms enables governments to depoliticize them and make them a matter of legal reasoning rather than a matter of winning or losing in party competition. Apart from initiating proceedings to amend the constitution, governments and parties in parliament use the Federal Constitutional Court as an arena to solve their conflicts. But given the increasingly detailed regulations in the constitution, the court can only confirm the status quo or demand constitutional amendments. This interplay of court judgements and constitutional reform creates a vicious cycle of change, which reduces the flexibility of German federalism (Benz 2008).

As a consequence, multilevel policy-making sometimes collides with constitutional rules constraining the power of federal or *Länder* governments or intergovernmental cooperation. One recent example shows the quandaries which the 2006 reform of the federal constitution has caused. When the federal government decided to support day care for children under the age of three years, it had to realize that it had lost its competence for providing grants to local governments. The reaction to this problem was telling. Because in this case the influential governments of the southern German *Länder* had a strong interest in federal money, the federal government with the support of *Länder* governments searched for a way to circumvent constitutional law. A special fund was established, which not only can be regarded as an infringement of the spirit of the constitution, but also contradicts rules of transparent public budgeting. With less detailed regulations of federal spending power, a flexible and more effective solution would have been possible.

6.3 Implicit Constitutional Change and Balance of Power

Certainly, implicit constitutional change can also be observed in the other countries compared in our research project. In Switzerland, the new constitutional rules on fiscal equalization needed to be implemented in legislation and administrative policy-making. So far no major conflicts or obstacles impeding this process have been reported. Regular evaluations by the federal department of finance and consultations on the results have indicated persisting support, despite rising criticism from financially strong Cantons.[2] Moreover, cooperation between Cantons has become now widespread practice (Bochsler 2009). One of the challenges that had to be met concerned the participation of parliaments and the application of referendum democracy in intercantonal policy-making. Provisions to ensure parliaments' participation have been made in all Cantons.[3] All in all the principles on the amended federal constitution guided the changes following the reform, and they also are reflected in the 2006 constitutional reform revising the rules of Swiss federalism in education policy. During the last years, the debate on a territorial reform of the Cantons has intensified. In line with the amended federal constitution, cantonal and city governments have responded to these ideas by introducing new forms of regional cooperation (Waldmann 2012).

In cases where amendments had been ratified after ineffective negotiations, limited adjustment occurred, not unlike the developments described for

[2] Neue Züricher Zeitung, 3 June 2015: Die Fehde um den Finanzausgleich; http://www.nzz.ch/schweiz/die-fehde-um-den-finanzausgleich-1.1855309 (last accessed 27 August 2015).

[3] See http://www.kantonsparlamente.ch/stadlin_tables/14 (last accessed 5 January 2014).

Germany. In Italy, the central government headed by Silvio Berlusconi tried to revise the previous reform by another constitutional change, yet it failed with this attempt due to a negative referendum. This stop-and-go policy revealed the political divide of the country, which continues to exist. It took until 2009 for the parliament to pass a fiscal equalization law required by the 2001 constitutional reform. This framework law defines the principles of fiscal federalism and needs to be implemented in legislative decrees. In contrast to the intentions of the 2001 reform, the fiscal crisis has compelled the central government to constrain fiscal autonomy of the regions. In France, significant changes in decentralization did not occur after the implementation of the 2002 reform, until the 2014 territorial reform reduced the number of the Regions. It is still open whether this step towards a consolidation will reinforce the regional level. The same holds true for Belgium, where the structures of the federation seem to be fixed until the Sixth State Reform passed in 2012. Currently, Regions and Communities are occupied with implementing this reform and adjusting new constitutional provisions to the increasingly complicated distribution of powers.

In contrast, due to the more flexible constitutional framework established by devolution laws in Great Britain, the Scottish and Welsh Parliaments and governments incrementally adopted powers, which had not been precisely defined in the 1997 constitutional act. In its response to the report of the McKay Commission evaluating the reform process, the government endorsed this evolutionary process arguing "that there has been a wide programme of change at a number of levels, following an incremental approach to reform. Within the broad scope of constitutional reform, a number of changes which represent major shifts have recently been implemented in the UK at all levels and some of which are still ongoing."[4] Conforming to the fragmented nature of devolution, the process of implicit constitutional change differs between the parts of the union. "Each part of the UK is developing in its own trajectory, each becoming increasingly firmly demarcated from the others, and little attention has been paid to the operation of the UK as a connected system of jurisdictions" (Jeffery 2012: 402). Although the process of implicit and fragmented constitutional change seems to have reached its limits, the government in London still rejects calls for a major and comprehensive reform.

In none of these four countries did the Constitutional Court determine constitutional evolution. Neither did courts shape the agenda of constitutional

[4] Government Response to the House of Commons Political and Constitutional Reform Committee, Fourth Report of Session 2012–13: Do we need a constitutional convention for the UK? Presented to Parliament by the Deputy Prime Minister by Command of Her Majesty November 2013 Cm 8749 p. 6; (https://www.gov.uk/government/uploads/system/uploads/attachment_data/file/264086/8749.pdf, last accessed 27 August 2015).

reforms nor were they extensively used as an arena to advance implicit change, in clear contrast to what we observed in Germany. Constitutional conflicts between governments in these countries undergoing a process of regionalization or federalization tend to be seen as political issues and not a matter that can be transformed into judicial terms (Erk 2011). Accordingly, implicit constitutional changes had more limited effects on the balance of power in these countries compared, for instance, to Canada and Germany.

In Austria and Spain, the deadlock of constitutional reform of the federation had different impacts on constitutional evolution. In Spain, the constitution opened up a wide leeway for implicit change, which was used to develop a federation. As César Colino explained:

> most changes of the Spanish system have occurred without explicit formal constitutional amendment, both through incremental adaptation of regional statutes and constitutional court interpretation of power distribution and responsibilities. Hence, without a single reform of Chapter VIII of the Constitution, the system has gradually transformed itself from an asymmetric decentralized system toward a largely symmetric federation, defined by the dominance of legislative concurrent powers and revenue-sharing as main funding model and may be transforming itself again into a more decentralized and asymmetric federation. (Colino 2009a: 263–4)

Hence, the dynamics of implicit constitutional change driven by successful reform processes in ACs offset the rigidity of the federal constitution. Yet the federal government so far has not been able to tame these dynamics coming from below. Meanwhile the "negative flipside of too much flexibility" (Colino and Olmeda 2012: 202) has become obvious. When in 2010 the Constitutional Court stepped in and tried to constrain the powers of the ACs, its decision caused considerable confusion among governments and experts. Hence, at least for a certain time, constitutional flexibility turned into stagnation and the imbalance of the federation prevailed. Yet, the central governments seem to counter constitutional stagnation by renewing intergovernmental politics. Based on an intergovernmental agreement, negotiated in the Fiscal and Financial Policy Council and parallel bilateral negotiations between the central government and governments of individual ACs, an agreement was found on a new fiscal equalization scheme (Blöchliger and Vammalle 2012: 114--21).[5] Whether this policy is sufficient to moderate nationalist forces in Catalonia is not yet certain.

[5] In contrast to the process leading to reforms of the AC Statutes, this process was neither regionally differentiated nor focused on party politics at the central level. Experts played a significant role, and the process was divided in multilateral and bilateral arenas of intergovernmental relations, before parliamentary proceedings started. As Blöchliger and Vammalle summarized: "The process for reforming the funding of ACs in Spain is complex, calling upon different bodies and institutions. Yet it may be argued that it is precisely this complexity that helped ensure the reform of the system, as

In Austria, constitutional change has been facilitated by the fact that Grand Coalition governments in the federal parliament are able to pass a law declared as part of the constitution. By explicit constitutional change, an extensive and detailed corpus of constitutional law emerged. This occurred without the wider public being involved and without any indication of constitutional moments. In fact, constitutional law and normal law are hardly distinct. Moreover, due to the legal and administrative tradition of the Austrian state, constitutional law and its changes and interpretation remained a task for lawyers and executives. "[A] technical and seemingly apolitical view of constitutional law that required expert knowledge made the constitution a domain of legal professionals, while political scientists and others did not engage in the debate or were not recognised as equal partners" (Konrath 2012: 336). This process of implicit constitutional change continued during and after the Convention process. Predominated by executives and experts, it brought about some changes in the federal system, including a change in fiscal relations, the system of Audit Courts modifying federal–*Länder* relations in fiscal control, and the organization of administrative courts. However, these changes concern more administrative affairs and did not really touch upon the federal system. The Convention barely left a mark on Austrian federalism, which still remains under continuous dispute.

Despite their differences, constitutional evolution in these cases confirms conclusions drawn from Canada and Germany, the cases we selected as particularly instructive examples. While dynamics of multilevel government consist of an interplay of explicit and implicit constitutional change, these processes only under particular conditions amount to a robust balance of power. Based on the two case studies, the following assumptions can be summarized.

First, as outlined in Chapter 2, a constitution of a multilevel government has to provide sufficient leeway for adjusting the balance of power without formal amendment. Certainly, principle-based constitutions, which evolved under the influence of the English common law, fulfill this condition more than rule-oriented constitutions emerging under the impact of the continental European tradition. Yet, regionalized governments or newly created federations, which are confronted by strong regionalist parties or claims for secessions from individual regions, also may define the distribution of powers between levels of government in a preliminary way or by general rules and procedures, as is exemplified by British devolution and federal Spain. In contrast, "old" and highly integrated federations in continental Europe usually tend to assign specific policies or tasks to levels of governments.

it allows for the opposition to speak out in the political sphere (parliament), for nuanced views to be expressed in more technical bodies, as well as for the final bilateral acceptance of the new system" (Blöchliger and Vammalle 2012: 119).

Austrian and German federal constitutions probably represent the most detailed ones, but they are also comparatively easy to amend. Therefore, not only the leeway, but also the need for implicit constitutional change is limited in these countries.

Second, implicit constitutional change promising to restore the balance of power in multilevel government requires institutions which allow for shifting politics and policy-making between arenas. While instability is caused by power migration in normal politics, a revision of this tendency can only be expected from processes that mobilize the power of institutional safeguards (Bednar 2009, 2013). Constitutional courts or institutions fulfilling comparable functions play a significant role. By elaborating principles or doctrines, they set frameworks for interpreting and applying the constitution. Whereas principles result from public discourses in political institutions, legal doctrines are defined by courts. They can be changed either fundamentally or incrementally (Baier 2006). Yet with their interpretation of constitutional law, courts usually follow trends in public opinion or the mainstream of political practice (Schapiro 2009; Vanberg 2004). In contrast, political decisions can have significant effects on constitutional evolution, if they depart from routine policy-making and relate to basic principles of governance. Parliaments may have the power to pass binding resolutions. Yet that they influence constitutional evolution by declarations, as we observed in the Canadian case, is rather an exception. As a rule, intergovernmental policy-making causes implicit change to a distribution of powers or modes of multilevel governance. Under normal circumstances, only incremental adjustments can be expected from these processes. Whether these changes increase an imbalance or lead to greater stability is uncertain. If central or regional governments are in a position to threaten with unilateral action (which at the regional level can mean secession) or if they can autonomously define the agenda of negotiations (as the ACs in Spain or the federal government in Austria), an evolution towards greater imbalance is highly probable. For these reasons, the existence of safeguards is a necessary but not a sufficient condition for a robust balance of power.

Third, in order to restore a balance of power, implicit change must be directed by renewed principles or guidelines. They cannot be established in normal political processes or by court rulings alone. Implicit constitutional change as such is constrained by the existing constitutional law, and it does not initiate a new path of evolution. However, a significant turn is possible if political practices affecting the meaning of constitutional norms are derived from a negotiated constitutional agreement or an amended constitutional law. Only if these negotiations depart from normal bargaining among executives or political parties and end with agreements justified by reasons and norms, they probably induce effective constitutional change. Therefore, we find a new balance of power in Canada and Switzerland, but not in the other cases, not even in countries where courts and politics could use leeway provided by a flexible constitution. Where processes are depoliticized and turned into disputes in courts, as in Germany, or where constitutional politics became a matter of experts and the executive, only incremental change can be expected to occur, depending on the degree of flexibility of the constitution.

Finally, significant constitutional changes need to be legitimized. Whereas legitimacy is guaranteed in explicit change of the constitutional law through amendment procedures, it regularly turns out uncertain when it comes to implicit constitutional change. Illegitimate change, which may be contested from the outset, cannot restore a balance of power, but rather constitutes a source of instability. Legitimacy is obviously lacking in cases of "unconstitutional implicit change" (Voigt 1997: 36–8). However, even if implicit change does not infringe constitutional law, it needs to be acknowledged by a wide majority of citizens or their legitimate representatives in parliaments.

From this point of view, the qualification of non-constitutional renewal in Canada as successful can be disputed. Although some of the changes had been triggered by resolutions of the federal parliament and were passed with an overwhelming majority, most resulted from intergovernmental agreements. Considering the predominance of ministers or civil servants in intergovernmental relations, scholars have long since criticized this "executive federalism" for lacking democratic legitimacy. This deficit should be disapproved even more in constitutional policy. Yet in contrast to other federal countries, Canadian intergovernmental relations are more open to the public. This in particular applies when intergovernmental agreements are concluded which affect the constitution of the federation. Jennifer Smith observed a clear contrast between normal intergovernmental politics shielded from parliaments and the public, and politics affecting fundamental questions of federalism: "The closed process of executive federalism can have the effect of immunizing controversies between the two levels of government from public debate, because the legislatures are excluded from these processes.... Paradoxically the very practice that normally closes out the public occasionally lets them in. When there is sharp, deep conflict between the governments, the public gets to see through the cracks" (Smith 2003: 106–7). Moreover, intergovernmental agreements are subject to parliamentary veto power. Due to the sovereignty of parliament, intergovernmental agreements are only binding if and as long as no parliament at the federal or provincial level decides against them. This was the case when the government of Quebec abstained from signing the Social Union Framework Agreement (SUFA) in order to maintain its autonomy in social policy, while other provincial parliaments silently consented to this accord. But the government of Quebec participated in activities resulting from the SUFA, and the opt-out of the province was in a way revoked by the 2004 Health Care Agreement.

Another source of legitimacy existed with the constitutional agreement itself. Although a majority of citizens in a majority of the provinces rejected the Charlottetown Accord, it was never put to the vote in parliaments according to the rules of constitutional amendment. To be sure, there were widespread debates, and many experts and politicians criticized the Accord as overloaded with diffuse declarations. Moreover, leaders of government and actors who negotiated the accord were apparently not very enthusiastic about the outcome, in particular the compromise settled with Quebec in the last stages of negotiations. Therefore, they did not sufficiently defend their decision. During the ratification campaign, few disputed points concerning the representation of provinces in federal institutions and the "distinct society" clause were highlighted, while issues on which a consensus was reached received much less attention. As a consequence, the confrontation on the redistribution of powers among the provinces trumped the agreement which had been achieved on basic issues like a reform of federal institutions (in particular the Senate reform) or the distribution of legislative and executive powers between the federation and the provinces. Although these agreements had been settled after extensive consultation with civil society organizations and citizens, after deliberation in federal and provincial parliaments, and after pragmatic negotiations among heads of governments, they shifted to the background in the referendum campaign. Following this turn of public debates, implicit constitutional change signified a return to the intergovernmental and parliamentary mode of constitutional policy and a departure from experiments of democracy by referendum. Actually, this implied a revival of the consensus negotiated among representatives of citizens. After Canadians had realized that too many veto-players could block ratification, they turned to the intergovernmental mode of constitutional change in order to find a new balance of their federal order, which they implemented in line with the negotiated accord. In retrospect, this process proved to be successful and did not provoke significant resistance either in parliaments or in society.

In Germany, legitimacy of implicit constitutional change exclusively derives from the widespread acceptance of the Federal Constitutional Court. Informal intergovernmental agreements or declarations of parliaments would not be considered a source from which constitutional norms could be achieved. For this reason, the Court has gained its role as agenda-setter in constitutional negotiations. Constitutional dynamics has been driven by the close interaction between intergovernmental politics and court proceedings. Yet it is rather the legitimacy of the rule of law than of democratic institutions which justifies this process. Accordingly, implicit constitutional change mainly results from decisions of judges or the community of lawyers interpreting the constitution.

6.4 Summary

The brief and selective account of implicit constitutional change expounded in this chapter corroborates the conclusion that arena differentiation supports constitutional change, whereas the concentration of constitutional policy in closely connected arenas or in a single arena increases rigidity. In Canada, where constitutional negotiations in the Charlottetown process combined parliamentary, consociational and intergovernmental processes, implicit change was fostered by parliamentary declarations, Supreme Court decisions and, most of all, intergovernmental negotiations. Aside from the ideas and norms resulting from constitutional negotiations, these institutional alternatives for dealing with constitutional problems created a potential for change and for restoring the balance of power. In none of the other cases did we find a similar flexibility due to an interplay of constitutional and non-constitutional change.

Germany represents a contrasting case. Here, the Constitutional Court not only constitutes the main source of implicit constitutional change, it also serves as a driving force of constitutional reform due to its actual power to define the agenda. The close interaction between proceedings in the court and constitutional amendment processes has increasingly reduced the flexibility of German federalism. It has turned constitutional politics into a process dominated by judicial review. To be sure, the interplay of politics and the Court allows decision makers to overcome joint-decision traps and contributes to the feasibility of constitutional amendments. However, these amendments follow a legalistic approach oriented towards rules rather than a political deliberation about norms, and they finally amounted to detailed regulations of the federal order. As a consequence, flexibility is reduced and, in the long run, the balance of power is at risk.

7

Explaining Success and Failure of Constitutional Policy

The previous Chapters 4, 5 and 6 summarized the results of our case studies on constitutional change in federal and regionalized governments. This chapter presents a systematic analysis of the causes and consequences of these processes, in order to evaluate the validity of the theory outlined above (Chapter 2). For this purpose, alternative theories or explanations will be included. As demonstrated in Chapter 5, ratification rules and ratification processes do not determine the outcome of constitutional policy. Rather, we have to consider them as conditions affecting negotiations. Accordingly, the following analysis focuses on those factors which influence processes of negotiation, and the quality of an amendment proposal or the outcome of constitutional policy. Beyond the scope of a reform compared to the intentions or the original agenda, this chapter intends to explain under which conditions constitutional change leads to balancing powers in a multilevel political system, as defined in Chapter 2 (section 2.2.4).

7.1 Method of Comparative Analysis

It goes without saying that the limited number of cases analyzed in this study does not allow us to derive generalizable explanations of constitutional change in federal or regionalized political systems. Moreover, the comparative study presented in this book does not allow us to identify all conditions affecting the balance of power in these multilevel governments. Yet we can use the results of our empirical research to check whether our theory holds compared to other theories.

According to our theoretical framework, a federal or multilevel system becomes robust if the balance of power between levels and institutions of government is explicitly renegotiated from time to time. Negotiations on principles, norms or rules of the constitutional framework can be considered a basic mechanism allowing adjustments to the constitutional compact when needed. In principle, they can lead to an agreement on a new balance of power, bring about an incremental modification to the status quo by a compromise among the decisive actors, or end in a deadlock, depending on whether participating actors tend to interact in the arguing, bargaining or confrontation mode. A theory explaining outcomes of constitutional policy therefore has to identify conditions for these modes of negotiations to evolve.

In our empirical research, we traced the processes of constitutional policy in order to find out the different arenas and sequences of negotiations and decision-making, the quality of the processes in the particular arenas and of the overall process of constitutional policy. Certainly, without participating in the negotiations and only by relying on reports by participants, it is difficult to clearly discern which type of negotiations had been practiced in the particular cases. Yet the information we collected is sufficient to describe the type of actors involved, their preferences and commitments, and the constraints under which they negotiated. Moreover, we can characterize those outcomes of constitutional negotiations which, with good reasons, can be linked to particular modes of negotiations.

Two sets of factors will be considered in the ensuing comparative analysis: First, we focus on organizational structures of constitutional negotiations that can be arranged to some extent by those actors initiating a constitutional reform, although these structures often emerge and change during the reform process. Decisions on these settings certainly are influenced by the institutional framework of the political system or can be traced back to distinct political cultures. However, neither these conditions nor amendment rules written down in a constitution ultimately determine structures and procedures of constitutional policy, while established practices can be shaped and modified. This in fact occurs in reality more often than not (for Belgium and Canada, see Petersohn 2013). Thus, when initiating constitutional negotiations, actors have to decide on the arrangement of the arena of constitutional reform, the set-up of specific arenas where particular issues are dealt with, the differentiation of the negotiation process, and the participants in the different arenas and stages of negotiations. Those participants can be selected from a wide range of executives, members of parliaments, party representatives, interest groups or civil society organizations. As explained above, we are primarily interested in these organizational conditions of constitutional negotiations, which are at the disposition of policy-makers. This set of conditions includes the different links between negotiation and ratification processes. To a certain degree, the relationship between these processes and arenas depends on the rules for constitutional amendment that are given and cannot be altered during a particular reform process. Yet the arrangement of negotiations also influences how these processes are linked and whether actors can anticipate potential vetoes or not.

The second category of conditions comprises those factors which must be taken as given by policy-makers. In this set, we find contextual conditions of historical legacies and the broader political system. They shape the underlying conflict structure of multilevel politics and the type of party system, which may integrate actors from different levels, institutions or policy sectors or may divide them into competing camps dissenting about the nature and direction of the needed constitutional amendments. Additionally, we consider time pressures on the reform negotiations a relevant condition. Those pressures might be caused by particular election outcomes, by deadlines for presenting results defined by constitutional rules or political decisions, following from terms of legislative institutions, or resulting from specific situations compelling a decision at a certain point in time. Finally, a change of government at the central level can trigger dynamics of constitutional policy.

We have to start the analysis by operationalizing these conditions displaying the potential factors of successful or failed constitutional reform. Although we are aware that effective constitutional change is caused by multiple conditions varying to certain degrees, the explanatory conditions are dichotomized in such a way that the presence of a condition is presumed to account for successful negotiation and its absence for failed negotiations. Following the logic of Qualitative Comparative Analyses (QCA), we do not search for the probability that individual "variables" have an impact on outcomes, but for combinations of conditions, which explain the modes of negotiations and the quality of outcomes of constitutional policy (Ragin 1987). Therefore, we classify the cases within a multidimensional analytical space, applying the organizational factors of negotiations and the contextual conditions in separate schemes.

At the same time, the limited empirical diversity of this study renders a formal analysis with QCA limited in its explanatory potential. Since we found only a small set of successful reforms and as we had to consider several conditions that constitute many different configurations, a QCA would only reveal negative results for particular theories, which can be proved as unconvincing. In order to reduce the number of conjunct conditions that explain successful negotiations, a comparative design including more cases and thus less hypothetical configurations would be necessary. Therefore, we applied QCA as a means to structuring the comparative analyses and as a prerequisite of multidimensional classification. The underlying approach of this method designed to search for configurations of conditions has guided the comparative analysis of the case studies. As will be explained in the ensuing sections, this analysis give us reasons to confirm the theory outlined in Chapter 2.

7.2 Conditions of Successful Constitutional Policy

As outlined above, the first set of conditions relating to the organization of constitutional negotiations is derived from institutional and actor-centered theories. The first step of our comparative analysis aims at confirming or disproving the theoretical framework outlined in Chapter 2. In a second step, alternative theories should be taken into consideration.

7.2.1 *Modifiable Conditions: The Organization of Constitutional Reform Processes*

The first of these conditions concerns the general set-up of the arena of constitutional politics and its delineation from arenas of normal or "constitutionalized" politics. It determines whether negotiations on constitutional issues can be protected from being exploited by actors pursuing particular policy interests or not. Constitutional politics is considered separate if it clearly differs from patterns of normal policy-making as regards formal structures, processes and actor constellation. Indicators of this separation are the establishment of a particular institution designed for negotiating a constitutional reform, the inclusion of actors usually not involved in legislative processes, or the relative power of these "external" actors. If negotiations took place in a separate arena of constitutional policy, cases are coded with 1, otherwise with 0. This condition of *separation between constitutional and normal politics* is abbreviated as *SepCP*.

Separation of constitutional and normal politics seems to be achieved by setting up a convention. However, as the Austrian case proves, the formal organization of a convention can mask a structure which actually is dominated by the political elite or political parties. We nevertheless coded the Austrian case with 1 due to the inclusion of actors from civil society and of experts. Moreover, the Convention constituted a distinct institution in Austrian government. This condition was also fulfilled in Canada and in Switzerland. In Canada, the Charlottetown process was organized as a particular process from the beginning. It included a broad variety of actors in distinct arenas. Even if experts and representatives from civil society participated only in consultations, their influence on constitutional negotiations should not be underrated. In Switzerland, initiators of the NFA process established a specific policy arena according to the mechanisms entrenched in the Swiss Constitution. Expert-dominated commissions, committees of high-ranking civil servants from federal and cantonal ministries, and consultation processes including representatives of different interest groups via the "*Vernehmlassung*" procedure constituted alternating centers of negotiation during the reform process. In all other cases, constitutional reforms were negotiated in the normal pre-legislative arenas, although the processes diverged to a certain extent from the standard procedures in legislation. As outlined above (section 4.1.2), the commission established for preparing the federalism reforms in Germany largely emulated normal policy-making in matters which the *Bundestag* and *Bundesrat* decide on an equal footing. The outline of the Reform Commission with thirty-two members delegated by the political parties in the *Bundestag* and by the *Bundesrat* reproduced the well-known composition of the interparliamentary conciliation committee ("*Vermittlungsausschuss*"). Experts and public hearings did not play a significant role. In Belgium, Great Britain, France, Italy, and Spain, party politics dominated negotiations unbalanced by actors from associations or civil society, even where governments attempted to give them a voice, as in France. In Spain and in Great Britain, as far as the Scottish devolution was concerned, separate arenas for constitutional policy-making were established at the regional level, but not at the central level. We consider these particular structures as regional differentiation (see Table 7.3).

The second condition refers to the organization of negotiation processes. We find cases in which all issues were dealt with at the same time. By leaving all pending questions open until the final decision was taken, this procedure was geared toward deal-making in order to settle conflicts. Constitutional amendment was regarded as a package determined to balance benefits and concessions among all interests involved. In contrast, processes proceeding in a well-designed sequence aim at finding a consensus. In such a *sequence* (abbreviated as *Sequ* and coded 1 if processes are divided in at least two phases), the most important issues are dealt with and decisions on them are fixed before other issues are addressed. According to our theory, the separation of negotiations on principles and negotiations on rules, as can be observed in the Swiss case, is most likely to lead to an effective agreement. A similar sequence was evident in the French reform, which started with a constitutional reform setting the basic rules and continued with the implementation of these principles in normal legislation. However, constitutional rules already revealed a compromise resulting from bargaining between the central government and the Senate. In Canada, this sequential logic was not as clearly visible, although the process aimed at clarifying basic principles first, before Prime Ministers settled more particular conflicts in intergovernmental negotiations. In any case, negotiations proceeded in a sequence. First, the federal government collected opinions from provincial governments and parliaments as well as citizens. After the government had—based on results of the Meech-Lake process—tabled a list of matters to the agenda, the consultation of civil society and parliaments at all levels was to identify possible proposals and solutions of basic matters of conflict, which afterwards were discussed among heads of the federal and provincial governments. In Spain, we again find a different sequence. Here the process shifted between the regional and the central level and gave the former the "first mover" advantage of defining the agenda of central negotiations. In Germany and Italy, sequences were not planned from the outset, but occurred by coincidence, when policy-makers responded to failure or deficits of previous reforms. In the German case, the limited result of the first reform led to a second stage of the reform. Both were linked not in a systematic way, but actually the first addressed mainly the distribution of powers and the second fiscal and administrative federalism. In Italy, the reform of 2001 resumed earlier processes of constitutional reform and continued them. Although these sequences were not the product of a particular design, they provided conditions for extending the scope of a reform and managing conflicts step-by-step. Yet they did not structure the reform process and affect its substance.

The third condition refers to differentiation of arenas of negotiations. It is visible in all cases, although the mode of differentiation and the consequences for internal negotiations as well as the processes linking the arenas vary.

- In most cases, negotiations in conventions, commissions or committees were passed to special subunits at a certain point. They worked on specific aspects, and usually focused on details. As a rule, these subunits served to manage the complexity of a reform. By assembling policy specialists or constitutional lawyers, they reduced the impact of party politics. Moreover, leaders of parties convened in exclusive meetings to settle compromises or package deals. Thus, functional differentiation implied a vertical structure, with the plenum being able to shift matters either down to specialized subunits, where specialists could find a common understanding of problems they were willing to solve and tended toward arguing, or shifting negotiations up to political leaders with the purpose to seal package deals or to find compromises. Functional differentiation is a common structure in negotiation and not a particular feature of constitutional negotiations. In all our cases, we found instances of specialization, and the role of leadership was important in each, although to a varying degree. Therefore, while both forms of functional differentiation seem to constitute an important condition for coming to agreements, it appears a regular feature in negotiations and therefore without explanatory value due to its ubiquity. For this reason, we excluded this condition from further consideration.
- Social differentiation (*SocDiff*) is based on a horizontal structure. In this case, actors from different institutional contexts, those representing the executive, parliaments and societal groups meet in distinct arenas in order to negotiate on a reform proposal. Social differentiation not only increases the range of actors providing information and pursuing

interests, but also requires communicative processes determined to transfer discussions from one arena into another. Both the variety of actors and the need for inter-arena communication increases the probability of arguing processes. In the case studies, we observed clear social differentiation only in Canada and Switzerland. In the Austrian Convention, representatives of civil society associations could participate, but did not play an independent role since they never met officially in a separate arena. The same holds true for the Scottish Convention, while in Catalonia, experts communicated in their own committee, and associations were involved in public hearings. At the central level, we find social differentiation of the arena where constitutional amendments were negotiated neither in Great Britain nor in Spain. At this level, parties and members of government took the lead. Therefore, *SocDiff* is coded as 0 for these cases.

- In addition to the conditions covered by our theoretical framework, we have to consider regional differentiation (*RegDiff*, coded 1 if it can be observed) of reform processes as an important structural dimension in our analysis. In this regard, processes in Great Britain and Spain stand out as particular cases. The separation of regional arenas increases the dynamics of reform processes, and this makes significant change more likely. Yet it also risks causing more imbalance if pressure from particular regions leads to asymmetric solutions without being sufficiently considered in the federal or central constitution. In Canada, the divide between Quebec and the other provinces found expression in a regional differentiation of processes, as long as Quebec did not participate in intergovernmental negotiations. Moreover, the province of Alberta threatened with a regional referendum. But all meetings at the federal level included representatives of all provinces. As long as the Premier of Quebec abstained from participating in intergovernmental negotiations, informal communication bridged this divide in negotiation structures. Moreover, parliamentary committees existed and public consultation took place either at the national level or in all parts of the country. At the end, a joint decision including all provinces was made at Charlottetown. The Belgian reform process also had a strong regional bias since only regional parties exist in this country. However, it was a federal process even in those instances when only the Brussels Region was concerned.

Finally, the linkage between constitutional negotiation and the ratification process (*NegRt*) constitutes a significant condition for reform. In Chapter 6, we distinguished cases of tight and loose coupling. According to theoretical reasoning, the former structure should make ratification more likely, but it also induces actors to anticipate vetoes. In loosely coupled processes, the risk of ratification failure needs to be reduced by intensive public communication aimed at convincing veto players, i.e. members of regional parliaments or citizens. Yet, more relevant are effects of loose coupling on constitutional negotiations. Lacking the immediate commitments to their parties in parliament or their government, actors are more likely to engage in arguing processes if they cannot control ratification processes. In five of the reform processes we studied, we found a clear differentiation between arenas of negotiation and ratification, mostly due to obligatory or consultative referendums. This applied for Switzerland, Canada, Italy, Great Britain and Spain which we coded 1 for *NegRt*. In Canada, the late decision on a referendum hardly had an impact on negotiations, but in this case, ratification in provincial parliaments is not under the full control of negotiating heads of governments since elections can change majorities. In Spain, the separation of regional reform processes (which usually are subject to a referendum) and ratification by the national parliament makes veto anticipation quite difficult as well.

When comparing the nine cases regarding the combinations of conditions (see Tables 7.1 and 7.2), one message becomes apparent. In Canada and Switzerland, where constitutional negotiations contributed to stabilizing the balance of power and to maintaining an appropriate balance between rigidity and flexibility of the federal order, negotiations on a renewal of the constitution went through different arenas and progressed in a consequential sequence, i.e. a sequence following an apparent logic. Moreover, the federal governments avoided a regional differentiation. They found a state-wide agreement with governments of the constituent units despite redistributive conflicts, which had to be solved in Switzerland, or conflicts about the nature of the federation as they prevailed in Canada. In both countries, ratification had no constraining effect on negotiations due to a loose coupling of arenas.

Table 7.1. Organizational conditions of constitutional policy

	SepCP	Sequ	SocDiff	RegDiff	NegRt[1]	Outc1 Scope[2]	Outc2 Balance[3]	Outc3 Imbalance[4]
CH	1	1	1	0	1	1	1	0
CAN	1	1	1	0	1	1	1	0
AUT	1	0	0	0	0	0	0	0
GER	0	0	0	0	0	0	0	0
IT	0	0	0	0	1	1	0	0
FR	0	1	0	0	0	0	0	0
BEL	0	0	0	0	0	0	0	1
GB	0	0	0	1	1	1	0	1
ESP	0	0	0	1	1	1	0	1

[1] Loose coupling 1, tight coupling 0.
[2] Scope of change (see Chapter 4, Table 4.1, intended scope and selectivity combined).
[3] Balance of power and flexibility (see Chapter 4, Table 4.2). A change towards balance is coded as 1, otherwise 0.
[4] Imbalance of power and flexibility (see Chapter 4, Table 4.2). A change towards imbalance is coded as 1, otherwise 0.

Table 7.2. Combined organizational conditions of constitutional negotiations

		SepCP (1)		SepCP (0)	
		NegRt (1)	NegRt (0)	NegRt (1)	NegRt (0)
Sequ (1)	SocDiff (1) RegDiff (0)	**CAN** **CH**			
	Socdiff (0) RegDiff (0)				FRA
Sequ (0)	SocDiff (0) RegDiff (0)		AUT	ITA	*BEL* GER
	SocDiff (0) RegDiff (1)			*GB* *ESP*	

Bold: more balanced, robust
Italics: more imbalanced, destabilized
Standard: rigidity or stagnation
Underlined: wide scope of change

The ratification failure in Canada can be explained by the fact that the referendum campaign was de facto decoupled from constitutional negotiations, since both processes were not sufficiently linked by communication of the reform proposal to the public. This stood in clear contrast to ratification in Switzerland, where both processes were linked by intense public communication in which negotiators had been strongly engaged. Yet ratification failure in Canada did not lead to instability. The federation got over the intermediate deadlock by implicit constitutional change. Although the conditions identified so far cover the reform process, it needs to be emphasized that the structures of policy-making leading to implicit change also combined different arenas (Parliament, Supreme Court, vertical, horizontal, bilateral and multilateral intergovernmental processes), thus also revealing a considerable complexity of the institutional setting. These findings give reason to conclude that a separation of normal and constitutional policy, a consequential sequence of negotiations, a differentiation of arenas including different groups of actors, a nation-wide process including all regional governments and societies, and a loose coupling between constitutional negotiations and ratification seem to constitute institutional conditions supporting a balance of multilevel government.

In Belgium, Germany, France and Italy, where constitutional reform ended with limited or, in the Italian case, significant changes but without an effective renewal of the balance of power, negotiations were concentrated to a large extent in one arena. The typical functional differentiation in this arena apparently facilitated compromises on particular issues, while the leaders of the different groups representing territorial or party political interests concluded package deals. Some particular circumstances promoted change or prevented deadlock situations. In Germany, the first Reform Commission ended without a proposal and the second commission was close to failure. Here, the change of the constitutional status quo depends on decisions of the Federal Constitutional Court or requests by the Court, which triggered agreements on the distribution of powers and a debt rule, which would not have been possible without this interplay between two arenas of constitutional policy. In Italy, the referendum allowed bypassing veto-power of the opposition in parliament, and this explains the scope of the reform. Moreover, the government profited from the work of a previous commission and finished an existing proposal. But ratification by referendum as such was not sufficient to generate more effective negotiations and a constitutional reform contributing to a balance of power. In France, the concentration of negotiations in the legislative arena counteracted the effects that may have resulted from the sequential process starting with constitutional amendment and followed by implementing legislation. In Belgium, the institutional framework and the set-up of the arena for constitutional negotiations revealed all the characteristic features of joint decision-making and lacked conditions favoring effective negotiations. Accordingly, we find no significant changes. Agreements reveal a bargain between regional parties, in this case at the cost of the central government and with the effect of a further destabilization of the federal balance.[1] These case studies confirm the assumption that, if negotiations on a constitutional amendment are concentrated in an arena where constitutional policy is not separated from normal policy-making, at best incremental change can be expected. A series of reform processes, which we observed in Belgium, Italy and Germany, can bring about an accumulation of amendments. Nonetheless, even this condition does not guarantee an improvement in the balance of power. If negotiations are concentrated in one arena dominated by parties and executives, bargaining prevails. Under these conditions, the effects of constitutional policy depend on contingent circumstances, but are in any case limited.

In Great Britain and Spain, the territorial organization of the state is still in flux, with significant changes resulting from regionally differentiated processes. The dynamics of change is mainly due to regionalization of constitutional policy and to proposals and claims formulated in particular regions. In both countries, we have traced the processes in the two most significant regions. If we compare the institutional conditions of constitutional negotiations in these regions, we find constellations which, according to our theoretical reasoning, include some factors contributing to success. This applies in particular to statute reform in Catalonia and to devolution in Scotland. The separation of the constitutional arena from normal politics may not

[1] The Sixth State Reform resulted in a wider scope of amendments. However, it did not deviate from the trend towards further decentralization and fragmentation of responsibilities. Hence, like the reform we included in our comparative case studies, it did not contribute to more stability and balance of power.

Table 7.3. Institutional conditions of regionally differentiated constitutional negotiations

	SepCP	Sequ	SocDiff	NegRt	Outc 1: Scope
AND	0	0	0	1	1
CAT	1	0	1	1	1
ESP—central level	0	0	0	0	1
SCOT	1	0	0	1	1
WALES	0	0	0	1	0
GB—central level	0	0	0	0	1

appear as clear as for instance in Canada. Nevertheless, it was symbolized by an expert commission in Catalonia and the Scottish Constitutional Convention. The strong role of experts and public hearings in Catalonia reveal a social differentiation, which was limited in Scotland despite the inclusion of civil society organizations in the Convention. The Scottish process went through different sequences, but more coincidentally shifted between the central and the regional level and did not follow a clear temporal organization. Apart from a similar back-and-forth between levels of governments, no sequence was observable in the other British regions either. All negotiations proceeded under the shadow of ratification in a regional referendum and in the national legislature.

In Table 7.3, the outcome of constitutional negotiations in Great Britain and Spain including the four regions is operationalized as scope of change. It was significant in three regions—the exception being Wales—and at the central level. Obviously, the growing nationalism in these regions encouraged a consensus among regional actors on autonomy claims against the central government. They were expressed not only by nationalist parties, but also by regional branches of state-wide parties. Therefore, the control of the center was limited, in Spain more than in Britain, because the central party leaders or the central government had no formal role in statute reforms of the ACs, whereas the British Labour Party initiated and the central government in formal terms organized and led negotiations in Scotland and Wales. Therefore, a significant pressure for change emerged within regional processes, but the responses to these changes ended up making the multilevel structures of the British and the Spanish governments even more instable after the reform processes. At the central level, conditions were not favorable for effective negotiations. Here, party politics dominated the reform process in the legislative arena. Lacking a coherent concept for the federation or the union as a whole, the reform ended with a patchwork of asymmetric changes and failed to enhance stability. In Spain, it was the Constitutional Court which finally drew attention to the principles holding the state together. The British parliament so far proved unable to find a constitutional framework for integrating the regionalized state.

The Austrian case confirms our assumptions, as the failed Convention process lacked all modes of differentiation which characterize the successful reforms in Switzerland and the fairly effective constitutional policy in Canada. The Convention established an arena where representatives of competing parties entered in bargaining processes and where *Länder* governments fought for powers against the central government. This constellation resembles the German case, where gradual change has been supported by a shift in policy-making between the political arena and the arena of constitutional judicial review. However, this was not the case in Austria.

7.2.2 *Given Conditions: The Political and Situational Context*

It is not only the limited number of cases which warrant caution against taking the findings drawn thus far from the comparative analysis for granted. The literature on federal dynamics and institutional change emphasizes other conditions. They are more or less endogenous and evolve independent of strategies or powers of policy-makers. As part of the context of politics and policy-making, they influence the type of constitutional conflicts, they constrain policy-making or open opportunities for entering new paths of constitutional negotiation or evolution, and they have an impact on the strategic behavior of actors participating in constitutional politics.

The first condition refers to basic challenges in a political system related to the structure of its territorial order. We distinguished in our case selection between countries where performance problems have to be solved, and those countries where problems of integration are at stake. In the first instance, problems are caused by the institutions of a multilevel government, in particular the division and sharing of powers and fiscal resources or modes of coordination. In a territorially integrated society, conflicts arise inside government between actors representing the central or regional level, with party politics constituting cross-cutting cleavages or reinforcing intergovernmental conflicts. The second type of problem is caused by economic or cultural divides in society. Following a society-centered view of federalism (Erk 2008), we can expect that these governments are confronted with continuous pressure for decentralization and autonomy of regional authorities.

Integration or disintegration of societies is regularly reflected in a party system. Yet immediate effects on constitutional policies can also be mentioned. First, the agenda of constitutional policy is different. In disintegrated societies, reforms of the territorial order refer to fundamental values framed as identities, minority rights or particular cultures. Therefore, questions of language policy, education, immigration or representation of regions in central legislation need to be addressed. Moreover, distributive conflicts on powers and resources are framed as problems of social justice, rather than as problems of efficiency. To put it in another way, actors are usually less willing to make compromises or engage in package deals, if basic values or social justice are affected. For this reason, scholars considering societal conditions of federalism expect that in divided, multination societies major constitutional reforms are doomed to fail or to instigate more conflicts than they solve. But due to the political tensions, they see continuous evolution of structures (Livingston 1956), and they assume that incremental change is more likely to end with a stable balance of power (Lerner 2011). In integrated societies, conflicts are framed in terms of relative costs and benefits governments perceive to result from a redistribution of powers and resources. Agreements on constitutional amendments can principally be achieved by compromises or package deals, by minimizing and levelling impacts for individual governments or by compensating negative effects (Scharpf et al. 1976: 62–6). In line with this reasoning, we code this condition (abbreviated as *Problem*) as 1, if performance problems predominated, and 0, if integration problems have to be solved.

The second theoretical approach emphasizes the role of parties and party systems. It has become quite popular in comparative federalism during the last decade. Scholars assume that parties determine federal dynamics and that party systems can explain whether a federal balance can be maintained or whether federal systems tend towards rigidity or flexibility.[2] Recently, scholars have tried to explain decentralization reforms by uncovering the preferences of parties in governments on governance structures or the allocation of powers (Alonso 2012; Bauer and Tatham 2014; Swenden and Toubeau 2013; Toubeau and Wagner 2015). However, while preferences are relevant for describing conflicts in constitutional negotiations, they do not tell us very much about how conflicts are solved. Therefore, the structure of the party system seems to be more relevant as a condition affecting processes of constitutional politics and policy-making. They can reflect and intensify intergovernmental or social conflicts, but party systems can also constitute arenas where disputes are settled. Scholars reflecting on the role of parties in multilevel governance or federalism do not tell us under which conditions a party system intensifies or moderates conflicts.

In order to consider these supposed causal relations, we include the type of party systems in our comparative analyses. Regarding constitutional reform, two dimensions seem to be relevant: The horizontal dimension (*HParty*)

[2] Scholars still dispute whether federal structures are shaped by party systems (Riker 1964) or whether parties adjust to existing federal structures (Chhibber and Kollman 2004; Detterbeck 2012; Thorlakson 2007). Probably different features of a party system should be explained by different theories. Parties integrated across levels of government often exist over a long time and need not adapt in processes of centralization or decentralization, since they profit from both directions of institutional changes. On the other hand, regionalization may give rise to regional parties and boost their development, and these parties compete with established central or vertically integrated parties (Thorlakson 2013).

describes the number of effective parties and their positions in an ideological spectrum. In pluralist party systems, coalitions are likely to be formed and parties are used to negotiate and find compromises. Moreover, in two-chamber legislatures, divergent majorities in both houses can compel parties to negotiate agreements. We find this condition, coded with 1, in Switzerland, Germany, Italy, Belgium and Austria. The intensity of party political disputes on constitutional reforms differed in these countries, and most intense conflicts among parties arose in Austria and Italy. However, the routines of negotiation in government should nonetheless favor compromises. In the other countries, though party politics is characterized by a confrontation between two major parties or party camps, coalitions are rarely formed and the organization of the legislature does not require party cooperation. These conditions even apply in countries where more than two effective parties exist and where the party system includes regional parties, like in Canada, France, Great Britain and Spain.

In view of conflicts between levels of government, the vertical dimension of party systems (*VParty*) is relevant. Integrated parties include actors from different levels in their organization and span boundaries of jurisdictions in intraparty politics. Therefore, they constitute an arena where conflicts can be dealt with. Differentiated party systems cannot fulfill this function. Rather they tend to reinforce conflicts between levels. This in particular occurs if strong regionalist parties are represented at the federal level or can control government in regions. Integrated party systems exist in Germany, France, Great Britain, and Austria. In Switzerland, cantonal party organizations decide on their policy independent of the central level. In matters of federalism, parties cannot effectively fulfill a coordinative function. Therefore, in contrast to Thorlakson (2009: 169), we label the Swiss party system territorially differentiated. Due to the strong role of regionalist parties in ACs, the Spanish party system will also be considered a differentiated party system. It is undisputed that the Canadian party system must be subsumed under this category as well.

The remaining two conditions refer to situations which can trigger change or constrain reform policy. First, a change of government (*GovCh*) has often been viewed as an event that releases energies for reform. A newly elected government usually intends to prove its legitimacy and performance by taking a new course in salient policies. A reform of the territorial order of the state can become one of the projects, if it is beneficial to implementing other substantial policies that are on the agenda of a new government. Yet, not every change in government necessarily implies a change in policy. According to the "partisan theory" of policy-making (Budge and Keman 1990; Schmidt 1983), this is only to be expected if elections bring about a shift from one party camp to another. Among the constitutional reforms included in our study, only the devolution in Great Britain was clearly induced by such a change in government. In France and Spain, the reform processes also started with a change in government. These cases are coded 1 for *GovCh*. In the other countries, results of elections did not produce a significant reform pressure. Governments either did not change at all or did not make constitutional policy a matter of priority. In federal systems, elections of regional parliaments can modify the majorities in institutions where constitutional amendments are ratified, as happened in Germany and France. These changes had been anticipated in negotiations. Whether and how they affect constitutional policy depends on the institutional conditions allowing for veto anticipation, i.e. on a causal mechanism different from the one triggered by change in central government. Therefore, we code these cases as *GovCh* 0.

A change in government can affect the scope of a reform agenda. Whether the promises of an agenda can be fulfilled depends on the political and institutional constraints of constitutional policy. Presumably, the influence of these constraints can be lowered if a shift in political majorities expresses a change in policy-making paradigms (Hall 1993). A newly elected government can attain the power necessary to transform such new ideas into policy that have evolved in party politics or public discourses over a longer time span (Benz 1984; Benz and Broschek 2013c). Thus, change of government can have the effect of a "critical juncture" in institutional development. Nonetheless, while these conditions can influence the scope of change, its impact on the balance of power depends on the structures and processes of constitutional politics, i.e. on how new ideas are converted into new constitutional norms and rules.

Besides changes in majorities in parliaments and in the party "complexion" of governments, constraints due to time pressure seems an important factor explaining constitutional change. While it can increase due to particular situations, for instance in a crisis, institutional conditions varying between states cause more or less time pressure (*Time*). In parliamentary systems, election periods usually define the time span available for a constitutional reform process, which reduces the period available for negotiations to a few years. In Canada, the threatening secession referendum announced by the government of Quebec put the federal government under pressure to accomplish a constitutional agreement in a rather short term. In Germany and in Austria, the Commission of the *Bundestag* and the *Bundesrat* and the Convention worked with a clear deadline, which was extended in Germany after crises in the negotiations occurred, whereas it was approximately applied in Austria. In Italy, constitutional provisions required the drafting of a reform bill at a specific time; otherwise, the whole project would have been cancelled. In Great Britain, there was significant public pressure on the Labour government to fulfill its pledges. In order to finish the project during the legislative period, the government immediately set the devolution process in motion. In Spain and in Belgium, substantial political pressure came from the regional level, while the term of the legislature did not set a tight temporal framework for a reform. Time was also not a problem for negotiations in France. Time limits were likewise rather irrelevant for negotiations of the Swiss fiscal equalization scheme. In Switzerland, no institutionalized deadlines exist, and negotiations proceed independently of elections or parliamentary terms. Accordingly, with overall fourteen years, the reform process extended over a far longer period compared to the other processes.

From a theoretical point of view, time pressure has two contradictory consequences. On the one hand, it reduces the capacities to collect and process information and the opportunities for extensive participation. On the other hand, actors facing a deadline are more inclined to make concessions in order to achieve an agreement. Therefore, we expect tight time constraints to reduce the effectiveness of constitutional negotiations with consequences both for the scope of a reform and the balance of power, although an agreement seems likely. Accordingly, we code with 1 those cases where no strict deadline or pressure from imminent elections existed. This applies to Switzerland, France, Belgium and Spain.

Beyond these factors related to the political system of states, pressure or impulses from the international context can affect constitutional policy. Following theories of federalism and policy-making, continental integration, internationalization or globalization should affect dynamics of territorial structures of governments. European integration, for instance, has often been said to have pushed for the "rise of regional authorities" and to trigger decentralization and regionalization (Hooghe et al. 2010: 59), at least after a period of centralization ended in the 1970s. The consequences have been studied in extensive research from different analytical perspectives. Whereas the multilevel governance approach has pointed to the political mobilization of regional actors in Europe and explained a structural transformation of European integration (Hooghe and Marks 2001; Marks 1996; Piattoni 2010: 20–2), other approaches in European studies focused on the effects on the distribution of power and the federal balance in member states (for example Schmidt 2006). The concept of Europeanization (Ladrech 2010) covers the impact of European integration on national governments in member states, which includes adjustments of constitutions. In Germany, one of the explicitly stated aims of the first reform of federalism (Federalism Reform I) was to adapt the distribution of powers and intergovernmental procedures to the requirements of European policy-making. Other federal constitutions or territorial organizations of the state had been adjusted during the process of European integration. Since 2008, the fiscal crisis changed conditions for national governance and led to pressure for centralization or multilevel coordination (Braun and Trein 2013). Among the cases studied in our research project, the second reform in Germany (Federalism Reform II) dealing with fiscal federalism was clearly affected by the financial crisis, which led to a revival of negotiations on the debt rule after several months of deadlock. The crisis also instigated demands for autonomy in Scotland and Catalonia, which increased instability of the territorial order in Great Britain and in Spain. However, these historical events or developments in the international context varied significantly between continents and in their time spans. Therefore, we cannot simply regard them as existing or absent. Moreover, they may have caused imbalances in multilevel structures and thus generated the problems constitutional policy had to address. Fiscal imbalances between territories and levels of governments increased significantly due to globalization and European integration of markets. Therefore, the international context causes the need for reform and shapes the agenda, but it cannot explain why states responded at different times and in different ways. Moreover, variations in the outcomes of constitutional reform or the achieved balance or remaining imbalance of federal or regionalized states cannot be traced back to these external conditions; rather it is the way governments respond to these conditions that must be considered.

The same holds true if we include another mechanism linking the international context and policy-making in nation states. Like changes in other policy fields, constitutional change can be induced by policy transfer (Dolowitz and March 2000; Evans 2009; Holzinger et al. 2007). While research on lesson drawing, policy diffusion and transfer started with studies on environmental policy, these concepts have also been applied to constitutional change. A comparative analysis of constitutional design in the nineteenth century led Zachary Elkins to the conclusion that "to understand the shaping of national constitutions in a given country, one must take into account the constitutional experiences and models of those countries that inspire its drafters" (Elkins 2010: 995). In our case studies, we indeed found some instances of policy transfer or at least endeavors of policy-makers to learn from external experiences. In Canada, models drawn from other countries stimulated the discussion on the Senate reform, although to no avail. The members of the Austrian Convention took into account the debates in Germany when searching for a new distribution of powers in the federal system. The German debt rule was designed with reference to a similar rule in the Swiss Constitution. Moreover, we found a number of indications that experts communicated information from abroad. Nonetheless, the effects of policy transfer remained limited, for an obvious reason: The problems and initial conditions varied, and the different agendas hardly overlapped. The particular organizations of reform processes set different filters for the processing of information from other countries. None of the reform projects was modeled after a constitution of another federation. For instance, when

Table 7.4. Context conditions of constitutional policy

	Problem[1]	HParty[2]	VParty[3]	GovCh[4]	Time[5]	Scope	Balance	Imbalance.
CH	1	1	0	0	1	1	1	0
CAN	0	0	0	0	0	1	1	0
AUT	1	1	1	0	0	0	0	0
GER	1	1	1	0	0	0	0	0
IT	1	1	0	0	0	1	0	0
FR	1	0	1	1	1	0	0	0
BEL	0	1	0	0	1	0	0	1
GB	0	0	1	1	0	1	0	1
ESP	0	0	0	1	1	1	0	1

[1] Performance problems 1, integration problems 0.
[2] HParty pluralist 1, dualist 0.
[3] VParty: integrated 1, differentiated 0.
[4] Change of government with significance for constitutional policy 1, otherwise 0.
[5] Time pressure for negotiations 0, otherwise 1.

Table 7.5. Combined external conditions of constitutional negotiations

		Problem (1)		Problem (0)	
		time (1)	time (0)	time (1)	time (0)
GovCH (1)	HParty (0) VParty (1)	FRA			*GB*
	HParty (0) VParty (0)			*ESP*	
GovCh (0)	HParty (1) VParty (1)		AUT GER		
	HParty (1) VParty (0)	**CH**	ITA	*BEL*	
	HParty (0) VParty (0)				**CAN**

Bold: more balanced, robust
Italics: more imbalanced, destabilized
Standard: rigidity or stagnation
Underlined: wide scope of change

German experts referred to concepts like dual or competitive federalism and argued on a comparative perspective, members of the Commission emphasized the particular features of German federalism. For these reasons, it appears that policy transfer had only marginal impact on the outcome of constitutional policy in the cases included in this study.

The results of our comparative analysis shown in Tables 7.4 and 7.5 do not support the assumptions on contextual conditions. The type of problems seems to have an impact on the reform outcome. Constitutional change in multilevel governments confronted with integration problems tends to be wider in scope, if we take into account implicit change in Canada, but the Belgian Fifth State Reform does not conform to this assumption. Obviously, integration problems make it difficult to restore a balance of power by a constitutional reform. Reforms in Belgium and Great Britain led to further disintegration, and, in Spain, the dynamics of explicit and implicit constitutional change caused a similar result. However, the Canadian case study tells another story. While a constitutional reform failed in ratification, governments proved able to find agreements and the federation could be stabilized. This finding is in accordance with the recommendation to avoid extensive constitutional reforms under these conditions (Lerner 2011). However, incremental evolution through implicit constitutional change alone does not guarantee achieving a balanced federation. Apparently, the challenge is to combine both tracks of change.

Remarkably, and in contrast to influential theories, results of this study indicate that structures of party systems cannot explain the outcome of constitutional policy. The assumption that a plurality of parties or established practices of negotiated politics favor effective constitutional negotiations is disconfirmed by the cases of Germany, Italy, Belgium and Austria. Sometimes, as in Belgium, parties were at least able to come to compromises despite deep divides in a federation (Sinardet 2012). But in other cases they formed coalitions along the lines of conflict among governments. Our research results also refute the hypothesis that an integrative party system facilitates a consensus on a federal balance. In Switzerland and Canada, a consensus was achieved despite differentiated party systems, while this outcome could not be observed in Germany, Austria, France and Great Britain, where parties function as linkage structures across levels of government. Apparently, when combined with concentration of parties in two competing camps, a vertically integrated party system can even cause confrontation in constitutional negotiations as we observed in Austria.

Finally, neither a change in government nor time pressure turned out to have significant effects on constitutional negotiations. Government change was a relevant factor only in the UK, where it worked in combination with the particular conditions of a majoritarian democracy. In general, this condition can explain that a reform project is initiated, but it cannot explain how reforms are made. As regards time constraints, the long duration of the Swiss reform process apparently allowed for a sequential process. In the other cases, we cannot discover a significant impact. Yet, it is safe to say that a consequential sequence of a reform process is hardly feasible under tight temporal constraints.

8

Conclusions

This study deals with a fundamental problem of multilevel governments, which we can observe both in federal and regionalized states, but also arises in transnational federations. These governments need a constitution determining the distribution of powers (according to the principles of self-rule or shared rule) and protecting the balance of power against ambitions of officeholders at the different levels to extend their domain. However, the distribution of power established in a constitution cannot be fixed for all times but has to be modified if it becomes too great an obstacle to fulfilling tasks of governments or to meeting new expectations of citizens. As tasks and expectations regularly change, multilevel constitutions must be flexible, either by allowing amendments of written rules or by allowing leeway for interpretation of norms implied by the wording of the constitution. Constitutionalizing multilevel government poses an evident dilemma. On the one hand, flexibility of a constitution can contradict the need to protect the balance of power, and it can be exploited to achieve "authority migration" in favor of powerful actors. On the other hand, constitutional rigidity can undermine stability if the necessary adjustments to social change fail and if an existing distribution of power prevents effective governance. This dilemma can only be solved by legitimized constitutional change. If constitutional rules defining how powers are distributed affect the way policies are made, and if the existing power structure is always subject to attempts of actors to manipulate it to their own benefit, constitutional policy becomes necessary to maintain the balance of power in a multilevel government.

This challenge for constitutional policy exists regardless of the reasons for dividing powers between different levels of government (Gerring et al. 2011; Marks and Hooghe 2009). Society-centered explanations point out the continuous conflict between communities struggling to preserve their cultural identities or economic resources with the center aiming at an integration of society in a larger territory. Accordingly, the need for changing a distribution of powers results from the dynamics of divided (multinational) societies. Functionalist theories of federalism or multilevel governance propose a division of responsibilities as a condition for efficient and accountable governance, a structure which should not be at the disposition of policy-makers. Those approaches suggesting a separation of powers are challenged by the experience that a "watertight" division is not feasible. If policies cut across levels in patterns of multilevel governance, the effective structure of power is always contested. If power sharing between levels of government is explained as a response to a rescaling of problems and increasing interdependence between jurisdictions, changes in transaction costs of coordination can affect the particular arrangement of shared rule. Therefore, decisions on specific policies regularly raise the question of which level of government should contribute in which way to fulfill a public task. Policy-making in multilevel governments always implies that actors find appropriate patterns of governance, and it is permanently accompanied by a struggle for power among actors representing governments. This unavoidable duality of politics causes the notorious instability of federalism (Riker 1964) or, in a more positive notion, dynamics of multilevel governance (Hooghe and Marks 2001). Designing strict constitutional rules as a means to protect against spontaneous change and thus avoid instability also prevents the positive effect of dynamics and ends in rigidity, which in turn can provoke political instability. Hence, instability and rigidity are complementary problems of a federal constitution.

Constitutional policy may provide the solution for these problems, but it is also affected by the intricacy of policy-making in multilevel structures. Generally, changing constitutional rules determining relations between different levels of governments implies a redistribution of power or resources among those actors who can exercise veto rights in joint decision-making, according to either amendment rules or their ability to influence or obstruct decisions. As either the central or the lower level governments must lose in a redistributive policy and as representatives of both sides have a say in constitutional policy, vetoes against decisions are likely if participants fail to reach a consensus or to find compromises or package deals. From the perspective of historical institutionalism—those emphasizing the advantages of (or "increasing returns" from) established institutions or those referring to the conservative effects of norms and discourses—gradual change seems to be possible, while theories adopting the framework of actor-centered institutionalism predict that deadlock is highly probable.

The results of our study do not confirm these expectations as generalizable and call for a qualification of the assumptions. First, most of the constitutional reform processes we analyzed ended with amendments, which in more than half of the nine cases were significant in scope. Moreover, in two cases, constitutional policy contributed to readjusting the balance of power and making the federation more robust, whereas, in other cases, changes caused more instability or rigidity. Therefore, we need to explain:

(1) why significant innovation occurs in a constellation of joint decision-making with powerful veto-players being involved in redistributive conflicts, and

(2) which conditions contribute to particular patterns of constitutional change appropriate to maintain or restore the balance of power in multilevel government.

8.1 Explaining the Scope of Change

To explain the scope of change, we need to look at processes of interaction and negotiations instead of focusing on given structural conditions. Institutions may enable collective action but they constrain constitutional change, for reasons outlined in institutionalist theories. This in particular applies to multilevel governments. In general, constitutions are complex rule systems, and the effects of significant change are difficult to estimate. However, if the distribution of power between governments is concerned, consequences are regularly obvious, and the more rules are addressed in constitutional policy, the more actors are affected and will defend their positions commensurately. Moreover, institutions created by constitutional rules evolve according to their own logics of reproduction resulting from the interplay of ideas and interaction (Broschek 2012), or communicative and coordinative discourses (Schmidt 2010). While they guide policy-making and legitimize the use of power, they nonetheless open opportunities and leave room for contests of actors who are interested in maintaining or extending their power. Therefore, the inherent elasticity of norms and their interpretation allows for adjustments to changing power relations and causes continuous gradual change. However, beyond changes in economic, societal or international conditions of multilevel governance, it is this continuity of incremental adjustment which requires that a formal process of amending constitutional rules is launched or needs to be launched. Dynamics of multilevel government are driven by these two mechanisms of constitutional policy, a policy which always cuts across boundaries of jurisdictions (Benz and Broschek 2013c: 379–81).

Veto-player theory and the model of joint-decision-making—the first dealing with division of powers among institutions of government or in party systems in general, the second focusing on German and European multilevel structures in particular—consider processes insofar as both approaches take into account the interplay of actors in their institutionalist framework. On this basis, they provide a coherent and parsimonious explanation. Yet the problem with veto-player theory is that it assumes fixed preferences of actors and, by taking veto power as the essential condition, overemphasizes ratification, i.e. the final decision on the issue of an agenda. It does not tell us much about the negotiation process, which determines the substance of what is subject to ratification. The joint-decision model, on the other hand, draws attention to negotiation, but does not sufficiently take into consideration that negotiations in normal policy-making and constitutional negotiations may proceed under quite different conditions, which to a certain extent can be shaped by policy-makers.

According to Elinor Ostrom's version of actor-centered institutionalism, collective choice on specific policies and constitutional choice signify distinct processes (Ostrom 2005). In principle, constitutional negotiations "reframe" a policy by addressing rules, norms and principles instead of particular interests and conflicts. The frame of reference of constitutional policy denotes a revised definition of problems, alters the issues that are on the agenda, extends the shadow of the future to be considered by policy-makers and increases the relevance of the policy. The concept of a "constitutional moment" (Ackerman 1991) refers to an explicit conversion of a policy frame occurring under particular historical circumstances. Yet even if constitutional amendments stand out as specific episodes in the ongoing process of governance, they do not always arise from such exceptional situations. In multilevel governance where they pertain to the distribution or sharing of powers, they often occur without attracting much public attention. In federalizing or regionalizing unitary governments, they usually signify a transformation of the political system evidently affecting citizens. But even in such processes, the distinction between normal and constitutional policy explicated in theory is not always followed in practice, if the transformation evolves in several steps of constitutional amendment. As has been revealed in our case studies, the joint-decision trap occurs precisely then, if normal intergovernmental or legislative politics and constitutional politics are fused and a constitutional amendment is negotiated among the same actors and in the same frame of reference as normal multilevel policy-making. This was obviously the case in Belgium, Germany and France, de facto also in Austria. Under these conditions, only incremental changes can be expected, and if—as in Austria—ambitions are higher and directed towards a comprehensive reform, negotiations and constitutional reform projects are doomed to end in deadlock.

Additional conditions for significant, non-incremental constitutional change can be observed in the other cases which revealed considerable shifts in the distribution of powers among levels of government, although constitutional policy was not clearly separated from normal policy-making. Most importantly, a comparatively large scope of reform is achievable if processes of negotiation and ratification are clearly separated, with the latter either including referendums or decisions of regional parliaments. As a consequence, negotiators cannot anticipate veto-players' presumed decisions and cannot take them into account when making compromises. Rather they have to find an agreement that promises to be attractive for a majority of voters or parties in regional parliaments. In regional parliaments, support for a constitutional reform is more likely if leaders of majority parties participate in negotiations, but the higher number of interests makes package deals or compromises on the lowest common denominator more difficult, and party politics can cause confrontation between representatives pursuing different ideological orientations. In order to win a majority in a referendum, negotiations have to be open to civil society organizations in order to turn the distribution of power into a matter of good governance for citizens. In any case, only substantial reform proposals will gain attention and mobilize citizens to an extent that promises acceptance for a constitutional amendment. However, mobilization also bears the risk of confrontation ending with a negative vote, as exemplified by the 1992 referendum in Canada. If veto anticipation is not possible, the outcome of ratification remains unpredictable. Hence, the differentiation of negotiations and ratification constitutes a necessary condition for significant constitutional change, but it is not a sufficient condition for this outcome.

A sequence of processes also contributes to increase the scope of change. As has been shown for Germany and Italy in this study, but can also be demonstrated by the history of federalization in Belgium (Petersohn 2013), change can accumulate during a series of reform processes. Even if a reform attempt fails at one point in time, proposals can be revived in later processes or issues can reappear on the agenda. However, a series of reforms can bring about contradicting changes. Instead, a sequential order of a reform process is more promising. Policy-makers, as can be observed in the Swiss reform of federalism, have the opportunity to design such an arrangement. Here, a first step served to fix a normative framework to define the conditions and set guidelines for further reform steps.[1] Moreover, a consequential temporal structure of constitutional policy is conducive to achieve significant change. Organizing the process accordingly entails defining the agenda at the outset, clarifying the general aims, ideas and principles in a second step, elaborating specific elements in a logical order and finally compiling the draft of an amendment bill. A sequential opening of negotiations and consultation to a wider set of actors contributes to this effect. Hence, sequences can reflect a strategy of incrementalism, but they can also support reform policies going beyond gradual evolution.

[1] Another case in point can be observed in the history of decentralization in France. In 1982 the Socialist government initiated a "loi locomotive" on decentralization which passed parliament and determined further steps to come (Loughlin 2007a: 65).

A further condition seems to come to the fore in cases of pending integration problems. In the affected countries, constitutional policy mobilized regional governments and parties aiming at autonomy from the center. By mobilizing the regional public and by turning distribution of power into a matter of rights and the preservation of cultural values instead of settling conflicts of interest among governments, these actors pushed for significant change and transformed societal cleavages into dynamics of constitutional politics. To achieve an agreement, central government was compelled to make concessions to these regions. In Great Britain and in Spain, governments tried to reduce the intensity of these conflicts by bilateral central–regional negotiations favoring regions with strong nationalist movements and regional parties, but they could never utterly control the process, in Spain less than in Great Britain. In Belgium, the central government was not at all in a position to direct the course of constitutional policy. Here, the Regions and Communities succeeded in extending their powers as long as they formulated common interests against the central government, although they failed to manage their conflicts when redistributive issues came to the fore. The need to find a qualified majority in a pluralist party system reduced the dynamics of constitutional policy as did the divergent interests between Flanders and Wallonia. Nonetheless, recent reforms brought about significant changes of the constitution after a decade of stagnation and a long blockade of the central government. In Canada, federal and provincial governments including organizations of Aboriginal people tried to find a new balance of power in constitutional policy for the whole federation. After the agreement was defeated in ratification, actors from the different levels continued to manage conflicts by dealing with constitutional issues in normal procedures of policy-making.

In general, integration problems lead to strong pressure for significant constitutional change. If imbalances in the distribution of powers between governments reflect conflicts in a disintegrated, multinational society articulated by regional parties, constitutional change becomes highly politicized and reform policy must respond to these fundamental issues by meaningful change. However, where regional parties directly participate in constitutional negotiations, they may cause a confrontation either due to their divergent ambitions for autonomy or due to conflicting redistributive interests. Therefore, reforms determined to hold together a federation can fail in absence of other conditions for success. In consequence, neither do integration problems explain an outcome nor do they constitute a necessary condition, since we also found a large scope of reform in Switzerland and Italy, where problems of performance dominated the agenda.

Thus, three particular conditions can explain the scope of change in a constellation of joint decision-making. First: if constitutional amendments are framed as a response to fundamental problems of governance or deep conflicts in a society, incremental adjustment of rules is not sufficient to meet expectations of the public. In contrast, if constitutional policy is framed as an internal affair of governments, gradual change is more likely, although other conditions may increase the scope of change. As a rule, these frames find expression in a particular organization of constitutional policy, so that the first one requires shifting politics and policy-making to a distinct constitutional arena, whereas the second one is inclined to permit a change in the agenda but not necessarily the structure of politics and policy-making. However, this set-up of distinct arenas is essential for achieving significant constitutional change. Second: if actors negotiating an agreement cannot anticipate decisions of veto-players, proposals for amendments must provide for effective innovation in order to convince those having a vote in ratification. In contrast, if veto anticipation is facilitated by structures linking ratification and negotiation in one arena (for example committees of parliaments), constitutional policy leads to decisions at the lowest common denominator, which is usually close to the status quo. Third: sequential processes can generate dynamics of reform if designed in an appropriate way. In contrast, attempts to cope with all issues at once usually end with limited change, either because they aim at package deals in bargaining processes or because the complexity of issues becomes unmanageable.

As regards scope of change, multilevel constitutional politics often results in the more significant redistribution of power than that forecasted by institutionalist or rational choice theories. Thus, the general assumption that complex institutional settings allow merely for gradual evolution needs revision. However, scope of change should not be equated with successful change. A significant modification in the distribution of powers between levels does not necessarily lead to a renewed or robust balance of power in a multilevel government. As several of our case studies demonstrated, such reforms can even trigger more imbalance, either by strengthening the central level, by threatening the integration of a state, or by reducing the flexibility of a constitution. Although we found many constitutional reform projects ending with ratification of amendments, only a few cases can be characterized as successful regarding the substance of the reform. Apparently, achieving a constitutional design appropriate for stabilizing a federal or multilevel order is more difficult than changing a constitution. Yet this finding does not justify the conclusion that constitutional policy is irrelevant in the context of solving the problem of instability or the dilemma of flexibility and rigidity. Rather it should motivate political scientists to uncover those conditions that are essential for finding a robust balance of power and to design an appropriate process of constitutional policy conducive to keep this balance.

8.2 Conditions of Successful Constitutional Policy

As constitutional policy in a multilevel government is targeted to maintain or restore the balance of power, its substance and direction is decisive for determining success or failure. These different outcomes result from constitutional negotiations on an amendment proposal rather than from ratification in formal procedures established by amendment rules. However, as we have found, even successful constitutional negotiations can fail in ratification, in particular since a differentiation between negotiations and ratification has proved a necessary condition for significant change, but a condition which makes a positive vote of decisive veto-players uncertain. Therefore, to explain robustness of a balance of power, three aspects must be taken into account:

- First: we need to demonstrate which conditions favor effective constitutional negotiations and produce an agreement sufficient to restore a constitutional balance.
- Second: we have to elucidate why successful negotiations can end in ratification failure and why ineffective or problematic compromises or package deals are often ratified.
- Finally: we must explain under which conditions proposals not ratified despite successful negotiations induce processes of constitutional evolution stabilizing a multilevel system that is threatened by disintegration or ineffective governance.

1. As outlined in the Introduction, a multilevel government can be considered robust if its constitution balances powers and allows for flexible revisions of this balance in order to correct authority migration or to meet functional needs of changing societies. Successful constitutional negotiations need to pursue these two goals of balance and flexibility concurrently. Therefore, in order to determine the quality of negotiations and the outcome resulting from them, we have to go beyond normative standards implied in rational choice theories of politics. They suggest a redistribution of power or other values to be acceptable if, on balance, all actors benefit more than they lose, so that negative consequences for individual participants can be compensated. However, constitutional policy is not only about interests of participating actors, but about maintaining or restoring the operation of a political system and about finding a new balance of power between institutions and levels. From a normative point of view, these changes cannot be justified by referring to actors' preferences. They have to conform to general purposes of a polity and to constitutional principles or shared ideas of how a polity should be organized. Although these principles and ideas cannot be defined merely on an abstract level but need to be clarified for particular

political systems, in general we can find out whether and to what extent they play a role in constitutional policy or whether actors pursue their own advantage. Therefore, the quality of constitutional negotiations depends on the mode of interaction, with arguing promising better results than bargaining (Elster 1995). Bargaining is defined as strategic action of negotiators aiming at individual interests, whereas arguing requires actors to refer to general principles and norms when they justify their claims. Leaving contingent factors like leadership or situations aside, our theoretical reasoning and empirical study demonstrate that the framing of constitutional problems and the structures of negotiations significantly affect modes of negotiation.

The substance of negotiations is influenced by the agenda, in particular by the way the issues addressed in constitutional policy are defined. Governments or parliaments usually raise problems of performance in multilevel governance. In negotiations, these actors reveal mixed motives: Even if they concur on a need for change, they try to defend their power in bargaining processes. This is exactly the situation which can lead constitutional policy into the joint-decision trap and which likely causes gradual evolution because actors prefer limited change to a deadlock. If constitutional issues are caused by conflicts in divided societies, they are usually raised by societal groups or regional parties. As a rule these actors challenge basic structures of a polity and do not accept an exclusion of issues. Two consequences result from this framing of problems: On the one hand, negotiations have to overcome a confrontation of identities and cultural values. On the other hand, agreements cannot be reached by compromises or package deals, but need to be justified by generalizable values. For this reason, bargaining is a risky strategy of negotiations. Nonetheless, central governments and state-wide parties often tend to defend the power of the center against regionalist demands or pressure for decentralization. Partial concessions in order to achieve gradual change often cause impasses or end with reforms which remain contested or induce further demands. Thus in constitutional negotiations aiming at problems of performance, bargaining carries the risk of increasing the rigidity of a constitution, whereas in multinational, divided societies, applying this mode is likely to increase instability.

Regardless of the framing of constitutional problems, the structure of constitutional negotiations is decisive for keeping the balance of federal or multilevel government. First, the type of arena and process differentiation is essential. Constitutional negotiations in Austria, Belgium, France, Germany, Italy and Spain took place in intergovernmental conferences, in committees of the legislative institutions responsible for deciding on amendments or commissions including executives and members of parliament. De facto committees incorporating executives or party leaders, who usually met in private meetings, settled conflicts. The Austria Convention included experts and delegates from *Länder* parliaments and civil society organizations. In fact, members acted as agents of parties, and ultimately the Convention worked like a joint committee of the two chambers of the federal legislature. A similar structure can be found in Germany, which hardly deviated from the committee type although it was established as a commission and included experts and representatives of regional parliaments and local governments. In France and Italy, parliamentary committees elaborated drafts for amendment legislation. Belgian state reforms were actually prepared by meetings of heads of governments and representatives of the parties. In Spain, processes in Autonomous Communities, where the reform started, varied, but the decisive approval of the central legislature was negotiated among governments and in a parliamentary committee. These structures of constitutional negotiations included veto-players, which turned negotiations right from the beginning into a process dealing with particular interests of these players. Members of committees, commissions and conferences are committed to their group or government, and other members identify each delegate as an agent standing for a particular position. For this reason, each negotiator expects bargaining tactics from the other side, and behaves accordingly, in order to avoid being exploited.

Participants involved in such negotiations know that agreements can only be found either by package deals or by excluding contested issues. However, actors aiming at package deals face several problems. First, they cannot fix an agreement on particular issues before everything is settled. Therefore, they are confronted by the whole complexity of constitutional reform during the process. Committees and commissions, and sometimes also intergovernmental conferences, respond to this challenge by working in subcommittees, with the consequence that they divide issues which finally should constitute part of a deal. The most serious obstacle for package deals, however, involves divisions among actors or conflicts within the coalitions of actors, which is quite common in multilevel governance. In Austria, Germany and France, the *Länder* or local governments did not agree on a common position, not unlike the parties in Belgium, Italy or Spain, which disagreed on basic issues or at least on details of constitutional amendments. Under these conditions, constitutional bargaining tends to fail or results in compromises on the lowest common denominator.

In the literature of constitution-making or constitutional amendment, scholars present "conventions" as alternatives to the parliamentary or intergovernmental organization of constitutional negotiations (Beyme 1968; Elster 1995: 395). They are open to delegates from civil society organizations or independent experts. In reality, institutions labelled convention can come closer to the committee or commission type, if it is turned into a venue of party politics. In cases revealing rather successful negotiations, a different model has been put in practice. Here, constitutional negotiations passed arenas separating intergovernmental, parliamentary and consociational negotiations. In contrast to the sectoral differentiation into subcommittees, the "multiple arena model" of constitutional negotiations is differentiated according to a "social" dimension. Each arena includes specific types of members, who show diverse negotiation behavior. In intergovernmental arenas, bargaining prevails, while in parliamentary committees, actors tend to refer to party ideologies. In negotiations including civil society or independent experts, arguing tends to become the predominating mode since actors need not defend power or fight for resources (Landwehr 2009; Landwehr and Holzinger 2010).

If constitutional negotiations take place in loosely coupled multiple arenas, two important effects can be expected. First: they clearly set apart constitutional negotiations and normal policy-making. But in contrast to conventions, this structure avoids a separation between both layers of policy-making and creates a kind of functional division of interrelated processes: Constitutional negotiations are oriented towards principles, rights and norms, but they remain linked to practical problems and experiences that find expression at least in the intergovernmental arena. Second: multiple arenas link processes of bargaining and arguing. Thus, particular interests concerning power and resources have to be considered, but reasoning on the general aim of constitutional policy and on principles and rules of governance has an impact as well.

Obviously, the relative impact of bargaining and arguing depends not only on a "social" differentiation, but also on a sequential differentiation of constitutional negotiations. In this regard, our case studies reveal two varieties. The Swiss reform process started in the executive, where we would expect bargaining to prevail, but where actually experts cooperating with consultants from the academic sector analyzed the effective problems to be addressed. In addition, actors managing the reform process decided on a clear functional distinction of two sequences. The first exclusively concerned the conceptual framework and guiding principles of the reform, while a second step of constitutional policy, following the agreement on principles and guidelines, focused on particular powers, rules for distributing fiscal resources and procedures for cooperation among Cantons. This sequence framed negotiations in a way that compelled all participants in negotiations to refer to the general ideas when justifying their claims. In the Charlottetown process in Canada, where we also find multiple arenas, the process started by open consultation and deliberation on constitutional issues in parliaments and civil society. This process influenced bargaining in the federal executive and, in a later stage, intergovernmental bargaining, but did not provide a consistent normative frame of reference for these ensuing sequences. In contrast to the Swiss process, Canadians put more emphasis on social differentiation, while sequencing was the prime organizing principle of constitutional negotiations in Switzerland. Apparently, this strategy turned out more successful. In both cases, loosely coupled multiple arenas were in place, beyond a differentiation between normal and constitutional policy-making.

Regarding the balance of a federation or a regionalized government, regional differentiation of constitutional negotiations has problematic consequences. Confronted by demands from distinct regions or regions striving for secession, central governments tend to bilateral negotiations with representatives of individual regions. These negotiations usually end with asymmetric constitutional arrangements, as can be observed in Spain and in Great Britain. Although asymmetric federalism has been praised as a solution for multinational societies (Agranoff 1999), such arrangements obviously increase instability if they are not justified by constitutional principles accepted in all parts of the federation or union. Yet regionally differentiated negotiations cannot achieve such a state-wide consensus, and if state-wide negotiations fail or are avoided, powers remain in imbalance. Stability may be increased by policy-specific asymmetries (opting out of individual regions from central legislation or intergovernmental agreements), that are, for instance, practiced in Canada in the context of implicit constitutional change. However, this practice evolved in a constitution which distributes powers on an equal basis to lower levels of government. If codified in the constitution, an asymmetric distribution of powers needs to be negotiated in a state-wide process of constitutional policy and, based on this process, must be approved as a constitutional principle.

2. As proved by the case studies summarized in Chapters 4 and 5, success or failure of constitutional negotiations does not definitively determine the ultimate outcome of a constitutional reform. Ineffective amendment bills may be ratified, and effective proposals may be voted down. In the second case, the joint-decision trap snaps shut. In the first case, consequences can be even worse, if destabilizing dynamics are induced by a reform, as can be observed, for instance, in Belgium and Great Britain, or if the rigidity of a constitution increases, as exemplified by German federalism. But if it is not the quality of negotiations that affects ratification, then which particular conditions do?

In accordance with previous research (Closa 2012a; Rasch and Congleton 2006; Lorenz 2005), our cases studies confirm that ratification rules do not explain variations in constitutional amendments. However, they imply different risks of failure which participating actors may take into account during constitutional negotiations and which therefore influence substantial outcomes, as outlined above (Chapter 5). Referendums can succeed or fail, depending on particular circumstances, in particular the quality of the referendum campaign. If regional parliaments have to approve constitutional amendments, there is also a high risk of failure since majorities can change during the course of a constitutional reform. Ratification in national parliaments seems to reduce this risk, even if the usual rules of federal systems requiring qualified majorities in two chambers of the legislature set high obstacles.

Ratification is rather likely if two conditions apply. First: amendment rules require ratification in the central legislature, and neither a referendum nor approval of regional parliaments is required. Second: proposals for amendments are negotiated in a committee of the central legislature or a commission established by the legislative chambers. These conditions applied to constitutional amendments in France and Germany. Depending on the amendment rules utilized, these structures also tend to arise in Belgium, if a reform is ratified as a special law, and in Austria, except in the rare case that one-third of the members in either of the legislative chambers demand a referendum. Under these conditions, members of committees or commissions negotiate by anticipating the positions of parties or governments, the votes of which are needed for passing an amendment law. Usually, veto-players support the proposals negotiated by their agents in committees, when they finally decide in ratifying institutions.

The risk of ratification failure is much higher in loosely coupled arenas. This applies if amendments are negotiated in constitutional conventions, which include independent experts or representatives from civil society, but also where a referendum or assent of regional parliaments is required as in the cases of federalism reform in Switzerland and Canada. The Swiss case of success is rather astonishing from this point of view. Particular conditions of consensus democracy in the country may have contributed to achieving this outcome. That ratification in a referendum failed in Canadian competitive democracy despite successful negotiations is less surprising. In Great Britain, where party competition influenced referendum campaigns, we found ratification failure in English Regions and a positive outcome in Scotland and Wales, while a nation-wide referendum did not take place. As is confirmed by the Spanish experience, regional referendums on decentralization of powers are more likely to succeed if regional parties support them.

As a consequence, amendments entailing ineffective proposals are not less likely than are negative votes in ratification on proposals promising effective solutions to problems. At a glance, exactly those conditions identified for favoring successful negotiations increase the risk of ratification failure. However, under particular circumstances, a meaningful constitutional reform improving the balance of power in multilevel government may succeed, if the structure of the negotiation process not only supports arguing among participants but also protects the impact of arguing against veto anticipation, and if this mode of deliberative policy-making can be transferred in ratification processes. Less than particular amendment rules, a decisive condition to accomplish an effective reform seems to be the inclusion of civil society in an appropriate setting or at least the reflection of a plurality of perspectives on the constitution during the negotiation process. Thus, whether referendums are recommendable depends on the particular circumstances. What is essential for guaranteeing a ratification of amendments leading to a more robust balance of power are structures of constitutional negotiations.

Moreover, even failure of ratification may not necessarily end in gridlock or stagnation, since agreements on a reform proposal resulting from effective negotiations can be implemented, to a certain extent, in implicit constitutional change. Depending on the particular formulation of constitutional law, rules on the distribution of powers between levels of government provide room for adjustment and interpretation. This room has ambivalent consequences and cannot allow for unlimited discretion. It can cause instability if exploited by individual governments, but it can also be used to restore the balance of power by constitutional evolution.

3. The concept of implicit constitutional change (Voigt 1999) relates to the possibility that constitutional rules can be altered through interpretation or application in practice without amending their wording. As has long been known and has been intensely discussed among legal scholars (Heard 1989; Marshall 1985), the substance and effects of rules depend not only on what is written on paper but also on how those who apply rules understand their meaning and intention. Furthermore, generally accepted norms shape the substance of a constitution and the application of its rules. In cases of divergent interpretation, parliamentary resolutions can provide for clarification, and courts can make binding decisions. In multilevel systems, intergovernmental treaties or agreements can also determine issues not regulated by the constitution. These modes of implicit constitutional change can be observed in all governments included in this comparative study. But as outlined above, they attained a particular relevance in Canada after the ratification of the Charlottetown Accord failed. Here, "non-constitutional renewal" has contributed to stabilizing the federation. In contrast, neither in Austria, where no reform was ratified, nor in Belgium, France, Germany or Italy, where ratified reforms did not prove effective in stabilizing multilevel government, can we so far observe a similar evolution, which would indicate a renewal by implicit constitutional change.

In Canada, the historical coincidence that in 1995 a very small majority of 50.6 percent of Quebec citizens voted "No" in the secession referendum contributed to this outcome. It paved the way for constitutional evolution of the existing federation. However, this event does not explain why the Canadian federal system became more stable after a crisis had broken out in the early 1990s. Arguably, three basic conditions must apply for problem-solving through implicit constitutional change.

- First: in contrast to ongoing shifts in power by "authority migration," parliamentary decisions and intergovernmental agreements in Canada could be justified by referring to ideas and principles derived from constitutional agreements negotiated in reform processes. The accords provided accepted guidelines for interpretation of constitutional rules and for political decisions contributing to implicit change of these rules. There is ample evidence that the Charlottetown Accord served as such a guideline. Even if the mode of multilevel governance returned to the old style of "executive federalism," the substance of the constitutional agreement was partially implemented, mainly by intergovernmental accords (Bakvis et al. 2009: 254–5).
- Second: implicit change has to result from procedures regarded as legitimate. Legitimacy can be generated by an institution responsible for deciding on constitutional issues, which usually is the role of a supreme or constitutional court. In multilevel systems, negotiated agreements can be considered an accepted practice of "treaty federalism." In contrast to constitutional federalism based on formal rules, such a concept of federalism emphasizes political processes of ongoing negotiation among independent governments as a constituent element of the political system (Hueglin 2000; 2013). Although Canadian federalism does not conform to this model in all respects, changes observable after the era of "mega-constitutional" reform indicate a trend in that direction. Legitimacy of intergovernmental agreements among governments depends on the support of parliaments, which turns agreements on constitutional issues into a kind of contract among states. In this respect, implicit constitutional change differs from the usual pattern of executive federalism in normal policy-making.
- Third: to allow for implicit change, multilevel governments need institutional structures which facilitate decision-making and are conducive to significant change. Canadian intergovernmental politics has proved more effective since the extent of institutionalization is low (Bolleyer 2009), voluntary negotiations prevail and gridlocks can be avoided by opt-outs (Painter 1991; Broschek 2009). Moreover, policy competition between governments, political parties and nations stimulates change. The Canadian polity is characterized by economic, social and cultural diversity and institutional tension between majority democracy and federalism. Under these conditions, ambiguity, i.e. the pragmatic acceptance of

> unsettled divergence, has appeared as one of the sources of stability (Bakvis et al. 2009: 258). Certainly, the other source was the political and social process of constitutional negotiations, making this ambivalence explicit in society and contributing to a shared understanding of the diversity and complexity of federalism.

Conditions for implicit constitutional change are different in other countries. In Germany, a powerful Federal Constitutional Court has driven the evolution of cooperative federalism, while intergovernmental policy-making risks falling into the joint-decision trap and allows only for incremental changes. Due to the increasing legitimacy deficit of intergovernmental bargaining and its limited effectiveness, governments and parties tend to leave the final word to the Court if they are not able to come to an agreement. Thereby, politics has a tendency to turn political issues into matters of constitutional policy-making by the judiciary. The consequence is an increasing constitutional regulation of multilevel governance while the norms of federalism remain disputed (Benz 2008). In Austria, implicit change has turned out as limited after reform policy had shifted to the executive arena and focused on administrative issues. Again, this can be explained by the lack of a legitimizing conception of federalism and the failure of constitutional negotiations. Moreover, incrementalism of intergovernmental relations prevailed. Under these conditions, a revision of centralization and the regular practice of executive federalism appear unlikely.

8.3 The Art of Keeping the Balance

As William Riker and others rightly discovered (Riker 1964; see also Filippov, Ordeshook and Shvetsova 2004), multilevel or federal systems are instable, and the performance of multilevel governance can be threatened by constitutional rigidity. Essential to achieving a robust distribution of powers is a "system of safeguards" (Bednar 2009), i.e. institutions and mechanisms that correct or counteract destabilizing tendencies or maintain flexibility. However, safeguards only trigger dynamics. They set out processes of constitutional policy, which aim at restoring or maintaining the balance of power, but they alone do not guarantee a balance to result from these processes.

Achieving a robust balance of power in a successful constitutional policy is not an easy task. As we have demonstrated by our case studies, instability and rigidity can prevail even after constitutional amendments and sometimes due to those amendments. Yet this does not mean that federalism must necessarily fail or become rigid, with governance becoming unavoidably ineffective. Constitutional change can be considered a process of joint decision-making, but it does not necessarily end in the joint-decision trap. Under certain circumstances, constitutional negotiations may fail to table an amendment proposal or a proposed amendment may be voted down in ratification. Yet under different circumstances, successful reform and ratification of amendment proposals are possible and do occur in practice, in contrast to what has been predicted by institutionalist or rational-choice theories. It depends on specific conditions whether constitutional policy attains this outcome. Furthermore, policy-makers have the authority to arrange the most significant of those conditions.

Keeping the balance in multilevel or federal governments depends on particular skills of policy-makers, and therefore can be called an art, because it requires designing an appropriate structural arrangement of arenas for making constitutional policy. As has been demonstrated in theory and empirical research in this study, the necessary balance of power and of stability and change results from an institutional framework reflecting the complexity of multilevel governance in constitutional policy. Complexity does not only lie in different levels, but also in a differentiation of arenas, i.e. more or less institutionalized venues of politics and policy-making defined by particular actor constellations and patterns of interaction. Moreover, "social" differentiation, which constitutes various actor constellations, is an additional source of change. The constraints and opportunities provided by this differentiated setting can lead actors to come to agreements in constitutional negotiations promising to stabilize a multilevel system against a concentration of powers or against disintegrative forces. As to deliberate change, a structure of loosely coupled multiple arenas, distinguishing constitutional from normal policy-making, separating decisions on general norms and particular rules, linking intergovernmental, parliamentary and consensual negotiations, and differentiating between the roles of negotiators (representatives elaborating a reform proposal) and veto-players (actors with the power to vote on a proposal in ratification procedures) seem to provide promising conditions for effective constitutional negotiations (i.e. negotiations which produce proposals for a substantial change working against causes of instability and contributing to renewal of the balance of power). However, the same conditions increase the risk of failure in ratification. In view of this dilemma, the interplay of constitutional and normal policy-making gains relevance. While "implicit constitutional change" can occur under all conditions due to the dynamics of multilevel governance, only change which follows effective constitutional negotiations and is guided by an accepted normative frame of reference contributes to stability.

Regarding a theory of constitutional change in multilevel governments, this study suggests a perspective linking the model of joint decision-making to a theory of "complex federalism" (Bednar 2009). In a structure consisting of loosely coupled multiple arenas, the trend of joint decision-making to end in deadlock and path dependency can be turned into dynamics of change driven by ideas, reasoning, competition and cooperation. To maintain and control these dynamics in a complex institutional setting is a challenge, which requires both analytical and practical skills. At this point, science turns into an art of managing multilevel governance. Constitutional policy must deal with many issues, it must include actors with different interests, action orientations and power, and it must finally end with a decision supported by a qualified majority. To find legitimacy for a balance of power, not only governments but also parliaments, parties and societal groups have to be given a say. To this end, the variety of possible outcomes must be maintained, but complexity must also be sufficiently reduced in order to avoid overload. Requisite variety (Ashby 1958), i.e. a degree of necessary complexity, can be accomplished by arena and process differentiation. Our research highlights this structuration of constitutional policy as an essential prerequisite for a stable multilevel political system, be it a federal or regional state or a transnational federation. It does not provide a blueprint for organizing constitutional negotiations or amendment procedures applicable under all conditions. Finding an appropriate design is the essence of the art of keeping the balance.

References

Ackerman, Bruce. 1991. *We the People: Foundations*, Cambridge, London: The Belknap Press of Harvard University Press.

Adam, Marc-Antoine, and Martin Fournier. 2012. "Constitutional Change in Canada after Charlottetown." In *Changing Federal Constitutions: Lessons from International Comparison*, edited by Arthur Benz and Felix Knüpling, Berlin: Barbara Budrich Publishers, 351–74.

Agranoff, Robert. 1999. *Accommodating Diversity: Asymmetry in Federal States*, Baden-Baden: Nomos.

Aja, Eliseo. 2003. *El Estado Autonómico: Federalismo y hechos diferenciales*, Madrid: Alianza.

Albert, Richard. 2009. "Nonconstitutional Amendments." *The Canadian Journal of Law and Jurisprudence* 22 (1), 5–47.

Albertazzi, Daniele, and Duncan McDonnell. 2005. "The Lega Nord in the Second Berlusconi Government: In a League of its Own." *West European Politics* 28 (5), 952–72.

Alcantara, Christopher. 2008. "To Treaty or Not to Treaty? Aboriginal Peoples and Comprehensive Land Claims Negotiations in Canada." *Publius: The Journal of Federalism* 38 (2), 343–69.

Alonso, Sonia. 2012. *Challenging the State: Devolution and the Battle for Partisan Credibility—A Comparison of Belgium, Italy, Spain, and the United Kingdom*, Oxford: Oxford University Press.

Ashby, W. Ross. 1958. "Requisite Variety and its Implications for the Control of Complex Systems." *Cybernetica* 1 (2), 83–99.

Auel, Katrin. 2008. "Still No Exit From the Joint Decision Trap: The German Federal Reform(s)." *German Politics* 17 (4), 424–39.

Bächtiger, André, and Dominik Wyss. 2013. "Empirische Deliberationsforschung: ein systematischer Überblick." *Zeitschrift für Vergleichende Politikwissenschaft* 7 (1), 155–81.

Baier, Gerry. 2006. *Courts and Federalism: Judicial Doctrine in the United States, Australia, and Canada*, Vancouver, Toronto: UBC Press.

Bakvis, Herman, and Roselle Hryciuk. 1993. "An Experiment in Intrastate Federalism: The Cabinet Committee on Canadian Unity." In *Canada: The State of the Federation 1993*, edited by Douglas M. Brown and Ronald L. Watts, Kingston, Ontario: Institute of Intergovernmental Relations, Queen's University, 117–50.

Bakvis, Herman, Gerald Baier, and Douglas Brown. 2009. *Contested Federalism: Certainty and Ambiguity in the Canadian Federation*, Toronto: Oxford University Press.

Baldini, Gianfranco, and Brunetta Baldi. 2014. "Decentralization in Italy and the Troubles of Federalization." *Regional and Federal Studies* 24 (1), 87–108.

Banting, Keith G., and Richard Simeon (eds.). 1985a. *Redesigning the State: The Politics of Constitutional Change,* Toronto: University of Toronto Press.

Banting, Keith G., and Richard Simeon. 1985b. "The Politics of Constitutional Change." In *Redesigning the State: The Politics of Constitutional Change,* edited by Keith G. Banting and Richard Simeon, Toronto: University of Toronto Press, 1–29.

Bartolini, Stefano. 2005. *Restructuring Europe: Centre Formation, System Building and Political Structuring Between the Nation State and the European Union,* Oxford: Oxford University Press.

Bassanini, Franco. 2012. "Federalising a Regionalised State: Constitutional Change in Italy." In *Changing Federal Constitutions: Lessons from International Comparison,* edited by Arthur Benz and Felix Knüpling, Berlin: Barbara Budrich Publishers, 229–48.

Batt, Lothar-Helge. 1996. *Die Grundgesetzreform nach der deutschen Einheit,* Opladen: Leske + Budrich.

Bauer, Michael, and Michael Tatham. 2014. "Support from Below? Regional Elites, Governance Preferences and Supranational Institutions." *Journal of Public Policy* 34 (2), 237–67.

Baus, Ralf Thomas, Annegret Eppler, and Ole Wintermann (eds.). 2008. *Zur Reform der föderalen Finanzverfassung in Deutschland. Perspektiven für die Föderalismusreform II im Spiegel internationaler Erfahrungen,* Baden-Baden: Nomos.

Beard, Charles. 1913. *An Economic Interpretation of the Constitution of the United States.* New York: Macmillan.

Bednar, Jenna. 2005. "Federalism as a Public Good." *Constitutional Political Economy* 16 (2), 189–205.

Bednar, Jenna. 2009. *The Robust Federation: Principles of Design,* New York: Cambridge University Press.

Bednar, Jenna. 2013. "Constitutional Change in Federations: The Role of Complementary Institutions." In *Federal Dynamics: Continuity, Change, and the Varieties of Federalism,* edited by Arthur Benz and Jörg Broschek, Oxford: Oxford University Press, 277–96.

Behiels, Michael. 2002. "Charlottetown: The Anatomy of Mega-Constitutional Politics." *Policy Options,* December 2002–January 2003, 65–9. http://policyoptions.irpp.org/wp-content/uploads/sites/2/assets/po/kyoto/behiels.pdf. (last accessed 16 August 2015).

Behnke, Nathalie. 2010. "Föderalismusreformen in Deutschland, Österreich und der Schweiz." In *Föderalismusreform in Deutschland,* edited by Julia von Blumenthal and Stephan Bröchler, Wiesbaden: VS Verlag für Sozialwissenschaften, 37–58.

Behnke, Nathalie, and Arthur Benz (eds.). 2009. *Federalism and Constitutional Change, "Publius: The Journal of Federalism" Special Issue 39 (2),* Oxford: Oxford University Press.

Béland, Daniel, and André Lecours. 2007. "Federalism, Nationalism and Social Policy Decentralization in Canada and Belgium." *Regional & Federal Studies* 17 (4), 405–19.

Benz, Arthur. 1984. "Zur Dynamik der föderativen Staatsorganisation." *Politische Vierteljahresschrift* 25 (1), 53–73.

Benz, Arthur. 1993. "Neue Formen der Zusammenarbeit zwischen den Ländern." *Die Öffentliche Verwaltung* 46 (1), 85–95.

Benz, Arthur. 1994. *Kooperative Verwaltung: Funktionen, Voraussetzungen und Folgen*, Baden-Baden: Nomos.

Benz, Arthur. 2000a. "Entflechtung als Folge von Verflechtung: Theoretische Überlegungen zur Entwicklung des europäischen Mehrebenensystems." In *Wie problemlösungsfähig ist die EU?*, edited by Edgar Grande and Markus Jachtenfuchs, Baden-Baden: Nomos, 141–63.

Benz, Arthur. 2000b. "Politische Steuerung in lose gekoppelten Mehrebenensystemen." In *Gesellschaftliche Komplexität und kollektive Handlungsfähigkeit*, edited by Raimund Werle and Uwe Schimank, Frankfurt, New York: Campus, 99–126.

Benz, Arthur. 2005. "Kein Ausweg aus der Politikverflechtung?: Warum die Bundesstaatskommission scheiterte, aber nicht scheitern musste." *Politische Vierteljahresschrift* 46 (2), 204–14.

Benz, Arthur. 2008. "From Joint Decision Traps to Over-regulated Federalism: Adverse Effects of a Successful Constitutional Reform." *German Politics* 17 (4), 440–56.

Benz, Arthur. 2011. "Escaping Joint Decision Traps: National and supranational experiences compared." In *The EU's Decision Traps: Comparing Policies*, edited by Gerda Falkner, Oxford: Oxford University Press, 199–216.

Benz, Arthur. 2013. "Dimensions and Dynamics of Federal Regimes." In *Federal Dynamics: Continuity, Change, and the Varieties of Federalism*, edited by Arthur Benz and Jörg Broschek, Oxford: Oxford University Press, 70–90.

Benz, Arthur. Forthcoming 2016. "The Federal Constitutional Court of Germany: Guardian of Unitarism and Federalism." In *Courts in Federalism*, edited by Nicolas Arony and John Kincaid, Toronto: University of Toronto Press.

Benz, Arthur, and Jörg Broschek (eds.). 2013a. *Federal Dynamics: Continuity, Change, and the Varieties of Federalism*, Oxford: Oxford University Press.

Benz, Arthur, and Jörg Broschek. 2013b. "Federal Dynamics: Introduction." In *Federal Dynamics: Continuity, Change, and the Varieties of Federalism*, edited by Arthur Benz and Jörg Broschek, Oxford: Oxford University Press, 1–33.

Benz, Arthur, and Jörg Broschek. 2013c. "Conclusion: Theorizing Federal Dynamics." In *Federal Dynamics: Continuity, Change, and the Varieties of Federalism*, edited by Arthur Benz and Jörg Broschek, Oxford: Oxford University Press, 366–88.

Benz, Arthur, and César Colino. 2011. "Constitutional Change in Federations: A Framework for Analysis." *Regional and Federal Studies* 21 (4), 377–402.

Benz, Arthur, and Felix Knüpling (eds.). 2012a. *Changing Federal Constitutions: Lessons from International Comparison*, Opladen, Berlin, Toronto: Barbara Budrich Publishers.

Benz, Arthur, and Felix Knüpling. 2012b. "Federalism and Constitutional Change: Lessons From Comparison." In *Changing Federal Constitutions: Lessons from International Comparison*, edited by Arthur Benz and Felix Knüpling, Berlin: Barbara Budrich Publishers, 395–412.

Benz, Arthur, Jessica Detemple, and Dominic Heinz. 2016. *Varianten und Dynamiken der Politikverflechtung*, Baden-Baden: Nomos.

Bergeron, Gérard. 1983. "Quebec in Isolation." In *And No One Cheered: Federalism, Democracy and the Constitution Act*, edited by Keith G. Banting and Richard Simeon, Toronto: Methuen, 59–73.

Beyme, Klaus von. 1968. *Die verfassungsgebende Gewalt des Volkes*, Tübingen: Mohr Siebeck.

Bickerton, James. 2010. "Deconstructing the New Federalism." *Canadian Political Science Review* 4 (2–3), 56–72.

Blair, Philip M. 1981. *Federalism and Judicial Review in West Germany,* Oxford: Clarendon Press.

Blair, Philip M., and Peter Cullen. 1999. "Federalism, Legalism and Political Reality: The Record of the Federal Constitutional Court." In *Recasting German Federalism: The Legacies of Unification,* edited by Charlie Jeffery, London, New York: Pinter, 119–54.

Blöchliger, Hansjörg, and Camila Vammalle. 2012. *Reforming Fiscal Federalism and Local Government: Beyond the Zero-Sum Game (OECD Fiscal Federalism Studies),* Paris: OECD.

Blümel, Barbara, and Christoph Konrath. 2009. *"Expertise 'Österreich-Konvent'"* Darmstadt: TU Darmstadt (unpublished report).

Bochsler, Daniel. 2009. "Neighborhood and Friends: When Swiss Cantonal Governments Cooperate with Each Other." *Regional and Federal Studies* 19 (3), 349–70.

Bogaards, Matthijs. 2005. "The Italian First Republic: 'Degenerated Consociationalism' in a Polarised Party System." *West European Politics* 28 (3), 505–20.

Bogdanor, Vernon. 1999. *Devolution in the United Kingdom,* Oxford: Oxford University Press.

Bogdanor, Vernon. 2005. *Joined-up Government,* Oxford: Oxford University Press.

Boismenu, Gérard. 1993. "When More Is Too Much." In *Canada: The State of the Federation 1993,* edited by Ronald L. Watts and Douglas M. Brown, Kingston, Ontario: Institute of Intergovernmental Relations, Queen's University, 45–60.

Bolleyer, Nicole. 2009. *Intergovernmental Cooperation: Rational Choices in Federal Systems and Beyond,* Oxford: Oxford University Press.

Bolleyer, Nicole, Wilfried Swenden, and Nicola McEwen. 2014. "A theoretical perspective on multi-level systems in Europe: Constitutional power and partisan conflict." *Comparative European Politics* 12 (4–5), 367–83.

Bourgaux, Anne-Emmanuelle. 2003. "L'évolution des modes de négociation institutionnelle ou la machine à explorer le temps institutionnel belge." In *Les Accords du Lambermont et du Lombard,* edited by ULB Centre de droit public, Brussels: Bruylant, 22–60.

Bradbury, Jonathan. 1998. "The Devolution Debate in Wales During the Major Governments: The Politics of a Developing Union State?" *Regional and Federal Studies* 8 (1), 120–39.

Bradbury, Jonathan. 2010. *"Country Profile: UK–Wales,"* Darmstadt: Technische Universität Darmstadt (unpublished report).

Bradbury, Jonathan, and James Mitchell. 2002. "Devolution and Territorial Politics: Stability, Uncertainty and Crisis." *Parliamentary Affairs* 55 (2), 299–316.

Bradbury, Jonathan, et al. 1996. "Policy Review Section." *Regional Studies* 30 (7), 689–712.

Brand, Jack, James Mitchell, and Paula Surridge. 1994. "Will Scotland come to the aid of the party?" In *Labour's Last Chance,* edited by Anthony Heath, Roger Jowell, and John Curtice, Aldershot: Dartmouth, 213–28.

Braun, Dietmar. 2009. "Constitutional Change in Switzerland." *Publius: The Journal of Federalism* 39 (2), 314–40.

Braun, Dietmar. 2011. "How Centralized Federations Avoid Over-centralization." *Regional and Federal Studies* 21 (1), 35–54.

Braun, Dietmar, and Philipp Trein. 2013. "Economic Crisis and Federal Dynamics." In *Federal Dynamics: Continuity, Change, and the Varieties of Federalism,* edited by Arthur Benz and Jörg Broschek, Oxford: Oxford University Press, 343–65.

Brauner, Günther. 2004. "Die österreichische Stromlösung im Spannungsfeld zwischen Oligopol und Wettbewerb." In *Österreichisches Jahrbuch für Politik 2004,* edited by Andreas Khol, Günther Ofner, Günther Burkert-Dottolo, and Stefan Karner, Vienna, Munich: Verlag für Geschichte und Politik, 415–32.

Bremers, Markus. 2001. *Die Gemeinsame Verfassungskommission: Warum gilt das Grundgesetz?,* Wiesbaden: VS Verlag für Sozialwissenschaften.

Brenner, Neil. 2004. *New State Spaces: Urban Governance and the Rescaling of Statehood,* Oxford: Oxford University Press.

Broschek, Jörg. 2009. *Der kanadische Föderalismus: Eine historisch-institutionalistische Analyse,* Wiesbaden: VS Verlag für Sozialwissenschaften.

Broschek, Jörg. 2011. "Pathways of Federal Reform: Australia, Canada, Germany, and Switzerland." *Publius: The Journal of Federalism* 45 (1), 51–76.

Broschek, Jörg. 2012. "Historical Institutionalism and Comparative Federalism." *World Political Science Review* 8 (1), 101–28.

Broschek, Jörg, and Rainer-Olaf Schultze. 2007. "Föderalismus und Föderalismusreform heute: Australien, Kanada, Schweiz, Deutschland im Vergleich." *Politische Bildung* 40 (1), 53–76.

Brown, Douglas M. 2012. "Fiscal Federalism: Searching for Balance." In *Canadian Federalism: Performance, Effectiveness, and Legitimacy,* edited by Herman Bakvis and Grace Skogstad, Don Mills, Ontario: Oxford University Press, 63–88.

Brown, Douglas M., and Robert Young. 1992. "Overview." In *Canada: The State of the Federation 1992,* edited by Douglas M. Brown and Robert Young, Kingston, Ontario: Institute of Intergovernmental Relations, Queen's University, 3–24.

Buchanan, James M., and Gordon Tullock. 1965. *The Calculus of Consent: Logical Foundations of Constitutional Democracy,* Ann Arbor: University of Michigan Press.

Budge, Ian, and Hans Keman. 1990. *Parties and Democracy: Coalition Formation and Government Function in Twenty States,* Oxford: Oxford University Press.

Bull, Martin, and Gianfranco Pasquino. 2007. "A Long Quest in Vain: Institutional Reforms in Italy." *West European Politics* 30 (4), 670–91.

Bulpitt, Jim. 1983. *Territory and Power in the United Kingdom,* Manchester: Manchester University Press.

Bundesrat. 2001. "Botschaft zur Neugestaltung des Finanzausgleichs und der Aufgaben zwischen Bund und Kantonen (NFA)." In *Schweizer Bundesrat Edition* 01.074, 2418–52, Berne. https://www.admin.ch/opc/de/federal-gazette/2002/2291.pdf (last accessed 30 August 2015).

Burgess, Michael. 2006. *Comparative Federalism: Theory and Practice,* London, New York: Routledge.

Burkhart, Simone. 2009. "Reforming Federalism in Germany: Incremental Changes instead of the Big Deal." *Publius: The Journal of Federalism* 39 (2), 341–65.

Busch, Andreas. 1999. "Das oft geänderte Grundgesetz." In *Demokratie in Ost und West,* edited by Wolfgang Merkel and Andreas Busch, Frankfurt: Suhrkamp, 549–74.

Bußjäger, Peter. 2003. "Verfassungsreform: ja, aber welche?" *Forum Parlament* 1, 56–9.

Bußjäger, Peter. 2005. "Klippen einer Föderalismusreform: Die Inszenierung Österreich-Konvent zwischen Innovationsresistenz und Neojosephinismus." In *Jahrbuch des Föderalismus 2005*, edited by Europäisches Zentrum für Föderalismus-Forschung Tübingen, Baden-Baden: Nomos, 403–26.

Bußjäger, Peter. 2009. *"Expertise 'Österreich-Konvent'"* Darmstadt: TU Darmstadt (unpublished report).

Bußjäger, Peter. 2012. "The 'Austrian Convention': The Failure of an Ambitious Reform." In *Changing Federal Constitutions: Lessons from International Comparison*, edited by Arthur Benz and Felix Knüpling, Berlin, Barbara Budrich Publishers, 97–117.

Cameron, David, and Richard Simeon. 2002. "Intergovernmental Relations in Canada: The Emergence of Collaborative Federalism." *Publius: The Journal of Federalism* 32 (2), 49–71.

Campaign for a Scottish Assembly. 1988. "A Claim of Right for Scotland." *Radical Scotland* 34 (Aug/Sept 1988), 17–20.

Canada. 1991. *Shaping Canada's Future Together: Proposals*, Ottawa: Minister of Supply and Services Canada.

Canada. 1992. *Status Report of the Multilateral Meetings on the Constitution*, Ottawa: Canadian Intergovernmental Conference Secretariat.

Canada, Senate and House of Commons. 1992. *Report of the Special Joint Committee on a Renewed Canada, 28 February 1992.*

Cappelletti, Fabio, Mario Fischer, and Pascal Sciarini. 2014. " 'Let's Talk Cash': Cantons' Interests and the Reform of Swiss Federalism." *Regional & Federal Studies* 24 (1), 1–20.

Caron, Jean-François, and Guy Laforest. 2009. "Canada and Multinational Federalism: From the Spirit of 1982 to Stephen Harper's Open Federalism." *Nationalism and Ethnic Politics* 15 (1), 27–55.

Cento Bull, Anna. 2002. "Verso uno stato federale?" In *Politica in Italia: I fatti dell'anno e le interpretazioni*, edited by Paolo Bellucci and Martin J. Bull, Bologna: il Mulino, 205–24.

Chhibber, Pradeep K., and Ken Kollman. 2004. *The Formation of National Party Systems: Federalism and Party Competition in Canada, Great Britain, India, and the United States*, Princeton: Princeton University Press.

Closa, Carlos. 2004. "The Convention method and the transformation of EU constitutional politics." In *Developing a Constitution for Europe*, edited by Erik Oddvar Eriksen, John Erik Fossum, and Agustín José Menéndez, London: Routledge, 183–206.

Closa, Carlos. 2012a. "Constitutional Rigidity and Procedures for Ratifying Constitutional Reforms in EU Member States." In *Changing Federal Constitutions: Lessons from International Comparison*, edited by Arthur Benz and Felix Knüpling, Berlin: Barbara Budrich Publishers, 281–310.

Closa, Carlos. 2012b. *Ratifying European Union Treaties: Processes and Actors*, London: Routledge.

Colino, César. 2009a. "Constitutional Change without Constitutional Reform: Spanish Federalism and the Revision of Catalonia's Statute of Autonomy." *Publius: The Journal of Federalism* 39 (2), 262–88.

Colino, César. 2009b. *"Expert Questionnaire for Country Profile: Spain-Catalonia,"* Darmstadt: TU Darmstadt (unpublished report).

Colino, César. 2011. "What Now for the Autonomic State? Muddling through Growing Tensions amidst the Aftermath of the Court's Ruling and the Painful Fiscal Crisis." In *Jahrbuch des Föderalismus 2011,* edited by Europäisches Zentrum für Föderalismus-Forschung Tübingen, Baden-Baden: Nomos, 309–22.

Colino, César. 2013. "Varieties of Federalism and Propensity for Change." In *Federal Dynamics: Continuity, Change, and the Varieties of Federalism,* edited by Arthur Benz and Jörg Broschek, Oxford: Oxford University Press, 48–69.

Colino, César, and José A. Olmeda. 2012. "The Limits of Flexibility for Constitutional Change and the Uses of Sub-national Constitutional Space: The Case of Spain." In *Changing Federal Constitutions: Lessons from International Comparison,* edited by Arthur Benz and Felix Knüpling, Berlin: Barbara Budrich Publishers, 191–209.

Commission on the Powers and Electoral Arrangements of the National Assembly for Wales. 2004. *Minutes of Proceedings of the evidence of Mr Ron Davies AM held at National Museum of Wales, Cathays Park, Cardiff on Thursday 26 September 2002.*

Congleton, Roger D., and Bjørn Erik Rasch. 2006. "Amendment Procedures and Constitutional Stability." In *Democratic Constitutional Design and Public Policy: Analysis and Evidence,* edited by Roger D. Congleton and Birgitta Swedenborg, Cambridge: MIT Press, 319–42.

Cook, Curtis. 1994. "Introduction: Canada's Predicament." In *Constitutional Predicament: Canada after the Referendum 1992,* edited by Curtis Cook, Montreal, Buffalo: McGill-Queen's University Press, 3–24.

Costa, Olivier, and Eric Kerrouche. 2009. "MPs under the Fifth Republic: Professionalisation within a Weak Institution." *West European Politics* 32 (2), 327–44.

Courchene, Thomas J. 2005. "Quebec and the Canadian Federation: From the 1980 Referendum to the Summit of the Canadas." In *Canada: The State of the Federation 2005. Quebec and Canada in the New Century,* edited by Michael Murphy, Montreal, Kingston, Ontario: McGill-Queen's University Press, 201–32.

Courchene, Thomas J. 2008. *Reflections on the Federal Spending Power: Practices, Principles, Perspectives,* Paper prepared for the Symposium "Open Federalism and the Spending Power," Queen's Law School and Queen's Institute for Intergovernmental Relations, January 25–6.

Crook, Richard, and James Manor. 2000. "Democratic Decentralization." In *OED Working Paper Series,* edited by World Bank Operations Evaluation Department, Washington, DC: The World Bank.

Czada, Roland. 1997. "Vertretung und Verhandlung: Aspekte politischer Konfliktregelung in Mehrebenensystemen." In *Theorieentwicklung in der Politikwissenschaft: Eine Zwischenbilanz,* edited by Arthur Benz and Wolfgang Seibel, Baden-Baden: Nomos, 237–59.

D'Onofrio, Francesco. 1997. "Relazione sulla Forma di Stato." In *Revisione della Seconda Parte della Costituzione, Commissione Parlamentare Per le Riforme Costituzionali: Progetto di legge Costituzionale,* edited by Camera dei Deputati and Senato della Repubblica, Rome: Testi Parlamentari 24.

Davidenkoff, Emmanuel. 2003. "L'Education hostile aux transferts." *Libération,* 26 March 2003.

Dawn, Oliver, and Carlos Fusaro (eds.). 2011. *How Constitutions Change: A Comparative Study,* Oxford: Hart Publishing.

De Figueiredo, Rui J., and Barry R. Weingast. 2005. "Self-enforcing federalism." *Journal of Law, Economics, and Organization* 21 (1), 103–35.

De Vries, Michiel S. 2000. "The Rise and Fall of Decentralization: A Comparative Analysis of Arguments and Practices in European Countries." *European Journal of Political Research* 38 (2), 193–224.

Delwit, Pascal, and Benoit Hellings. 2002. "La nouvelle réforme de l'État: processus, contenu, méthode." *Administration Publique* 26, 99–106.

Denver, David. 2002. "Voting in the 1997 Scottish and Welsh Devolution Referendums: Information, Interests and Opinions." *European Journal of Political Research* 41 (6), 827–43.

Deschouwer, Kris. 1999. "From Consociation to Federation: How the Belgian Parties Won." In *Party Elites in Divided Societies: Political Parties in Consociational Democracy*, edited by Kurt R. Luther and Kris Deschouwer, London, New York: Routledge, 74–107.

Deschouwer, Kris. 2009. *The Politics of Belgium: Governing a Divided Society*, Basingstoke: Palgrave Macmillan.

Deschouwer, Kris, and Min Reuchamps. 2013. "The Belgian Federation at a Crossroad." *Regional and Federal Studies* 23 (3), 261–70.

Detterbeck, Klaus. 2012. *Multi-Level Party Politics in Western Europe*, Basingstoke, New York: Palgrave Macmillan.

Deubel, Ingolf. 2009. "Föderalismusreform II: Zur Reform der föderalstaatlichen Finanzverfassung/Reforming Fiscal Federalism." *Zeitschrift für Staats- und Europawissenschaft* 7 (2), 218–34.

Di Giovacchino, Rita. 2005. *Il libro nero della Prima Repubblica*, Rome: Fazi Editori.

DiMaggio, Paul J., and Walter W. Powell. 1991. "Introduction." In *The New Institutionalism in Organizational Analysis*, edited by Walter W. Powell and Paul J. DiMaggio, Chicago, University of Chicago Press, 1–40.

Dolowitz, David, and David March. 2000. "Learning From Abroad: The Role of Policy Transfer in Contemporary Policy-Making." *Governance* 13 (1), 5–24.

Donovan, Mark. 1995. "The Politics of Electoral Reform in Italy." *International Political Science Review* 16 (1), 47–64.

Dörfer, Bert-Sebastian. 2010. *Bundesverfassungsgericht und Bundesstaat*, Berlin: Duncker & Humblot.

Ebert, Werner, et al. 2010a. "Der politische Prozess." In *Die neuen Schuldenregeln im Grundgesetz: Zur Fortentwicklung der bundesstaatlichen Finanzbeziehungen*, edited by Christian Kastrop, Gisela Meister-Scheufelen, and Margaretha Sudhof, Berlin: Berliner Wissenschaftsverlag, 62–88.

Ebert, Werner, et al. 2010b. "Ausgangslage und Entstehungsgeschichte der Reform." In *Die neuen Schuldenregeln im Grundgesetz: Zur Fortentwicklung der bundesstaatlichen Finanzbeziehungen*, edited by Christian Kastrop, Gisela Meister-Scheufelen, and Margaretha Sudhof, Berlin: Berliner Wissenschaftsverlag, 124–49.

EFD. 2004. *Neugestaltung des Finanzausgleichs und der Aufgabenteilung zwischen Bund und Kantonen (NFA)*, Bern: Eidgenössisches Finanzdepartement (EFD).

Elkins, Zachary. 2010. "Diffusion and the Constitutionalization of Europe." *Comparative Political Studies* 43 (8/9), 969–99.

Elkins, Zachary, Tom Ginsburg, and James Melton. 2009. *The Endurance of Constitutions*. Cambridge: Cambridge University Press.

Elster, Jon. 1995. "Forces and Mechanisms in the Constitution-Making Process." *Duke Law Journal* 45 (2), 364–96.

Elster, Jon. 1998. "Deliberation and Constitution Making." In *Deliberative Democracy*, edited by Jon Elster, Cambridge, New York: Cambridge University Press, 97–122.

Erdos, David. 2009. "Charter 88 and the Constitutional Reform Movement: a Retrospective." *Parliamentary Affairs* 62 (4), 537–51.

Erk, Jan. 2008. *Explaining Federalism: State, Society and congruence in Austria, Belgium, Canada, Germany and Switzerland*, London, New York: Routledge.

Erk, Jan. 2011. "The Sociology of Constitutional Politics: Demos, Legitimacy and Constitutional Courts in Canada and Germany." *Regional & Federal Studies* 21 (4/5), 523–38.

Erk, Jan, and Lawrence Anderson. 2009. "The Paradox of Federalism: Does Self-Rule Accommodate or Exacerbate Ethnic Divisions?" *Regional & Federal Studies* 19 (2), 191–202.

Evans, Mark (ed.). 2009. *New Directions in the Study of Policy Transfer: Special Issue of Policy Studies 2009*, Abingdon: Routledge.

Fabbrini, Sergio and Marco Brunazzo. 2003. "Federalizing Italy: The Convergent Effects of Europeanization and Domestic Mobilization." *Regional & Federal Studies* 13 (1), 100–20.

Fabre, Elodie. 2008. "Party Organization in a Multi-level System: Party Organizational Change in Spain and the UK." *Regional & Federal Studies* 18 (4), 309–29.

Falkner, Gerda (ed). 2011. *The EU's Decision Traps: Comparing Policies*, Oxford: Oxford University Press.

Fedele, Marcello. 2010. *Né uniti né divisi: Le due anime del federalismo all'italiana*, Rome: Donzelli Editore.

Fiedler, Franz. 2005. *Bericht des Österreich-Konvents*, Vienna: Büro des Österreich-Konvents.

Filippov, Mikhail, Peter C. Ordeshook, and Olga Shvetsova. 2004. *Designing Federalism: A Theory of Self-sustainable Federal Institutions*, New York: Cambridge University Press.

Fischer, Manuel. 2012. *Entscheidungsstrukturen in der Schweizer Politik zu Beginn des 21. Jahrhunderts*, Zürich, Chur: Rüegger Verlag.

Fischer-Hotzel, Andrea. 2013. *Vetospieler in territorialen Verfassungsreformen: Britische Devolution und französische Dezentralisierung im Vergleich*, Baden-Baden: Nomos.

Fix, Elisabeth. 1999. *Italiens Parteiensystem im Wandel: Von der Ersten zur Zweiten Republik*, Frankfurt, New York: Campus.

Flinders, Matthew. 2010. *Democratic Drift: Majoritarian Modification and Democratic Anomie in the United Kingdom*, Oxford: Oxford University Press.

Foley, Michael. 1989. *The Silence of Constitutions*, New York: Routledge.

Fossum, John-Erik, and Augustino Menendez. 2010. *The Constitution's Gift: A Constitutional Theory for a Democratic European Union*, Lanham: Rowman & Littlefield.

Freiburghaus, Dieter. 2005. "Bedingungen für eine gelingende Föderalismusreform: Die Neugestaltung des Finanzausgleichs und der Aufgabenteilung zwischen Bund und

Kantonen in der Schweiz." In *Jahrbuch des Föderalismus 2005*, edited by Europäisches Zentrum für Föderalismusforschung, Baden-Baden: Nomos, 506–15.

Freiburghaus, Dieter. 2009. *Expertise "Neugestaltung des Finanzausgleichs und der Aufgabenteilung zwischen Bund und Kantonen."* Darmstadt: TU Darmstadt (unpublished report).

Freiburghaus, Dieter. 2012. "Swiss Federalism, Fiscal Equalisation Reform and the Reallocation of Tasks." In *Changing Federal Constitutions: Lessons from International Comparison*, edited by Arthur Benz and Felix Knüpling, Berlin: Barbara Budrich Publishers, 53–79.

Friedrich, Carl Joachim. 1968. *Trends of Federalism in Theory and Practice*, New York: Praeger.

Fusaro, Carlo. 1998. "The Politics of Constitutional Reform in Italy: A Framework for Analysis." *South European Society and Politics* 3 (2), 45–74.

Gagnon, Alain-G., and François Rocher. 1992. "The Multilateral Agreement: A Betrayal of the Federal Spirit." In *Canada: The State of the Federation 1992*, edited by Douglas M. Brown and Robert Young, Kingston, Ontario: Institute of Intergovernmental Relations, Queen's University, 117–27.

Galligan, Brian. 2008. "Processes for Reforming Australian Federalism." *University of South Wales Law Journal* 31 (2), 617–42.

Galligan, Dennis J., and Mila Versteeg. 2013. "Theoretical Perspectives on the Social and Political Foundations of Constitutions." In *Social and Political Foundations of Constitutions*, edited by Dennis Galligan and Mila Versteeg, Cambridge: Cambridge University Press, 42–8.

Gamble, Andrew. 2006. "The Constitutional Revolution in the United Kingdom." *Publius: The Journal of Federalism* 36 (1), 19–35.

Garrec, René. 2002. "Rapport no 27." Sénat: Session Ordinaire de 2002–2003. http://www.senat.fr/rap/l02-027/l02-027.html (last accessed 23 January 2016).

Gaudin, Jean-Pierre. 2004. *L'action publique: Sociologie et politique.* Paris: Presses de la Fondation Nationale des Sciences Politiques.

Gay, Oonaugh. 1998. "The Scotland Bill: Devolution and Scotland's Parliament." *Library Research Papers 98/1* (House of Commons).

Gerring, John, et al. 2011. "An Institutional Theory of Direct and Indirect Rule." *World Politics,* 63 (3), 377–433.

Gibbins, Roger. 1989. "Senate Reform: Always the Bridesmaid, Never the Bride." In *Canada: The State of the Federation 1989*, edited by Ronald L. Watts and Douglas M. Brown, Kingston, Ontario: Institute of Intergovernmental Relations, Queen's University, 193–210.

Ginsburg, Tom, Zachary Elkins, and Justin Blount. 2009. "Does the Process of Constitution Making Matter?" *Annual Review of Law and Social Science* 5 (5), 201–23.

Göler, Daniel. 2006. *Deliberation: Ein Zukunftsmodell europäischer Entscheidungsfindung? Analyse der Beratungen des Verfassungskonvents 2002–2003*, Baden-Baden: Nomos.

Gomez-Reino Cachafeiro, Margarita. 2000. "A Territorial Cleavage in Italian Politics? Understanding the Rise of the Northern Question in the 1990s." *South European Society and Politics* 5 (3), 80–107.

Gontcharoff, Georges. 2004. "Une loi gigantesque et complexe." *Territoires* 451, 12–14.

González, Alfredo, and Lourdes López Nieto. 2008. "The Role of Political Parties in the Estado Autonómico." In *Intergovernmental Relations in Democratic Spain: Interdependence, Autonomy, Conflict and Cooperation*, edited by Lourdes López Nieto, Madrid: Dykinson, 105–27.

Goodin, Robert E. 2008. *Innovating Democracy: Democratic Theory and Practice After the Deliberative Turn*, Oxford: Oxford University Press.

Government of Canada. 1991. *Shaping Canada's Future Together: Federal Constitutional Proposals*, Ottawa.

Government of Québec. 1985. *Draft Agreement on the Constitution: Proposals by the Government of Québec*, Québec City: Government of Québec.

Grande, Edgar. 2002. "Parteiensystem und Föderalismus. Institutionelle Strukturmuster und politische Dynamiken im internationalen Vergleich." In *Föderalismus: Analysen in entwicklungsgeschichtlicher und vergleichender Perspektive. Politische Vierteljahresschrift, Sonderheft 32*, edited by Arthur Benz and Gerhard Lehmbruch, Wiesbaden: Westdeutscher Verlag, 179–212.

Grotz, Florian. 2005. "'Europäisierung' der Bundesstaatsreform? Zur Übertragung des EU-Konventsmodells in Deutschland und Österreich." *Politische Vierteljahresschrift* 46 (1), 110–31.

Grotz, Florian, and Klaus Poier. 2010. "Zwischen Gemeinschaftsprojekt, Tauschgeschäft und Symbolpolitik: Die Initiativen zu 'großen' Bundesstaatsreformen in Deutschland, Österreich und der Schweiz." *Zeitschrift für Vergleichende Politikwissenschaft* 4 (2), 233–59.

Guibernau, Montserrat. 2000. "Spain: Catalonia and the Basque Country." In *Democracy and Cultural Diversity*, edited by Michael O'Neill and Dennis Austin, Oxford: Oxford University Press, 55–68.

Guibernau, Montserrat. 2013. "Secessionism in Catalonia: After Democracy." *Ethnopolitics* 12 (4), 368–93.

Haegel, Florence. 2002. "Faire l'Union: la refondation des partis de droite après les élections de 2002." *Revue française de science politique* 52 (5–6), 561–76.

Hämmerle, Katrin. 2005. "'Niemand soll sagen können, er wäre nicht gehört worden . . .': Betrachtungen zum Österreich-Konvent aus Sicht der Zivilgesellschaft." *Österreichische Zeitschrift für Politikwissenschaft* 34 (4), 367–80.

Hall, Peter A. 1993. "Policy Paradigms, Social Learning, and the State: The Case of Economic Policymaking in Britain." *Comparative Politics* 25 (3), 275–96.

Hart, Herbert L. A. 1994. *The Concept of Law*, Oxford: Oxford University Press.

Hawkes, David C. 1985. "Negotiating Aboriginal Self-Government." In *Canada: The State of the Federation*, edited by Peter M. Leslie, Kingston, Ontario: Institute of Intergovernmental Relations, Queen's University, 151–72.

Hay, Colin. 2006. "Constructivist Institutionalism." In *The Oxford Handbook of Political Institutions*, edited by R.A.W. Rhodes, Sarah A. Binder, and Bert A. Rockman, Oxford: Oxford University Press, 56–74.

Heard, Andrew J. 1989. "Recognizing the Variety among Constitutional Conventions." *Canadian Journal of Political Science* 22 (1), 63–81.

Hechter, Michael. 1975. *Internal Colonialism. The Celtic fringe in British National Development*, Berkeley: University of California Press.

Heinemann-Grüder, Andreas (ed.). 2002. *Federalism doomed? European Federalism between Integration and Separation*, New York et al.: Berghan Books.

Heinz, Dominic. 2012. "Varieties of Joint Decision Making: The Second Federal Reform." *German Politics* 21 (1), 129–42.

Heinz, Dominic. 2014. "Stabilitätsrat und Politikverflechtung in der Haushaltspolitik: Institutionelle Reform mit Politikwechsel?" *Zeitschrift für Politik* 61 (special issue 6), 181–203.

Héritier, Adrienne. 1999. *Policy-Making and Diversity in Europe: Escaping Deadlock*, Cambridge: Cambridge University Press.

Héritier, Adrienne. 2007. *Explaining Institutional Change in Europe*, Oxford: Oxford University Press.

Hesse, Joachim J., and Arthur Benz. 1990. *Die Modernisierung der Staatsorganisation: Institutionspolitik im internationalen Vergleich: USA, Grossbritannien, Frankreich, Bundesrepublik Deutschland* (1st ed.), Baden-Baden: Nomos.

Hoffmann-Martinot, Vincent. 2003. "The French Republic: One Yet Divisable." In *Reforming Local Government in Europe*, edited by Norbert Kersting and Angelika Vetter, Opladen: Leske + Budrich, 157–83.

Hoffmann-Martinot, Vincent. 2005. "Zentralisierung und Dezentralisierung." In *Länderbericht Frankreich: Geschichte, Wirtschaft, Politik, Gesellschaft*, edited by Adolf Kimmel and Henrik Uterwedde, Bonn: Bundeszentrale für politische Bildung, 323–41.

Holzinger, Katharina. 2001. "Verhandeln statt Argumentieren oder Verhandeln durch Argumentieren? Eine empirische Analyse auf der Basis der Sprechakttheorie." *Politische Vierteljahresschrift*, 42 (3), 414–46.

Holzinger, Katharina, Helga Jörgens, and Christoph Knill (eds.). 2007. *Transfer, Diffusion und Konvergenz von Politiken: Politische Vierteljahresschrift, Sonderheft 38* Wiesbaden: VS Verlag für Sozialwissenschaften.

Hombrado, Angustias. 2011. "Learning to Catch the Wave? Regional Demands for Constitutional Change in Contexts of Asymmetrical Arrangements." *Regional & Federal Studies* 21 (4–5), 479–501.

Hooghe, Liesbet. 2004. "Belgium. Hollowing the Centre." In *Federalism and Territorial Cleavages*, edited by Ugo M. Amoretti and Nancy Bermeo, Baltimore: John Hopkins University Press, 55–92.

Hooghe, Liesbet, and Gary Marks. 2001. *Multi-level Governance and European Integration*, Lanham: Rowman & Littlefield.

Hooghe, Liesbet, and Gary Marks. 2009. "A Postfunctionalist Theory of European Integration: From Permissive Consensus to Constraining Dissensus." *British Journal of Political Science* 39 (1), 1–23.

Hooghe, Liesbet, Gary Marks, and Arian H. Schakel. 2010. *The Rise of Regional Authority: A Comparative Study of 42 Democracies*, New York: Routledge.

Hornig, Eike-Christian. 2011. *Die Parteiendominanz direkter Demokratie in Westeuropa*, Baden-Baden: Nomos.

Horowitz, Donald L. 1985. *Ethnic Groups in Conflict*, Berkeley, Los Angeles: University of California Press.

Hörtenhuber, Helmut, and Wolfgang Steiner. 2004. "'Der Österreich-Konvent': Vorgeschichte, Aufgaben und Erwartungen." In *Österreichisches Jahrbuch für Politik 2003*, edited by Andreas Khol, Günther Ofner, Günther Burkert-Dottolo, and Stefan Karner, Vienna, Munich: Verlag für Geschichte und Politik, 247–60.

Hueglin, Thomas O. 1999. *Early Modern Concepts for a Late Modern World: Althusius on Community and Federalism*, Waterloo, Ontario: Wilfrid Laurier University Press.

Hueglin, Thomas O. 2000. "From Constitutional to Treaty Federalism: A Comparative Perspective." *Publius: The Journal of Federalism*, 30 (4), 137–53.

Hueglin, Thomas O. 2008. "Working around the American Model: Canadian Federalism and the European Union." In *The Comparative Turn in Canadian Political Science*, edited by Linda A. White, Richard Simeon, Robert Vipond, and Jennifer Wallner, Vancouver, Toronto: UBC Press, 140–57.

Hueglin, Thomas O. 2013. "Comparing Federalisms: Variations or Distinct Models?" In *Federal Dynamics: Continuity, Change, and the Varieties of Federalism*, edited by Arthur Benz and Jörg Broschek, Oxford: Oxford University Press, 27–47.

Hueglin, Thomas O., and Alan Fenna. 2006. *Comparative Federalism: A Systematic Inquiry*, Peterborough, Ontario: Broadview Press.

Hurley, James Ross. 1996. *Amending Canada's Constitution: History, Processes, Problems and Prospects*, Ottawa: Supply and Services Canada.

Institute of Intergovernmental Relations (ed.). 2006. *Open Federalism: Interpretations, Significance*, Kingston, Ontario: Institute of Intergovernmental Relations.

Jacobs, Dirk, and Marc Swyngedouw. 2003. "Territorial and Non-territorial Federalism in Belgium: Reform of the Brussels Capital Region, 2001." *Regional & Federal Studies* 13 (2), 127–39.

Jacques, Charles-Xavier, and Charles Boromée. 2001. "La Conférence intergouvernementale et interparlementaire du renouveau institutionnel." *Courrier hebdomadaire* No.1707–1708, Brussels: CRISP.

Jeffrey, Brooke. 2006. "From Collaborative Federalism to New Unilateralism: Implications for the Welfare State." In *Continuity and Change in Canadian Politics*, edited by Hans J. Michelmann and Christine de Clercy, Toronto: University of Toronto Press, 117–46.

Jeffrey, Brooke. 2014. *Dismantling Canada: Stephen Harper's New Conservative Agenda*, Montreal, Kingston: McGill-Queen's University Press.

Jeffery, Charlie. 1995. "The Non-Reform of the German Federal System after Unification." *West European Politics* 18 (2), 252–72.

Jeffery, Charlie. 2009. "Devolution in the United Kingdom: Problems of a Piecemeal Approach to Constitutional Change." *Publius: The Journal of Federalism* 39 (2), 289–313.

Jeffery, Charlie. 2012. "The United Kingdom: The Shifting Territorial Constitution." In *Jahrbuch des Föderalismus 2012*, edited by Europäisches Zentrum für Föderalismusforschung Tübingen, Baden-Baden: Nomos, 391–402.

Jeffery, Charlie and Daniel Wincott. 2006. "Devolution in the United Kingdom: Statehood and citizenship in transition." *Publius: The Journal of Federalism* 36 (1), 3–18.

Johnston, Richard, André Blais, Elisabeth Gidengil, and Neil Nevitte. 1993. "The People and the Charlottetown Accord." In *Canada: The State of the Federation 1993*, edited by Ronald L. Watts and Douglas M. Brown, Kingston, Ontario: Institute of Intergovernmental Relations, Queen's University, 19–43.

Johnston, Richard, André Blais, Elisabeth Gidengil, and Neil Nevitte (eds.). 1996. *The Challenge of Direct Democracy: The 1992 Canadian Referendum*, Montreal: McGill-Queen's University Press.

Jones, James Barry. 2000. "Post Referendum Politics." In *The Road to the National Assembly for Wales*, edited by James Barry Jones and Denis Balson, Cardiff: University of Wales Press.

Jones, Peter. 1997a. "A Start to a New Song: The 1997 Devolution Referendum Campaign." *Scottish Affairs* 21 (Autumn), 1–16.

Jones, Peter. 1997b. "Labour's Referendum Plan: Sell-Out Or Act Of Faith." *Scottish Affairs* 18 (Winter), 1–17.

Jones, R. Merfyn, and Ioan Rhys Jones. 2000. "Labour and the Nation." In *The Labour Party in Wales*, edited by Duncan Tanner, Chris Williams, and Deian Hopkin, Cardiff: University of Wales Press, 241–63.

Kaltenborn, Markus. 2012. "Constitutional Amendment Rules in Federal and Unitary States." In *Changing Federal Constitutions: Lessons from International Comparison*, edited by Arthur Benz and Felix Knüpling, Berlin: Barbara Budrich Publishers, 271–80.

Keating, Michael. 1993. "Spain: Peripheral nationalism and state response." In *The Politics of Ethnic Conflict Regulation*, edited by John McGarry and Brendan O'Leary, London, New York: Routledge, 204–25.

Keating, Michael. 1998. *The New Regionalism in Western Europe: Territorial Restructuring and Political Change*, Cheltenham, Northampton, MA: E. Elgar.

Keating, Michael. 2004. "The United Kingdom: Political Institutions and Territorial Cleavages." In *Federalism and Territorial Cleavages*, edited by Ugo M. Amoretti and Nancy Bermeo, Baltimore: Johns Hopkins University Press, 155–79.

Keating, Michael. 2009. *The Independence of Scotland: Self-Government and the Shifting Politics of Union*, Oxford: Oxford University Press.

Keating, Michael, and Alex Wilson. 2009. "Renegotiating the State of Autonomies: Statute Reform and Multi-level Politics in Spain." *West European Politics* 32 (3), 536–58.

Keating, Michael, and Alex Wilson. 2010. "Federalism and Decentralisation in Italy," *PSA-Conference*, Edinburgh.

Kilper, Heiderose, and Roland Lhotta. 1996. *Föderalismus in der Bundesrepublik Deutschland*, Opladen: Leske + Budrich.

Kincaid, John. 2002. "Federalism in the U.S.: A Continual Tension Between Persons and Places." In *Föderalismus: Analysen in entwicklungsgeschichtlicher und vergleichender Perspektive*, edited by Arthur Benz and Gerhard Lehmbruch, Wiesbaden: Westdeutscher Verlag, 134–56.

Kincaid, John. 2005. "Comparative Observations." In *Constitutional Origins, Structure and Change in Federal Countries*, edited by John Kincaid and G. Alan Tarr, Montreal, Kingston: McGill-Queen's University Press, 409–48.

Kincaid, John. 2012. "The Relevance of Constitutional Change in Federal Systems." In *Changing Federal Constitutions: Lessons from International Comparison*, edited by Arthur Benz and Felix Knüpling, Berlin, Barbara Budrich Publishers, 31–50.

Kingdon, John W. 1984. *Agendas, Alternatives, and Public Policies*, Boston: Little, Brown.

Kisker, Gunter. 1989. "The West German Federal Constitutional Court." *Publius: The Journal of Federalism* 19 (4), 35–52.

Konrath, Christoph. 2005. "Dann bleibt es eben so: Föderalismus und Kompetenzverteilung als Themen des Österreich-Konvents." *Österreichische Zeitschrift für Politikwissenschaft* 34 (4), 351–66.

Konrath, Christoph. 2012. "Austria After the Austrian Convention." In *Changing Federal Constitutions: Lessons from International Comparison*, edited by Arthur Benz and Felix Knüpling, Berlin: Barbara Budrich Publishers, 333–50.

Kriesi, Hanspeter, and Alexander H. Trechsel. 2008. *The Politics of Switzerland. Continuity and Change in a Consensus Democracy*, Cambridge: Cambridge University Press.

Kymlicka, Will. 1995. *Multicultural Citizenship: A Liberal Theory of Minority Rights*, Oxford: Oxford University Press.

Kymlicka, Will. 2007. *Multicultural Odysseys: Navigating the New International Politics of Diversity*, Oxford: Oxford University Press.

Lachmuth, Annemarie, Haral Georgii, and Sarab Borhanian. 2006. *Föderalismusreform 2006: Grundgesetzänderungen. Synopse. Dokumentation*, Berlin: Deutscher Bundestag Wissenschaftliche Dienste 313/06.

Ladrech, Robert. 2010. *Europeanisation of National Politics*, Basingstoke: Palgrave Macmillan.

Laffin, Martin, and Alys Thomas. 1999. "The United Kingdom: Federalism in Denial?" *Publius: The Journal of Federalism* 29 (3), 89–107.

Laforest, Guy. 1991. "L'esprit de 1982." In *Le Québec et la Restructuration du Canada 1980–1992: Enjeux et perspectives*, edited by Louis Balthazar, Guy Laforest and Vincent Lemieux, Saint-Laurent: Les éditions du Septentrion, 147–63.

Laforest, Guy. 1992. "Robert Bourassa et la maîtrise du temps." In *Canada: The State of the Federation 1992*, edited by Douglas M. Brown and Robert Young, Kingston, Ontario: Institute of Intergovernmental Relations, Queen's University, 53–75.

Laforest, Guy. 2014. *Interpreting Quebec's Exile Within the Federation*, Brussels et al.: P.I.E. Peter Lang.

Lagasse, Nicolas. 2009. *"Expertise Lambermont Agreement in Belgium,"* Darmstadt: TU Darmstadt, (unpublished report).

Landau, Martin. 1973. "Federalism, Redundancy, and System Reliability." *Publius. The Journal of Federalism* 3 (3), 173–96.

Landwehr, Claudia. 2009. *Political Conflict and Political Preferences: Communicative Action Between Facts, Norms and Interests*, Colchester: ECPR-Press.

Landwehr, Claudia, and Katharina Holzinger. 2010. "Institutional Determinants of Deliberative Interaction." *European Political Science Review* 2 (3), 373–400.

Laski, Harold. 2005 [1939]. "The Obsolence of Federalism." In *Theories of Federalism: A Reader*, edited by Dimitrios Karmis and Norman Wayne, New York: Palgrave Macmillan, 193–205.

Lazar, Harvey. 1998. "Non-Constitutional Renewal: Towards a New Equilibrium in the Federation." In *Canada: The State of the Federation 1997: Non-Constitutional Renewal*, edited by Harvey Lazar, Kingston, Ontario: Institute of Intergovernmental Relations, Queen's University, 3–35.

Le Lidec, Patrick. 2005. "Pouvoir de blocage et blocage de pouvoir: Le Sénat de la V. République." *Pouvoirs Locaux*, 67 (4), 81–6.

Le Lidec, Patrick. 2012. "Decentralisation and Territorial Reforms in France: How Constitutional Constraints Impact Strategies for Reform." In *Changing Federal Constitutions: Lessons from International Comparison*, edited by Arthur Benz and Felix Knüpling, Berlin: Barbara Budrich Publishers, 249–67.

Lecours, André, and Daniel Béland. 2013. "The Institutional Politics of Territorial Redistribution: Federalism and Equalization Policy in Australia and Canada." *Canadian Journal of Political Science* 46 (1), 93–113.

Lehmbruch, Gerhard. 2000. *Parteienwettbewerb im Bundesstaat*, Stuttgart: Kohlhammer.

Lemco, Jonathan. 1991. *Political Stability in Federal Governments*, New York: Praeger.

Lerner, Hanna. 2011. *Making Constitutions in Deeply Divided Societies*, Cambridge: Cambridge University Press.

Lieberman, Robert. 2002. "Ideas, Institutions, and Political Order: Explaining Political Change." *American Political Science Review* 96 (4), 697–712.

Lienbacher, Georg. 2005. "Verfassungsreform durch Konventsmethode?" *Journal für Rechtspolitik* 13 (1), 42–51.

Lienbacher, Georg. 2008. "Der erste Teil der Verfassungsreform," *Journal für Rechtspolitik* 16 (2), 77–84.

Lijphart, Arend. 2012. *Patterns of Democracy: Government Forms and Performance in Thirty-Six Countries*, 2nd rev. ed., New Haven, London: Yale University Press.

Linder, Wolf. 2010. *Swiss Democracy: Possible Solutions to Conflict in Multicultural Societies*, Basingstoke: Palgrave Macmillan.

Lippi, Andrea. 2011. "Evaluating the 'Quasi Federalist' Programme of Decentralisation in Italy since the 1990s: A Side-effect Approach." *Local Government Studies* 37 (5), 495–516.

Livingston, William S. 1956. *Federalism and Constitutional Change*, Oxford: Clarendon Press.

Livingston, William S. 1967. "A note on the nature of federalism." In *American Federalism in Perspective*, edited by Aaron Wildavsky, Boston: Little, Brown, 33–40.

Lorenz, Astrid. 2004. "Stabile Verfassungen? Konstitutionelle Reformen in Demokratien." *Zeitschrift für Parlamentsfragen* 35 (3), 448–68.

Lorenz, Astrid. 2005. "How to Measure Constitutional Rigidity: Four Concepts and Two Alternatives." *Journal of Theoretical Politics* 17 (3), 339–61.

Lorenz, Astrid. 2008. *Verfassungsänderungen in etablierten Demokratien: Motivlagen und Aushandlungsmuster*, Wiesbaden: VS Verlag für Sozialwissenschaften.

Lorenz, Astrid. 2011. "Constitutional Negotiations in Federal Reforms: Interests, Interaction Orientation, and the Prospect of Agreement." *Regional and Federal Studies* 21 (4/5), 407–25.

Loughlin, John. 2007a. *Subnational Government: The French Experience*, Basingstoke: Palgrave Macmillan.

Loughlin, John. 2007b. "Reconfiguring the State: Trends in Territorial Governance in European States." *Regional & Federal Studies* 17 (4), 385–403.

Loughlin, John. 2009. "The 'Hybrid' State: Reconfiguring Territorial Governance in Western Europe." *Perspectives on European Politics and Society* 10 (1), 49–66.

Loughlin, John. 2013. "Reconfiguring the Nation-state: Hybridity vs. Uniformity." In *Routledge Handbook of Regionalism and Federalism*, edited by John Loughlin, John Kincaid and Wilfried Swenden, London, New York: Routledge, 3–18.

Loughlin, John, and Guy B. Peters. 1997. "State Traditions, Administrative Reform and Regionalization." In *The Political Economy of Regionalism*, edited by Michael Keating and John Loughlin, London: Routledge, 41–62.

Lusztig, Michael, and Colin Knox. 1999. "Good Things and Small Packages: Lessons from Canada for the Northern Irish Constitutional Settlement." *Nations and Nationalism* 5 (4), 543–63.

Lutz, Donald S. 1994. "Toward a Theory of Constitutional Amendment." *American Political Science Review* 88 (2), 355–70.

Lutz, Donald S. 2006. *Principles of Constitutional Design*, Cambridge: Cambridge University Press.

Lynch, Peter. 1996. "The Scottish Constitutional Convention 1992–5." *Scottish Affairs* 15 (Spring), 1–16.

MacWhirter, Ian. 1995. "Doomsday Two: The Return of Forsyth." *Scottish Affairs* 13, 15–26.

McAllister, Laura. 1999. "The Road to Cardiff Bay: The Process of Establishing the National Assembly for Wales." *Parliamentary Affairs* 52 (4), 634–48.

McAllister, Laura. 2000. "The New Politics in Wales: Rhetoric or Reality?" *Parliamentary Affairs* 53 (3), 591–604.

McAllister, Laura. 2005a. "Proving the Potential of Independent Commissions: A Critical Review of the Richard Commission on the Powers and Electoral Arrangements of the National Assembly for Wales." *Public Management* 83 (2), 493–512.

McAllister, Laura. 2005b. "The Value of Independent Commissions: An Insider's Perspective on the Richard Commission." *Parliamentary Affairs* 58 (1), 38–52.

McFadden, Jean. 1995. "The Scottish Constitutional Convention." *Public Law* (Summer), 215–23.

McGarry, John, and Brendan O'Leary. 2009. "Must Pluri-National Federations Fail?" *Ethnopolitics* 8 (1), 5–26.

McLean, Iain, and Alistair McMillan. 2005. *State of the Union*, Oxford: Oxford University Press.

McRae, Kenneth D. 1986. *Conflict and Compromise in Multilingual Societies: Belgium*, Waterloo: Wilfried Laurier University Press.

McWhinney, Edward. 1981. *Constitution-making: Principles, Process, Practice*, Toronto: University of Toronto Press.

Magnette, Paul, and Kalypso Nicolaidis. 2004. "The European Convention: Bargaining in the Shadow of Rhetoric." *West European Politics*, 27 (3), 381–404.

Magone, José M. 2009. *Contemporary Spanish Politics*, 2nd ed., London, New York: Routledge.

Mahoney, James, and Kathleen Thelen. 2010. "A Theory of Gradual Institutional Change." In *Explaining Institutional Change: Ambiguity, Agency, and Power*, edited by James Mahoney and Kathleen Thelen, Cambridge: Cambridge University Press, 1–37.

Maiz, Ramon, Francisco Caamaño, and Miguel Azpitarte. 2010. "The Hidden Counterpoint of Spanish Federalism: Recentralization and Resymmetrization in Spain (1978–2008)." *Regional & Federal Studies* 20 (1), 63–82.

Manow, Philip, and Simone Burkhart. 2006. "Kompromiss und Konflikt im parteipolitisierten Föderalismus der Bundesrepublik." *Zeitschrift für Politikwissenschaft* 16 (3), 807–24.

Manow, Philip, and Simone Burkhart. 2007. "Legislative Self-Restraint Under Divided Government In Germany, 1976–2002." *Legislative Studies Quarterly* 32 (2), 167–91.

Margedant, Udo. 2008. *Probleme der Föderalismusreform in Deutschland: der gegenwärtige Stand der Reformen und der Auftrag der Föderalismus-Kommission II*, Sankt Augustin: Konrad Adenauer Stiftung.

Marks, Gary. 1996. "An Actor-Centred Approach to Multi-Level Governance." *Regional & Federal Studies* 6 (2), 20–38.

Marshall, Geoffrey. 1985. "What are Constitutional Conventions?." *Parliamentary Affairs* 38 (1), 33–9.

Marzelier, Christiane. 2004. *Décentralisation Acte II: Chroniques des assises des libertés locales*, Paris, Budapest, Turin: l'Harmattan.

Mazzoleni, Martino. 2009. "The Italian Regionalisation: A Story of Partisan Logics." *Modern Italy* 14 (2), 135–50.

Meekison, J. Peter. 1993. "Let There Be Light." In *Canada: The State of the Federation 1993*, edited by Ronald L. Watts and Douglas M. Brown, Kingston, Ontario: Institute of Intergovernmental Relations, 61–85.

Mendelson, Matthew, Andrew Parkin, and Maurice Pinard. 2005. "A New Chapter or the Same Old Story? Public Opinion in Quebec from 1996–2003." In *Canada: The State of the Federation 2005*, edited by Michael Murphy, Montreal, Kingston: McGill-Queen's University Press, 25–52.

Meyer, John W., and W.R. Scott. 1983. *Organizational Environments: Ritual and Rationality*, Beverly Hills: Sage.

Miller, William L. 1998. "The Periphery and its Paradoxes." *West European Politics* 21 (1), 167–96.

Milne, David. 1992. "Innovative Constitutional Processes: Renewal of Canada Conferences, January–March 1992." In *Canada: The State of the Federation 1992*, edited by Douglas M. Brown and Robert Young, Kingston, Ontario: Institute of Intergovernmental Relations, Queen's University, 27–51.

Ministère de l'Intérieur, de l'Outre-Mer et des Collectivités Territoriales. 2009. "Assises des libertés locales, 28 février 2003 au Zénith de Grand-Quevilly, Minutes de la Réunion de synthèse nationale." http://www.interieur.gouv.fr/sections/a_l_interieur/les_collectivites_locales/decentralisation/assises-libertes./assises/downloadFile/attachedFile_1/minutes_assises.pdf, (last accessed 9 June 2009).

Mitchell, James. 2007. "The Evolution of Devolution: Labour's Home Rule Strategy in Opposition." *Government and Opposition* 33 (4), 479–96.

Mitchell, James. 2009a. *Devolution in the UK*, Manchester: Manchester University Press.

Mitchell, James. 2009b. *"Scotland's Constitutional Moment,"* Darmstadt: TU Darmstadt, (unpublished report).

Mitchell, James. 2012. "Britain's Constitutional Moment." In *Changing Federal Constitutions: Lessons from International Comparison*, edited by Arthur Benz and Felix Knüpling, Opladen, Berlin, Toronto: Barbara Budrich Publishers, 213–28.

Mitchell, James. 2014. *The Scottish Question*, Oxford: Oxford University Press.

Moore, Carolyn, and Wade Jacoby (eds.). 2009. *German Federalism in Transition? Reforms in a Consensual State*, London: Routledge.

Moravcsik, Andrew. 1997. "Warum die Europäische Union die Exekutive stärkt: Innenpolitik und internationale Kooperation." In *Projekt Europa im Übergang*, edited by Klaus Dieter Wolf, Baden-Baden: Nomos, 211–69.

Moreno, Luis. 2001. "Ethnoterritorial Concurrence in Multinational Societies: The Spanish Comunidades Autónomas." In *Multinational Democracies*, edited by Alain G. Gagnon and James Tully, Cambridge: Cambridge University Press, 201–21.

Moreno, Luis, and César Colino. 2010. "Kingdom of Spain." In *Diversity and Unity in Federal Countries*, edited by Luis Moreno and César Colino, Montreal, Kingston: McGill-Queen's University Press, 289–319.

Morgan, Kevin, and Geoff Mungham. 2000. *Redesigning Democracy: The Making of the Welsh Assembly*, Bridgend: Poetry Wales Press.

Nagel, Klaus-Jürgen. 2005. "Verfassungs- und Statutsreformen in Spanien: ein föderalistischer Frühling?" In *Jahrbuch des Föderalismus 2005*, edited by Europäisches Zentrum für Föderalismus-Forschung Tübingen, Baden-Baden: Nomos, 458–74.

Nassaux, Jean-Paul. 2001. "Le groupe de travail sur le fonctionnement des institutions bruxelloises: Deuxième phase et accord dit du Lombard." *Courrier hebdomadaire* 1716–1717, Brussel: CRISP.

Négrier, Emmanuel. 2000. "The Changing Role of French Local Government." In *The Changing French Political System*, edited by Robert Elgie, London: Frank Cass Publishers, 120–41.

Newell, James L., and Martin J. Bull. 2002. "Italian politics after the 2001 General Election: Plus ça change, plus c'est la même chose?" *Parliamentary Affairs* 55 (4), 626–42.

Nicolaïdis, Kalypso. 2001. "Conclusion: The Federal Vision Beyond the Federal State." In *The Federal Vision: Legitimacy and Levels of Governance in the United States and the European Union*, edited by Kalypso Nicolaïdis and Robert Howse, Oxford: Oxford University Press, 443–84.

Niechoj, Torsten. 2010. "'Es muss Schluss sein mit der dauernden Schuldenmacherei'. Die Neuregelung der Finanzverfassung im Zuge der Föderalismusreform II." *Zeitschrift für Staats- und Europawissenschaften* 8 (1), 59–88.

North, Douglas. 1990. *Institutions, Institutional Change and Economic Performances*, Cambridge: Cambridge University Press.

Obinger, Herbert, Stephan Leibfried, and Francis G. Castles. 2005. *Federalism and Welfare State: New World and European Experiences*, Cambridge: Cambridge University Press.

Oettinger, Günther H. 2009. "Föderalismuskommission II: Ergebnisse und Bilanz." *Zeitschrift für Staats- und Europawissenschaft* 7 (7), 6–13.

Olmeda, José A. 2009. *"Country profile: Reforming the Andalusian Statute of Autonomy in 2006,"* Darmstadt: TU Darmstadt, (unpublished report).

Olsen, Johan P. 2013. "The Institutional Basis of Democratic Accountability." *West European Politics*, 36 (3), 447–73.

Onoma, Ato Kwamena. 2010. "The Contradictory Potential of Institutions: The Rise and Decline of Land Documentation in Kenya." In *Explaining Institutional Change. Ambiguity, Agency, and Power*, edited by James Mahoney and Kathleen Thelen, Cambridge: Cambridge University Press, 63–93.

Orte, Andreu, and Alex Wilson. 2009. "Multi-level Coalitions and Statute Reform in Spain." *Regional & Federal Studies* 19 (3), 415–36.

Osborne, David, and Ted Gaebler. 1993. *Reinventing Government*, New York: Addison-Wesley.

Osmond, John. 1995. "The Contradictions of Welsh Politics." *Scottish Affairs* 11 (Spring), 31–47.

Ostrom, Elinor. 1990. *Governing the Commons: The Evolution of Institutions for Collective Action*, Cambridge: Cambridge University Press.

Ostrom, Elinor. 2005. *Understanding Institutional Diversity*, Princeton: Princeton University Press.

Pagano, Guiseppe. 2000. "Les résolutions du Parlement flamand pour une réforme de l'État." *Courrier hebdomadaire du CRISP* 5/2000 (1670–1671), 1–83.

Painter, Martin. 1991. "Intergovernmental Relations in Canada: An Institutional Analysis." *Canadian Journal of Political Science* 24 (2), 269–88.

Palermo, Francesco. 2004. "Föderalisierungstendenzen in Italien." In *Föderalismus in Europa III, Zukunftsforum Politik, Nr. 64*, edited by U. Margedant, Sankt Augustin: Konrad Adenauer Stiftung, 43–71.

Palermo, Francesco, and Matteo Nicolini. 2010. *"Country Profile Italy,"* Darmstadt: TU Darmstadt, (unpublished report).

Papillon, Martin. 2008. "Canadian Federalism and the Emerging Mosaic of Aboriginal Multilevel Governance." In *Canadian Federalism: Performance, Effectiveness, and Legitimacy*, edited by Herman Bakvis and Grace Skogstad, Don Mills, Ontario: Oxford University Press, 291–313.

Papillon, Martin, and Richard Simeon. 2004. "The Weakest Link? First Minister Conferences in Canadian Intergovernmental Relations." In *Canada: The State of the Federation 2002*, edited by J. Peter Meekison, Hamish Telford, and Harvey Lazar, Montreal, Kingston: McGill-Queen's University Press, 113–40.

Pasquier, Romain. 2004. *Vers une maturité politique des régions françaises? 1986–2004: dix-huit ans de démocratie régionale*, Boulogne: Institut de la Décentralisation.

Pasquier, Romain. 2005. "Sénat, régionalisation et cumul des mandats: trois piliers pour un acte III?" *Pouvoirs locaux* 67, 115–18.

Pasquier, Romain. 2009. *"La réforme constitutionnelle de 2003 en France,"* Darmstadt: TU Darmstadt, (unpublished report).

Pasquier, Romain. 2015. *Regional governance and Regional Power in France: The Dynamics of Political Space*, New York: Palgrave Macmillan.

Paterson, Lindsay, Alice Brown, and David McCrone. 1992. "Constitutional Crisis: The Causes and Consequences of the 1992 Scottish General Election Result." *Parliamentary Affairs* 45 (4), 627–39.

Peach, Ian. 2007. "Building or Severing the Bonds of Nationhood?: The Uncertain Legacy of Constitution Making in the Mulroney Years." In *Transforming the Nation: Canada and Brian Mulroney*, edited by Raymond B. Blake, Montréal, Kingston: McGill-Queen's University Press, 80–112.

Peters, Guy B., Jon Pierre, and Desmond King. 2005. "The Politics of Path Dependency: Political Conflict in Historical Institutionalism." *Journal of Politics* 62 (4), 1275–300.

Petersohn, Bettina. 2011. "Konfliktakkommodierung bis zur Selbstaufgabe? Stabilität und Dynamik der Verfassungsentwicklung in Belgien." *Politische Vierteljahresschrift* 52 (2), 195–219.

Petersohn, Bettina. 2013. *Konfliktregulierung in multinationalen Demokratien. Föderalismus und Verfassungsreformprozesse in Kanada und Belgien im Vergleich*, Baden-Baden: Nomos.

Petersohn, Bettina, Nathalie Behnke, and Eva Rhode. 2015. "Negotiating Territorial Change in Multinational States: Party Preferences, Negotiating Power and the Role of the Negotiation Mode." *Publius: The Journal of Federalism* 45 (4), 626–52.

Piattoni, Simona. 2010. *The Theory of Multi-Level Governance: Conceptual, Empirical, and Normative Challenges*, Oxford: Oxford University Press.

Pierson, Paul. 2000. "Increasing Returns, Path Dependence and the Study of Politics." *American Political Science Review* 94 (2), 251–67.

Poirier, Johanne. 2004. "Intergovernmental Agreements in Canada: At the Crossroads between Law and Politics." In *Canada: The State of the Federation 2002*, edited by J. Peter Meekison, Hamish Telford, and Harvey Lazar, Montreal, Kingston: McGill-Queen's University Press, 425–62.

Poirier, Johanne. 2008. "Une source paradoxale du droit constitutionnel canadien: les ententes intergouvernementales." *Revue québécoise de droit constitutionnel* 1. http://www.aqdc.org/volumes/pdf/poirier-une_source_paradoxale.pdf, (last accessed 5 January 2014).

Popelier, Patricia, and Bea Cantillon. 2013. "Bipolar Federalism and the Social Welfare State: A Case for Shared Competences." *Publius: The Journal of Federalism* 43 (4), 626–47.

Putnam, Robert. 1994. *Making Democracy Work: Civic Traditions in Modern Italy*, Princeton: Princeton University Press.

Québec. 1991. "An Act respecting the process for determining the political and constitutional future of Québec (As assented to on June 20, 1991)." *(2001) Québec's Positions on Constitutional and Intergovernmental Issues. Doc. 25*, Québec City.

Québec Liberal Party. 1991. *A Québec Free To Choose: Report of the Constitutional Committee of the Québec Liberal Party*, Montréal: Québec Liberal Party.

Raffarin, Jean-Pierre, and Pierre-Luc Séguillon. 2007. *10 + 1 questions à Jean-Pierre Raffarin sur la décentralisation*, Paris: Michalon.

Ragin, Charles C. 1987. *The Comparative Method: Moving beyond Qualitative and Quantitative Strategies*, Berkeley, Los Angeles: University of California Press.

Ragin, Charles C. 2000. *Fuzzy-set Social Science*, Chicago, London: University of Chicago Press.

Ranson, Stewart, and John Stewart. 1994. *Management for the Public Domain: Enabling the Learning Society*, Basingstoke: Palgrave Macmillan.

Rasch, Bjørn E., and Roger D. Congleton. 2006. "Amendment Procedures and Constitutional Stability." In *Democratic Constitutional Design and Public Policy: Analysis and Evidence*, edited by Roger D. Congleton and Birgitta Swedenborg, Cambridge: MIT Press, 319–42.

Rawlings, Richard. 1998. "The New Model Wales." *Journal of Law and Society* 25 (4), 461–509.

Rawlings, Richard. 2003. *Delineating Wales: Constitutional, Legal and Administrative Aspects of National Devolution*, Cardiff: University of Wales Press.

Rawls, John A. 1999. *A Theory of Justice*, rev. ed. Cambridge: Harvard University Press.

Rémond, Bruno. 2007. "La région, une France d'avenir." *Commentaire* 30 (118), 447–58.

Renzsch, Wolfgang. 2008. "Föderalismusreform, zweite Stufe - warum und was." In *Jahrbuch des Föderalismus 2007*, edited by Europäisches Zentrum für Föderalismusforschung Tübingen, Opladen: Nomos, 109–20.

Rey, Alfred. 1994. "Finanzföderalismus zwischen Bund, Kantonen und Gemeinden." In *Finanzföderalismus*, edited by Franz Eng, Alexander Glatthard and Beat H. Koenig, Bern: Emissionszentrale der Schweizer Gemeinden, 12–29.

Rhinow, René. 2003. "Auswirkungen der Neugestaltung des Finanzausgleichs und der Aufgabenteilung zwischen Bund und Kantonen (NFA) auf die Parlamente." *Parlament* 6, 5–9.

Riker, William H. 1964. *Federalism. Origins, Operation, Significance*, Boston, Toronto: Little, Brown.

Rocher, François. 2009. "The Quebec–Canada Dynamic or the Negotiation of the Ideal of Federalism." In *Contemporary Canadian Federalism*, edited by Alain-G. Gagnon, Toronto: University of Toronto Press, 81–131.

Roeder, Philip G. 2009. "Ethnofederalism and the Mismanagement of Conflicting Nationalisms." *Regional & Federal Studies* 19 (2), 203–19.

Roller, Elisa, and Pieter Van Houten. 2003. "A National Party in a Regional Party System: The PSC-PSOE in Catalonia." *Regional & Federal Studies* 13 (3), 1–22.

Röttgen, Norbert, and Henner J. Boehl. 2007. "Abweichung statt Zustimmung – Die Re-Adjustierung des Verhältnisses von Bundestag und Bundesrat durch Änderung des Artikels 84 GG." In *Die Reform des Bundesstaates: Beiträge zur Arbeit der Kommission zur Modernisierung der bundesstaatlichen Ordnung 2003/2004 und bis zum Abschluss des Gesetzgebungsverfahrens 2006*, edited by Rainer Holtschneider and Walter Schön, Baden-Baden: Nomos, 17–35.

Roux, Christophe. 2008. "Italy's Path to Federalism: Origins and Paradoxes." *Journal of Modern Italian Studies* 13 (3), 325–39.

Russell, Peter H. 2004. *The Constitutional Odyssey: Can Canada Become a Sovereign People?*, 3rd ed., Toronto: University of Toronto Press.

Sala, Gemma. 2014. "Federalism without Adjectives in Spain." *Publius: The Journal of Federalism* 44 (1), 109–34.

Saward, Michael. 2010. *The Representative Claim*, Oxford: Oxford University Press.

Schapiro, Robert A. 2009. *Polyphonic Federalism: Toward the Protection of Fundamental Rights*, Chicago, London: University of Chicago Press.

Scharpf, Fritz W. 1988. "The Joint Decision Trap: Lessons from German Federalism and European Integration." *Public Administration* 66 (3), 239–78.

Scharpf, Fritz W. 1991. "Games Real Actors Could Play: The Challenge of Complexity." *Journal of Theoretical Politics* 3 (3), 277–304.

Scharpf, Fritz W. 1992. "Koordination durch Verhandlungssysteme: Analytische Konzepte und institutionelle Lösungen." In *Horizontale Politikverflechtung: Zur Theorie von Verhandlungssystemen*, edited by Arthur Benz, Fritz W. Scharpf, and Reinhard Zintl, Frankfurt, New York: Campus, 51–96.

Scharpf, Fritz W. 1997. *Games Real Actors Play: Actor-centered Institutionalism In Policy Research*, Boulder: Westview Press.

Scharpf, Fritz W. 2006. "Recht und Politik in der Reform des Föderalismus." In *Politik und Recht (PVS-Sonderheft 36)*, edited by Michael Becker and Ruth Zimmerling, Wiesbaden: VS Verlag für Sozialwissenschaften, 307–32.

Scharpf, Fritz W. 2009. *Föderalismusreform. Kein Ausweg aus der Politikverflechtungsfalle?*, Frankfurt: Campus.

Scharpf, Fritz W. 2010. "Verfassungsreform mit Vetospielern." In *Die Gemeinschaftsaufgaben von Bund und Ländern in der Wissenschafts- und Bildungspolitik: Analysen und Erfahrungen*, edited by Margrit Seckelmann, Stefan Lange, and Thomas Horstmann, Baden-Baden: Nomos, 23–36.

Scharpf, Fritz W. 2011. "The JDT Model: Context and Extensions." In *The EU's Decision Traps. Comparing Policies*, edited by Gerda Falkner, Oxford: Oxford University Press, 217–36.

Scharpf, Fritz W., and Matthias Mohr. 1994. "Efficient Self-Coordination in Policy Networks: A Simulation Study." *MPIfG Discussion Paper* 94 (1), 1–61.

Scharpf, Fritz W., Bernd Reissert, and Fritz Schnabel. 1976. *Politikverflechtung: Theorie und Empirie des kooperativen Föderalismus in der Bundesrepublik*, Kronberg/Ts.: Scriptor.

Scharpf, Fritz W., Bernd Reissert, and Fritz Schnabel. 1978. "Policy Effectiveness and Conflict Avoidance in Intergovernmental Policy Formation." In *Interorganizational Policy Making: Limits to Coordination and Central Control*, edited by Kenneth Hanf and Fritz W. Scharpf, London: Sage, 57–112.

Scheller, Henrik. 2008. "Politikverflechtung als Funktionsvoraussetzung des Bundesstaates? Zum Umgang mit dem Faktischen in der deutschen Föderalismusdiskussion." *dms: der moderne staat* 1 (2), 469–83.

Schmidt, Manfred G. 1983. "The Welfare State and the Economy in Periods of Economic Crisis: A Comparative Study of Twenty-Three OECD Nations." *European Journal of Political Research* 11 (1), 1–26.

Schmidt, Vivien A. 1990. *Democratizing France: The Political and Administrative History of Decentralization*, Cambridge: Cambridge University Press.

Schmidt, Vivien A. 2006. *Democracy in Europe: The EU and National Polities*, Oxford: Oxford University Press.

Schmidt, Vivien A. 2010. "Taking ideas and discourse seriously: explaining change through discursive institutionalism as the fourth 'new institutionalism'." *European Journal of Political Research* 2 (1), 1–25.

Schneider, Hans-Peter. 2013. *Der neue deutsche Bundesstaat. Bericht über die Umsetzung der Föderalismusreform I*, Baden-Baden: Nomos.

Scottish Constitutional Convention. 1990. *Towards Scotland's Parliament: A Report to the Scottish People by the Scottish Constitutional Convention*, Edinburgh: The Convention.

Scottish Constitutional Convention. 1995. *Scotland's Parliament: Scotland's Right*, Edinburgh: The Convention.

Scottish Liberal Democrats. 1990. *Sovereignty and Integration: Home Rule for Scotland*, (White paper Scottish Liberal Democrats, no. 1), Edinburgh: Scottish Liberal Democrats.

Secretary of State for Scotland. 1997. *Scotland's Parliament: Presented to Parliament by the Secretary of State for Scotland by Command of Her Majesty July 1997*, London: The Scottish Office.

Senato della Repubblica—Servizio Studi (ed.). 2001. *La legge costituzionale 18 ottobre 2001, n. 3. Scheda di lettura*, Rome: https://www.senato.it/documenti/repository/leggi_e_documenti/approfondimenti/dossier/XIV/Dossier%20n.%2070.pdf. (last accessed 20 May 2015).

Simeon, Richard. 2006. *Federal–Provincial Diplomacy. The Making of Recent Policy in Canada*, 3rd ed., Toronto: University of Toronto Press.

Simeon, Richard. 2009. "Constitutional Design and Change in Federal Systems: Issues and Questions." *Publius: The Journal of Federalism* 39 (2), 241–61.

Simeon, Richard, and Daniel-Patrick Conway. 2001. "Federalism and the management of conflict in multinational societies." In *Multinational Democracies*, edited by Alain-G. Gagnon and James Tully, Cambridge: Cambridge University Press, 338–65.

Sinardet, Dave. 2010. *"Expertise on the Fifth State Reform in Belgium (2000/01)."* Darmstadt: TU Darmstadt (unpublished report).

Sinardet, Dave. 2012. "Federal Reform and Party Politics: The Case of the Fifth Belgian State Reform." In *Changing Federal Constitutions: Lessons from International Comparison*, edited by Arthur Benz and Felix Knüpling, Berlin: Barbara Budrich Publishers, 135–60.

Smith, Jennifer. 2003. *Federalism*, Vancouver: UBC Press.

Soifer, Hillel David. 2012. "The Causal Logic of Critical Junctures." *Comparative Political Studies* 45 (12), 1572–97.

Stein, Michael B. 1993. "Tensions in the Canadian Constitutional Process: Elite Negotiations, Referendums and Interest Group Consultations, 1980–1992." In *Canada: The State of the Federation 1993*, edited by Ronald L. Watts and Douglas M. Brown, Kingston, Ontario: Institute of Intergovernmental Relations, Queen's University, 87–116.

Stein, Michael B. 1997. "Improving the Process of Constitutional Reform in Canada: Lessons from the Meech Lake and Charlottetown Constitutional Rounds." *Canadian Journal of Political Science* 30 (2), 307–38.

Stepan, Alfred. 1999. "Federalism and Democracy: Beyond the U.S. Model." *Journal of Democracy* 10 (4), 19–34.

Stolz, Klaus. 1999. "Labour in British Territorial Politics. (Lots of) Continuity and (Maybe Some) Change." In *The return of Labour. A turning point in British politics*, edited by Hans Kastendiek, Richard Stinshoff, and Roland Sturm, Berlin: Philo, 221–33.

Streeck, Wolfgang, and Kathleen Thelen. 2005. "Introduction: Institutional Change in Advanced Political Economies." In *Beyond Continuity: Institutional Change in Advanced Political Economies*, edited by Wolfgang Streeck and Kathleen Thelen, Oxford: Oxford University Press, 1–39.

Struck, Peter, and Günther H. Oettinger. 2008. *Eckpunkte zur Modernisierung der Bund-Länder-Finanzbeziehungen. Vorschlag der Vorsitzenden*, Berlin: Kommission zur Modernisierung der Bund-Länder-Finanzbeziehungen.

Stünker, Joachim. 2007. "Zur Entwicklung der Neufassung von Artikel 72 Abs. 2 GG (Erforderlichkeitsklausel) und Artikel 72 Abs. 3 GG (Abweichungsrechte)." In *Die Reform des Bundesstaates: Beiträge zur Arbeit der Kommission zur Modernisierung der bundesstaatlichen Ordnung 2003/2004 und bis zum Abschluss des Gesetzgebungsverfahrens 2006*, edited by Rainer Holtschneider and Walter Schön, Baden-Baden: Nomos, 91–103.

Swenden, Wilfried. 2013. "Conclusion: The Future of Belgian Federalism—Between Reform and Swansong?" *Regional and Federal Studies* 23 (3): 369–82.

Swenden, Wilfried, Marleen Brans, and Lieven De Winter. 2006. "The Politics of Belgium: Institutions and Policy under Bipolar and Centrifugal Federalism." *West European Politics* 29 (5), 863–73.

Swenden, Wilfried, and Bart Maddens (eds.). 2009. *Territorial Party Politics in Western Europe*, New York: Palgrave Macmillan.

Swenden, Wilfried, and Simon Toubeau. 2013. "Mainstream Parties and Territorial Dynamics in the UK, Spain and India." In *Federal Dynamics: Continuity, Change, and the Varieties of Federalism*, edited by Arthur Benz and Jörg Broschek, Oxford: Oxford University Press, 277–96.

Taylor, Charles. 1992. *Multiculturalism and the Politics of Recognition: An Essay*, Princeton: Princeton University Press.

Thelen, Kathleen. 1999. "Historical Institutionalism in Comparative Politics." *Annual Review of Political Science* 2, 369–404.

Thelen, Kathleen, and Sebastian Karcher. 2013. "Resilience and Change in Federal Institutions: The Case of the German Federal Council." In *Federal Dynamics: Continuity, Change, and the Varieties of Federalism*, edited by Arthur Benz and Jörg Broschek, Oxford: Oxford University Press, 117–39.

Thoenig, Jean-Claude. 2005. "Territorial Administration and Political Control: Decentralization in France." *Public Administration* 83 (3), 685–708.

Thomas, Alys. 1999. "Politics in Wales: A New Era?" In *Wales Today*, edited by David Dunkerley and Andrew Thompson, Cardiff: University of Wales Press.

Thomas, David M. 1999. *Explaining Constitutional Change: A Positive Economics Approach*, Cheltenham: Edward Elgar.

Thomas, David M. 2003. *Whistling Past the Graveyard: Constitutional Abeyances, Quebec and the Future of Canada*, Toronto: University of Toronto Press.

Thorlakson, Lori. 2005. "Federalism and the European Party System." *Journal of European Public Policy* 12 (3), 468–87.

Thorlakson, Lori. 2007. "An Institutional Explanation of Party System Congruence: Evidence from Six Federations." *European Journal of Political Research* 46 (1), 69–95.

Thorlakson, Lori. 2009. "Patterns of Party Integration, Influence and Autonomy in Seven Federations." *Party Politics* 15 (2), 157–77.

Thorlakson, Lori. 2013. "Dynamics of Change in Federal Representation." In *Federal Dynamics: Continuity, Change, and the Varieties of Federalism*, edited by Arthur Benz and Jörg Broschek, Oxford: Oxford University Press, 229–48.

Tierney, Stephen. 2009. "Federalism in a Unitary State: The Paradox too Far." *Regional and Federal Studies* 19 (2), 237–53.

Tierney, Stephen. 2014. *Constitutional Referendums: The Theory and Practice of Republican Deliberation*, Oxford: Oxford University Press.

Toffler, Alvin. 1970. *Future Shock*, New York: Bantam Books.

Toubeau, Simon, and Emanuele Massetti. 2013. "The Party Politics of Territorial Reforms in Europe." *West European Politics* 36 (2): 297–316.

Toubeau, Simon, and Markus Wagner. 2015. "Explaining Party Positions on Decentralization." *British Journal of Political Science* 45 (1): 97–119.

Treisman, Daniel. 2007. *The Architecture of Government: Rethinking Political Decentralization*, Cambridge: Cambridge University Press.

Trench, Alan. 2008. "Finding a Voice for Wales: Assessing Three Phases of Constitutional Development in Wales." *ECPR Joint Session of Workshops* (Université de Rennes II. https://ecpr.eu/Filestore/PaperProposal/13e7e37d-ff23-41fe-98b4-0b63120348e9.pdf (last accessed 20 April 2016).

Tsebelis, George. 1990. *Nested Games: Rational Choice in Comparative Politics*, Berkeley: University of California Press.

Tsebelis, George. 2002. *Veto Players: How Political Institutions Work*, Princeton: Princeton University Press.

Tully, James. 1995. *Strange Multiplicity: Constitutionalism in an Age of Diversity*, Cambridge: Cambridge University Press.

Tully, James. 2001. "Introduction." In *Multinational Democracies*, edited by Alain-G. Gagnon and James Tully, Cambridge: Cambridge University Press, 1–33.

Ulram, Peter, and Fritz Plasser. 2005. "Ruhe und Unruhe: Die Bundespräsidentenwahl und die Wahlen zum Europäischen Parlament 2004." In *Österreichisches Jahrbuch für Politik 2004*, edited by Andreas Khol, Günther Ofner, Günther Burkert-Dottolo, and Stefan Karner, Linz: Böhlau, 3–27.

Van Houten, Pieter. 2009. "Authority in Multilevel Parties: A Principal-Agent Framework and Cases from Germany and Spain." In *Territorial Party Politics in Western Europe*, edited by Wilfried Swenden and Bart Maddens, Basingstoke: Palgrave Macmillan, 167–82.

Van Morgan, Sydney. 2006. "Plaid Cymru: The Party of Wales: The New Politics of Welsh Nationalism and the Dawn of the 21st Century." In *Autonomist Parties in Europe: Identity Politics and the Revival of Territorial Cleavages*, vol. 1, edited by Lieven de Winter, Margarita Gómez-Reino Cachafeiro, and Peter Lynch, Barcelona: Institut de Ciènces Polítiques I Socials.

Vanberg, Georg. 2004. *The Politics of Constitutional Review in Germany*, Cambridge: Cambridge University Press.

Vanberg, Victor, and James M. Buchanan. 1989. "Interests and Theories in Constitutional Choice." *Journal of Theoretical Politics* 1 (1), 49–62.

Voigt, Stefan. 1997. "Positive Constitutional Economics: A Survey." *Public Choice* 90 (1), 11–53.

Voigt, Stefan. 1999. *Explaining Constitutional Change: A Positive Economics Approach*, Cheltenham: Edward Elgar.

Waldmann, Bernhard. 2012. "Der schweizerische Föderalismus vor territorialen Herausforderungen." In *Jahrbuch des Föderalismus 2012*, edited by Europäisches Zentrum für Föderalismusforschung Tübingen, Baden-Baden: Nomos, 331–45.

Wales Labour Party. 1989. *The Future of Local Government*, Cardiff: Wales Labour Party.

Wales Labour Party. 1995. *Shaping the Vision*, Cardiff: Wales Labour Party.

Wales Labour Party. 1997. *Representing Wales*, Cardiff: Wales Labour Party.

Watts, Ronald L. 1996. "Canada: Three Decades of Periodic Federal Crises." *International Political Science Review* 17 (4), 353–71.

Watts, Ronald L. 2008. *Comparing Federal Systems*, 3rd ed., Kingston, Montréal: McGill-Queen's University Press.

Watts, Ronald L. 2013. "Typologies of Federalism." In *Routledge Handbook of Regionalism and Federalism*, edited by John Loughlin, John Kincaid, and Wilfried Swenden, London, New York: Routledge, 19–33.

Wettstein, Gérard. 2002. "Die Neugestaltung des Finanzausgleichs und der Aufgaben (NFA): Erfolgsfaktoren und Hürden aus Sicht der Projektleitung." *Leges* 2, 35–54.

Wettstein, Gérard. 2009. *"Country Expertise Switzerland NFA."* Darmstadt: TU Darmstadt, (unpublished manuscript).

Wettstein, Gérard. 2012. "Why Federal Reform Succeeded in Switzerland." In *Changing Federal Constitutions: Lessons from International Comparison*, edited by Arthur Benz and Felix Knüpling, Berlin: Barbara Budrich Publishers, 81–96.

Wolf, Klaus Dieter. 2000. *Die Neue Staatsräson: Zwischenstaatliche Kooperation als Demokratieproblem in der Weltgesellschaft*, Baden-Baden: Nomos.

Wright, Kenyon. 1997. *The People Say Yes: The Making of Scotland's Parliament*, Argyll: Argyll Publishing.

Zahariadis, Nikolaos. 2007. "The Multiple Streams Framework: Structure, Limitations, Prospects." In *Theories of the Policy Process*, 2nd ed., edited by Paul A. Sabatier, Boulder: Westview Press, 65–92.

Ziblatt, Daniel. 2006. *Structuring the State: The Formation of Italy and Germany and the Puzzle of Federalism*, Princeton: Princeton University Press.

Zimmermann-Steinhart, Petra. 2004. "Akt II der französischen Dezentralisierung: Konsequenzen für das politische System und die Gesellschaft." In *Jahrbuch des Föderalismus 2004*, edited by Europäisches Zentrum für Föderalismus-Forschung Tübingen, Baden-Baden: Nomos, 219–34.

Zimmermann-Steinhart, Petra. 2006. "Dezentralisierung in Frankreich, Acte II: Mehr Aufgaben, weniger Handlungsspielraum für die Gebietskörperschaften?" In *Jahrbuch des Föderalismus 2006*, edited by Europäisches Zentrum für Föderalismus-Forschung Tübingen, Baden-Baden: Nomos, 336–44.

Index